"Rogers combines a passionate commitment to the religious liberty guarantees in the First Amendment with a principled but also practical approach to how we can live together in peace and respect each other's rights. These pages are anchored in her extensive experience—as a lawyer, scholar, and White House official. They are inspired by the hope that even in a fractious political time, we can still make progress in resolving at least some of our conflicts. That hope urgently needs to be rekindled."

—E. J. Dionne Jr., *Professor in the Foundations of Democracy and Culture, Georgetown University*

"The present moment in American society is calling people of faith to our civic duty of discerning a way forward to strengthen America's future as a land of freedom, opportunity, tolerance, and civility. Our public discourse has become more polarized and less constructive as we often speak at one another through electronic devices, rather than speaking with our fellow human beings. The potential for people of faith to work across differences holds great promise so long as we foreground our shared commitment to faith and work to understand the boundaries laid out in our Constitution. With clear explanations and fascinating examples, this is a bookshelf essential for all who are interested in religion's role in American public life."

—Julie Schonfeld, *CEO Emeritus of The Rabbinical Assembly and Founder and CEO of Leading Ethics LLC*

"This is a magisterial book written by an extraordinary scholar and practitioner. All of us who are interested both in what the Constitution has to say about religion in our country and in how those words have been read, parsed, interpreted, and implemented are indebted to Rogers. She helps us to understand why religious freedom is so important and how we can best defend it when it is threatened."

—Amir Hussain, *Professor of Theological Studies, Loyola Marymount University*

"Melissa Rogers is a national treasure for her leadership and scholarship on the intersection of faith and public policy. I benefited greatly from her leadership when she chaired President Obama's inaugural Advisory Council on Faith-Based and Neighborhood Partnerships, on which I served, and in her role as Special Assistant to President Obama. She continues to lead in this area with *Faith in American Public Life*. It is an engaging, accessible, and informative must-read for all who exercise their faith in the public square."

—Frederick A. Davie, *Executive Vice-President, Union Theological Seminary*

"Filled with both cogent arguments and historical anecdotes, *Faith in American Public Life* is an invaluable, accessible resource for any pastor or religious leader endeavoring to understand more deeply the role that faith can play in American public life. At a time in our nation's history when some Christians are claiming religious liberty only for themselves, Melissa Rogers reminds us of religion's prophetic role in calling people and nations to exercise what Abraham Lincoln poetically described as 'the better angels of our nature.'"

—Julie Pennington-Russell, *Senior Pastor, First Baptist Church of the City of Washington, D.C.*

"A careful and meticulous study, one that has enormous value to scholars but also to general readers who are interested in this important topic. What sets this book apart is the careful scholarship as well as the breadth of the treatment, taking the analysis up to the present. Rogers covers all of the relevant cases, providing historical as well as cultural context."

—Randall Balmer, *John Phillips Professor in Religion and Director of the Society of Fellows, Dartmouth College*

Faith in American Public Life

Melissa Rogers

BAYLOR UNIVERSITY PRESS

The Library of Congress has cataloged this book under ISBN
978-1-4813-0970-7.

CONTENTS

FOREWORD

E. J. Dionne Jr.

One of the tragedies of our politics is that religious liberty has been transformed from a bedrock American principle into a partisan and ideological slogan.

If any idea should unite our currently fractious nation, it is a commitment to the rights of conscience. No American wants government to dictate what are (or are not) acceptable beliefs about the most important things. No one wants the state to interfere with religious practice or with the right to believe—or not believe—in God.

Moreover, the structure of the First Amendment takes care to guard against two very different dangers to religious faith. It declares that "Congress shall make no law respecting an establishment of religion" and also that it must avoid "prohibiting the free exercise thereof." Embedded in these words is a "freedom from" and a "freedom to." Government cannot promote religion or favor one faith over another. And government must leave citizens free to pursue their ultimate concerns as they see fit.

These two clauses reinforce each other, but there is a certain tension between them—a tension that has led to fierce arguments over how they interact and whether one takes priority. This tension explains many of the arguments we have had about religion and government from the outset, and it helps define some of the polarization we are witnessing today.

On the one side, the "no establishment" obligation is sometimes interpreted as meaning that the federal government should never become involved with any religious organization. This penalizes religion and raises serious challenges to longstanding direct or indirect government partnerships with religious groups in pursuit of common public goals. Non-establishment can thus become a battering ram against free exercise.

On the other hand, the obligation to guarantee "free exercise" is sometimes extended to a view that government must allow businesses to infringe on employees' rights or religious groups to use government grant money to buy sacred texts or conduct worship services. In this view, failing to do so amounts to a government veto of religion itself. Such an approach can lead to government imposition of religion, preferences for some faiths over others, and excessive entanglement between government and religion. Free exercise can thus be transformed into a cudgel against non-establishment.

Melissa Rogers is deeply aware of the limits of views such as these (which I have presented in a highly compressed though, I hope, not inaccurate way). These pages make clear that she combines a passionate commitment to *both* guarantees in the First Amendment with a deeply principled but also highly practical approach to how we can live together in peace and respect each other's rights.

As a Baptist, she believes religious freedom for all is both a theological and legal mandate. As a lawyer, she sees the First Amendment's Establishment and Free Exercise Clauses as, in Justice William Brennan's words, "co-guarantors" of this right. Few people in the public sphere have been as consistent as Rogers has in defending both halves of the guarantee. When she worked for the Baptist Joint Committee for Religious Liberty, she helped file friend-of-the-court-briefs with the Supreme Court against state-sponsored prayers and government-subsidized religion *and* in support of religious expression by students and other religious speakers on government property. This is in keeping with her view that the First Amendment is a "both/and," not an "either/or," proposition.

Too often, the areas of law and policy discussed here are not taken as seriously as they should be by policymakers. There is a strong default to evade or avoid these issues, given the passions they arouse. And when they do pay close attention, politicians and their lieutenants often consult only with those who share their ideological or religious perspectives. Neither approach is adequate because neither provides a basis for policies that uphold our shared rights in consensual ways that can be sustained across administrations. Few know this better than Rogers, and few have worked harder to find common ground. These pages are anchored in her extensive experience—as a lawyer, scholar, and White House official. They are inspired by the hope that even in a fractious political time, we can still make progress in resolving at least some of our conflicts.

That hope urgently needs to be rekindled. As a nation, we confront a cycle of backlash and counter-backlash that threatens to undermine the good will and mutual understanding required to preserve our basic freedoms.

It should especially trouble us (and it certainly troubles Rogers) that over the last decade, "religious liberty" has often been reduced to a political slogan, and a highly ideological one at that. This problem has become particularly acute in the Trump Era. Religious liberty is defiled when demands to protect Christians are accompanied by calls to ban Muslims from entering the country. Religious liberty, as Rogers insists, is indivisible. Defending the rights of any faith tradition requires defending the rights of all traditions.

What does religious liberty mean, Rogers asks, to an administration that prosecutes individuals whose religious convictions drive them to provide humanitarian assistance to undocumented immigrants in the desert and demands that a Roman Catholic diocese surrender part of its property for a border wall it opposes because of its faith?

Religious liberty has been invoked to resist advances in LGBTQ rights, and as a battering ram against the Affordable Care Act. Rogers is acutely sensitive to free exercise concerns, including those of religious conservatives. She advocated for a much stronger exemption for religious institutions than the Obama administration initially offered from the ACA's requirement that most employers provide cost-free contraception coverage to their female employees, while also insisting that employees receive such coverage by other means. But when the administration gave ground and endorsed a broader exemption, she was also critical of those who asserted a broad right for virtually all employers to deny women this coverage and effectively extinguish this entitlement for their female employees. A fair resolution to this issue and so many others in the religious sphere requires finding a balance between competing and legitimate rights claims.

Rogers' strengths, as a scholar and a public servant, are rooted in her empathetic imagination. This is her extraordinary gift at a moment when the nation is going through a crisis created in large part by a widespread failure of empathy. In the White House, she developed a reputation among outside groups of widely varying views as a person who could not only listen but actually hear. Her interlocutors knew of her capacity for sympathetic understanding of views she did not hold herself. This served the country and the administration well. It enabled a series of Obama Era reforms of faith-based programs championed during George W. Bush's administration that won assent from conservatives as well as progressives. Both sides knew Rogers was not interested in partisan victories. She sought to promote innovative approaches to lifting up people in need that were consistent with their religious rights and the rights of taxpayers not to find themselves underwriting religious views that are not their own. At the same time, she understood the desire of religious service providers to maintain the integrity of their organizations. It was an extraordinary feat. Many in the administration realized that because Rogers was there, unnecessary battles were avoided and misunderstandings were minimized. She will be remembered not only for the breadth of her visible accomplishments, but also for what we did not see: the waste of vast amounts of energy on fruitless, fractious conflicts.

I have worked with Rogers on these issues for nearly two decades, so I consider it a privilege to offer this foreword. Collaborating with her is a joy not simply because she is a generous colleague, but also because she enjoys intellectual give-and-take. Agreeing with her is easy because she is so persuasive and so consistently reasonable. But disagreeing with her—we are not often far apart in our views, but we have had occasional differences—can be even more enriching. Precisely because she can get inside the view she is disagreeing with, her critiques are always constructive rather than caustic. And she is always willing to put her own ideas at risk. We have changed each other's mind on some issues: I have joked that thanks to our dialogues, I think a bit more like a Baptist than I used to, and she thinks a bit more like a Catholic. All of which means that I appreciate this book most of all because it gives a wide readership a chance to get to know how an extraordinary progressive woman of faith thinks and reasons and—that word again—empathizes.

Where Rogers and I most agree is in our shared desire for left, right, and center, and for more secular and more religious people, to follow Isaiah's call to come and reason together on how to preserve religious liberty. The issues she grapples with are questions on which most of us see only partially and imperfectly. We bring a lot of baggage to just about everything touching on religion. Rogers wants us to unpack our bags, appreciate the grandeur of the First Amendment, and do the very best we can to defend each other's rights.

E. J. DIONNE JR. is University Professor in the Foundations of Democracy and Culture at Georgetown University, a senior fellow at the Brookings Institution, and a columnist for the *Washington Post*. His books include *Our Divided Political Heart* and (with Norman J. Ornstein and Thomas E. Mann) *One Nation After Trump*.

ACKNOWLEDGMENTS

My deep gratitude goes to President Barack Obama for the extraordinary honor of serving him and the country. I would also like to thank my friends and colleagues from the Obama administration for the opportunity to work with and learn from them.

My career in this field began more than twenty years ago, when Brent Walker and the late James Dunn of the Baptist Joint Committee for Religious Liberty offered me my first opportunity to work on issues related to religious freedom and the separation of church and state. Their generous offer and mentorship changed my life. I will always be deeply grateful for them and for Oliver ("Buzz") Thomas, Larry Chesser, and so many other fine Baptists who taught me about the Baptist tradition of defending and extending God-given religious liberty for all.

Profound thanks also go to E. J. Dionne for many years of friendship, collaboration, and inspiration. E. J. has taught me much about religion, policy, and politics, and also about what it means to seek to serve as a voice for public justice. E. J.'s eloquent contribution to this book is a great gift.

Bill Leonard, Nathan Hatch, the late Gail O'Day, Jill Crainshaw, John DiIulio, Bill Galston, and Darrell West, among many others from the Wake Forest University and Brookings Institution communities, have offered steadfast support and encouragement. They have my heartfelt thanks, as do Seymour and Kate Weingarten for their longstanding friendship and good counsel.

I am fortunate to have many other friends who are also wise, brilliant, and generous. Their generosity included taking the time to read portions of this manuscript and offer their feedback or to simply discuss ideas with me. These friends include David Beckman, Tom Berg, Kara Bobroff, Alan Brownstein, John Carr, Brian Corbin, John DiIulio, E. J. Dionne, Lanae Erickson, Richard Foltin, Steve Green, Derrick Harkins, Hoda Hawa, Jennifer Hawks, Charles Haynes, Holly Hollman, Richard Katskee, Brian Kaylor, Kathleen Leslie,

Michael Lieberman, Dan Mach, Benjamin Marcus, Elliot Mincberg, Bill Marshall, Steve Pomper, David Saperstein, Matthew Soerens, Adam Taylor, Amanda Tyler, and Brent Walker. I also would like to thank the many other experts and journalists whose work I have cited. Of course, no one should be held responsible for the views expressed here but me.

It is difficult to articulate my thanks for my friend Carey Newman of Baylor University Press because he played such an essential and varied role in the development of this book. I simply could not have launched, much less sustained and completed, this project without Carey's expert guidance and support. I also want to thank the staff of Baylor University Press for their invaluable assistance. It has been a special honor and pleasure to work again with the press of my alma mater.

I am enormously grateful to my families of faith and pastors over the years. They have nurtured and encouraged me in countless ways.

My parents, Lu Rogers and Bill Rogers, have loved and supported me every day of my life. No one could have a better sibling or siblings-in-law. I would like to thank them and the rest of my wonderful family for who they are and for all they have taught me.

I also treasure and thank my husband and our sons for their constant love and support. Their presence in my life is a daily reminder that I am blessed beyond measure. Thanks be to God.

INTRODUCTION

Religion's Role in American Public Life

When Pope Francis accepted President Obama's invitation to visit the United States, the president provided clear instructions to his staff: the visit should not be simply a moment in time or a photo op. Instead, President Obama wanted the visit to have lasting value. He asked his staff to identify specific steps the U.S. government could take, both on its own and with others, to advance some of the values he and Pope Francis share.[1]

President Obama's charge launched a series of consultations. White House staff traveled to the Vatican to meet with leaders there and began conversations with religious and humanitarian groups in the United States about the visit. External meetings were matched by internal ones. Staff throughout the Obama administration met regularly to consider goals that were ambitious yet feasible, and the president and senior advisors reviewed plans for the visit as they took shape.[2]

Three ethical and policy pillars emerged from these conversations. The first pillar was the imperative to stand in solidarity with people in crisis, including refugees and persecuted religious minorities. The second pillar was promoting sustainable development, including advancing an agenda to end extreme poverty, expand peace, and encourage good governance. The third pillar was protecting our "common home," as Pope Francis said in his 2015 encyclical—to be good stewards of the earth and its resources.[3]

To further these goals, the Obama administration significantly elevated the number of refugees the United States could accept, without cutting any corners on the rigorous security checks each refugee undergoes before entering the country.[4] Religious and humanitarian organizations asked the Obama administration to raise the ceiling for refugees, and they then helped the U.S. government reach those goals.

To promote religious freedom, the administration created a new post at the State Department to advocate for religious minorities in the Near East and South and Central Asia. Training for diplomats on religious liberty was expanded, and a new civil society conference was launched to stand "for the universal right of all people to practice their faiths in peace and in freedom."[5]

In consultation with faith-based and humanitarian groups, the United States Agency for International Development (USAID) issued a plan for ending extreme poverty. As a complement to policy initiatives such as the Climate Action and Clean Power Plans, the Obama administration formed an array of partnerships with religious and community groups to promote climate resiliency at home and abroad.

On September 23, 2015, the White House announced these and other steps, and an estimated crowd of eleven thousand gathered on the South Lawn to join President Obama in welcoming Pope Francis to the United States.[6] Participants included people of many different faiths and none, all of whom rose before dawn in order to clear security in time for the celebration.[7] The ceremony began at 9:32 a.m., shortly after Pope Francis' black Fiat zipped onto the South Lawn.[8] When the arrival ceremony ended and President Obama escorted Pope Francis off the stage, someone yelled, "We love you, Pope Francis!"[9] The crowd broke into laughter and applause. And long after Pope Francis left the White House, the work on shared values continued.

This collaboration involving the U.S. government, the Vatican, and religious and other civil society organizations is one high-profile example of how faith communities and government can work together to promote the common good. Our Constitution rightly recognizes that religion can play a prominent role in American public life, including through cooperation with government.

Religious communities serve their neighbors, sometimes by partnering with the state. People of faith gather in public parks and on sidewalks and streets for demonstrations and devotional events. Voices of the faithful are heard in workplaces and public schools. Homeowners and houses of worship place religious signs and symbols on their front lawns.

Faith is visible, vital, and vocal in the United States. According to the Pew Research Center, "Americans pray more often, are more likely to attend weekly religious services and ascribe higher importance to faith in their lives than adults in other wealthy, Western democracies, such as Canada, Australia and most European states . . . ."[10]

While the Constitution *prohibits* government-backed religion, it *protects* the rights of religious individuals and organizations to promote their faith. And rather than undermining faith, the limits the Constitution places on government's involvement in religion help to preserve faith's integrity and influence. The bar on governmental promotion of faith assists religious communities in retaining control over their messages, thus helping to ensure their authenticity. When religious communities are independent and authentic, they can be credible and influential.

Prohibiting government-backed religion, while *protecting* the rights of individuals and organizations to promote their faith; *barring* governmental preferences for particular religions, while *welcoming* collaboration with people of all faiths and none for the common good—principles like these have made the United States exceptional.

This book describes these and other principles that define the relationship between government and religion and offers recommendations for observing them in various sectors of American public life. The legal rules of the United States are not perfect, nor have they been perfectly applied. The American legal framework, however, has produced remarkable freedom. This framework has helped to create a country in which people of many different faiths and beliefs live together peacefully and often cooperatively, and where religion can be a powerful force for good in society.

Special attention is given to the role of policymakers. Members of the legislative and executive branches must carry out constitutional commands, including religious liberty guarantees. The relationship between religion and government is as important as any other legal or policy issue, yet policymakers often do not have the training, much less staffing plans, to address them. Further, government officials often adopt one of two faulty approaches to religion-related issues: they either give scant attention to these issues, hoping they can mostly be avoided; or they pay close attention but only consult with and respond to those with shared ideological or religious perspectives. Both approaches must change.

This book also warns about certain contemporary threats to religious freedom and pluralism in the United States. The most serious and urgent threat includes hostility against and attacks on religious minorities in this country. Some political leaders—most prominently, the current president of the United States—are willing to engage in fear-mongering on factors like religion, race, and ethnicity and to use dehumanizing language and violent rhetoric or imagery in attempts to defeat opponents and silence critics. Given current polarization, such tactics amount to throwing a lit match on dry kindling. Americans must take action now to counter these threats.

Other contemporary challenges to religious freedom include a dangerous mix: overreaching on free exercise issues coupled with efforts to shrink the constitutional prohibition on government advancement of religion. The answer to this challenge is not to do the opposite—undervalue religious exercise and inflate the Establishment Clause. Neither is protecting only religious practices we like, which is a danger on all sides. Each of these concerns must be taken seriously, and this book offers suggestions for doing so.

The Constitutional Framework

Any discussion of religion and American public life must begin with the Constitution. Article VI of the Constitution bars religious tests for public office. The first sixteen words of the First Amendment are: "Congress shall make no law respecting an establishment of religion, or prohibiting the free exercise thereof." The first clause is known as the Establishment Clause, and the second as the Free Exercise Clause.

Candor requires the recognition that the same Constitution that included these majestic religious liberty guarantees also sought to blot out the humanity of some Americans, including by restricting their ability to practice their faith. The Constitution allowed slavery and the slave trade to continue and counted slaves as only three-fifths of a person, for example.[11] Slaveholding states tightly regulated the religious practices of slaves and of black churches and repressed any religious leadership, black or white, that opposed slavery.[12]

Americans eventually corrected these monstrous errors in the Constitution's text by adopting the Thirteenth, Fourteenth, and Fifteenth Amendments. But much work remained—and still remains—to be done to align American practices with its promises on racial equality. With the Fourteenth Amendment, states were barred from abridging citizens' privileges or immunities and from depriving any person of equal protection or "life, liberty, or property, without due process of law." In time, the U.S. Supreme Court confirmed that the protections of the First Amendment, including both of its religion clauses, apply to the states through the Fourteenth Amendment.[13]

The content of the First Amendment's religion clauses is complementary. Under the Establishment Clause, the government may not promote or denigrate religion or prefer one faith over another. Neutrality among faiths must be coupled with "benevolent neutrality" toward religion generally.[14] It is not the government's role to foster faith; this is the job of religious individuals and institutions themselves. The flip side is that governmental decisions must not be based in hostility toward religion or appear to be so.

The Establishment Clause also prohibits the government from deciding or taking sides on theological issues. As James Madison wisely recognized, "the Civil Magistrate" is not "a competent Judge of Religious Truth."[15] The Establishment Clause is "a co-guarantor, with the Free Exercise Clause, of religious liberty."[16]

Under the Free Exercise Clause, the government cannot target religion for mistreatment, either overtly or covertly. If religiously motivated conduct is restricted because it endangers the state's interests, yet a similar amount of nonreligious conduct that endangers the state's interest in the same way is not, free exercise concerns are implicated.[17] When coupled with supporting laws, the Constitution promises a wide berth for Americans not just to believe but also to practice their faith, both individually and within communities.[18]

Providing robust protection for free exercise is a necessary complement to a strong constitutional prohibition on government promotion of religion. Working together, these clauses create a healthy separation of church and state, ensuring that religion and government are meaningfully independent.

The First Amendment's protections are counter-majoritarian—they are aimed at ensuring that all have equal citizenship, no matter their faith or lack thereof, no matter whether one belongs to the most popular faith or the religion that is the smallest minority. In the ringing words of Justice Robert Jackson, "One's right to life, liberty, and property, to free speech, a free press, freedom of worship and assembly, and other fundamental rights may not be submitted to vote; they depend on the outcome of no elections."[19]

The Constitution's guarantees strengthen the United States by allowing it to tap the talents of all its citizens and by encouraging civic unity across religious differences. When religious beliefs and affiliations, or lack thereof, are irrelevant to one's standing in the political community, the United States can draw on Americans' strengths, whether they are Baptists, Buddhists, or Baha'is.

Religious liberty has been central to our country's history and still matters greatly today. Whether and how to pray—that is a citizen's choice, not one to be made by government. To hire or fire a minister is a religious community's call, not that of government. The state may not pass the collection plate for religious items and activities. The government has no say in decisions about the organization or membership of congregations. And the right to speak out on public issues belongs to religious speakers as much as secular ones.

Rights like these are inalienable. They are also timeless. Religious freedom remains key to human dignity and flourishing.

The recent rise in the number of Americans claiming no religious affiliation does not change this calculus. Choosing not to affiliate with a religious denomination does not necessarily mean an individual is not engaging in religious or spiritual practices.[20] And, of course, the choice not to embrace a faith is a decision that must be as protected as any religious choice.

The Constitution's religious liberty guarantees have fostered an atmosphere in which groups of different faiths and beliefs not only coexist; they also make common cause. The Circle of Protection, for example, unites Protestant and Catholic leaders who focus on ending hunger and poverty.[21] The Refugee Council USA (RCUSA) is a coalition of twenty-five U.S.-based nongovernmental organizations, including diverse faith-based organizations, that seeks to protect and welcome refugees and promote excellence in the refugee resettlement program.[22] Members of the RCUSA include Church World Service, Episcopal Migration Ministries, Hebrew Immigration Aid Services (HIAS), Lutheran Immigration and Refugee Services, the Multifaith Alliance for Syrian Refugees, the United States Conference for Catholic Bishops, and World Relief, an evangelical organization.[23] Interaction is an alliance of nongovernmental organizations that works on behalf of the poor and vulnerable around the world.[24] Members of Interaction include the Adventist Development and Relief Agency, the African Methodist Episcopal Church Service and Development Agency, American Jewish World Service, Buddhist Tzu Chi Foundation, Catholic Relief Services, Islamic Relief USA, Mennonite Central Committee, Seva Foundation, United Methodist Committee on Relief, and World Vision, an evangelical organization.[25] The unique American system of religious freedom helps to produce this kind of teamwork.

A Legacy at Risk

Some signal American achievements on religious freedom and pluralism are at risk. The most fundamental danger is hostility against and attacks on religious minorities and certain communities of racial or ethnic minorities that are also defined by their religious identities, like predominantly African American churches.

Of course, the history of the United States is stained by chapters of governmental and nongovernmental oppression and discrimination against such minorities. The United States claimed territory by driving Native Americans from their homelands. America's record includes other forms of oppression and discrimination against a variety of faiths, including Native Americans, predominantly African American religious communities, Jews, Catholics, Jehovah's Witnesses, Muslims, and members of the Church of Jesus Christ of Latter-day Saints. Tragically, there has been a spike in hostility against and attacks on various minorities today.[26]

On October 27, 2018, a man with an assault rifle entered the Tree of Life synagogue in Pittsburgh, Pennsylvania, and killed eleven worshippers.[27] The attack is believed to be the deadliest one on American Jews in U.S. history.[28] The gunman was an anti-Semite, and one of his latest fixations appears to have been the Jewish community's compassionate response to immigrants and refugees.[29] We have also seen the evil of anti-Semitism in other attacks on and threats against synagogues and Jewish community centers, in toppled gravestones in Jewish cemeteries,[30] and in slurs on social media.[31] We have heard it in the chants of neo-Nazis and other white supremacists marching through Charlottesville.[32]

In November 2018, a gunman tried to enter a historically black church, First Baptist Church of Jeffersontown, Kentucky, shortly after a noon-day Bible study concluded. The doors of the church were locked, a precaution taken in the wake of the attack on Mother Emanuel African Methodist Episcopal Church in 2015 in Charleston, South Carolina, so the gunman was thwarted. The killer left the church and went to a nearby grocery store, where he brutally gunned down two African American shoppers, while telling some white customers he was sparing them due to their skin color. There have been at least ninety-four attacks on predominantly African American churches since the 1950s.[33]

Hatred also prompted a man to taunt a girl in a hijab on a Portland, Oregon, commuter train in May 2017 and then stab three of the girl's defenders, two fatally.[34] American Muslims and Sikhs are harassed regularly in public places today.[35] A wide variety of anti-Muslim activities are on the rise, like attacks on houses of worship, statements by government officials denouncing Islam, and serious consideration of anti-Muslim laws. Seven hundred and fifty-seven unique incidents of such activities were documented from 2012 to August 2018, with a dramatic increase since late 2015.[36] Some officeholders have even argued that Islam is not a religion in order to seek to deny it First Amendment protections.[37] Hostility and discrimination against individuals and groups because of their faith is inexcusable, particularly when carried out by political candidates and governmental officials.[38]

Religion-based hate crimes—crimes against people or property motivated by an offender's bias against a religion—rose 23 percent from 2016 to 2017, with a 37 percent increase in crimes targeting Jews and Jewish institutions.[39] According to the Anti-Defamation League, the 1,564 religion-based hate crimes that were reported in 2017 is the second-highest number of such hate crimes ever, with more being reported only in 2001 in the wake of the 9/11 terrorist attacks.[40] The Sikh Coalition has estimated that American Sikhs experienced an average of one hate crime per week in 2018.[41]

President Donald Trump has made these matters much worse. When President Trump was asked about a violent demonstration in Charlottesville, Virginia, by the Ku Klux Klan, neo-Nazis, and other white supremacists, one that drew counter-protestors, Trump blamed the violence on "many sides" and said "some very fine people" marched with the white supremacists.[42] He has also fomented fear about undocumented immigrants and refugees and used dehumanizing language to describe them.[43]

During the 2016 presidential campaign, then-candidate Trump called for Muslims to be banned from entering the United States simply because they are Muslims.[44] President Trump has never apologized for that statement, much less retracted it.[45] At a White House dinner for evangelicals in the summer of 2018, President Trump told the group, "This Nov. 6 election is very much a referendum on not only me, it's a referendum on your religion . . . ."[46] If the GOP loses, Trump said, Democrats "will overturn everything that we've done and they'll do it quickly and violently . . . ."[47]

A member of Trump's cabinet, Secretary of Housing and Urban Development Ben Carson, has said that Muslims should not serve as president.[48] Roy Moore, the former judge and failed Trump-backed candidate for U.S. senator from Alabama, has insisted that Muslims should not be permitted to serve in any public office.[49] Numerous other Trump administration appointees and affiliates have made anti-Muslim comments. Former national security advisor Michael Flynn, for example, referred to Islam as "a cancer" and claimed a "fear of Muslims is rational."[50] Media have reported that Sebastian Gorka, who worked at the White House until August 2017, told an introductory-level class for staff of the Federal Bureau of Investigation that "there is no such thing as mainstream Muslims—only those radicalized and those soon to be radicalized."[51]

The president of the United States has a special duty to condemn such expressions of bigotry and prejudice in the strongest possible terms and treat them as disqualifiers for public service. Yet President Trump appointed or endorsed all of these men.

It is no defense to cite the fact that groups like ISIS, and those it inspires, have committed heinous attacks around the world and in the United States. The appropriate response is to combat terrorism, not to discriminate against Muslims. Just as it would be wrong to blame the Christian community for the fact that the man who attacked the Tree of Life synagogue cited Bible verses and Jesus Christ to try to justify murder, it is wrong to blame the Muslim community for those who cite the Qur'an and Allah to do the same.[52]

While there can be good-faith differences about some religious freedom issues, the principle of equal treatment for all faiths is not one of them. Rhetoric and actions like these have endangered lives and done enormous damage to the best traditions of religious freedom and pluralism. An unwillingness to defend the principle that the government must treat all faiths equally is support for religious privilege, not religious liberty. To fear-monger on factors like religion, race, and ethnicity is to forsake core values enshrined in the Constitution.

Every American must treat an attack on any faith as an attack on their own faith or beliefs. As Rev. Dr. Martin Luther King Jr. said: "Injustice anywhere is a threat to justice everywhere. We are caught in an inescapable network of mutuality, tied in a single garment of destiny."[53] Taking this approach is not only the right thing to do; it is the smart thing to do. Every faith is a minority somewhere in the United States, and rapidly changing demographics may convert today's religious majorities to tomorrow's religious minorities.[54] Anyone can become the target of prejudice and violence as times and public opinion change and as demagogues come and go. Further, when the United States protects religious minorities at home, including Muslims, the government strengthens its hand when pressing other countries, such as Muslim-majority countries, to protect religious minorities abroad.[55] And every American benefits when all citizens are free to participate in public life, no matter their faith or background.

Fear-mongering and hostility, hate crimes and discrimination are certainly the most inexcusable and urgent threats to religious freedom and pluralism, but they are not the only ones. Other contemporary challenges include a dangerous mix: overreaching on free exercise issues coupled with attempts to shrink the constitutional prohibition on governmental advancement of religion.

An ascendant agenda would allow big businesses to impose religion on their employees and blow gaping holes in civil rights protections. The Department of Labor, for example, is proposing a major expansion of the religious exemption for federal contractors from employment nondiscrimination obligations, one that would cover at least some large commercial entities.[56] The Department of Health and Human Services has waived religious nondiscrimination requirements in order to permit government subgrantees to refuse to work with potential foster parents who do not share their religious beliefs. This will allow an evangelical subgrantee, for example, to turn away Catholics and Jews, among others.[57] And three federal agencies have issued rules permitting even publicly traded businesses to deny their female employees the cost-free contraception coverage to which they are entitled under federal law, if those businesses cite a religious objection to providing this coverage. Under this policy, the government would not ensure that others would extend such coverage to these women. In other words, Trump administration rules could allow the religious objections of corporate bosses to end their female employees' entitlement to benefits that help reduce unintended pregnancies and abortions.

On the one hand, the Department of Justice forcefully defends free-exercise claims like these.[58] On the other, the department prosecutes individuals who provide water and other humanitarian and medical aid to undocumented immigrants in the desert because of their faith.[59] The administration is also reportedly demanding "immediate possession" of at least some of the land where a historic Catholic mission sits for use in its planned border wall, despite the diocese's religious objections.[60] Administration officials never mention claims like these when they discuss religious liberty. It also does not appear that the administration has made any effort to reconsider its positions in the face of strong religious objections. One need not defend every free exercise claim to take a principled approach. But it is striking to see how differently free exercise claims are treated when they do not align with the administration's policy agenda.[61]

Meanwhile, the Department of Justice's guidance on religious liberty, which is currently being implemented across the federal government, mentions free exercise roughly five times as often as the no-establishment command and completely ignores the constitutional bar on governmental promotion of religion generally.[62] And at the Supreme Court, some justices are calling for decades of Establishment Clause precedent to be overturned. Justice Clarence Thomas believes the Establishment Clause should not even apply to the states. If it does, Thomas says, the Clause should only prohibit laws that involve "the type of actual legal coercion that was a hallmark of historical establishments of religion," like a state statute requiring individuals to attend or subsidize a church.[63]

Justice Neil Gorsuch, with Justice Thomas joining him, would reverse precedent so that Americans would be unable to challenge governmental monuments or symbols containing religious imagery, as long as the state does not force anyone to pray or bow down before them.[64] Moreover, these justices argue, "a practice consistent with our nation's traditions is just as [constitutionally] permissible whether undertaken today or 94 years ago."[65] Under this theory, the United States government could erect a 32-foot tall Latin cross monument today as a memorial for military service members who gave their lives in Afghanistan and Iraq.

– It is easy to see why such a memorial would not seem to honor service members who were not Christians. What may be less obvious is that this kind of memorial also distorts the Christian message. The Latin cross is the symbol of the sacrifice and resurrection of Jesus Christ and biblical promises of eternal life. When individuals, including individual soldiers who are buried in Arlington Cemetery, request that the cross be placed on their headstones, the cross communicates that message. But when the government appropriates the cross, saying it represents sacrifice for the United States, it secularizes and nationalizes this sacred symbol.

Similar concerns would arise if the Court were to chip away at precedent prohibiting government-sponsored prayers and other forms of religious expression, and these concerns must be considered given the newly configured Supreme Court.[66] When the government sponsors religious messages, it tends to suppress or moderate expression that seems to challenge the state's agenda. In these and other ways, faith can become a creature of the state, warped and weakened. And as the government's big megaphone amplifies its preferred religious message, it is likely to drown out competing messages reflecting a more authentic religious witness. Governmental sponsorship of prayers and other religious messages also generally lead to state favoritism for certain faiths. Communities simply will not tolerate governmental sponsorship of all religions, and officials will respond to this social fact. These are some of the reasons the Supreme Court has said: "[T]here is a crucial difference between *government* speech endorsing religion, which the Establishment Clause forbids, and *private* speech endorsing religion, which the Free Speech and Free Exercise Clauses protect."[67] The Court's reference to "private speech" means speech attributable to nongovernmental institutions and individuals.

The Supreme Court has also wisely drawn a line prohibiting religious use of government grant funds. What the state funds, it regulates, even if what it funds is religious. Further, the use of government grant money for certain sacred texts or forms of worship would generate fierce opposition. This line, therefore, has guarded against government meddling in faith and de facto preferences for some religions over others, while also protecting liberty of conscience.

This constitutional rule, however, may be vulnerable now too.[68] Indeed, support may be growing for the notion that the Constitution not only permits but requires the government to allow houses of worship and other religious entities to use such aid for religious items or activities, if doing so could be said to serve some secular purpose and if grants are given to a broad range of religious and nonreligious bodies alike.[69] A ruling of this kind would have the head-spinning effect of transforming what has long been prohibited by the Establishment Clause to be required by the Free Exercise Clause.

These challenges must be addressed, but the answer is not to underprotect religious exercise and inflate the Establishment Clause. Some government officials have done the former by crafting religious exemptions from laws and policies that demonstrate little understanding of faith and freedom. In 2011, for example, three federal agencies adopted an exceedingly narrow definition of the religious organizations that would be exempt from the Affordable Care

Act's requirement that most employers provide their employees with cost-free contraception coverage. To be exempt, religious organizations had to meet *all* of the following criteria: (1) have the inculcation of religious values as their purpose; (2) primarily employ persons who shared their religious tenets; (3) primarily serve persons who shared their religious tenets; and (4) be a house of worship or closely associated body, a convention or association of churches, or a religious order.[70] Such requirements could have had the effect of pressuring religious bodies to violate a basic tenet of their faith—serving all people, no matter their faith, background, or beliefs. The federal agencies were right to be attentive to the fact that most women are entitled to cost-free contraception coverage under the Affordable Care Act, but this policy was the wrong way to do so.[71] President Obama insisted that this policy be changed. While the new policy was ultimately not acceptable to all, it was a genuine effort to find common ground.[72]

Also, some government officials have erred by presuming that religious beliefs and practices are insincere and that everything they would define as "intolerance" can and should be eradicated by the state. The chairman of the independent United States Civil Rights Commission (USCRC) seemed to do so in a 2016 report, while also casting aspersions on religious freedom generally. The USCRC chairman said, "The phrases 'religious liberty' and 'religious freedom' will stand for nothing except hypocrisy so long as they remain code words for discrimination, intolerance, racism, sexism, homophobia, Islamophobia, Christian supremacy or any form of intolerance."[73] Government officials certainly may share their views on law and policy, and they must reject some requests for religious exemptions. But they should do so without disparaging people's faith or appearing to call into question an entire First Amendment right.

Similarly, government leaders cross a line when they call for religious beliefs to change. In remarks to a 2015 global women's conference, for example, former secretary of state and then–presidential candidate Hillary Clinton gave a speech promoting education and reproductive rights for women and said, "[D]eep-seated cultural codes, religious beliefs and structural biases have to be changed."[74] Again, it is fair to debate law and policy and appropriate to deny certain requests for religious exemptions. But it is emphatically not the place of government to say that faith must change.

Other threats to religious freedom are attacks on common-ground initiatives. Common-ground initiatives should not be confused with efforts to broker compromises. Compromises happen when people on different sides of an issue agree to meet somewhere in the middle. Common-ground projects, on the other hand, involve participants in searches for positions that both sides agree on, even as they disagree on other issues. Significant progress can be made on religious freedom issues when leaders bring diverse individuals together to seek common ground.

In 2009, for example, President Obama assembled a group of religious and community leaders who differed in their religious affiliations, political persuasions, and views on church-state issues. President Obama asked these leaders to seek common ground regarding rules governing partnerships the state forms with faith-based organizations to serve people in need. After painstaking work, the group found important consensus items, including the belief that protections for the religious liberty of social service beneficiaries should be augmented. President Obama then embraced these recommendations through an executive order.

In 2018, however, President Trump struck these religious liberty protections with his own executive order. While Trump said he was promoting religious liberty, he actually dealt the cause a blow. President Trump broke with the usual presidential pattern of honoring the work of common-ground initiatives and undermined support for the many partnerships the government has with faith-based entities.[75]

President Trump is also wrong to claim that perhaps his "greatest contribution to Christianity—and other religions"[76] would be to "totally destroy" the rules[77] barring tax-exempt 501(c)(3) organizations, including tax-exempt 501(c)(3) religious organizations, from endorsing or opposing political candidates.[78] Unsurprisingly, the most vocal proponents of President Trump's initiative are politicians.[79] Candidates, not congregations, would be the primary beneficiaries of such a change. If passed, this legislation could result in government officials subtly pressuring congregations and other religious organizations for endorsements in exchange for certain governmental benefits, like zoning and other land-use permits. As Trevor Potter, one of President George H. W. Bush's appointees to the Federal Election Commission, has said, revising tax laws in this way also could effectively convert houses of worship and other faith-based bodies into "super dark money groups"—tax-exempt bodies that allow anonymous donors to funnel tax-deductible political donations through them.[80] And at a time when Russians and other foreign-state actors are seeking to manipulate U.S. elections, the United States should not create a legal path for religion-themed front operations.

PRESERVING AND PERFECTING A SYSTEM THAT HAS SERVED US WELL

This book suggests steps policymakers and civil society leaders can take to meet such challenges and to preserve and advance progress that has been made under religious liberty guarantees and the best traditions of religious engagement in American public life.

In her final opinion as a justice of the U.S. Supreme Court, Justice Sandra Day O'Connor reflected on some of these guarantees and traditions. Justice O'Connor wrote:

> Reasonable minds can disagree about how to apply the Religion Clauses in a given case. But the goal of the Clauses is clear: to carry out the Founders' plan of preserving religious liberty to the fullest extent possible in a pluralistic society. By enforcing the Clauses, we have kept religion a matter for the individual conscience, not for the prosecutor or bureaucrat. At a time when we see around the world the violent consequences of the assumption of religious authority by government, Americans may count themselves fortunate: Our regard for constitutional boundaries has protected us from similar travails, while allowing private religious exercise to flourish . . . . Americans attend their places of worship more often than do citizens of other developed nations, and describe religion as playing an especially important role in their lives. Those who would renegotiate the boundaries between church and state must therefore answer a difficult question: Why would we trade a system that has served us so well for one that has served others so poorly?[81]

Americans should not trade the system that has served us so well. Instead, Americans should work diligently to preserve and perfect it.

How to Read This Book

Readers can read this book in one of two ways. The first way would be the traditional approach—reading the book from beginning to end. Most chapters focus on federal law and policy in a particular area, with a strong emphasis on key Supreme Court cases.

As readers make their way through the chapters, some questions may arise. For example, some readers might wonder why dissenting as well as majority Supreme Court opinions, and even aspects of cases that have subsequently been overruled, are sometimes discussed. The chapters aim not only to communicate key points of law but also to provide a sense of the varied values at stake in many of these cases. The tensions among these values usually do not go away, even when one set of concerns wins the day at the Court.

It is also worth noting that the Court normally is simply considering whether a given resolution of an issue passes legal muster, not whether there is another available resolution that might dignify more interests or otherwise produce a more equitable result. As policymakers do their work, they should always consider whether their solutions could create a greater measure of fairness for all interests at stake.

Readers should know what this book is and is not. The book aims to serve as an accessible guide to some key aspects of federal law and policy that are relevant to religion's role in public life. All references to the Constitution and the Supreme Court are to the United States Constitution and the United States Supreme Court. The book is not a guide to state and local law and policy, and it is not a legal treatise or an exhaustive treatment of church-state issues. Also, the book offers a set of recommendations for readers' consideration. It does not offer legal advice, nor does it opine on, much less resolve, every controversy.

Some readers may wonder why segments of the book contain a disproportionate amount of material regarding activities that took place during the administration of President Barack Obama. The answer is that the author served as the chair of President Obama's inaugural Advisory Council on Faith-Based and Neighborhood Partnerships from 2009 to 2010 and as a member of the White House staff during President Obama's second term (2013–2017). Thus, while a wide range of presidents and policies are discussed, the author's greatest familiarity is obviously with President Obama's administration.

The second way to read this book is to do a speed-read. On the page before each chapter, summary points of law and policy are presented. These points are the "bottom line up front," sometimes abbreviated as BLUF. Public servants sometimes insert a BLUF section at the top of briefing memos to showcase key points and conclusions and to allow a reader to read only the BLUF section if he or she does not have time to read the rest of the memo. The speed-read should also include the recommendations at the end of the chapters and the conclusion, which offer additional reflections on how to defend religious freedom and promote a healthy role for religion in American public life today.

Notes on Terminology

As explained in chapter 2, the term "religion" is used in this book as the United States Supreme Court has employed it. Purely for stylistic reasons, the terms "religion" and "faith" are used interchangeably.

As also explained in chapter 2, the Supreme Court generally uses the term "public" to refer to the government. When the Supreme Court refers to "public property," for example, it means government-owned property. When quoting the Supreme Court, this book uses the term "public" in this way.

Otherwise, however, the book uses the term "public" more broadly to refer to "an activity or place that is visible or accessible to a wide variety of people."[82] The focus of the book is "on religious expression and activity that occurs in places and spheres that are visible and accessible to people generally rather than on religious expression and activity that occurs behind the closed doors of homes or houses of worship."[83]

The phrase "religion in American public life" or "religion in the American public square" is used here, therefore, to refer to instances in which religious individuals, institutions, expression, or practices play roles in realms beyond homes or houses of worship. Some of these realms are specifically governmental, such as religious gatherings on state-owned property, religious expression in governmental workplaces, and lobby visits religious individuals and organizations make to the offices of elected officials. Faith-based partnerships with government to serve people in need are another form of religious participation in American public life. The term "faith in public life" also is used to refer to the roles religious individuals, institutions, expression, and practices play in certain nongovernmental spheres such as op-eds in newspapers by clergy or other religious leaders, invitations to officials to speak to religious gatherings, employees' requests for accommodation of their religious beliefs and observance in secular nongovernmental workplaces, and discussions of faith on Twitter or television.

As this book makes clear, different legal rules may apply depending on the relevant actors or the particular sphere where the religious expression or practice occurs. Article VI and the First Amendment to the Constitution apply only to government. Some federal statutes do the same, such as the Religious Land Use and Institutionalized Persons Act (RLUIPA) and the Religious Freedom Restoration Act (RFRA). Other federal laws and policies, however, bind both governmental and nongovernmental entities, including religious bodies. These laws include a range of civil rights measures, such as prohibitions on employment discrimination, that apply to nongovernmental bodies due to their effect on interstate commerce. Other laws require nongovernmental organizations that wish to gain a certain governmental benefit to abide by specific rules, such as the Internal Revenue Service's requirement that certain tax-exempt entities not engage in electioneering. This book focuses mostly on laws that only restrain government, but it also includes discussion of some laws that bind nongovernmental bodies as well.

RELIGION AND THE CONSTITUTION

Historical Origins

Religious tests for public office were common when the delegates met at the Constitutional Convention in Philadelphia. At the convention, the delegates decided there should be no religious tests for federal officeholders and inserted such a ban in Article VI. The religious-test ban protects religious freedom in two ways. It ensures that the government cannot disqualify aspiring officeholders simply because of their religious beliefs and affiliations, or lack thereof. Also, by permitting officeholders to swear or affirm their support for the Constitution, the clause allows those whose scruples prohibit them from taking an oath to make an affirmation instead.

When the Constitutional Convention was concluding, George Mason, a delegate from Virginia, suggested an addition to the Constitution: a preface with a bill of rights. The proposal was rejected, but popular demand for a bill of rights resulted in the drafting of such a document by the First Congress.

The first sixteen words of what became the First Amendment are: "Congress shall make no law respecting an establishment of religion, or prohibiting the free exercise thereof." The first clause is called the Establishment Clause and the second is called the Free Exercise Clause.

The First Amendment, including the Establishment and Free Exercise Clauses, was originally intended to apply only to the federal government. The

Supreme Court subsequently confirmed, however, that the Fourteenth Amendment to the Constitution had the effect of applying the religion clauses to the states. This move by the Court is commonly known as the "incorporation doctrine." To understand the history surrounding the religion clauses, therefore, one must look to the adoption of the First and the Fourteenth Amendments.

There has been, and continues to be, debate about aspects of the clauses' historical meaning and how that meaning should shape the law today. Incorporation of the Establishment Clause has been challenged, most notably by Supreme Court Justice Clarence Thomas, and defended by others. There have also been arguments on and off the Court over whether the framers intended the Establishment Clause to ban federal funding for religion generally or only to bar government aid that preferred some faiths over others, thus permitting "nonpreferential aid for religion." Additionally, commentators have considered what the historical record says about governmental expression involving religion. With regard to the Free Exercise Clause, scholars have disagreed about whether original meaning supports mandatory exemptions for religious individuals and institutions even from neutral, generally applicable laws and policies when those laws and policies unnecessarily burden religious practices.

An "originalist" is someone who believes "that the proper way to interpret the Constitution is to determine what the Constitution meant when it was adopted and to give it that meaning today."[1] One need not be an originalist, however, to be interested in, and appreciative of, the history surrounding the adoption of constitutional provisions. Non-originalists do not necessarily agree that this history should define our understanding of constitutional provisions, but they usually agree it is important.[2]

The origins of the Constitution's religious liberty guarantees refer to their initial framing and ratification. As originally adopted, these guarantees applied only to the federal government.

To understand the historical origins of the First Amendment's religion clauses, however, one must also consider the "second adoption" of these clauses—the application of the religion clauses to states and localities through the post–Civil War Fourteenth Amendment.[3] The history of the religious liberty guarantees reverberates through battles at the U.S. Supreme Court and beyond.[4]

A Ban on Religious Tests for Public Office

Religious tests for public office were common at the time the delegates met at the Constitutional Convention in Philadelphia.[5] Oliver Ellsworth (1745–1807), a convention delegate who would later become a U.S. senator and serve as the third chief justice of the U.S. Supreme Court,[6] defined such tests:

> A religious test is an act to be done, or profession to be made, relating to religion (such as partaking of the sacrament according to certain rites and forms, or declaring one's belief of certain doctrines) for the purpose of determining whether his religious opinions are such, that he is admissible to a publick office.[7]

England's Test Act of 1672 required all officeholders to profess a belief against transubstantiation in communion and to receive sacraments aligned with the practices of the Church of England.[8] This test specifically targeted Catholics and had the effect of excluding most other non-Anglicans as well.[9]

Similar restrictions were common in the American colonies and, later, the states. When the delegates met in Philadelphia to craft the Constitution, a number of states banned non-Christians from public office, and some even banned non-Protestants.[10] The Pennsylvania Constitution, for example, required officeholders to make the following profession:

> I do believe in one God, the Creator and Governor of the Universe, the Rewarder of Good and Punisher of the Wicked. And I do acknowledge the Scriptures of the Old and New Testament to be given by Divine Inspiration.[11]

While the delegates to the Constitutional Convention met in Philadelphia, they received a letter about the Pennsylvania oath requirement from Jonas Phillips, a former member of the Philadelphia militia and a founder of Mikveh Israel, a Jewish synagogue.[12] Phillips explained that the oath requirement had the effect of excluding Jewish Americans from public office and violated civil liberties that were supposedly secured by another part of the state constitution.[13] Phillips implored the delegates not to include such a religious test in the new constitution. He placed special emphasis on the contributions Jewish Americans had made to the Revolution. American Jews, like other Americans, should be able to exercise the rights for which they had fought. Phillips said:

> It is well known among all the Citizens of the 13 united states that the Jews have been true and faithfull whigs, & during the late Contest with England they had been foremost in aiding and assisting the States with their lifes & fortunes, they have supported the cause, have bravely fought and bled for liberty which they can not Enjoy.

Therefore if the honourable Convention shall in their Wisdom think fit and alter the said oath & leave out the words to viz —and I do acknowledge the scriptures of the new testament to be given by divine inspiration, then the Israelites will think themself happy to live under a government where all Religious societys are on an Equal footing—I solicit this favour for myself my children & posterity, & for the benefit of all the Israelites through the 13 united states of America.[14]

There was scant discussion of religious tests at the Constitutional Convention and no recorded debate.[15] Roger Sherman of Connecticut thought it unnecessary to rule out these tests with a constitutional provision—"the prevailing liberality [was] a sufficient security [against] such tests."[16] Other delegates, however, expressed concern about the potential exclusion of non-Christians and others through religious-test oaths.[17] The delegates ultimately decided that, while officeholders should be required to swear or affirm that they would support the Constitution, no religious test should be part of that oath or affirmation for federal officeholders.[18] Luther Martin, a Maryland delegate, said this provision "was adopted by a great majority of the convention, and without much debate."[19]

The test ban drew much more attention during the ratification debates, however. Delegates in some states objected to the fact that officeholders would not be required to profess a belief in God or Jesus Christ, for example, and that Catholics would not be excluded from federal office.[20] Other delegates defended the test ban, arguing that such tests were "useless and counterproductive."[21] Oliver Ellsworth said:

[T]he sole purpose and effect of [the ban on religious tests for office] is to exclude persecution, and to secure to you the important right of religious liberty . . . . In our country every man has a right to worship God in that way which is most agreeable to his own conscience. If he be a good and peaceable citizen, he is liable to no penalties or incapacities on account of his religious sentiments; or in other words, he is not subject to persecution.[22]

Another argument, however, may have been decisive. If a religious test were to be imposed, no one could be sure that the test they preferred would be adopted.[23]

In any case, the test ban was inserted in Article VI of the Constitution. The ban protects religious freedom in two ways. It ensures that the government cannot disqualify aspiring federal officeholders simply because of their religious beliefs and affiliations, or lack thereof. Also, by permitting officeholders to swear or affirm their support for the Constitution, the clause allows those whose scruples prohibit them from taking an oath to make an affirmation instead. The delegates added the latter protection mostly in an effort to respect the consciences of Quakers, some of whom were prominent.[24] Members of other small faiths also believed the Bible prohibits the swearing of oaths.[25] Including the option of affirming rather than swearing was exceedingly minor as a drafting matter. Yet it sent a powerful signal of respect for the rights of conscience, including those of religious minorities.

Article VI had the effect of widening the circle of inclusion in American politics. Moving forward, the federal government would not be deprived of talented national leaders for irrelevant reasons.[26] James Madison said: "[T]he door of this part of the federal government is open to merit of every description, whether native or adoptive, whether young or old, and without regard to poverty or wealth, or to any particular profession of religious faith."[27] Baptist minister John Leland, a leading opponent of governmental establishments, concurred:

> The federal constitution certainly had the advantage of any of the state constitutions, in being made by the wisest men in the whole nation, and after an experiment of a number of years trial upon republican principles; and that constitution forbids Congress ever to establish any kind of religion, or require any religious test to qualify any officer in any department of federal government. Let a man be Pagan, Turk, Jew or Christian, he is eligible to any post in that government.[28]

As the delegates finished their work, Article VI's ban on religious tests stood as the only mention of religion in the Constitution.

"[N]ot a Shadow of Right in the General Government to Intermeddle with Religion"?

When the Constitutional Convention was concluding, George Mason, a Virginia delegate, suggested an addition to the document: a preface with a bill of rights.[29] Concerned about the potential of the Constitution to encroach on civil rights and liberties, Mason argued that a bill of rights "would give great quiet to the people, and, with the aid of the state declarations, a bill might be prepared in a few hours."[30] Massachusetts delegate Elbridge Gerry made a motion to establish a committee to draft such a bill of rights.[31] The motion, however, was rejected.[32] The decision was undoubtedly based partially on the merits of the matter, but it is also likely that a more mundane reason played a role. The delegates had been at their painstaking and secretive labors in Philadelphia for an entire summer. They were tired and ready to go home.[33]

Once again, what was a minor matter at the Constitutional Convention became a major one in the ratification debates. Antifederalists made the case for adding a bill of rights to the Constitution, including protections for religious freedom. Federalists, however, insisted that a bill of rights was unnecessary. "There is not a shadow of right in the general government to intermeddle with religion. Its least interference with it would be a most flagrant usurpation," James Madison argued.[34] Proponents of a free exercise amendment had sound reasons for rejecting such arguments, however. As Professor Michael McConnell, a former federal appellate judge and leading First Amendment scholar, has explained:

> The federal government would exercise plenary regulatory authority in the territories, the District of Columbia, and the military. Its powers of taxation, spending, immigration and naturalization, copyright, international trade, bankruptcy, and relations with Indian tribes and foreign governments could, with little imagination, be expected to affect the exercise of religion. The potential of the necessary and proper clause might be viewed—and was viewed, according to Madison—as the most threatening of all. Thus, a federal government bent on religious oppression could accomplish such oppression under pretext of one of the enumerated powers. Moreover, the argument that the lack of enumerated power could serve as a sufficient assurance of religious liberty offered no comfort to those who understood free exercise of religion to entail exemption from otherwise legitimate general legislation. Such legislation is by definition within the enumerated powers of the federal government.[35]

The argument that religious liberty protections were unnecessary simply did not stand up to scrutiny.

The Federalists' other main argument was that the systems of federalism and checks and balances, as well as the existence of multiple faiths in the United States, would guard against governmental mischief in this area. When delegates argued that state laws would be sufficient to protect individual rights, George Mason noted that "[t]he Laws of the U.S. are to be paramount to State Bills of Rights."[36] When Madison argued that "the multiplicity of sects" was "the best and only security for religious liberty in any society; for where there is such a variety of sects, there cannot be a majority of any one sect to oppress and persecute the rest,"[37] Antifederalists demurred. A multiplicity of faiths might guard against rank religious discrimination by the federal government, but it would not stop the federal government from burdening religious practices with its wide-ranging powers through "ignorance or indifference."[38]

In August 8, 1789, the Committee of the United Baptist Churches of Virginia wrote to President Washington to express its concern about the new Constitution's lack of protection for religious freedom but also its confidence in Washington's leadership.[39] The Baptists noted that they had personal experience with "mobs, fines, bonds and prisons" in Virginia "under the regal government."[40] Attempting to reassure them, President Washington responded:

> If I could have entertained the slightest apprehension that the Constitution framed by the Convention where I had the honor to preside, might possibly endanger the religious rights of any ecclesiastical society, certainly I would never have placed my signature to it; and if I could now conceive that the general government might even be so administered, as to render the liberty of conscience insecure, I beg you will be persuaded, that no one would be more zealous than myself, to establish effectual barriers against the horrors of spiritual tyranny, and every species of religious persecution. For you, doubtless, remember, I have often expressed my sentiments, that any man, conducting himself as a good citizen, and being accountable to God alone for his religious opinions, ought to be protected in worshiping the Deity according to the dictates of his own conscience.[41]

The debate in Virginia, along with a threat to his own electoral prospects, eventually changed James Madison's mind.[42] After Madison announced his candidacy for Congress, he learned that some Virginians, including many Baptists, would vote for his opponent, James Monroe, if Madison did not support the addition of a bill of rights to the Constitution. Expecting a tight race, Madison announced his full support for a bill of rights generally and protections for the rights of conscience specifically, gaining strong support from Virginia Baptists and narrowly winning a congressional seat.[43]

After the states ratified the Constitution in 1788, James Madison began drafting a bill of rights.[44] On September 25, 1789, Congress approved twelve amendments to be sent to the states for ratification.[45] Ten of these amendments were ratified on December 15, 1791, becoming part of the Constitution.[46] The amendments became known as the Bill of Rights.

"Congress Shall Make No Law . . . ."

The first sixteen words of what became the First Amendment are: "Congress shall make no law respecting an establishment of religion, or prohibiting the free exercise thereof." There has been, and continues to be, debate about aspects of the clause's original meaning and how that meaning should shape the law today.

To the framers of the Bill of Rights, concerns about religious establishments centered on questions about government aid for religion. Some argue that the framers intended the Establishment Clause only to bar government aid that preferred some faiths over others, thus permitting "nonpreferential aid for religion." In a dissenting opinion in a 1985 Supreme Court case, for example, Justice William Rehnquist argued:

> It would seem from th[e] [historical] evidence that the Establishment Clause of the First Amendment had acquired a well-accepted meaning: it forbade establishment of a national religion, and forbade preference among religious sects or denominations. Indeed, the first American dictionary defined the word "establishment" as "the act of establishing, founding, ratifying or ordaining," such as in "[t]he episcopal form of religion, so called, in England." The Establishment Clause did not require government neutrality between religion and irreligion, nor did it prohibit the Federal Government from providing nondiscriminatory aid to religion. There is simply no historical foundation for the proposition that the Framers intended to build the "wall of separation" that was constitutionalized in *Everson*.[47]

The argument that the framers intended generally to ban federal funding for religion, however, is the much more defensible claim.[48] The First Congress repeatedly rejected drafts of the Establishment Clause that would have codified the view that nonpreferential aid was permitted.[49] Instead, the body adopted a broad statement of the Establishment Clause. The final draft does not bar only the establishment of a national religion or the establishment of a particular denomination or sect. Instead, the First Amendment says there can be no law respecting an establishment of *religion*.[50]

As Justice David Souter has said:

> What we thus know of the Framers' experience underscores the observation of one prominent commentator, that confining the Establishment Clause to a prohibition on preferential aid "requires a premise that the Framers were extraordinarily bad drafters—that they believed one thing but adopted language that said something substantially different, and that they did so after repeatedly attending to the choice of language." We must presume, since there is no conclusive evidence to the contrary, that the Framers embraced the significance of their textual judgment. Thus, on balance, history neither contradicts nor warrants reconsideration of the settled principle that the Establishment Clause forbids support for religion in general no less than support for one religion or some.[51]

Also, while the framers focused on financial forms of government support for religion, that does not mean prohibiting nonfinancial forms of state-backed faith is inconsistent with the Clause's original meaning. As Professor Douglas Laycock, one of the foremost scholars of the religion clauses, has said, "[W]e are not unfaithful to the Framers' intent when we apply their principle to analogous problems."[52]

The Supreme Court has not spoken with one voice on such issues, but Court majorities have implemented these basic understandings of the Establishment Clause. In other words, Court majorities have read the Establishment Clause to prohibit the government from advancing or denigrating religion generally as well as from preferring one faith over another, whether the matter involves government aid or expression.[53]

Of the two religion clauses, the Establishment Clause drew the most attention in the First Congress and the ratifying state conventions. The First Congress also considered, however, several drafts of the Free Exercise Clause,[54] and aspects of the original meaning of that clause have been hotly debated as well.

One argument regarding the original meaning of the Free Exercise Clause focuses on whether the clause was intended to protect not only faith-based beliefs and practices but also ethical or moral beliefs and practices not anchored in religion.[55] The word "religion" is used only once in the First Amendment. It would be odd, therefore, for that word to have two different meanings—prohibiting the establishment of religion only, while at the same time protecting the free exercise of religion as well as nonreligious conscientious beliefs and practices.[56]

Perhaps the most vigorously debated issue regarding the original meaning of the Free Exercise Clause, however, is whether that clause was intended to require exemptions for individuals and organizations from religiously neutral and generally applicable laws when those individuals and organizations assert religious objections to compliance with such laws. Must religious objectors to military combat, for example, be exempted from such requirements, if the state has no narrowly tailored compelling interest for refusing such an exemption? The Court has left this history largely unexplored, and scholarship to date suggests it is not conclusive.[57]

As ratified in 1791, the Bill of Rights applied only to the federal government, leaving states unencumbered by the Establishment and Free Exercise Clauses. States that had religious establishments were free to continue them.[58] But states gradually abandoned their establishments, with Massachusetts being the last to do so in 1833.[59] Approximately a century later, the Supreme Court found that the adoption of the Fourteenth Amendment in the wake of the Civil War had the effect of applying the religion clauses to the states. Thus, the historical meaning of these clauses now had two locus points: the adoption of the First and the Fourteenth Amendments.

The Establishment and Free Exercise Clauses Apply to the States

In July 1868, the states ratified the Fourteenth Amendment to the Constitution. The first section of the Fourteenth Amendment declares:

No state shall make or enforce any law which shall abridge the privileges or immunities of citizens of the United States; nor shall any state deprive any person of life, liberty, or property, without due process of law; nor deny to any person within its jurisdiction the equal protection of the laws.

In the 1940s, the Supreme Court held that the religion clauses of the First Amendment applied to states as well as to the federal government through the Fourteenth Amendment.[60] This move by the Court is commonly known as the "incorporation doctrine."[61] The Court said:

The fundamental concept of liberty embodied in that [Fourteenth] Amendment embraces the liberties guaranteed by the First Amendment. The First Amendment declares that Congress shall make no law respecting an establishment of religion or prohibiting the free exercise thereof. The Fourteenth Amendment has rendered the legislatures of the states as incompetent as Congress to enact such laws.[62]

There is little resistance to the notion that the Free Exercise Clause applies to states through the Fourteenth Amendment.[63] Also, no one disputes that the Establishment Clause was initially intended to apply only to the federal government. The question that triggers fierce debate is whether the Court acted appropriately when it applied the Establishment Clause to the states under the incorporation doctrine.

When the Supreme Court specifically held that the Establishment Clause applied to states through the Fourteenth Amendment,[64] it provided scant reasoning to support its decision, thus leaving the holding vulnerable to attack.[65] To say the Court did not do enough at the outset to justify the incorporation of the Establishment Clause is not to say, however, that this doctrine cannot be justified.

Justice Potter Stewart questioned the incorporation of the Establishment Clause in a case that triggered a spectacular backlash against the Court: the 1963 ruling striking down a requirement that Pennsylvania schools begin each day with Bible readings—*Abington Township v. Schempp.*[66] In his dissent, Justice Stewart argued that the circumstances leading to the adoption of the Establishment Clause "strongly suggest" that the clause "was primarily an attempt to insure that Congress not only would be powerless to establish a national church, but would also be unable to interfere with existing state establishments."[67] Stewart accepted "the proposition that the Fourteenth Amendment has somehow absorbed the Establishment Clause . . . ."[68] Yet, Justice Stewart claimed, "it is not without irony that a constitutional provision evidently designed to leave the States free to go their own way should now have become a restriction upon their autonomy."[69]

Justice William Brennan responded to Justice Stewart's arguments in his opinion agreeing with the Court's decision in *Schempp*. Whatever the framers of the First Amendment's Establishment Clause had intended, Brennan said, the framers of the Fourteenth Amendment could not have intended that the clause protect state establishments of religion.[70] Justice Brennan explained:

> For it is clear on the record of history that the last of the formal state establishments was dissolved more than three decades before the Fourteenth Amendment was ratified, and thus the problem of protecting official state churches from federal encroachments could hardly have been any concern of those who framed the post–Civil War Amendments.[71]

Brennan also responded to the argument that the "liberty" guaranteed by the Fourteenth Amendment could not incorporate the Establishment Clause because that clause only protects states' rights, not individual freedom. Do not "underestimate[] the role of the Establishment Clause as a co-guarantor, with the Free Exercise Clause, of religious liberty," Brennan warned.[72] The framers of the Constitution "did not entrust the liberty of religious beliefs to either clause alone."[73]

Approximately forty years later, Justice Clarence Thomas picked up the thread of Justice Stewart's argument.[74] But instead of accepting the notion that the Fourteenth Amendment "somehow absorbed" the Establishment Clause, Justice Thomas challenged it. Thomas addressed the issue in a case testing the constitutionality of the words "under God" in the Pledge of Allegiance as a violation of the Establishment Clause: *Elk Grove Unified School District v. Newdow*. The Supreme Court found that Michael Newdow, the man who brought the claim, lacked standing to sue. Thomas agreed that Newdow should lose his case, but he disagreed about the grounds for such a decision. In a separate opinion concurring only in the Court's judgment, Justice Thomas said the pledge did not come close to violating the Establishment Clause, in part because the Establishment Clause "resists incorporation."[75] Thomas explained:

> I accept that the Free Exercise Clause, which clearly protects an individual right, applies against the States through the Fourteenth Amendment. But the Establishment Clause is another matter. The text and history of the Establishment Clause strongly suggest that it is a federalism provision intended to prevent Congress from interfering with state establishments. Thus, unlike the Free Exercise Clause, which does protect an individual right, it makes little sense to incorporate the Establishment Clause.[76]

According to Justice Thomas, "The best argument in favor of incorporation would be that, by disabling Congress from establishing a national religion, the Clause protected an individual right, enforceable against the

Federal Government, to be free from coercive federal establishments."[77] Thomas, however, rejected this argument, too:

> [E]ven assuming that the Establishment Clause precludes the Federal Government from establishing a national religion, it does not follow that the Clause created or protects any individual right. For the reasons discussed above, it is more likely that States and only States were the direct beneficiaries. Moreover, incorporation of this putative individual right leads to a peculiar outcome: It would prohibit precisely what the Establishment Clause was intended to protect—*state* establishments of religion. Nevertheless, the potential right against federal establishments is the only candidate for incorporation.[78]

The application of the Establishment Clause to the states needs to be reconsidered, Justice Thomas said.[79]

Unsurprisingly, Justice Thomas' opinion in the *Newdow* case drew responses, including responses from legal scholars who poked holes in his arguments.[80] While the framers of the First Amendment clearly did not intend the Establishment Clause to apply to the states, scholars said, they also did not necessarily intend to protect state establishments, which were already crumbling at the time the Constitution was adopted.[81] The framers simply left this matter to the states.

Also, scholars emphasized that the Establishment Clause was never simply a federalism provision or even merely a structural restraint on government's power.[82] By restraining the government from establishing religion, the clause protects individual liberties from incursion. In other words, when the government is barred from establishing religion, that bar creates freedom for all who might have otherwise been subject to such an establishment. When the Establishment Clause was initially adopted, it created that kind of liberty from federal establishments. When Congress prohibited states from establishing religion, the Establishment Clause created individual liberty from those establishments too.

Extending that kind of freedom was a perfectly sensible step to take, and that is what Congress did after the Civil War by applying the Establishment Clause to states through the Fourteenth Amendment.[83] Further, the drafters and ratifiers of the Fourteenth Amendment raised concerns about the Southern states' violation of no-establishment principles, including these states' regulation of the religious freedom of slaves and black churches and their repression of any religious leadership, black or white, that opposed slavery.[84] Slaves were not permitted to have their own ministers, and they could not hold worship services if whites were not present, for example.[85] Professor Kurt Lash has observed: "By 1860, the South had erected the most comprehensive religious establishment to exist on American soil since Massachusetts Bay."[86]

These justifications provide ample support for the Supreme Court's incorporation of the Establishment Clause against states through the Fourteenth Amendment.[87] "At the very least," as one scholar has said, "one may reasonably conclude that slave-state action to promote proslavery Christianity violated both free exercise and anti-establishment norms and that the concern of members of the Reconstruction Congresses to eliminate this practice reflected an intention to apply both [establishment and free exercise] norms to the states."[88]

While a handful of church-state cases reached the U.S. Supreme Court before 1940, the pace picked up after the Court recognized that the First Amendment's religion clauses applied to states too.[89] In time, the incorporation doctrine brought some of the most significant church-state cases before the highest court in the land.

2

RELIGION AND THE CONSTITUTION

Some Key Concepts and Cases

The Constitution prohibits the government from disqualifying aspiring officeholders due simply to their religious beliefs and affiliations, or lack thereof. The state cannot adopt a set of religious beliefs and attempt to hold officeholders accountable to those beliefs. This ban obviously has the effect of protecting those who do not claim a belief in God or any religious commitments. It also protects believers from whatever religious tests governmental bodies might decide to impose.

The First Amendment's religion clauses place special limits on government that pertain to religion. For example, both religion clauses bar the government from interfering with the ability of religious organizations to make employment decisions regarding their ministers. This protection is often called the "ministerial exception."

Under the Establishment Clause, the government may neither promote nor denigrate religion. The government also cannot prefer one or more faiths over others. These principles extend far beyond an explicit governmental preference for Baptists, Buddhists, or Baha'is. Neutrality requirements are not satisfied, for example, simply by ensuring that a law or government policy is neutral on its face. Text that is facially neutral will not save a policy if discrimination lurks behind it. The Court has applied these and related Establishment Clause principles to governmental aid programs and expression.

Under the Free Exercise Clause, laws may not target religious beliefs and practices. Federal statutes, including the Religious Freedom Restoration Act (RFRA) and the Religious Land Use and Institutionalized Persons Act (RLUIPA), provide stronger protections for free exercise. Under RFRA, for example, the federal government may not substantially burden religious exercise unless it has a compelling reason for doing so, and only if the government advances that interest by the means that is least restrictive of religious exercise. At the same time, the Establishment Clause places certain limits on religious exemptions. Under the Establishment Clause, for example, the government must consider the burdens or harms a religious exemption might impose on those who do not benefit from it. The Court has invalidated religious exemptions that have failed to strike an appropriate balance.

The First Amendment's religion clauses sometimes compel the government to take certain actions and sometimes forbid the state from doing so. At other times, however, neither clause commands a result, giving the government the freedom to act or not, as it chooses.

Justice Robert Jackson famously said the U.S. Supreme Court is "not final because we are infallible, but we are infallible only because we are final."[1] Like the Court's other decisions, its rulings on religious freedom are infallible only in this sense. Even so, those rulings have rightly protected a robust role for faith in public life and done much to secure religious freedom for all.

To interpret and apply the Constitution's provisions, the Supreme Court considers their original meaning, text, structure, and undergirding values. Taking into account its previous decisions, known as "precedent," is another tool the Court uses. When the Court seeks to maintain continuity with its prior decisions, it emphasizes the doctrine known as "stare decisis," which means "to stand by things decided."[2] A review of some of the broad strokes of First Amendment precedent sets the stage for closer examinations of relevant decisions and issues in specific contexts.[3]

RELIGION AND THE CONSTITUTIONAL FRAMEWORK

The Constitution mentions religion twice, once in Article VI and once in the First Amendment. Article VI requires officeholders to support the Constitution, while prohibiting religious tests for public office. Individuals may not be disqualified from public office simply because of their religious beliefs and affiliations, or lack thereof.

The first sixteen words of the First Amendment are: "Congress shall make no law respecting an establishment of religion, or prohibiting the free exercise thereof." The first clause is known as the Establishment Clause, and the second as the Free Exercise Clause. Both clauses place special limits on government that pertain to religion.

The Supreme Court has never adopted a definition of the term "religion" as a constitutional matter, although it has sometimes spoken to these issues.[4] In a case involving a federal statute, for example, the Court interpreted the term "religious training or belief." The statute excused individuals from combatant training and service if they opposed war due to their "religious training or belief" and defined that term as "an individual's belief in a relation to a Supreme Being involving duties superior to those arising from any human relation, but [not including] essentially political, sociological, or philosophical views or a merely personal moral code."[5] The Court interpreted that term in the following way:

> Under the 1940 [Selective Training and Service] Act, it was necessary only to have a conviction based upon religious training and belief; we believe that is all that is required here. Within that phrase would come all sincere religious beliefs which are based upon a power or being, or upon a faith, to which all else is subordinate or upon which all else is ultimately dependent. The test might be stated in these words: A sincere and meaningful belief which occupies in the life of its possessor a place parallel to that filled by the God of those admittedly qualifying for the exemption comes within the statutory definition. This construction avoids imputing to Congress an intent to classify different religious beliefs, exempting some and excluding others, and is in accord with the well-established congressional policy of equal treatment for those whose opposition to service is grounded in their religious tenets.[6]

This expansive reading of the statutory language, therefore, was due at least in part to the Court's interest in ensuring that the statute was not applied in a way that discriminated against some beliefs that were rooted in religion.

In a subsequent First Amendment case involving the Amish community, the Court recognized that the Amish had free exercise rights, but said such protections did not extend to other "way[s] of life, however virtuous or admirable," if they were "based on purely secular considerations."[7] Practices that were merely philosophical did not qualify. Similarly, in another Free Exercise Clause case, the Court said: "Only beliefs rooted in religion are protected by the Free Exercise Clause, which, by its terms, gives special protection to the exercise of religion."[8]

In sum, the precise borders of a constitutional definition of the term "religion" remain unsettled. Rather than exploring those borders, this book focuses on expression and activities that the Supreme Court has said are covered by the Constitution's religious liberty guarantees.

No Religious Tests

Roy Reed Torcaso was born in 1910 in Enumclaw, Washington, to a Catholic father and a Protestant mother. Torcaso, however, did not embrace a faith as an adult.[9] While Torcaso was working as a bookkeeper, his boss urged him to become a notary public. As one who aspired to hold office in the state of Maryland, Torcaso was required to swear the following oath:

> In the presence of Almighty God, I, Roy R. Torcaso, do solemnly promise and declare that I will support the Constitution of the United States; and that I will be faithful and bear true allegiance to the State of Maryland, and support the Constitution and Laws thereof; and that I will, to the best of my skill and judgment, diligently and faithfully without partiality or prejudice execute the office of Notary Public of The State of Maryland
>
> In and For Montgomery County
>
> according to the Constitution and Laws of this State.
>
> I, Roy R. Torcaso, do declare that I believe in the existence of God.[10]

Torcaso refused. "The point at issue," Torcaso said, "is not whether I believe in a Supreme Being, but whether the state has a right to inquire into my beliefs."[11]

The state of Maryland rejected Torcaso's bid to serve as a notary public. The Maryland Constitution generally prohibited religious tests for public office, but it made an exception for requiring a belief in God. Maryland's highest court upheld the application of a religious test to Torcaso, saying he was not required to do anything because no one had to hold public office.[12]

Torcaso asked the Supreme Court to review the lower court's decision, and the Court agreed to do so. Torcaso won his case.

In an opinion written by Justice Black, the Court ruled that Maryland's test violated First Amendment protections for beliefs regarding religion. The Court forcefully rejected the notion that there was no constitutional violation because no one was required to hold public office:

> The fact . . . that a person is not compelled to hold public office cannot possibly be an excuse for barring him from office by state-imposed criteria forbidden by the Constitution. This was settled by our holding in *Wieman v. Updegraff*. We there pointed out that whether or not "an abstract right to public employment exists," Congress could not pass a law providing

"'. . . that no federal employee shall attend Mass or take any active part in missionary work.'"[13]

The Court handed down its ruling in June 1961. In August 1961, Mr. Torcaso became a notary public after swearing to uphold the laws of the state and the federal Constitution, with no mention of religion. His first official act was to witness his daughter's application to take an exam to be a ham radio operator.[14]

The Supreme Court decided this case under the First Amendment, not under Article VI's clause banning religious tests.[15] But the case clearly illustrates the fact that the Constitution prohibits the government from disqualifying aspiring officeholders due simply to their religious beliefs and affiliations, or lack thereof. The state cannot adopt a set of religious beliefs and attempt to hold officeholders accountable. No governmental power gets to be an arbiter of what is sacred or dictate the content of consciences. These protections obviously have the effect of protecting those who do not claim a belief in God or any religious commitments. They also protect believers from whatever religious tests governmental bodies might decide to impose.

The Establishment Clause

The Establishment Clause bars the government from establishing religion—any religion. Many mistakenly view this clause as a limit on religion. Not so. It is a limit on governmental involvement in religion, not on religion itself. In other words, it is a limit on government's power that in turn protects the freedom of nongovernmental organizations and individuals. The government is barred from promoting faith, and that creates freedom for individuals and organizations to do so or not, as they wish.

"The First Amendment," the Court has said, "mandates governmental neutrality between religion and religion, and between religion and nonreligion."[16] Under the U.S. Constitution, there are no second-class faiths, and the government may neither promote nor denigrate religion.[17]

"The clearest command of the Establishment Clause is that one religious denomination cannot be officially preferred over another," the Court has said.[18] These principles extend far beyond an explicit governmental preference for Baptists, Buddhists, or Baha'is. Neutrality requirements are not satisfied, for example, simply by ensuring that a law or government policy is neutral on its face. The Establishment Clause "forbids subtle departures from neutrality, 'religious gerrymanders,' as well as obvious abuses."[19] Text that is facially neutral will not save a policy if discrimination lurks behind it.[20]

Under the First Amendment, the government also may not decide theological matters.[21] In his *Memorial and Remonstrance against Religious Assessments*,

James Madison argued that "Civil Magistrate[s]" are not "competent Judge[s] of Religious Truth."[22]

The Establishment Clause obviously protects nonreligious people and those who practice small or minority faiths. Governmental establishments of religion would clearly harm the consciences of atheists and agnostics and individuals who practice faiths that are not endorsed by the state.

But the Establishment Clause also protects the integrity of faiths that would otherwise be established by the state. Governmental establishments not only harm nonreligious people and minority faiths; they also harm the faith, or faiths, the state chooses to back. An historical example helps to illuminate this point.

In American's founding era, Baptists identified several ways in which state establishments corrupted the faith the government embraced, whether they were establishments of a single faith or multiple faiths, and even when Baptists would receive a share of state support. Virginia Baptists, for example, said the Virginia establishment substituted accountability to the state for accountability to God. They fiercely opposed a proposal whereby citizens would be required to support the pastor of their choice.[23]

In a statement published on Christmas Day in 1776, Virginia Baptists declared:

> We believe that Preachers should be supported only by *voluntary Contributions* from the People, and that a general Assessment (however harmless, yea useful some may conceive it to be) is pregnant with various Evils destructive to the Rights and Privileges of religious Society . . . .
>
> If, therefore, the State provides a Support for Preachers of the Gospel, and they receive it in Consideration of their Services, they must certainly when they Preach act as Officers of the State, and ought to be Accountable thereto for their Conduct, not only as Members of civil Society, but also as *Preachers.* The Consequence of this is, that those whom the State employs in its Service, it has a Right to *regulate* and *dictate to*; it may judge and determine *who* shall preach; *when* and *where* they shall preach; and *what* they must preach . . . .
>
> Sorry should we be to see the *Seeds of Oppression* sown by the Hand of Power amongst us, and as we think it our Duty, to our utmost *in a legal Way*, to retard, or if possible, to prevent the luxuriant Growth of a Plant that has always brought forth the most *bitter and baneful Fruit* wherever it has been cultivated . . . .[24]

Baptist minister John Leland echoed these sentiments. Leland was born in Massachusetts in 1754 and spent some of his later years there,[25] but he lived most of his adult life in Virginia, where he served as a preacher and an advocate for religious freedom.[26] Rev. Leland also was known for his support for Thomas Jefferson and the gift he and others personally gave President Jefferson in 1802—a mammoth cheese weighing 1,238 pounds.[27] Regarding religious establishments, Pastor Leland said:

> Experience, the best teacher, has informed us, that the fondness of magistrates to foster Christianity, has done it more harm than all the persecutions ever did. Persecution, like a lion, tears the saints to death, but leaves Christianity pure: state establishment of religion, like a bear, hugs the saints, but corrupts Christianity, and reduces it to a level with state policy.[28]

To determine whether the Establishment Clause has been violated, the Supreme Court has used a variety of tests and standards.[29] Consider a government grant program that is open to nonprofits, including religious nonprofits. Establishment Clause standards in this context include a general bar on the use of direct aid for religious items, expression, or activities like the purchase of sacred texts or the conduct of worship services.[30]

A somewhat different set of rules applies to indirect aid programs, like programs that provide vouchers to families who can then use those vouchers at religious or nonreligious schools. An indirect aid program must also have a secular purpose and be neutral with regard to religion. But when aid recipients spend their vouchers at religious schools, the aid may be used by the schools for religious items, expression, and activities. In cases like these, the Court has said, any advancement of religion is properly attributable to voucher recipients, not to the state.[31]

The Supreme Court's Establishment Clause precedent has dealt with not only governmental aid but also governmental expression. "[T]here is a crucial difference between *government* speech endorsing religion, which the Establishment Clause forbids, and *private* speech endorsing religion, which the Free Speech and Free Exercise Clauses protect," the Court has noted.[32] As used here, the term "private" means speech attributable to nongovernmental organizations and leaders—not speech "in private."

If speech is attributable to the government, it cannot advance or denigrate religion or prefer one faith over others. But if speech promoting or denigrating religion, or preferring one faith over another, is attributable to nongovernmental organizations and individuals, then it is protected. The Court has held, for example, that public schools cannot organize or sponsor prayers, but they must also protect students' rights to pray voluntarily on campus, whether before, during, or after the school day.[33]

While the Constitution prohibits government-backed religion, it protects the rights of religious individuals and organizations to promote their faith. Governmental neutrality toward religion creates space and freedom for individuals and nongovernmental organizations to share their faith and beliefs as they wish. When the government is barred from promoting faith, expressions of faith can be authentic, not coerced. The First Amendment, therefore, protects religious expression directly and indirectly, by safeguarding the rights of religious organizations and individuals to speak and by ensuring that the state cannot advance or denigrate religion.

Other countries have taken a different approach, attempting to build unity by seeking to erase religious differences in public life. Under the French system of *laïcité*, for example, French schoolchildren are prohibited from wearing a yarmulke or hijab to public school.[34] In contrast, while American public schools themselves are barred from advancing or denigrating religion, students generally have the right to express their faith by wearing religious garb to school. Rather than attempting to promote unity by mandating uniformity, the United States builds unity by prohibiting the government from backing religion but protecting the rights of individuals to promote their faith.

Nonetheless, one still hears the claim that the Supreme Court has banished religion from the public square. A few who make this claim may actually favor a religion-free public square, one where religious expression does not take place on public property and where religious voices are silenced in the debate of public affairs. Others argue that the Supreme Court has driven faith from American public life in an attempt to impugn the Court. No matter their motivations, their claim is false.

The most generous reading of the false claim that the Supreme Court has kicked religion out of the public square is that those who make such a claim are confused about the meaning of the term "public." The Supreme Court uses the term "public" as a legal term of art, meaning "governmental." Common usage of this term, however, is much different. Public expression, activities, or places are usually understood to mean expression, activities, and places that can be seen or accessed by people generally.[35] Put simply, when the Court has rightly said that public entities—meaning governmental entities—should not promote religion, some may have wrongly heard that religion has no role in public life.[36] When discussing religion's role in the public square, keeping these matters in mind is critical.

The Free Exercise Clause

The freedom to believe is important, but it must be accompanied by a freedom to act on those beliefs. The Free Exercise Clause protects exercise—action. Like all other human freedoms, the right to practice one's faith is not absolute. Yet it is a broad freedom that protects not only popular religious beliefs but also unpopular ones, especially when one considers a variety of federal statutes protecting the free exercise of religion.

The freedom to practice one's faith individually is the starting place. The Court has repeatedly recognized that an individual's understanding of his or her faith need not conform to any religious community's standard—even that of his or her own religious community—in order to be protected. In a case involving Eddie Thomas, a Jehovah's Witness and factory worker, for example, Thomas said his religious convictions prevented him from producing turrets for military tanks. In its opinion, the Supreme Court noted that a lower court "appear[ed] to have given significant weight to the fact that another Jehovah's Witness had no scruples about working on tank turrets; for that other Witness, at least, such work was 'scripturally' acceptable." The Court rebuked the lower court for doing so, saying:

> Intrafaith differences of that kind are not uncommon among followers of a particular creed, and the judicial process is singularly ill equipped to resolve such differences in relation to the Religion Clauses. One can, of course, imagine an asserted claim so bizarre, so clearly nonreligious in motivation, as not to be entitled to protection under the Free Exercise Clause; but that is not the case here, and the guarantee of free exercise is not limited to beliefs which are shared by all of the members of a religious sect. Particularly in this sensitive area, it is not within the judicial function and judicial competence to inquire whether the petitioner or his fellow worker more correctly perceived the commands of their common faith. Courts are not arbiters of scriptural interpretation.[37]

In both Establishment and Free Exercise cases, the Court has recognized that the government should not attempt to make theological judgments, acknowledging that "[i]t is not within the judicial ken to question the centrality of particular beliefs or practices to a faith, or the validity of particular litigants' interpretations of those creeds."[38] The state also should not judge an individual's free exercise by the theological convictions of his or her co-religionists.

An individual's religious practices ought not to be held to any communal standard, but the freedom to practice religion as a community is essential. Some religious practices can be done only in groups, like certain forms of Jewish prayer.[39] Similarly, religious communities must have the freedom to build institutions—not only houses of worship, but also schools and seminaries, social service bodies, hospitals, and parachurch ministries that educate and advocate. These institutions represent the faith and inculcate it in rising generations.

The rights of religious communities includes the right to select ministers free from any interference by the state.[40] Indeed, as the Court has explained, both of the First Amendment's religion clauses bar the government from interfering with a religious community's employment decisions regarding its ministers, a doctrine often known as the "ministerial exception":

> The members of a religious group put their faith in the hands of their ministers. Requiring a church to accept or retain an unwanted minister, or punishing a church for failing to do so, intrudes upon more than a mere employment decision. Such action interferes with the internal governance of the church, depriving the church of control over the selection of those who will personify its beliefs. By imposing an unwanted minister, the state infringes the Free Exercise Clause, which protects a religious group's right to shape its own faith and mission through its appointments. According the state the power to determine which individuals will minister to the faithful also violates the Establishment Clause, which prohibits government involvement in such ecclesiastical decisions.[41]

Free exercise and free speech rights also include the right to express one's faith on public issues. The Court has recognized: "Adherents of particular faiths and individual churches frequently take strong positions on public issues . . . . Of course, churches as much as secular bodies and private citizens have that right."[42] Additionally, the Court has held that ministers may not be excluded from public office because they are clergy.[43] As Justice Brennan put it: "Religionists no less than members of any other group enjoy the full measure of protection afforded speech, association, and political activity generally."[44]

The Free Exercise Clause prohibits the government from denying a generally available benefit to an entity or individual solely on account of its religious identity or affiliation, unless there is an interest of the highest order justifying such a denial. The Court found in 2017 that there was no such interest in *Trinity Lutheran Church v. Comer*, a case involving a provision of the Missouri constitution that prohibited a Lutheran preschool and day care center from receiving a grant under the state's playground resurfacing program because they were part of a church.[45] The parties agreed that Missouri law was stricter than the First Amendment's Establishment Clause. In other words, neither party argued that the Establishment Clause *required* Missouri to exclude the church from the program. At the same time, the parties disagreed about whether the First Amendment's Free Exercise Clause *allowed* the state to do so. In a narrow decision, the Supreme Court ruled against the state of Missouri.[46] The state's exclusion of the church due to its religious character was unconstitutional. At the same time, four of the justices who joined the Court's majority opinion noted that the case did not involve religious uses of government funding.

From the early 1960s to 1990, the Supreme Court required the government to meet a demanding standard in a range of cases brought under the First Amendment's Free Exercise Clause. When it substantially burdened religious exercise, the state had to justify that burden with a compelling interest. Further, the government usually had to show that it was advancing that interest in a way that put only the lightest possible burden on the religious practice. This test is called the "compelling interest test."[47]

In its 1990 decision in *Employment Division v. Smith*, however, the Court abruptly ended this practice. The Constitution's Free Exercise Clause did not require application of the compelling interest test when laws and policies were neutral toward religion and generally applicable. Applying the compelling interest test to all free exercise claims would "court[] anarchy," the Court said.[48]

To be neutral, a law must not target faith, either overtly or covertly. To be generally applicable, a law must not restrict only conduct that is religiously motivated. Also, a law is not generally applicable if religiously motivated conduct is restricted because it endangers the state's interests, yet a similar amount of nonreligious conduct that endangers the state's interest in the same way is not.[49] When the city of Hialeah, Florida, for example, enacted animal slaughter laws aimed at suppressing religious practices of members of the Santeria faith, the Court struck them down.[50]

Other federal law sometimes requires the government to exempt organizations and individuals with religious objections from even neutral and generally applicable policies. The Religious Freedom Restoration Act (RFRA) prohibits the federal government from substantially burdening religious exercise unless it has a compelling reason for doing so, and only if the government pursues that interest in a manner that puts the lightest possible burden on religious exercise.[51] Also, the Religious Land Use and Institutionalized Persons Act (RLUIPA) applies the compelling interest test to religious land use and zoning matters and cases in which the religious exercise claims are made in the context of government institutionalization, such as state prisons and immigrant detention centers.[52] These are statutes, not constitutional provisions, but they provide significant protection for religious practices.

The Establishment Clause places certain limits on religious exemptions or accommodations from laws and policies. The government's aim must be to lift burdens on religious exercise, and it must ensure that exemptions or accommodations do not privilege any particular religion or single out any faith for disadvantageous treatment, for example. Also, the state has to "take adequate account of the burdens a requested [religious] accommodation may impose on" people who do not benefit from the accommodation.[53] "[A]n accommodation must be measured so that it does not override other significant interests," the

Court has said.[54] The Court has sometimes invalidated religious exemptions when those accommodations have failed to strike an appropriate balance.[55]

"Play in the Joints"

The First Amendment's religion clauses sometimes compel the government to take certain actions and sometimes forbid it from doing so. At other times, however, neither clause commands a result, giving the government the freedom to act or not, as it chooses. The Supreme Court has put it this way: neither "governmentally established religion [n]or governmental interference with religion" is acceptable. But, "[s]hort of those expressly proscribed governmental acts[,] there is room for play in the joints productive of a benevolent neutrality which will permit religious exercise to exist without sponsorship and without interference."[56]

Government may accommodate religious practices even when it is not legally required to do so, if such accommodations do not violate the Establishment Clause. In other words, the state may accommodate religion when such accommodations are neither required nor prohibited by the Constitution.[57] Citing this doctrine, the Court has upheld Congress' decision to allow religious organizations to hire only individuals of a particular faith, despite prohibitions on religion-based employment decisions by other employers.[58]

The state can also refuse to fund certain activities even when the Establishment Clause does not require such a refusal, so long as the Free Exercise Clause does not prohibit it. The Court has permitted the state of Washington, for example, to retain its policy of refusing to allow participants in a scholarship program to use program proceeds to pursue a degree in theology.[59] Washington's policy was based on an article in its constitution.[60] The Establishment Clause did not force the state to adopt this policy—the clause allows such indirect aid to support religious activities if the program is one of genuine, independent choice.[61] Nonetheless, Washington's more stringent policy remained valid. The policy did not demonstrate hostility toward religion but rather simply demonstrated an interest in ensuring that tax funds were not used to support the clergy, the Court noted. In a case like this one, a state could observe stricter limits on government funding than the Constitution requires.

"Different Facets of [a] Single Great and Fundamental Freedom"

The First Amendment's two religion clauses—the Establishment and Free Exercise Clauses—represent "only different facets of [a] single great and fundamental freedom," Justice Wiley Rutledge said.[62] The state protects religious freedom by barring the government from advancing or denigrating religion and charging it with protecting the free exercise of faith.

These revolutionary propositions are countermajoritarian—they are aimed at ensuring that all have equal citizenship, no matter their faith or lack thereof, no matter whether one belongs to the most popular faith or the religion that is the smallest minority. In the ringing words of Justice Robert Jackson:

> The very purpose of a Bill of Rights was to withdraw certain subjects from the vicissitudes of political controversy, to place them beyond the reach of majorities and officials and to establish them as legal principles to be applied by the courts. One's right to life, liberty, and property, to free speech, a free press, freedom of worship and assembly, and other fundamental rights may not be submitted to vote; they depend on the outcome of no elections.[63]

This system of religious freedom has made it possible for religious groups to feel welcome in the United States and to build institutions and communities here, even when they are few in number.

As Father John Courtney Murray explained, First Amendment protections are "the American solution to the problem put by the plurality of conflicting religions within the one body politic."[64] The religion clauses, Murray said, "are not articles of faith but articles of peace."[65] These articles do not demand that Americans affirm each other's faith commitments. They demand only that Americans affirm one another's right to make such commitments, or not. Americans will never be able to unite around religious convictions, but that kind of unity is not necessary to build a strong nation. Citizens can unite across religious differences to advance shared ideals like establishing justice, ensuring domestic tranquility, promoting the general welfare, and securing the blessings of liberty for all.[66]

3

FAITH AND 1600 PENNSYLVANIA AVENUE

The Role of Religion in the White House

Government officials do not surrender their rights to practice their faith when they take the oath of office. Religion may also intersect with public service in other permissible ways. Considering how faith has intersected with the service of presidents is one way to explore such issues. Perhaps the most visible way presidents have practiced their faith while serving the nation is through attendance at houses of worship.

Presidents and other high-ranking government officials also have sometimes practiced their faith by speaking about it, including in public remarks. As Supreme Court Justice John Paul Stevens has noted, "when [government] officials deliver public speeches, we recognize that their words are not exclusively a transmission from the government because those oratories have embedded within them the inherently personal views of the speaker as an individual member of the polity."

The White House is often called the "People's House," a place that "belongs to all who call this country home." For that reason, presidents have observed a growing number of religious holidays at the White House, both with official statements and events.

Another intersection of religion and the White House involves religious organizations' activism on public policy. Just as labor, business, civil rights, environmental, and women's groups seek to engage government officials on public issues that are important to them, so do religious organizations. That is the right of religious leaders and communities under the First Amendment.

In the White House, staffing has evolved from managing engagement with religious communities and religion-related policy issues in informal ways to establishing more formal teams with specific responsibilities. In 2001, President George W. Bush opened the first White House Office of Faith-Based and Community Initiatives. President Barack Obama continued this office, while putting his own stamp on the office's name, policies, and activities.

In October 1800, President John Adams was making his way from Philadelphia to Washington, D.C., to take occupancy of what was known then as the President's House. The building was not yet finished—the paint and plaster were still wet, furniture was sparse, and closet doors were missing. But the President's House was the largest house in America at the time, and it looked grand even as it sat in a field strewn with stones and rubble.[1]

Around midday on Saturday, November 1, two commissioners from the District of Columbia were inspecting the main floor when President Adams' carriage rolled up to the south entrance. The commissioners and workers unceremoniously welcomed Adams to his new home, which later became known as the White House.[2]

The next morning, President Adams wrote a letter to his wife, Abigail:

My dearest friend

We arrived here last night, or rather yesterday, at one o Clock and here we dined and Slept. The Building is in a State to be habitable. And now We wish for your Company . . . .

Before I end my Letter I pray Heaven to bestow the best of Blessings on this House and all that shall hereafter inhabit it. May none but honest and wise Men ever rule under this roof . . . .[3]

When he served as president, Franklin Delano Roosevelt had Adams' prayer carved into the wooden mantelpiece in the State Dining Room. President Truman retained this inscription when the White House was remodeled during his time of service. Subsequently, President John F. Kennedy had the inscription carved into a new marble mantelpiece.[4]

From the nation's early days, religion has had a role in the service of presidents and the conduct of the White House. Exploring the intersections of faith and the presidency is one way to better understand how the Constitution speaks to issues of religion and public service.

Practicing Faith while Serving as President

Government officials do not surrender their rights to practice their faith when they take the oath of office. Perhaps the most visible way presidents have practiced their religion while serving the nation is through attendance at houses of worship. George Washington attended church almost every Sunday when he was president, usually worshipping at Episcopal churches but also attending other houses of worship.[5] Thomas Jefferson certainly was not an orthodox Christian,[6] yet he too frequently attended church while serving as president, including some church services that were held on government property.[7]

John Quincy Adams, the second child of John and Abigail Adams, attended church two times each Sunday and visited almost every congregation in the District of Columbia at least once.[8] During his presidency, Abraham Lincoln rented a pew at New York Avenue Presbyterian Church and regularly attended services there.[9] William McKinley worshiped at Metropolitan Methodist Church in Washington, D.C.,[10] and invited friends and members of Congress to the White House on Sunday evening for "hymn sings."[11]

While president, Franklin Delano Roosevelt also served as a vestryman in Saint James Episcopal Church in Hyde Park, New York.[12] President Roosevelt apparently interrupted White House meetings sometimes to discuss church business with other members of Saint James.[13] Nevertheless, Roosevelt attended church only about once a month as president. He did not like being the focus of attention during services. "I can do almost everything in the 'Goldfish Bowl' of the President's life," Roosevelt said, "but I'll be hanged if I can say my prayers in it."[14]

President Harry Truman, a sometime attender at First Baptist Church of the District of Columbia, agreed.[15] He said, "People ought to go to church to worship God—not to see some mortal."[16] Nevertheless, Truman thought he had his bases covered in the religion department. As he told his wife, Bess: "I had a Presbyterian bringing up, a Baptist education, and Episcopal leanings, so I reckon I ought to get to heaven somehow."[17]

Dwight David Eisenhower, who was named for both his father and American evangelist Dwight L. Moody, joined National Presbyterian Church the second Sunday after his inauguration.[18] President Eisenhower was baptized in a private ceremony that same day, becoming the only president to be baptized while in office.[19] Eisenhower had not been a member of a church as an adult until then and had thought that he would not join one as president so as not to seem to do it for the wrong reasons. But he changed his mind, apparently at least in part because he came to believe that his membership and attendance at church would set a good example for his fellow Americans.[20] In 1959, President Eisenhower invited Nikita Khrushchev, who was his guest at Camp David at the time, to attend church with him. Khrushchev declined the invitation, but Eisenhower traveled twenty-five miles to attend church anyway.[21]

John F. Kennedy often worshiped at St. Stephen's Church near his home in Middleburg, Virginia, while president.[22] Kennedy nevertheless had some run-ins with his church. The Vatican reportedly questioned some of then-senator Kennedy's statements about the separation of church and state during the 1960 campaign, prompting Kennedy to say: "Now I understand why Henry VIII set up his own church."[23] President Richard Nixon, the nation's second Quaker president, famously organized his own worship services at the White House.[24]

President Carter attended church every Sunday, at First Baptist Church of the District of Columbia when he was in town and elsewhere when he was out of town.[25] While on the campaign trail, then-governor Carter referred to himself as "a born-again Christian Baptist Sunday-school-teacher deacon."[26] Carter taught Sunday School before, during, and after his time in the White House.[27] President Clinton and the First Family regularly attended Foundry United Methodist Church in the District of Columbia.[28] While Bill Clinton is a Baptist, his wife, Hillary, is a longtime Methodist.[29]

During his time of service, President Obama and his family worshiped at a variety of churches in the Washington, D.C., area,[30] and at Evergreen Chapel at Camp David, which was dedicated on April 11, 1991, during the presidency of George H.W. Bush.[31] President Obama began a tradition of holding an Easter Prayer Breakfast at the White House.[32] He invited Christian leaders of different political, theological, and denominational stripes for this time of fellowship and reflection. The president spoke about his faith at these gatherings, with Vice President Biden sometimes joining him in doing so.[33]

Other presidents and high-ranking government officials also have some-times discussed their faith in public remarks. As Supreme Court Justice John Paul Stevens has noted, "[W]hen [government] officials deliver public speeches, we recognize that their words are not exclusively a transmission from *the* government because those oratories have embedded within them the inherently personal views of the speaker as an individual member of the polity."[34]

In his first inaugural address, President McKinley echoed Micah 6:8 when he said, "God will not forsake us so long as we obey His commandments and walk humbly in His footsteps."[35] Dwight Eisenhower began and ended his presidency with public prayers.[36]

As president, John F. Kennedy quoted Rev. Phillips Brooks saying, "Do not pray for tasks equal to your powers. Pray for powers equal to your tasks."[37] In his inaugural address, Kennedy memorably said: "[H]ere on earth God's work must truly be our own."[38]

Since the National Prayer Breakfast was established in 1953, every president has accepted the invitation to speak there.[39] The National Prayer Breakfast is not sponsored or organized by the White House, however. Private-sector volunteers and members of Congress who participate in unofficial prayer groups plan the breakfast and select the invitees. The program includes prayers and scripture readings by members of Congress, musical performances, and a keynote speech by a prominent leader, after which the president speaks.

In his final remarks to this gathering as president on February 4, 2016, President Obama offered reflections on a verse from Second Timothy: "For God has not given us a spirit of fear, but of power and of love and of a sound mind."[40] The president said:

> I pray that by His grace, we all find the courage to set such examples in our own lives—not just during this wonderful gathering and fellowship, not just in the public piety that we profess, but in those smaller moments when it's difficult, when we're challenged, when we're angry, when we're confronted with someone who doesn't agree with us, when no one is watching. I pray, as Roma* so beautifully said, that our differences ultimately are bridged; that the God that is in each of us comes together, and we don't divide.
>
> I pray that our leaders will always act with humility and generosity. I pray that my failings are forgiven. I pray that we will uphold our obligation to be good stewards of God's creation—this beautiful planet. I pray that we will see every single child as our own, each worthy of our love and of our compassion. And I pray we answer Scripture's call to lift up the vulnerable, and to stand up for justice, and ensure that every human being lives in dignity.[41]

President Obama notably spoke about faith at other times, including his remarks on grace at the funeral of Rev. Clementa Pinckney, one of nine victims of an attack on members of Mother Emanuel Church in Charleston, South Carolina, as church members gathered for Wednesday night prayer and Bible study on June 17, 2015.[42] President Obama did not just speak at this gathering; he sang. As he remembered the victims and spoke about the role of God's grace, President Obama began to sing the beloved hymn "Amazing Grace." Surprised mourners only missed a beat or two before joining in.

"The People's House"

Religion also intersects with the White House because it is the "People's House," a place that "belongs to all who call this country home."[43] For that reason, presidents have honored a growing number of religious holidays there.

In December 1805, President Thomas Jefferson invited guests to dinner at the White House, including the Muslim ambassador to the United States from Tunisia.[44] Jefferson's invitation noted that "dinner will be on the table precisely at sun-set."[45] The timing of the dinner recognized the fact that the ambassador was observing Ramadan and thus was fasting during daylight hours.[46] In 1996, the Clinton White House hosted an Eid-al-Fitr celebration, a Muslim celebration marking the end of Ramadan. And in November 2001, President George W. Bush hosted an Iftar dinner for Muslim leaders at the White House.[47] Presidents have also long sent greetings to mark Jewish high holy days and hosted Hanukkah celebrations.[48]

Continuing a tradition that began on the campaign trail, President Obama and the First Lady held a Seder dinner in the private residence each year.[49] In addition to visiting synagogues and a mosque, the Obamas celebrated many other religious holidays at the White House, including lighting the menorah at Hanukkah; hosting an Iftar dinner; and recognizing Diwali, a holiday celebrated by Hindus, Sikhs, Jains, and Buddhists.[50] President Obama also followed the White House tradition of issuing statements to recognize a range of religious holidays. In 2016, President Obama made a statement marking Vesak, a holiday observed by Buddhists, for the first time.[51] White House celebrations also honored Guru Nanak Dev Ji, a Sikh leader.[52]

When he was on the campaign trail, Donald Trump claimed Americans would be saying "Merry Christmas" again if he won the presidency.[53] "With Trump as your president," the candidate said, "we are going to be celebrating Merry Christmas again, and it's going to be done with a big, beautiful tax cut."[54] Once he became president, Trump said he was bringing Christmas back.[55]

Christmas never left. Christians have been celebrating Christmas for over a thousand years, and they have never needed a tax cut to do so. Government officials have routinely recognized Christmas too. Presidents have presided over the lighting of the National Christmas Tree since 1923, for example.[56] A crèche has been displayed at Christmas in the White House since it was donated in 1967.[57] Presidents have extended annual Christmas greetings to Christians, both at home and abroad.[58] During the 2015 Christmas season, President Barack Obama issued a statement on persecuted Christians that concluded:

We join with people around the world in praying for God's protection for persecuted Christians and those of other faiths, as well as for those brave men and women engaged in our military, diplomatic, and humanitarian efforts to alleviate their suffering and restore stability, security, and hope to their nations. As the old Christmas carol reminds us:

> The Wrong shall fail,
> The Right prevail,
> With peace on earth, good-will to men.[59]

Such greetings are part of a host of statements made by elected officials to recognize seasons and events that are important to American communities.

FAITH, THE PRESIDENCY, AND PUBLIC POLICY

Another intersection of religion and the White House involves religious organizations' activism on public policy. Just as labor, business, civil rights, environmental, and women's groups seek to engage government officials on public issues that are important to them, so do religious organizations. That is the right of religious leaders and organizations under the First Amendment. As the Supreme Court has recognized:

> Adherents of particular faiths and individual churches frequently take strong positions on public issues . . . . Of course, churches as much as secular bodies and private citizens have that right.

To cite just two of the most famous examples of such engagement with presidents: President George Washington received a letter from leaders at Touro Synagogue in Newport, Rhode Island, about the new Constitution, and Washington responded.[60] Thomas Jefferson responded to a letter from the Danbury Baptist Association about the same topic, noting that the religion clauses of the First Amendment had built a wall of separation between church and state.[61]

Especially in modern times, engagement between presidents and religious leaders includes presidents initiating contact with faith communities, particularly about key presidential initiatives. In 1935, for example, Franklin Roosevelt sent a letter to "representative clergyman"—about 120,000 of them—to ask for advice about the impact of his new administration's social security legislation and public works programs, conditions in their communities, and ways government could better serve people who were struggling.[62] On June 11, 1963, after Alabama governor George Wallace attempted to stop blacks from enrolling in the University of Alabama, John F. Kennedy gave a televised address to the nation, announcing that he was submitting a wide-ranging civil rights bill to Congress. Six days after that address, on June 17, President Kennedy met with a large group of religious leaders (including Protestants, Catholics, and Jews)—both white and black—to seek their help in advancing racial equality as a moral issue.[63]

Religious leaders met with President Obama to discuss a wide range of public policy issues, including comprehensive immigration reform, voting rights, criminal justice reform, the Ebola disease, and religious freedom.[64] President Obama met with the Dalai Lama multiple times,[65] and he sometimes participated in religious conferences, including a panel discussion on poverty at Georgetown University that was organized by Catholics and evangelicals.[66]

As president, Obama visited Pope Benedict and Pope Francis at the Vatican and hosted Pope Francis when he came to the United States for the first time in 2015.[67] In addition to heading the Catholic Church, the pope is the head of Vatican City, making him "a civil chief of state like any other monarch of a small state recognized under international law."[68]

When Pope Francis accepted President Obama's invitation to visit the United States, the president provided clear instructions: He did not want the visit to be simply a moment in time or a photo op. Instead, President Obama wanted the visit to have lasting value. He asked his staff to look for specific steps the government could take, either on its own or with others, to advance some of the values he and Pope Francis share.

One of the areas that Obama administration staff examined was the number of refugees that could be admitted to the United States. President Obama wanted to raise that ceiling significantly due to the growing global refugee crisis, without cutting any corners on the rigorous vetting system for each and every refugee who is being considered for admission to the United States.[69] Pope Francis had been, and continues to be, a strong advocate for refugees.

During President Obama's second term in office, the plight of refugees drew increasing attention.[70] In early September 2015, for example, heartbreaking pictures were published of the body of a three-year-old refugee from Syria, Alan Kurdi. Kurdi and his family had boarded a boat in an attempt to escape the civil war in Syria, but he, his mother, and his brother drowned. Alan's tiny body washed up on a shore in Turkey, and photographers captured the awful moment. The picture drew worldwide attention to the plight of refugees.[71]

At the start of each fiscal year, the president, in consultation with Congress, makes a determination about the maximum number of refugees that may be admitted to the country that year.[72] In September 2015, the Obama administration announced that the United States would aim for a large increase in the number of carefully screened refugees who would be resettled here, including by faith-based groups. In fiscal year 2016, the president determined that the United

States should aim to admit at least 85,000 refugees, including at least 10,000 Syrian refugees.[73] The United States ultimately admitted 84,995 refugees in fiscal year 2016.[74] During fiscal year 2017, the Obama administration announced, up to 110,000 refugees would be admitted, without any lessening of the onerous security checks that refugees go through before they enter the country.[75] Until President Trump took office, the United States was on track to reach President Obama's goal, which would have been the highest number of refugees admitted to the country in any year since 1994.[76] But refugee admissions began to drop drastically after President Trump took office in January 2017.[77]

With the Obama administration's moves, the United States was able to welcome more persecuted people from around the globe to American shores, exert moral leadership on this important matter, and make a significant contribution to the global refugee crisis. American participation in a robust, global system of refugee resettlement has helped to advance human rights and to prevent crises and conflicts around the world.[78] And by increasing the number of refugees it would admit and resettle, the United States strengthened its diplomatic toolkit. U.S. officials were better able to push other countries to increase the number of refugees they admit, for example.[79]

Religious organizations first asked the Obama administration to raise the ceiling of refugees who could be admitted. They then helped the U.S. government reach its goals. The evangelical World Relief organization, for example, resettled refugees at a record rate in fiscal year 2016, more than doubling the number of refugees it resettles in a typical month.[80] World Relief partnered with more than one thousand churches to do so.[81]

President Obama and his administration also worked alongside religious leaders as well as faith-based and humanitarian organizations to secure the release of missionary Kenneth Bae and Pastor Saeed Abedini, both American citizens. Bae was arrested in November 2012 while leading a tour group in North Korea and was charged with engaging in "antigovernment activities." He was sentenced to a fifteen-year prison term and sent to a labor camp.[82] Saeed Abedini is an Iranian American Christian pastor who was arrested by the government of Iran in the summer of 2012. In January 2013, Abedini was sentenced to eight years in prison, reportedly on charges of "undermining national security" through religious gatherings in Christian homes in Iran.[83]

In his remarks at the 2014 National Prayer Breakfast, President Obama said "promoting religious freedom is a key objective of U.S. foreign policy."[84] He added that "no nation on Earth does more to stand up for the freedom of religion around the world than the United States of America," and he pledged that his administration would take steps to ensure that that would continue to be the case.[85] In the final portion of his remarks, President Obama lifted up the plight of Kenneth Bae and Pastor Abedini and called for prayers for and the release of these two men as well as all other prisoners of conscience.[86] President Obama said:

> [L]et us never forget those who are persecuted today, among them Americans of faith. We pray for Kenneth Bae, a Christian missionary who's been held in North Korea for 15 months, sentenced to 15 years of hard labor. His family wants him home. And the United States will continue to do everything in our power to secure his release because Kenneth Bae deserves to be free.

> We pray for Pastor Saeed Abedini. He's been held in Iran for more than 18 months, sentenced to eight years in prison on charges relating to his Christian beliefs. And as we continue to work for his freedom, today, again, we call on the Iranian government to release Pastor Abedini.[87]

The Obama administration subsequently continued its work on these cases, including by staying in close touch with these Americans' family and friends.[88]

The following November, U.S. Director of National Intelligence James Clapper brought Kenneth Bae back home along with another American who had been held by North Korea, Matthew Miller.[89] At the 2015 National Prayer Breakfast, President Obama gratefully marked the moment. "Last year, we joined together to pray for the release of Christian missionary Kenneth Bae, held in North Korea for two years," the president said. "And today, we give thanks that Kenneth is finally back where he belongs—home, with his family." President Obama also vowed "to keep up this work—for Pastor Abedini and all those around the world who are unjustly held or persecuted because of their faith."[90]

In 2016, Iran finally released Pastor Saeed Abedini. In his remarks at the National Prayer Breakfast in February 2016, President Obama noted that the gathering had prayed together that Abedini might be freed. And President Obama was able to say that Pastor Abedini, who had been "imprisoned for no crime other than holding God in his heart," was "now home safe."[91] These were victories not just for these men, their families, and the U.S. government but also for the many others who prayed and pressed for their release.

White House Staffing on Religion-Related Matters

During the nineteenth and early twentieth centuries, presidents generally seem to have managed engagement with religious communities and religion-related policy issues in informal ways. Staff with other responsibilities handled these matters, either because staff had some affinity for them or because the president or senior staff asked them to do so or both.

In 1956, however, President Eisenhower organized a formal team with the specific responsibility of handling religion-related issues. Eisenhower appointed

Rev. Frederic Fox, a Congregationalist minister, to serve as a special assistant and coordinate existing staff working on issues touching on faith. These staff members included Eisenhower's chief of staff and press secretary, who apparently handled issues relating to religion on behalf of the president; his speechwriter; and liaisons to the Christian and Jewish communities.[92] Fox was reportedly the first ordained minister to work in the White House since Rev. Edward Neil served as correspondence secretary for President Abraham Lincoln.[93] Led by Fox, this Eisenhower team responded to citizens who wrote about religious matters; drafted speeches and other communications addressing religious topics; served as liaisons to religious groups; and accompanied Eisenhower or represented him at religious gatherings.[94]

Subsequent presidencies appear to have continued the religious liaisons role and sometimes included the role of a religiously informed speechwriter or communications staffer.[95] Brooks Hays, president of Southern Baptist Convention from 1957 to 1959, served as special assistant to President Kennedy for intergovernmental affairs and as a liaison to Protestant groups.[96] Deputy Special Counsel Myer Feldman played a similar role for the Jewish community during the Kennedy administration.[97] Bill Moyers, an ordained Baptist minister, served in a variety of capacities during the Lyndon B. Johnson administration, including that of press secretary, and another Baptist minister, Robert Maddox, served as President Carter's liaison to religious communities.[98] The Obama White House had similar liaisons and added a new one for American Muslim, Buddhist, Hindu, and Sikh communities.

Some presidents have also added staff to help ensure that religious liberty guarantees are respected, both by White House operations and by the executive branch as a whole. President Eisenhower reportedly consulted with his Jewish community liaison on questions involving church-state issues.[99] During the Clinton administration, the portfolio of at least one of the deputies of the Domestic Policy Council included policy issues touching on religion, and the White House Counsel's Office included a constitutional scholar with expertise on church-state issues.[100]

Also during the Clinton administration, Father Joe Hacala was appointed to serve as the head of a new office at the Department of Housing and Urban Development—the Center for Community and Interfaith Partnerships.[101] The goal of the center was to work with community and faith-based organizations on housing and economic development.[102]

President George W. Bush built on this tradition when he opened the White House Office of Faith-Based and Community Initiatives in 2001, with staff dedicated to fostering partnerships with religious and secular groups to serve people in need.[103] President Bush also opened Centers for Faith-Based and Neighborhood Partnerships at eleven federal agencies.[104]

President Obama continued these White House and agency offices, while putting his own stamp on them.[105] Staff assigned to lead the White House office also worked with administration colleagues on policy issues that had religious aspects, including the implementation of federal regulations that impacted religious bodies.[106] The Obama administration expanded the capacity of additional agencies to work with faith-based and community groups, both at home and abroad. Secretary Kerry opened an Office of Religion and Global Affairs at the State Department.[107] As Secretary Kerry said: "We ignore the global impact of religion . . . at our peril."[108] The Environmental Protection Agency dedicated staff to forming such partnerships for the first time, and the Peace Corps inaugurated a new initiative to partner with faith and community organizations.[109]

Many presidents have sought to increase religious diversity among their appointees. In 1956, President Eisenhower appointed Justice William Brennan, a Catholic, to serve on the Supreme Court.[110] President John F. Kennedy appointed two Jewish leaders to the cabinet for the first time—Arthur Goldberg served as Secretary of the Department of Labor, and Abraham Ribicoff served as Secretary of the Department of Health, Education, and Welfare.[111] Richard Nixon appointed Father Ted Hesburgh, a Catholic priest, to head the U.S. Civil Rights Commission.[112] President Bush appointed members of the Church of Jesus Christ of Latter-day Saints to public office, including appointing Michael Leavitt to serve as Secretary of the Department of Health and Human Services.[113] President Obama appointed the first non-Christian Ambassador at Large for International Religious Freedom: Rabbi David Saperstein.[114] Presidents who have expanded religious diversity among their appointees have advanced the spirit of Article VI of the Constitution, which prohibits religious tests for public office.

RECOMMENDATIONS: EXERCISING CONSTITUTIONAL RIGHTS WHILE PRESERVING, PROTECTING, AND DEFENDING THE CONSTITUTION

Government officials retain their constitutional rights to express their faith. They also take on the duty to "preserve, protect and defend the Constitution." Relying on the following principles will help them fulfill that pledge and build greater unity among the American people.

(1) Affirm that there are no second-class faiths under the Constitution.

Government officials should affirm that there are no second-class faiths under our Constitution. Both policymaking and engagement must be consistent with this bedrock principle. Officials should welcome people of all faiths, and none, to the table for conversation and insist that no religion is preferred over another. Taking affirmative steps to include members of minority groups is a key part of this task. Maintaining an advisory board, even unofficially, that is comprised of members of only one faith group, or only a subset of one faith group, is inappropriate.[115]

(2) Promote the common good, not religion.

The government's role is not to advance faith; that is the job of religious individuals and institutions themselves. The government's role is to promote secular ends, even as the state recognizes that these same ends are seen as deeply spiritual by some with whom it works. Both the state and the religious sector can work together to promote the common good.

(3) Recognize that the religious sector is neither the master nor the servant of the state.

Rev. Dr. Martin Luther King said that the church "is not the master or the servant of the state, but rather the conscience of the state."[116] Government officials should invite religious leaders to engage in conversation or participate in an initiative rather than instructing them to do so. Neither government officials nor their staff should attempt to tell religious leaders what their sacred texts mean or what their theology should be.[117] No president or other public servant should ever refer to cardinals of the Catholic Church, for example, as "my cardinals."[118] Government officials should not assume that they may speak from the pulpit or that they will be specially recognized during worship services or other religious gatherings. The flip side is that religious communities are not the master of the state. Thus, the government should never take orders from religious leaders or communities.

(4) High-ranking government officials should feel free to speak publicly about their personal religious beliefs and practices, always doing so in ways that are consistent with the spirit of the Constitution.

Governmental officials do not have to leave their faith behind when they take the oath of office. High-ranking officials may speak about their personal faith publicly.[119] Officials should always speak about their religious beliefs and practices in ways that are consistent with the spirit of the Constitution. Government leaders should make clear, for example, that they will protect the right of every American to practice their faith or to practice no faith at all.

(5) Staff for religious literacy and religious liberty.

Policymakers need staff who are religiously literate and know how to engage religious communities. Leaders simply cannot understand our nation or world without understanding religion. Officials also need staff, including both political appointees and civil servants, who understand and appreciate the religious liberty guarantees of the Constitution and other laws. Issues related to these guarantees arise across government on a regular basis. The American commitment to religious liberty requires policymakers to take such issues as seriously as any other constitutional mandate, including by hiring staff with adequate expertise to handle them.

(6) While on the campaign trail, political candidates should describe their vision for religious freedom and religion's role in American public life.

Political candidates should describe their vision for religious freedom and religion's role in American public life. Presidential candidates can make a particularly important impact by doing so.

The leadership of the president of the United States can generate enormous attention, catalyze conversations, and set precedent for officials across the country. One of the most effective ways to ensure presidential leadership on an issue is for the candidate to address it during a campaign. By starting a dialogue and making commitments on the campaign trail, a candidate articulates a vision and a roadmap for his or her presidency. Taking a public position during the campaign also creates accountability for the president once in office.

Some will say that asking candidates to address religious freedom and religion's role in public life is the equivalent of asking them to stick their hands in a hornet's nest. After all, these issues can be divisive. Moreover, critics would say, the reward for taking this approach could be small because a significant share of the voters who prioritize these matters may disagree with some of the candidate's stands.

The truth is that there is no way for candidates to avoid these issues. Religious freedom and religion's role in public life may have been sleepy issues in the past. No more. The real choice for presidential candidates, therefore, is between affirmatively tackling these issues or merely reacting to them. The former approach is far superior, from the standpoint of both principle and strategy. The American traditions of religious freedom and pluralism have played key roles in shaping our country for the better, and they should continue to do so. The only question is how we should move forward, and that is a question candidates should answer.

RELIGION, POLICY, AND POLITICS

Barring Religious Tests—
Protecting Rights to Engage in Policy and Politics

Article VI of the Constitution states that public officials "shall be bound by oath or affirmation" to support the Constitution, "but no religious test shall ever be required as a qualification to any office or public trust under the United States." If the government requires aspiring officeholders to affirm or disavow religious beliefs or affiliations in order to hold public office, it violates the Constitution.

The First Amendment places some restrictions on the policy choices government officials make. Government action must have a secular purpose, for example. The mere fact that a law coincides with religious tenets, however, does not invalidate it.

The Constitution protects the rights of religious leaders to run for office and religious communities to speak out on public issues. It bars government officials from taking sides in theological debates. As James Madison said, no "Civil Magistrate" is "a competent Judge of Religious Truth."

The First Amendment places no limits on the political activities of religious organizations, but an organization, whether religious or nonreligious, that wishes to qualify for and maintain status as a 501(c)(3) tax-exempt organization must comply with certain restrictions on its political activities that apply to all 501(c)(3) organizations. Section 501(c)(3) organizations must not engage in campaign activity for or against candidates for elective political office, for example. Such Internal Revenue Code restrictions apply only to actions attributable to the 501(c)(3) organization, not to actions attributable to individuals. 501(c)(3) organizations can play unbiased, educational roles regarding elections.

In 1983, the Supreme Court rejected an Establishment Clause challenge to a state legislature's longtime practice of opening the legislative day with a prayer offered by a state-employed chaplain. In 2014, the Supreme Court held that legislative bodies generally do not violate the Constitution by exposing constituents to prayers that they would rather not hear, as long as they need not participate. At the same time, the Court observed: "If the course and practice over time shows that the invocations denigrate nonbelievers or religious minorities, threaten damnation, or preach conversion," then that "would present a different case than the one presently before the Court."

In May 2018, Attorney General Jeff Sessions announced the Trump administration's family separation policy.[1] Sessions said:

> [T]he Department of Homeland Security is now referring 100 percent of illegal Southwest Border crossings to the Department of Justice for prosecution. And the Department of Justice will take up those cases.

> I have put in place a "zero tolerance" policy for illegal entry on our Southwest border. If you cross this border unlawfully, then we will prosecute you. It's that simple . . . .

> If you are smuggling a child, then we will prosecute you and that child will be separated from you as required by law.[2]

The Trump administration was wrong when it claimed that the Obama administration had had the same policy.[3] When a federal agency presented a policy of this kind to the Obama administration, the administration immediately rejected it as "immoral."[4]

The Trump administration also was wrong in its belief that Americans would tolerate such a policy. As stories began to emerge about babies, toddlers, and other children being separated from their families by U.S. government officials at the border, countless Americans—including religious leaders of almost every theological, ideological, and political stripe—rose up to condemn and demand an end to this horrific policy. Denominations issued statements, pastors took to their pulpits, and religious communities poured into the streets to challenge the policy in theological, ethical, and moral terms.[5]

Such criticism drew a pointed response from Attorney General Jeff Sessions. In a speech made in his capacity as the nation's top law enforcement official, Sessions said: "[T]he Apostle Paul and his clear and wise command in Romans 13, to obey the laws of the government because God has ordained them for the purpose of order." Sessions' remarks were circulated by the Department of Justice with the title *Attorney General Sessions Addresses Recent Criticisms of Zero Tolerance by Church Leaders.*[6]

There are at least two problems with General Sessions' statement. The first problem is that the nation's top law enforcement official lectured religious leaders about the meaning of their faith. Sessions suggested that religious leaders' interpretations of their own sacred texts were wrong. Instead of lecturing Christians about the Bible, General Sessions should have consulted the writings of James Madison, who said no "Civil Magistrate" is "a competent Judge of Religious Truth."[7]

A second problem with General Sessions' response is that it appeared, whether intentionally or unintentionally, to be an attempt to claim divine authority for the administration's actions and to silence the voices of critics, including religious leaders. One certainly would not be crazy for hearing something like the following message in Sessions' words: "God has ordained us to execute the law, so get back in line." That message is as wrong as it is ominous.

In the United States, governmental officials must protect the rights of religious leaders to speak on public issues, not try to prevent them from doing so. And officials must never suggest that the workings of the government cannot be questioned because they are God-ordained.

Adhering to these and other basic rules can help government officials as well as religious and other civil society leaders to avoid unforced errors and unnecessary blowback when religion, policy, and politics mix. Attention to the values undergirding American law can also aid leaders in building greater unity across a country with citizens of many different faiths and beliefs.

RELIGIOUS TESTS FOR PUBLIC OFFICE—FORMAL AND INFORMAL

Article VI of the Constitution states that public officials "shall be bound by oath or affirmation" to support the Constitution, "but no religious test shall ever be required as a qualification to any office or public trust under the United States." When the government requires aspiring officeholders to affirm or disavow religious beliefs or affiliations in order to hold public office, it violates the Constitution.

There is little danger today that formal test oaths will reemerge, but that does not mean that there are no remaining concerns in this area. In 2018, President Trump appointed a man to serve as acting attorney general of the United States who appears to believe it is appropriate to ask judicial nominees' whether they are "people of faith" and disqualify them if they do not hold "a biblical view of justice."[8] When Whitaker was asked whether he was referring to the Old or New Testament of the Bible, he indicated he was referring to the latter.[9] "[W]hat I know," Whitaker said, "is as long as they have that world view, that they'll be a good judge."[10] But, Whitaker continued, "if they have a secular world view, where this is all we have here on Earth, then I'm going to be very concerned about that judge."[11]

When he was running for president, Ben Carson said he "would not advocate that we put a Muslim in charge of this nation" because Islam is not "consistent with the Constitution."[12] Former Alabama judge and U.S. Senate candidate Roy Moore opposed the seating of Muslim congressman Keith Ellison, simply because Ellison is Muslim and took the oath of office on a Qur'an, which Moore said was like taking an "oath on *Mein Kampf*."[13] President Trump appointed Carson to serve as Secretary of Housing and Urban Development and backed Moore in his Senate bid.

Other challenges have arisen in the context of actual U.S. Senate confirmation hearings. Certain candidates for public office must first be nominated by the president and then confirmed by the Senate. To be confirmed, those candidates must testify before a committee of senators under oath. In that setting, senators sometimes ask candidates about their religious beliefs.

One case involved Amy Coney Barrett, who was serving as a law professor at Notre Dame University Law School when she was nominated for a federal judgeship.[14] While in law school, Barrett coauthored a law review article with one of her professors stating that a faithful Catholic judge must recuse herself from certain death penalty cases due to the Catholic Church's teachings against capital punishment.[15] In the article, the co-authors said: "We focus on Catholic judges not because their church has set a better example, but because it is the one we belong to."[16] Leaders of several advocacy organizations brought this article to the attention of senators and asked them to probe Barrett's views.[17]

During Barrett's confirmation hearing, Senator Feinstein questioned Barrett about this law review article. Unfortunately, Senator Feinstein handled the questioning badly, and some of her statements were deeply problematic. At one point, Senator Feinstein said to Barrett: "[T]he dogma lives loudly within you, and that's of concern . . . ."[18]

It is not unfair or wrong for a senator to ask a nominee about law review articles she or he has written, but when the article touches on the nominee's personal religious beliefs, or lack thereof, senators need to proceed with great care. Senators should not take it upon themselves to characterize a nominee's religious beliefs and practices. They also should not ask any questions that might suggest that they would qualify or disqualify a nominee simply because of her or his faith, or lack thereof. Asking open-ended, neutral questions is best. Senators could have asked Barrett what she intended to say with this article and the relevance of those views, if any, for her potential service as a federal judge.

When nominees have not written such law review articles or books, senators are best served by simply asking every nominee whether he or she would be unable to support the Constitution for any reason, including any personal beliefs or affiliations. That way, senators can seek assurance that nominees will uphold the Constitution without seeming to single out any nominee due to his or her religious beliefs and affiliations, or lack thereof. Of course, senators are also free to ask nominees about their views on any legal issue and to support or oppose them for such views.

"[T]he Democratic Party's Candidate for President Who Happens Also to Be a Catholic"

Article VI clearly does not apply to the judgments citizens make in the voting booth, but voting against a candidate for public office simply because of his or her faith affiliation, or lack thereof, reflects bias and deprives our nation of talented leaders.

When John F. Kennedy ran for the White House in 1960, some Americans vigorously opposed him because he was Catholic. Certain Protestants in particular argued that Kennedy might take orders from the pope or other members of the Catholic hierarchy, thus undermining the separation of church and state.[19]

On September 12, 1960, Kennedy went to the proverbial lion's den—a gathering of Protestant ministers in the Bible Belt known as the Greater Houston Ministerial Association. "I believe in an America where the separation of church and state is absolute, where no Catholic prelate would tell the president (should he be Catholic) how to act, and no Protestant minister would tell his parishioners for whom to vote; where no church or church school is granted any public funds or political preference; and where no man is denied public office merely because his religion differs from the president who might appoint him or the people who might elect him,"[20] Kennedy began. He continued:

I believe in an America that is officially neither Catholic, Protestant nor Jewish; where no public official either requests or accepts instructions on public policy from the Pope, the National Council of Churches or any other ecclesiastical source; where no religious body seeks to impose its will directly or indirectly upon the general populace or the public acts of its officials; and where religious liberty is so indivisible that an act against one church is treated as an act against all.

For while this year it may be a Catholic against whom the finger of suspicion is pointed, in other years it has been, and may someday be again, a Jew—or a Quaker or a Unitarian or a Baptist. It was Virginia's harassment of Baptist preachers, for example, that led to Jefferson's statute of religious freedom. Today, I may be the victim, but tomorrow it may be you—until the whole fabric of our harmonious society is ripped apart at a time of great national peril.

Kennedy insisted that a president's "views on religion are his own private affair, neither imposed by him upon the nation, nor imposed by the nation upon him as a condition to holding that office." He "would not look with favor upon a president working to subvert the First Amendment's guarantees of religious liberty. Nor would our system of checks and balances permit him to do so." Deftly turning the tables, Kennedy then cautioned that he also would not "look with favor upon those who would work to subvert Article VI of the Constitution by requiring a religious test—even by indirection. For if they disagree with that safeguard, they should be openly working to repeal it."[21]

Then-senator Kennedy insisted that he was "not the Catholic candidate for president" but rather "the Democratic Party's candidate for president who happens also to be a Catholic." He promised that if there were ever a time when his office would require him "to either violate my conscience or violate the national interest, then I would resign the office; and I hope any other conscientious public servant would do likewise," although he stressed that he did not expect such a situation to arise.

After his remarks, Kennedy answered questions from the audience, including whether he could attend Protestant services, his relationship to the Catholic hierarchy, and whether Catholics believed it was acceptable to lie under certain circumstances.[22] (Kennedy's answer to the last question was a clear "no.") Taking his leave of the group, Kennedy said:

I don't want anyone to think because they interrogate me on this very important question, that I regard that as unfair questioning or unreasonable or that somebody who is concerned about the matter is prejudiced or bigoted. I think this fight for religious freedom is basic in the establishment of the American system, and therefore any candidate for the office, I think, should submit himself to the questions of any reasonable man. (Applause.)

My only objection would be—my only limit to that would be if somebody said regardless of Senator Kennedy's position, regardless of how much evidence he has given that what he says he means, I still would not vote for him because he is a member of that Church—I would consider that unreasonable. What I would consider to be reasonable in an exercise of free will and free choice is to ask the candidate to state his views as broadly as possible, investigate his record to see whether he states what he believes and then to make an independent, rational judgment, as to whether he could be entrusted with this highly important position. So I want you to know that I am grateful to you for inviting me tonight. I am sure I have made no converts to my Church. (Laughter.) But I do hope that at least my view, which I believe to be the view of my fellow Catholics, who hold office, I hope it may be of some value in at least assisting you to make a careful judgment. Thank you. (Applause.)[23]

Despite Kennedy's eloquence and his eventual political success, his candidacy did not settle this issue. In 2011, for example, the Pew Research Center found that 25 percent of all voters, and 34 percent of white evangelical Protestants, said that the fact that a political candidate is a member of the Church of Jesus Christ of Latter-day Saints (sometimes known as "Mormons") would make them less likely to vote for that candidate.[24] Opposing a candidate merely because of his or her faith affiliation, or lack thereof, is inconsistent with the spirit of Article VI.

The First Amendment on Faith, Policy, and Politics

The First Amendment places some restrictions on the policy choices government makes. State action must have a secular purpose, for example.[25] In 1985, the Court found that a particular moment-of-silence law whose sole purpose was to promote prayer in public schools failed this test.[26] But the mere fact that a law coincides with religious tenets does not invalidate it. The Supreme Court has rejected the claim, for example, that a federal law's denial of government funding for certain medically necessary abortions violates the religion clauses of the First Amendment.[27] The taxpayers who brought this claim alleged that a federal law, the Hyde Amendment, violated the Establishment Clause because "it incorporates into law the doctrines of the Roman Catholic Church concerning the sinfulness of abortion and the time at which life commences."[28] A statute does not violate the Establishment Clause because it "happens to coincide or harmonize with the tenets of some or all religions," the Court said.[29]

While the First Amendment places certain restrictions on the policy choices government officials make, it does not restrict the rights of religious individuals and organizations to engage in policymaking and politics. Instead, both the Free Exercise and the Free Speech Clauses protect the rights of religious individuals and institutions to participate in these processes.[30]

People of faith exercise such freedoms every day, both individually and through action by single-faith organizations, multifaith entities, and bodies that include both religious and nonreligious members. During the past two years, many religious Americans have repeatedly lifted their voices on public issues. Clergy and other religious leaders have joined counterprotestors in standing against members of the Ku Klux Klan, neo-Nazis, and other white supremacists who were demonstrating in Charlottesville, Virginia, for example.[31] People of faith across theological and political lines pressed Congress to pass legislation shielding "Dreamers"—undocumented young adults who were brought to the United States as children—from deportation and creating a pathway for them to become citizens.[32] Faith-based organizations filed friend-of-the-court briefs in several high-profile cases pending before the U.S. Supreme Court.[33] Ministers and religious leaders kicked off a Poor People's Campaign, modeled on the campaign initially launched by Rev. Dr. Martin Luther King Jr. in 1968.[34] Religious communities have been virtually unanimous in insisting on an end to President Trump's policy of separating children from their families when they cross the nation's Southwest border without papers.[35]

The United States protects the rights of religious communities to play such roles in public life, and the United States is a far better country for doing so. The Constitution prohibits government-backed religion, but it protects the rights of religious individuals and organizations to promote their faith. This formula is one of the things that makes the United States exceptional.

In *McDaniel v. Paty*, a case decided in 1978, the Court held that ministers may not be excluded from public office because they are clergy.[36] Rev. Paul McDaniel, an ordained minister of a Baptist church in Chattanooga, Tennessee, filed as a candidate to serve as a delegate to the state constitutional convention. An opposing candidate, Selma Cash Paty, sued for a judgment that state law disqualified McDaniel from serving in this office. The relevant provision from the Tennessee Constitution, first enacted in 1796, said:

> Whereas Ministers of the Gospel are by their profession, dedicated to God and the care of Souls, and ought not to be diverted from the great duties of their functions; therefore, no Minister of the Gospel, or priest of any denomination whatever, shall be eligible to a seat in either House of the Legislature.[37]

This provision had been interpreted to apply to candidates for delegate to the state's 1977 limited constitutional convention.[38] After a Tennessee court held that this provision of state law violated the First and Fourteenth Amendments to the federal Constitution, and declared McDaniel eligible for the office of delegate, McDaniel's name remained on the ballot. He was elected by an overwhelming margin.

After the election, however, the Tennessee Supreme Court reversed the lower court. The Tennessee provision barring ministers from serving in public office did not burden McDaniel's religious beliefs, the Tennessee Supreme Court ruled. Rev. McDaniel had made the choice to serve as a minister, and that was what excluded him from serving in public office, the court said.[39]

The U.S. Supreme Court disagreed. A Court plurality noted that James Madison believed that such provisions "punish[ed] a religious profession with the privation of a civil right[.]"[40] Baptist preacher John Leland concurred. In 1790, Leland wrote:

> To have one branch of the legislature composed of clergyman as is the case in some European powers is not seemly—to have them entitled to seats of legislation, on account of their Ecclesiastical dignity, like the bishops of England is absurd. But to declare them ineligible, when their neighbors prefer them to any others, is depriving them of the liberty of free citizens, and those who prefer them, the freedom of choice . . . . Things should be so fixed in government, that there should be neither degrading checks, nor alluring baits in the states to the sacred work.[41]

Other states had had similar restrictions on their books in the past, but Tennessee was the only state that still excluded ministers from particular public offices.[42] Tennessee had violated McDaniel's First Amendment right to exercise his faith freely, the Court said.[43]

In an opinion concurring in the judgment, Justices Brennan and Marshall argued that the Establishment Clause as well as the Free Exercise Clause dictated the result.[44] Unlike the Court plurality, Justices Brennan and Marshall also said the Court's ruling in the *Torcaso v. Watkins* case dictated the outcome:

> [Tennessee's restriction preventing clergy from running for public office] imposes a unique disability upon those who exhibit a defined level of intensity of involvement in protected religious activity. Such a classification as much imposes a test for office based on religious conviction as one based on denominational preference. A law which limits political participation to those who eschew prayer, public worship, or the ministry as much establishes a religious test as one which disqualifies Catholics, or Jews, or

Protestants. Because the challenged provision establishes as a condition of office the willingness to eschew certain protected religious practices, *Torcaso v. Watkins*, compels the conclusion that it violates the Free Exercise Clause.[45]

Justice Brennan concluded: "Religionists no less than members of any other group enjoy the full measure of protection afforded speech, association, and political activity generally."[46] Rev. McDaniel served as a delegate to Tennessee's constitutional convention in 1977 and later on the Hamilton County Commission for twenty years.[47]

While the Constitution protects the right of religious leaders to run for office and the right of religious communities to speak out, it bars government officials from intervening in theological debates.[48] It is beyond the government's ken to say what is true or false as a theological matter. Likewise, the Supreme Court has said, "Courts are not arbiters of scriptural interpretation."[49] The same is true for other divisions of government.

Similarly, politicians and government leaders cross a line when they call for religious beliefs to change. In remarks to a 2015 global women's conference, for example, former secretary of state and then–presidential candidate Hillary Clinton gave a speech promoting education and reproductive rights for women and said, "[D]eep-seated cultural codes, religious beliefs and structural biases have to be changed."[50] Of course, it is fair to debate law and policy and appropriate to deny certain requests for religious exemptions. But it is emphatically not the place of government to say that faith must change.

A Quid Pro Quo: Rules for Tax-Exempt Organizations

While the First Amendment places no limits on the political activities of religious organizations, an organization, whether religious or nonreligious, that wishes to qualify for and maintain status as a 501(c)(3) tax-exempt organization needs to comply with certain restrictions on its political activities that apply to all 501(c)(3) organizations.[51] Section 501(c)(3) organizations are exempt from federal income tax, and donors generally may deduct the contributions they make to such groups.[52] Section 501(c)(3) organizations must not engage in campaign activity for or against candidates for elective political office.[53] Also, lobbying cannot constitute a substantial amount of their activities. In other words, this is a "quid pro quo" arrangement: the "quid" is the benefits of status as a 501(c)(3) tax-exempt organization, and the "quo" is restrictions on an organization's electioneering and lobbying activities.

The restrictions allow 501(c)(3) organizations to play unbiased, educational roles regarding elections. Organizations may conduct nonpartisan voter registration and get-out-the-vote activities. Tax-exempt 501(c)(3) organizations may educate voters on issues through public forums, including candidate debates, and voter guides that are unbiased. These organizations may discuss issues of public importance during the election season. The IRS has noted that these organizations "may take positions on public policy issues, including issues that divide candidates in an election for public office." At the same time, the IRS has said that such organizations "must avoid any issue advocacy that functions as political campaign intervention."[54]

If leaders of such organizations make comments in official organization publications or at official functions, those comments are attributable to the organization. Outside that context, leaders may become involved in campaigns and endorse candidates so long as they "do not in any way utilize the organization's financial resources, facilities, or personnel, and clearly and unambiguously indicate that the actions taken or the statements made are those of the individuals and not of the organization."[55]

The IRS has never revoked a congregation's tax-exempt status due to comments made from the pulpit.[56] The only time the IRS has stripped a church of its tax-exempt status for violating these rules occurred when a New York church placed full-page ads in several national newspapers in 1992 asking Christians not to vote for then–presidential candidate Bill Clinton.[57]

"Ceremonial Prayer": Prayers before Legislation Sessions

The place of faith in policy and politics has sometimes centered on the role of official prayer before legislative sessions. In 1983, the Supreme Court rejected a claim that the Nebraska legislature's longtime practice of opening the legislative day with a prayer offered by a state-employed chaplain violated the First Amendment's Establishment Clause.[58] Writing for the Court in *Marsh v. Chambers*, Chief Justice Burger noted: "In light of the unambiguous and unbroken history of more than 200 years, there can be no doubt that the practice of opening legislative sessions with prayer has become part of the fabric of our society."[59] The Court cited the fact that the Continental Congress opened with prayer, as did the First Congress.[60] Legislative prayer is a practice that has been seen as consistent with disestablishment and religious liberty since the founding, the Court observed.

Expressing great reluctance to scrutinize the content of prayers, the Court said the substance of the prayers were "not of concern to judges where, as here, there is no indication that the prayer opportunity has been exploited to proselytize or advance any one, or to disparage any other, faith or belief."[61] The

Court subsequently observed that the legislative prayers at issue in *Marsh* did not have the impermissible effect of affiliating the government with any specific faith because the chaplain said he had "removed all references to Christ" from his prayers after he received a complaint from a Jewish legislator.[62]

Justices Brennan, Marshall, and Stevens vigorously dissented from the *Marsh* ruling.[63] Justices Brennan and Marshall argued that legislative prayers had the preeminent purpose and primary effect of advancing religion and also excessively entangled church and state. The fact that legislative practice was part of American history should not override the fact that such prayer violated the First Amendment, they insisted. "[T]he Constitution is not a static document whose meaning on every detail is fixed for all time by the life experience of the Framers," according to Justices Brennan and Marshall.[64] "Prayer is serious business—serious theological business," these justices said, and devout people might object to legislative prayers for theological reasons, including the fact that they were organized and sponsored by government.[65]

In 2014, the Supreme Court returned to the subject of legislative prayer. The Court considered the constitutionality of the Town of Greece's (New York) practices regarding prayers that were offered before the monthly meetings of its town board. Prior to 1999, the town board observed a moment of silence before its meetings began.[66] In 1999, the recently elected town superintendent, John Auberger, instituted a new practice: inviting clergy to offer prayers, a practice Auberger had appreciated when he served in the county legislature.[67]

In a typical meeting, Superintendent Auberger would call the meeting to order, and the town clerk would announce the board members.[68] Then Auberger would ask the board members and town residents in attendance to stand for the recitation of the Pledge of Allegiance.[69] Next, Auberger would introduce that month's prayer-giver, who stood in the front of the room facing the audience and offered a prayer over the public address system.[70] After the prayer, Auberger would thank the clergy person for being the town's "chaplain of the month" and usually present him or her with a commemorative plaque.[71] Then the board would take up its other business, including discussions of topics as varied as traffic conditions, municipal contracts, accommodations for the disabled, community awards and recognitions, special land-use permits, zoning ordinances, and licenses.[72]

To find religious leaders who were willing to offer prayers in this setting, staff for the Greece town board first contacted members of religious organizations that were listed in a community guide published by the city's chamber of commerce.[73] Staff then created a list of clergy who had agreed to pray at board meetings, and they used this list as the pool for future prayer-givers, sometimes supplementing it with additions from updated community guides or the town newspaper.[74]

The congregations located in Greece were primarily Christian.[75] Staff generally did not contact houses of worship that were near the town but outside its borders.[76] Town staff said they never declined to contact an organization due to its religious affiliation.[77] Until 2008, when the litigation began, all those who had prayed at town meetings were Christian.[78] Greece had no written policy on prayer at board meetings. The town offered no guidelines to those offering prayers about the content of their prayers, and it never asked to review prayers in advance.[79]

In 2007, two residents of Greece, Linda Stephens and Susan Galloway, who objected to the prayers began complaining to town leadership.[80] After these complaints, a Wiccan priestess, the chairman of the local Baha'i congregation, and a Jewish layperson offered prayers, along with Christian clergy.[81] In 2008, Stephens and Galloway sued the town, claiming it violated the Establishment Clause by associating itself with Christianity.[82]

The trial court rejected the plaintiffs' claim, but the appellate court reversed this decision, finding that the town's "prayer practice impermissibly affiliated [it] with a single creed, Christianity."[83] The Supreme Court agreed to hear the case and reversed the appellate court's decision by a vote of five to four, saying Greece's prayer practices did not violate the Establishment Clause.[84]

Writing for the Court majority, Justice Kennedy said, "An insistence on nonsectarian or ecumenical prayer as a single, fixed standard is not consistent with the tradition of legislative prayer outlined in the Court's cases."[85] The Court noted: "Government may not mandate a civic religion that stifles any but the most generic reference to the sacred any more than it may prescribe a religious orthodoxy."[86] Instead, once the government made prayer part of the legislative program, it had to take a hands-off approach, allowing the prayer giver "to address his or her own God or gods as conscience dictates, unfettered by what an administrator or judge considers to be nonsectarian."[87]

Nevertheless, that does not mean there are no limits on the content of legislative prayers, Kennedy said.[88] Courts must consider the prayer practice as a whole, with a focus on whether prayer was being used to proselytize or advance or disparage any faith. "If the course and practice over time shows that the invocations denigrate nonbelievers or religious minorities, threaten damnation, or preach conversion," then that "would present a different case than the one presently before the Court."[89] Also, the Court found that the town had made "reasonable efforts" to include all of the congregations within its borders and welcome everyone who wanted to pray. So long as the town did not discriminate, it was not required to search for prayer-givers beyond its borders, the Court said. "The quest to promote 'a diversity of religious views' would require the town 'to make wholly inappropriate judgments about the number of religions [it] should sponsor and the relative frequency with which it should sponsor each,' a form of government entanglement with religion that is far more troublesome than the current approach."[90]

In a section of the opinion that Justices Scalia and Thomas did not join, Justice Kennedy said the evidence in the case did not indicate that the town had compelled its citizens to engage in prayer.[91] A different analysis would be required if the town had instructed citizens to participate in prayers, criticized those who did not participate, or suggested that a citizen's participation or nonparticipation in the prayers might affect the board's decision-making on policy issues, Justice Kennedy said.[92] "Offense . . . does not equate to coercion," and "an Establishment Clause violation is not made out any time a person experiences a sense of affront from the expression of contrary religious views in a legislative forum, especially where, as here, any member of the public is welcome to turn to offer an invocation reflecting his or her own convictions."[93] The justices concluded that legislative bodies generally do not violate the Constitution "merely by exposing constituents to prayer they would rather not hear and in which they need not participate."[94] The prayers at issue in the case had a permissible purpose, Justice Kennedy said:

> Ceremonial prayer is but a recognition that, since this Nation was founded and until the present day, many Americans deem that their own existence must be understood by precepts far beyond the authority of government to alter or define and that willing participation in civic affairs can be consistent with a brief acknowledgment of their belief in a higher power, always with due respect for those who adhere to other beliefs.[95]

Justice Kagan authored the principal dissent in the *Greece* case, with Justices Ginsburg, Breyer, and Sotomayor joining. While registering her agreement with the 1983 *Marsh* decision, Kagan noted that the meetings of the Greece town board were "a kind of hybrid" of legislative and adjudicative functions.[96] That put a special burden on the government in this case. Kagan explained:

> The government (whether federal, state, or local) may not favor, or align itself with, any particular creed. And that is nowhere more true than when officials and citizens come face to face in their shared institutions of governance. In performing civic functions and seeking civic benefits, each person of this nation must experience a government that belongs to one and all, irrespective of belief. And for its part, each government must ensure that its participatory processes will not classify those citizens by faith, or make relevant their religious differences.[97]

Justice Kagan posed a hypothetical to make her point. Assume a Muslim member of the Greece community went before the board to address traffic conditions or seek a zoning variance to build an addition to her home. Assume also that a Christian minister led participants in board meetings in prayer that evening, asking citizens to bow their heads and pray "in the name of God's only son, Jesus Christ."[98] Such circumstances would likely create a dilemma for a Muslim member of the town, Kagan noted, because she would not want to betray her faith, show disrespect to her neighbors, or antagonize board members who held the power to make a decision about her requests. Justice Kagan said:

> Everything about that situation, I think, infringes the First Amendment. (And of course, as I noted earlier, it would do so no less if the Town's clergy always used the liturgy of some other religion.) That the Town Board selects, month after month and year after year, prayer givers who will reliably speak in the voice of Christianity, and so places itself behind a single creed. That in offering those sectarian prayers, the Board's chosen clergy members repeatedly call on individuals, prior to participating in local governance, to join in a form of worship that may be at odds with their own beliefs. That the clergy thus put some residents to the unenviable choice of either pretending to pray like the majority or declining to join its communal activity, at the very moment of petitioning their elected leaders. That the practice thus divides the citizenry, creating one class that shares the Board's own evident religious beliefs and another (far smaller) class that does not. And that the practice also alters a dissenting citizen's relationship with her government, making her religious difference salient when she seeks only to engage her elected representatives as would any other citizen.[99]

Prayers could be offered in this setting, Justice Kagan said, but the town must take more care to ensure that the prayers are inclusive. The town board could have invited clergy of different faiths to serve as chaplains on a rotating basis. That way, "[w]hen one month a clergy member refers to Jesus, and the next to Allah or Jehovah . . . the government does not identify itself with one religion or align itself with that faith's citizens, and the effect of even sectarian prayer is transformed."[100] In any case, the Town of Greece had allowed "government-sponsored worship" to divide citizens along religious lines, in violation of the Establishment Clause.[101]

In his concurring opinion, Justice Alito, joined by Justice Scalia, highlighted Kagan's suggestion that the town had the option of inviting clergy of many different faiths to pray on a rotating basis. If that would solve the problem, Justice Alito said, then the dissent's objection was "really quite niggling,"[102] amounting only to the claim that the town board's staff "did a bad job in compiling the list of potential guest chaplains."[103] Further, requiring more exactitude from towns like Greece would have the effect of ending prayer practices all together, Alito argued, simply because towns did not use "what might best be termed a 'best practice' standard."[104] In other words, towns would excise prayers from proceedings due to concern that their content might not pass constitutional muster.

Justice Kagan shot back. She certainly was not suggesting that prayer should be excluded from the proceedings, Kagan said. Moreover, reducing the problem presented by these facts as some "sort of bureaucratic glitch" was telling:

> Every month for more than a decade, the Board aligned itself, through its prayer practices, with a single religion. That the concurring opinion thinks my objection to that is "really quite niggling" says all there is to say about the difference between our respective views.[105]

While Justice Alito referred somewhat derisively to a "best practice" standard for legislative prayer, Justice Breyer provided some suggestions along these lines in his concurring opinion. Breyer noted, for example, that the town could have posted its prayer policy on its website, along with the dates and times of upcoming meetings. Further, both on its website and before introducing that month's prayer-giver at meetings, the town could have made it clear that anyone was welcome to pray before future board meetings. The town could have sent this information to congregations of all faiths that were close to the town's borders (and thus could include citizens of Greece among their members).[106] While governmental bodies are not required to take such steps under the *Town of Greece* decision, doing so would be a way to seek to honor all of their citizens and increase the likelihood that they would not be sued.

Governmental officials, it should also be said, are always free to meet informally for prayer before they begin their official business. The Constitution places no limits on the content of such unofficial prayers.

RECOMMENDATIONS: MANAGING INTERSECTIONS OF FAITH, POLICY, AND POLITICS

Steps for government officials

Government officials have a duty to "preserve, protect and defend the Constitution." Relying on the following set of principles, as well as those described in the previous chapter, will help government officials fulfill that pledge and build greater unity among Americans.

(1) Steer clear of theological debates.

James Madison said no "Civil Magistrate" is "a competent Judge of Religious Truth."[107] It is beyond the government's ken to say what is true or false as a theological matter. Likewise, the Supreme Court has said, "Courts are not arbiters of scriptural interpretation."[108] The same is true for other divisions of government. It is not the job of government to pass judgment on the rightness or wrongness of religious beliefs and practices or to tell Americans that they need to change their religious convictions.

(2) Do not apply, or even appear to apply, religious tests to aspiring officeholders.

Government officials should not suggest that individuals are qualified or disqualified for public office due to their religious beliefs and affiliations, or lack thereof, much less actually apply, or appear to apply, religious tests to prospective officeholders. In confirmation hearings, a best practice for government officials is to ask *all* nominees if any of their personal beliefs or affiliations would render them unable to support the Constitution. That way, officials can seek assurance that nominees will uphold the Constitution without seeming to single out any nominee due to his or her religious beliefs and affiliations, or lack thereof. Of course, officials are also free to ask nominees about their views on any legal or policy issue and to support or oppose them for such views, even if those views spring from religious convictions.

(3) Reject proposals to "totally destroy" the rules that bar electioneering and substantial lobbying by tax-exempt 501(c)(3) entities, including religious tax-exempt 501(c)(3) entities.

Organizations that are tax-exempt under Section 501(c)(3) of the Internal Revenue Code, including congregations and other religious entities, cannot endorse or oppose candidates for elective public office, nor can they do a substantial amount of lobbying. Such organizations may speak out on public issues, and clergy can endorse candidates in their individual capacities. But 501(c)(3) organizations are not permitted to electioneer for or against candidates, if they wish to keep their tax-exempt status.

President Trump has pledged to "totally destroy" these rules,[109] and he has claimed that this would be perhaps his "greatest contribution to Christianity—and other religions."[110] Yet, as *Christianity Today* magazine has noted, this issue is rarely discussed even among white evangelicals.[111] Unsurprisingly, the most vocal proponents of President Trump's initiative are politicians.[112] Candidates, not congregations, would be the principal beneficiaries of such a change. Under Trump's policy, candidates who are officeholders might attempt to subtly pressure religious bodies in an attempt to get political endorsements. A city councilperson might, for example, push congregational leaders for an endorsement in exchange for a zoning permit the congregation needs. Also, if 501(c)(3) organizations are permitted to make campaign donations, houses of worship could turn into new magnets for tax-deductible "dark money."[113] And at a time when Russians and other foreign-state actors are seeking to manipulate U.S. elections, the United States should not create a legal path for religion-themed front operations.

(4) Include religious leaders in meaningful discussions of public issues.

Government officials usually meet with a wide variety of community leaders, including representatives from veterans, business, labor, and civil rights groups, for example. Religious communities also care deeply about a broad array of public issues, and governmental leaders should meet with them too. Forming relationships with religious leaders and including them in substantive discussions of public policy should be the aim, not simply summoning leaders for photo ops and blessings of deals that they have had no opportunity to shape. Government officials should also consult with leaders of intentionally secular groups, like secular humanists.

(5) Do not limit religious engagement to the "usual suspects."

Some government officials only engage religious communities with whom they are politically aligned. That is a mistake. Officials must serve their entire constituency, including the parts of the religious sector that did not vote for them and do not agree with them on most policy issues. Engagement with religious communities should aim to identify and advance common ground and commit to respectful, ongoing dialogue where there are differences.

(6) Consult widely and seek common ground before making policy decisions.

Policymakers should seek to ensure that diverse stakeholders are given meaningful opportunities to offer their views before decisions are made. All interested communities should be notified about ways to provide input and given sufficient time to do so, for example.[114] Policymakers should weigh this feedback carefully and seek common ground. To be sure, often there is no comprehensive common-ground solution on controversial issues. But there is usually at least some common ground, and there are always opportunities to build greater understanding and trust.[115] Special deference should be given across administrations to policies that were developed through a bona fide common-ground process.

(7) Promote inclusive practices regarding government-sponsored prayers before legislative sessions.

The Supreme Court has upheld the practice of government-organized prayers before legislative sessions. While the Court has not required legislative bodies to take specific steps to promote inclusion in this practice, such bodies can and should do so as a way of supporting religious freedom for all and diminishing the likelihood of lawsuits. Legislative bodies can post their prayer policies and also the dates and times of upcoming meetings on their websites, for example. Further, before introducing the person who will give the prayer at a given session, a leader could invite audience members to flag their interest in future prayer opportunities and encourage the audience to make these opportunities known to other community members.

Steps for religious and other civil society leaders

The First Amendment does not apply to the activities of civil society, including religious leaders and organizations, but civil society leaders' advocacy on public issues should respect certain core principles of religious freedom. To some extent, the following steps describe the informal, civil society "flip side" of the legal responsibilities the government bears. Also, the following practical tips may help such leaders and organizations to engage government more effectively.

(1) Respect and protect religious liberty for all.

Protecting religious freedom for all is not just the government's duty. Americans should also seek to protect each other's rights. One need not believe that all faiths are equally true to engage in such advocacy. One only needs to believe that every human being has dignity and inalienable rights of conscience that must be respected. In particular, members of faiths that would be considered the majority religion in a given area should demonstrate leadership by demanding protection for members of the smallest religious minorities and nonreligious groups. Members of the majority religious group, for example, could insist that government officials implement inclusive legislative prayer practices. Doing so would not be an endorsement of other religions but rather an endorsement of religious liberty for all.

(2) Promote policies that advance the common good, not ones that benefit only co-religionists or advance some narrow theological end.

Government alone bears the responsibility for ensuring that laws and policies comply with the Constitution. Nevertheless, religious leaders demonstrate respect for religious freedom when they ensure that the policies they advocate would benefit people of all faiths and of none.

(3) Understand religion's role.

Rev. Dr. Martin Luther King said the church "is not the master or the servant of the state, but rather the conscience of the state."[116] The religious sector should not seek to control or be subservient to the government. Instead, the religious sector should focus on calling the state to heed "the better angels of our nature," in the memorable words of President Abraham Lincoln.[117]

(4) Develop a written policy regarding invitations to government officials and political candidates to speak at meetings.

The time to develop a policy on whether a government official or political candidate should be invited to speak at a religious gathering is well before any such invitations are extended. Policies should be in writing, based on theology, and consistent with law and ethics. Policies should include directions about the process to be used to extend such invitations, if any, including who should do so and under what circumstances. Similarly, policies should provide instructions for handling requests by governmental officials or candidates to speak to, or be recognized in, religious services or other meetings.

(5) Protect the integrity of religious witness.

Engaging with government should not come at the cost of the integrity of faith. Sometimes, religious communities become so enamored with access to powerful people in government that they still their own prophetic voices. Religious communities may refuse to call out even egregious moral and ethical violations by policymakers as well as their unjust policies, because those same officials are making other policy just the way their communities like it.

The use of double standards—faulting someone outside the party or faction for certain behavior, for example, yet giving someone inside their favored party or faction a pass for the same or similar behavior—is a problem. Consider one example: In 2011, only 30 percent of white evangelicals believed "an elected official who commits an immoral act in their personal life can still behave ethically and fulfill their duties in their public and professional life."[118] By 2016, however, that number had risen to 72 percent,[119] meaning "[w]hite evangelicals are now more tolerant of immoral behavior by elected officials than the average American."[120] Of course, President Donald Trump, a thrice-married admitted adulterer who has been accused of many ethical violations and sexual assault, was elected president in 2016, with 81 percent of white evangelicals supporting him.[121] Protecting the integrity of religion's witness is an essential act of faith and helps to preserve the power of religion in public life.

(6) Be engaged, not used.

Religious leaders must be on guard against being used rather than engaged by government. Religious communities can take proactive and practical steps to protect their independence. For example, religious leaders generally should avoid standing behind government officials at public events if they do not have advance knowledge of what will be said. Religious leaders should also ask if government officials plan to use their name or picture in any way, either before, during, or after an event. If so, leaders should insist on approving such materials before they are released. John Carr—who served for over twenty years as director of the Department of Justice, Peace and Human Development at the United States Conference of Catholic Bishops—well summarized the right approach for religious leaders. Carr said, "We need to be political, but not partisan. We need to be principled, but not ideological. We need to be civil, but not soft. We need to be engaged, and not used."[122]

(7) Servants of God, not spokespersons for God.

At a meeting of the Baptist Joint Committee for Religious Liberty, Representative Barbara Jordan was asked how to articulate Christian values in public life. Jordan responded:

> You would do well to pursue your causes with vigor, while remembering that you are *a servant of God, not a spokesperson for God*—a servant of God, not a spokesperson for God—and remembering that God might well choose to bless an opposing point of view for reasons that have not been revealed to you.

Regardless of one's faith or denomination, these are wise words for religious leaders in the public sphere.

(8) Do not wait for an invitation from government officials to engage with them.

At the earliest opportunity, religious leaders and organizations who are interested in collaborating with government should introduce themselves to government officials at all levels. Religious leaders should share statements they make about public issues and invite conversation on those issues. Doing so will lay a foundation for collaboration on shared aims in the future.

(9) Understand the secular aspects of the issues.

Religious leaders should be knowledgeable about and conversant with the secular aspects of the issues they are discussing. Also, people of faith should never assume any religious knowledge on the part of any government official or staff person. Instead, religious leaders should ensure that their arguments are accessible to people without any religious knowledge or commitments.

(10) Know your audience.

Part of what politicians do is look at life through a political prism. They consider whether adopting a particular policy will help them get reelected or gain more popularity. For this and other reasons, religious leaders should always build the broadest coalition possible around their proposals, including unusual allies. While religious leaders should not base their agenda on polls, they should be aware that politicians are concerned about polls, and they should help government officials to see how taking the desired action will not only be right thing: it will also help them to succeed. Being specific, clear, and concise is another important part of knowing an audience of politicians and government officials.

(11) Find a balance between prophetic and pragmatic.

In interactions with government, religious leaders need to find a balance between the prophetic and pragmatic. If government officials are not inclined to adopt a proposal wholesale, consider whether there are pieces of it that might make a meaningful difference, if adopted.

(12) Recognize that a good idea is not enough.

If civil society leaders wish to work with government, they need to understand that the fact that a proposal is a good idea is usually not enough to get it implemented. A proposal must also rank high on government officials' priority lists, have strong support, and have the capacity to be executed by government, for example. If proposals do not currently meet such tests, proponents can act to increase the likelihood that their proposals will do so in the future.

(13) Go upstream.

People run for office because they want to accomplish something. Candidates use their campaigns to showcase and sell their agenda. Then, if the candidate is fortunate, he or she is elected and gains the opportunity to execute an agenda. Once elected, governmental officials are acutely aware of keeping their campaign promises. Other agenda items are often not considered as high a priority.

Thus, if civil society leaders want their ideas to be implemented by government officials, they should seek to ensure that such ideas become part of politicians' campaign promises. Religious organizations can do so without engaging in electioneering or partisan politics. The Circle of Protection, a group of Christian leaders that focus on ending hunger and poverty, created one model for doing so. In recent elections, this group asked all presidential candidates to produce a three-minute video "telling the American people what you would do as president to offer help and opportunity to hungry and poor people in the United States and around the world."[123] The Circle of Protection then shared these materials with their networks as a way of doing nonpartisan electoral education. This model does not involve the religious community in electioneering, yet it helps prompt politicians to make commitments on issues that are important to them long before politicians take office.

RELIGIOUS EXPRESSION
ON GOVERNMENT PROPERTY

Prohibiting Government Speech Endorsing Religion—
Protecting Nongovernmental Religious Speech

The U.S. Supreme Court has said, "[T]here is a crucial difference between government speech endorsing religion, which the Establishment Clause forbids, and private speech endorsing religion, which the Free Speech and Free Exercise Clauses protect." Speech that is attributable to the government cannot promote or denigrate religion or prefer one faith over others. If such speech is attributable to nongovernmental organizations and individuals instead, it is protected.

When a religious group holds a protest or a meeting in a public park just as other nongovernmental groups do, it is generally understood that religious expression is attributable to the group, not the state, and thus is constitutionally protected. Also, when a public university opens its campus to student clubs, student religious clubs must be as welcome as student nonreligious clubs. This principle is often called the "equal access" rule.

Some governmental expression containing religious elements is nevertheless permissible. The Court has found, for example, that the Establishment Clause did not prohibit a city from erecting a Christmas display that included many seasonal elements in addition to a nativity scene. In 2005, the Court refused to order the removal of a longstanding government monument with the Ten Commandments that was surrounded by other secular monuments, partially due to concern that removal of the monument would send a signal of hostility to faith. And in 2019 the Court upheld the constitutionality of a large, longstanding cross memorial on government land. While the cross is undoubtedly a symbol of Christianity, the Court said, this memorial to soldiers who died in World War I also had other meanings and thus did not violate the Establishment Clause.

The Court has struck down school-sponsored religious exercises at public schools. In addition to invalidating school-organized prayers and Bible readings in the classroom, the Court has invalidated practices such as school-sponsored prayers by clergy during middle school graduation exercises.

At the same time, public schools are not "religion-free zones." Students generally are free to pray individually or in groups, read scriptures, and discuss their faith at public schools, for example. Middle and high school students may form religious clubs that meet on school property during non-instructional time if other extracurricular student clubs are permitted to do so. Students may discuss their religious beliefs in schoolwork where other personal views may be expressed. And while public schools cannot preach, they can teach about religion. Academic study of sacred texts or of religion's role in world history, for example, is consistent with the First Amendment.

The National Mall in Washington, D.C., may be the most well-known public park in the United States. Indeed, the mall is often called "America's front yard."[1] The monuments on the mall tell part of the American story.[2] The protests, marches, and other gatherings that take place there are equally important.[3]

Religious voices have been among those who have gathered on the mall to protest, practice their faith, and demonstrate how their religion fits into the American experience. In 1943, for example, rabbis marched to call for a stop to the persecution of Jews in Europe.[4] Rev. Dr. Martin Luther King Jr. shared his dream of racial equality during the 1963 March on Washington for Jobs and Freedom.[5] Opponents of abortion held the first March for Life in the wake of the U.S. Supreme Court's decision in *Roe v. Wade.*[6] Pope John Paul II celebrated Mass on the mall during his first papal visit to the United States.[7] The Million Man March took place on the mall in 1995.[8] Two years later, an evangelical men's group, Promise Keepers, had a daylong revival service there.[9] In 2017, Christian women held a rally to seek God's guidance for the nation;[10] diverse clergy marched to recommit to the principles that Rev. Dr. Martin Luther King Jr. advanced;[11] and Native Americans built a symbolic camp at the Washington Monument to protest the U.S. government's treatment of indigenous people.[12] These public protests and marches are among those that have demonstrated the power of faith in America's front yard.

Such expression is protected speech under the First Amendment. As the Supreme Court has said, "[T]here is a crucial difference between *government* speech endorsing religion, which the Establishment Clause forbids, and *private* speech endorsing religion, which the Free Speech and Free Exercise Clauses protect."[13] In other words, speech that is attributable to the government cannot promote or denigrate religion or prefer one faith over others. If such speech is attributable to nongovernmental organizations and individuals instead, it is protected.

A set of Supreme Court cases provides guidance on how to distinguish between protected and prohibited religious expression on government property, including public parks and public schools as well as other government buildings. Some of these cases are complex and even confusing, in part because they produced multiple opinions and a spate of sometimes heated disagreements on the Court. Still, some basic rules can be extracted from these cases, and these cases confirm that religion has not been kicked out of American public life. While the Constitution prohibits government-backed religion, it protects the rights of religious individuals and organizations to promote their faith, including on government property. The Constitution ensures that our nation provides ample space for faith to flourish, without governmental support or interference.

EQUAL ACCESS FOR RELIGIOUS SPEAKERS

Government property such as public parks, streets, and sidewalks has traditionally been open to speech and debate.[14] Nongovernmental groups and individuals are generally permitted to express themselves there, including through religious activities and speech, subject to what are called "time, place, and manner" restrictions. Such restrictions do not apply to the content of the expression, only to the speech's timing and form as well as where it takes place. In this context, it is usually understood that religious expression is attributable to nongovernmental speakers, not the state, and thus is constitutionally protected.[15]

Also, when the government opens up other property to nongovernmental expression on a wide range of topics, the state generally must welcome religious as well as nonreligious speech there.[16] A case involving the University of Missouri–Kansas City (UMKC) is instructive.[17] UMKC opened its property for speech when it permitted registered student groups to meet on campus, subject to certain time, place, and manner restrictions.[18] At the same time, the school prohibited the use of university buildings (except chapels) "for purposes of religious worship or religious teaching either by student or non-student groups."[19] Both the Constitution and Kansas law required this prohibition, UMKC said. Citing this policy, the school rejected the request of a registered student club known as Cornerstone to meet on campus. Cornerstone's meetings typically included activities like an opening prayer, singing, reading scripture, and Bible commentary.[20] While the club identified itself as Christian, its meetings were open to the public, including students of any faith or no faith.[21]

In 1977, Cornerstone sued UMKC, saying the school's policy violated its free speech and religious liberty rights. Students who belonged to Cornerstone noted a number of ways in which the school's policy impacted their club. "Having to explain that we have to meet off campus tends to make students think that there is something 'wrong' with us and that there is something wrong with religion since it has been banished from campus," the students said.[22]

In *Widmar v. Vincent*, the U.S. Supreme Court ruled in Cornerstone's favor.[23] The university did not have to exclude Cornerstone in order to protect the school's secular nature, the Court said. The school had opened up its facilities to registered student groups for the exchange of ideas. Over a hundred student groups, including Cornerstone, were registered with the school and thus eligible to use the school's property. The school was not endorsing the goals of the other student groups, including the Students for a Democratic Society and the Young Socialist Alliance, by allowing them to meet on campus. UMKC also would not endorse the goals of religious groups by doing so. "[B]y creating a forum the University does not thereby endorse or promote any of the particular ideas aired there," the Court noted.[24]

The fact that the Christian student club's activities could be described as "worship" did not put those activities beyond the Constitution's protection.[25] Singing, teaching, and reading are forms of speech, and there is no clear distinction between such expression and worship, the Court said. In any case, the government would not be competent to draw such lines in this context. "Merely to draw the distinction would require the university—and ultimately the courts—to inquire into the significance of words and practices to different faiths, and in varying circumstances by the same faith."[26] That task would inevitably, and unconstitutionally, entangle government with faith.[27]

In the *Widmar* case, the Court required UMKC to afford Cornerstone the same access to campus facilities that all other registered student groups enjoyed. This decision did not enable UMKC to control the expression of Cornerstone or any other student club. The Court recognized that the school was simply administering a forum, not endorsing any of the speech by participants in that forum.[28]

The Court considered a related case in 1993 involving a New York school district that allowed after-hours use of school property for social, civic, and recreational purposes.[29] Given this policy, the Court said the school district could not exclude an evangelical church from using those facilities to show a religiously oriented film on family values. "The film series involved here no doubt dealt with a subject otherwise permissible under [the school district's access policy], and its exhibition was denied solely because the series dealt with the subject from a religious standpoint."[30] Thus, the school's policy violated the First Amendment's prohibition on governmental regulation of speech favoring some viewpoints over others.[31]

Nongovernmental expression in government forums also includes unattended displays—signs or symbols erected by nongovernmental speakers on government property for a set period of time.[32] In 1995, the Court held that these kinds of religious expression by nongovernmental speakers also generally must be treated the same as secular speech by nongovernmental speakers.[33]

In 2010, the Supreme Court considered a case in which a state law school refused to grant a religious club an exemption from its general nondiscrimination policy.[34] The Hastings College of Law required registered student organizations (RSOs) to accept students as members or leaders regardless of a student's status or beliefs. The Christian Legal Society (CLS) sued the school, arguing that the CLS club should be permitted to choose its leaders based on its statement of faith.

By a five-to-four vote, the Court rejected the Christian Legal Society's free-speech and expressive-association claims. RSOs at the law school receive several benefits, including the ability to use the school's name and logo, a share of mandatory student-activity fees, and use of school communications channels and facilities for meeting space. Through its RSO program, the Court said, the law school was simply "dangling the carrot of subsidy, not wielding the stick of prohibition."[35] The Court also drew other contrasts with its decision in the *Widmar* case. Whereas UMKC "singled out organizations for disfavored treatment because of their points of view, Hastings' all-comers requirement draws no distinction between groups based on their message or perspective," the Court said.[36] Taking issue with a dissenting opinion by Justice Alito, the Court majority insisted: "Those who hold religious beliefs are not 'singled out'; those who engage in discriminatory *conduct* based on someone else's religious status and belief are singled out."[37] The "all-comers" policy was reasonable and viewpoint neutral, according to the Court. As the Court also noted, however, schools are not required to adopt such "all-comers" policies.[38] Whatever their policies on these issues, public schools must enforce them uniformly, not selectively.[39]

The "Plastic Reindeer Rule"

The First Amendment protects the right of nongovernmental organizations and individuals to promote their faith in the public square, but the Establishment Clause generally prohibits the government from promoting or denigrating faith or preferring one religion over another. Permanent monuments displayed on government property usually constitute government speech, including monuments paid for by nongovernmental sources but donated and then displayed on government property.[40] Also, temporary displays by government, including seasonal displays that include some religious elements, are government speech. To determine whether such monuments or displays violate the Establishment Clause, the Supreme Court has applied a variety of tests.[41] This section and the following one demonstrate how the Court's thinking on these issues has evolved.

In 1984, the Court considered a Christmas display including a nativity scene, or crèche, that was erected by the city of Pawtucket, Rhode Island.[42] The city erected the display in a park owned by a nonprofit organization and located in a shopping district. In addition to the nativity scene, the display included a Christmas tree and reindeer pulling Santa's sleigh, among other secular seasonal items.[43]

The question in this case, *Lynch v. Donnelly*, was whether the Establishment Clause prohibited the city from including the crèche in the display. In an opinion written by Chief Justice Warren Burger, the Court found it did not. The city had a secular purpose for including the crèche in the display—celebrating Christmas and recognizing its origins. Including the crèche did not advance religion, or Christianity specifically, any more than programs allowing government funds to support textbooks and transportation for schools, including religious schools, the Court said, although it did not explain the factors that differentiated cases falling on the right side of the line from those that did not. The display also did not create excessive entanglement between religion and government.[44]

Justice O'Connor concurred in the Court's judgment in *Lynch* but wrote separately to suggest "a clarification" of Establishment Clause doctrine. "The Establishment Clause prohibits government from making adherence to a religion relevant in any way to a person's standing in the political community," O'Connor said.[45] Government violates that principal when it endorses or disapproves of religion: "Endorsement sends a message to nonadherents that they are outsiders, not full members of the political community, and an accompanying message to adherents that they are insiders, favored members of the political community. Disapproval sends the opposite message."[46] Endorsement should be judged by a "reasonable observer" standard, one who is "deemed aware of the history and context of the community and forum in which the religious display appears."[47] Under this standard, Justice O'Connor said, she would have found that the city had a legitimate secular purpose for including the crèche in the display—to celebrate a public holiday with traditional symbols, some of which are religious.[48] The fact that cities commonly had such celebrations added to

O'Connor's conclusion that they usually were not understood by the reasonable observer as an endorsement of religion.[49]

The dissenters in the case—Justices Brennan, Marshall, Blackmun, and Stevens—argued that such displays not only damaged government but also harmed faith. In his dissenting opinion, which Justice Stevens joined, Justice Blackmun said that, while the mayor of Pawtucket had admittedly "undert[aken] a crusade to 'keep "Christ" in Christmas,'" the Court's ruling had "relegated [the crèche] to the role of a neutral harbinger of the holiday season, useful for commercial purposes, but devoid of any inherent meaning and incapable of enhancing the religious tenor of a display of which it is an integral part. The city has its victory—but it is a Pyrrhic one indeed."[50] Justice Brennan voiced similar concerns: "To suggest, as the Court does, that [a crèche] is merely 'traditional,' and therefore no different from Santa's house or reindeer is not only offensive to those for whom the crèche has profound significance, but insulting to those who insist for religious or personal reasons that the story of Christ is in no sense a part of 'history' nor an unavoidable element of our national 'heritage.'"[51]

Skeptical Court-watchers refer to the *Lynch* ruling as "the plastic reindeer rule."[52] To make a governmental display of a crèche constitutional, simply add some plastic reindeer to it.

Five years later, a different Christmas display was before the Court in *Allegheny County v. American Civil Liberties Union*. The *Allegheny* case involved a crèche that was given to the county by the Holy Name Society, a Roman Catholic group, to display during the Christmas holiday season.[53] The nativity scene included a banner proclaiming, "Gloria In Excelsis Deo!"[54] The county displayed the crèche on the Grand Staircase of the county courthouse, framed by a fence lined with red and white poinsettia plants. The fence bore a plaque, which said: "This Display Donated by the Holy Name Society."[55] No other figures or decorations appeared on the Grand Staircase.

By displaying the nativity scene in this particular setting, the Court held, "the county sen[t] an unmistakable message that it supports and promotes the Christian praise to God that is the crèche's religious message."[56] The Court was careful to note that "[t]he Grand Staircase does not appear to be the kind of location in which all were free to place their displays for weeks at a time, so that the presence of the crèche in that location for over six weeks would then not serve to associate the government with the crèche."[57] The county was not administering a forum that was open to all. Instead, the county was selectively featuring the crèche display.

The *Allegheny County* case also involved another display at a city-county building about a block away. This display included a Hanukkah menorah, which was owned by Chabad, a Jewish group, and a city-owned Christmas tree. At the foot of the tree, the city placed a message from the mayor, saying: "During this holiday season, the city of Pittsburgh salutes liberty. Let these festive lights remind us that we are the keepers of the flame of liberty and our legacy of freedom."[58] Taking all these factors into account, Justice Blackmun said, it was not "sufficiently likely" that Pittsburgh residents would perceive the display as an endorsement or disapproval of their individual religious beliefs and practices.[59] The Court struck down the display where the nativity scene stood alone but upheld the display that included the menorah among other signs and symbols.

The divisions on the Court in the *Allegheny* case make even lawyers' eyes glaze over. In addition to Justice Blackmun's opinion, Justice O'Connor wrote an opinion concurring in part and concurring in the judgment, with Justices Brennan and Stevens partially joining.[60] Justice Brennan wrote an opinion concurring in part and dissenting in part, with Justices Marshall and Stevens joining.[61] Justice Kennedy wrote an opinion agreeing with the Court's ruling regarding the tree, menorah, and sign but deeply disagreeing with the rationale and result regarding the crèche display on the Grand Staircase.[62] Chief Justice Rehnquist and Justices White and Scalia joined Kennedy's opinion.[63]

The opinions are not only fractured; portions of them are laced with vitriol. In his opinion, Justice Blackmun harshly criticized the majority opinion written by former chief justice Burger in *Lynch* just five years earlier. Because Blackmun and Burger had once been close friends, Blackmun's attack on Burger's opinion was even more notable.[64] In a section of the opinion that Justices O'Connor, Brennan, and Marshall did not join, Blackmun said: "The rationale of the majority opinion in *Lynch* is none too clear," citing the lack of "a sound analytical framework for evaluating governmental use of religious symbols" in the opinion.[65] Justices Blackmun and Kennedy traded barbs. The Court majority's view of the Establishment Clause, Kennedy charged, "reflect[ed] an unjustified hostility toward religion, a hostility inconsistent with our history and our precedents . . . ."[66] In response, Justice Blackmun said that "nothing could be further from the truth, and the accusations could be said to be as offensive as they are absurd."[67] When Justice Kennedy said the "endorsement" test, which the Court used to decide the case, was "flawed in its fundamentals and unworkable in practice,"[68] Justice Blackmun insisted that the test Kennedy had proposed was no better.[69] In another retort to Blackmun, Kennedy went out of his way to insert a favorable name-check of former chief justice Burger, saying he "accept[ed] and indeed approve[d] both the holding and the reasoning of Chief Justice Burger's opinion in *Lynch* . . . ."

Setting aside the merits of these rulings, the multiplicity of opinions in these cases—and, to some extent, their tone—caused frustration. Two 2005 decisions regarding Ten Commandments exhibitions and a 2019 case involving a memorial to soldiers killed in the First World War continued to put the Court's divisions on display.

Two Ten Commandments Cases and a World War I Memorial

In *McCreary County v. ACLU,* the Supreme Court struck down governmental displays of the Ten Commandments that had recently been posted on the walls of Kentucky courthouses.[70] The original displays consisted of the Ten Commandments by themselves. After the counties were sued, they added other materials to the displays. The Supreme Court found "ample support" for the lower court's conclusion that the display had a predominantly religious purpose.[71] "When the government acts with the ostensible and predominant purpose of advancing religion," the Court noted, "it violates that central Establishment Clause value of official religious neutrality, there being no neutrality when the government's ostensible object is to take sides."[72] The Court was careful to note, however, that its ruling was not a flat prohibition on integrating a sacred text into a governmental display regarding American law or history.[73]

On the same day that the Supreme Court handed down its decision in *McCreary County,* the Court also issued its ruling in another Ten Commandments case, *Van Orden v. Perry.* The Court upheld a forty-year-old monument inscribed with the Ten Commandments that was one of seventeen monuments and twenty-one historical markers appearing on the grounds of a state capitol.[74] The monument had "a mixed but primarily nonreligious purpose" and primary effect, Justice Breyer said, and had not been challenged for forty years.[75] The vote was five to four in both the *McCreary County* and *Van Orden* cases, but only Justice Breyer was in the Court majority both times. Concurring only in the result in *Van Orden,* Breyer described it as a "borderline case," one on the knife's edge of constitutionality.[76] Breyer said a decision to remove the longstanding Texas monument "based primarily upon on the religious nature of the tablets' text would, I fear, lead the law to exhibit a hostility toward religion that has no place in our Establishment Clause traditions."[77]

The Court handed down these decisions on June 27, 2005. On July 1, 2005, Justice Sandra Day O'Connor announced she would retire from the bench after twenty-four years of service at the Supreme Court.[78] O'Connor had reportedly been willing to stay on the Court another year and expected Chief Justice Rehnquist, who was suffering from cancer, to retire in the summer of 2005.[79] Toward the end of the Court's 2005 term, however, Rehnquist surprised O'Connor by saying he wanted to stay another year. There should not be two vacancies on the Court at the time, he counseled.[80] The chief's point was clear: O'Connor should either retire now or serve two more years.[81] Given her husband's failing health, O'Connor decided to announce her departure after the 2005 term concluded.[82]

President George W. Bush moved swiftly to nominate then-appellate-judge John Roberts to take O'Connor's seat.[83] But before Roberts' confirmation hearings began, Chief Justice Rehnquist passed away.[84] Two days later, on September 6, President Bush withdrew Roberts' nomination to serve as an associate justice and instead nominated him to serve as the chief justice of the U.S. Supreme Court.[85]

In his September 2005 confirmation hearings, then-judge John Roberts discussed the Court's decisions in the *McCreary County* and *Van Orden* cases.[86] Roberts said: "I think everyone would agree that the religion jurisprudence under the First Amendment, the Establishment Clause and the Free Exercise Clause[,] could be clearer."[87] The Court issued rulings in two Ten Commandments cases, Roberts noted, but "[o]nly one [j]ustice thinks both [rulings] are right."[88]

Justice Breyer was the one justice who thought both Ten Commandments decisions were right. Breyer's opinion in the *Van Orden* case suggested the outlines of an imperfect but potentially workable compromise: refrain from insisting on the removal of longstanding monuments or displays like the one at issue in *Van Orden*, while halting efforts to erect or post new ones.[89]

In 2019, the Supreme Court revisited these issues in a case involving a thirty-two-foot tall cross monument that was erected in 1925 in Bladensburg, Maryland, as a memorial to soldiers from the area who gave their lives in the First World War.[90] The monument and land were initially owned by private organizations, but they were transferred to the state due to traffic-safety concerns. The government spent approximately $117,00 maintaining the monument and budgeted another $100,000 for renovations and repairs.

In 2012, members of the American Humanist Association challenged the constitutionality of the monument under the Establishment Clause. In *American Legion v. American Humanist Association*, the Supreme Court rejected the challenge by a vote of 7-2.

Writing for five of the seven justices, Justice Alito said longstanding monuments, symbols, and practices share several characteristics. Identifying their original purpose or purposes may be challenging, the purpose and message they convey may change over time, and removing them may not appear to be neutral. Thus, "[R]etaining established, religiously expressive monuments, symbols, and practices is quite different from erecting or adopting new ones," according to the Court. "The passage of time gives rise to a strong presumption of constitutionality."[91]

Turning to the case at hand, the Court concluded:

The cross is undoubtedly a Christian symbol, but that fact should not blind us to everything else that the Bladensburg Cross has come to represent. For some, that monument is a symbolic resting place for ancestors who never returned home. For others, it is a place for the community to gather and honor all veterans and their sacrifices for our Nation. For others still, it is a historical landmark. For many of these people, destroying or defacing the Cross that has stood undisturbed for nearly a century would not be neutral and would not further the ideals of respect and tolerance embodied in the First Amendment. For all these reasons, the Cross does not offend the Constitution.[92]

Notably, the Court found no evidence that Jewish soldiers from the area were deliberately left off the list of names that appear on a plaque affixed to the monument or that their names were included on that plaque against their family's wishes.[93]

The five justices who joined Justice Alito's opinion agreed on this much but not much more. Four of those justices (Chief Justice Roberts and Justices Breyer, Alito, and Kavanaugh) rejected application of the *Lemon* test in favor of an approach "that focuses on the particular issue at hand and looks to history for guidance."[94]

In a separate concurring opinion that Justice Kagan joined, however, Justice Breyer said his understanding of the Court's opinion was that it did not "adopt a 'history and tradition test' that would permit any newly constructed religious memorial on public land."[95] The case would be different, Breyer said, "if the Cross has been erected only recently, rather than in the aftermath of World War I," or "if there were evidence that the organizers had 'deliberately disrespected' members of minority faiths . . . ."[96]

And while she too looks to history for guidance, Justice Kagan also wrote separately to say she "prefer[red] at least for now to do so case-by-case, rather than to sign on to any broader statements about history's role in Establishment Clause analysis."[97] Kagan also set herself apart from the other four justices by emphasizing that, while she agreed "that rigid application of the *Lemon* test does not solve every Establishment Clause problem," she believes that the "test's focus on purposes and effects is crucial in evaluating government action in this sphere—as this very [lawsuit] shows."[98]

Other justices were ready not only to bury the *Lemon* test entirely but also to throw other hunks of Establishment Clause doctrine into the grave with it. In a separate concurring opinion, Justice Kavanaugh set forth an additional presumption of his own: "If the challenged government practice is not coercive *and* if it (i) is rooted in history and tradition; or (ii) treats religious people, organizations, speech, or activity equally to comparable secular people, organizations, speech, or activity; or (iii) represents a permissible legislative accommodation or exemption from a generally applicable law, then there ordinarily is no Establishment Clause violation."[99]

Concurring only in the judgment, Justice Thomas reiterated his view that the Establishment Clause should not apply to the states and that, even if it did apply, there was no violation here because only laws that force people to act or not to act violate that Clause.[100] Justice Gorsuch, with Justice Thomas joining him, also concurred only in the judgment, arguing that individuals who object to monuments and displays do not sustain concrete injuries and thus should not be permitted to bring lawsuits in such cases. Thomas and Gorsuch rejected the *Lemon* test too. But they also rejected their colleagues' distinction between "longstanding" monuments and new ones, insisting that "a practice consistent with our nation's traditions is just as permissible whether undertaken today or 94 years ago."[101]

Justice Ginsburg vigorously dissented, with Justice Sotomayor joining her. The cross is the preeminent symbol of Christianity, she noted. The Court's decision did real damage to Establishment Clause values, the dissenters said:

> Decades ago, this Court recognized that the Establishment Clause of the First Amendment to the Constitution demands governmental neutrality among religious faiths, and between religion and nonreligion. Numerous times since, the Court has reaffirmed the Constitution's commitment to neutrality. Today the Court erodes that neutrality commitment, diminishing precedent designed to preserve individual liberty and civic harmony in favor of a "presumption of constitutionality for longstanding monuments, symbols, and practices."[102]

"Recognizing that a Latin cross does not belong on a public highway or building," however, "does not mean the monument must be 'torn down,'" the dissenters noted.[103] It might have been possible to move the monument to private land or transfer the land on which it sits to private parties.

At least two matters seem plain after the Court's ruling in *American Legion v. American Humanist Association*. First, the case raises many questions, including how old a monument, symbol, or practice must be in order to be considered "longstanding." Second, while there are growing calls on the Court for major changes to Establishment Clause doctrine, the *American Legion* decision left much of that doctrine intact.

Public Schools: Not "Religion-Free Zones"

In 1962, the Supreme Court struck down a public school district's practice of requiring a state-written prayer to be said in elementary schools each day: "[T]he constitutional prohibition against laws respecting an establishment of religion must at least mean that in this country it is no part of the business of government to compose official prayers for any group of the American people to recite as a part of a religious program carried on by government."[104] The following year, the Court struck down state-organized Bible readings at the beginning of the public school day.[105] The purpose and primary effect of these exercises was to advance religion, thus violating the Establishment Clause. In both of these cases, the Court found that the exercises were unconstitutional even though students could opt out of them. The Court also noted that the cases involved impressionable children, a factor that has always been taken into account in this area.

These decisions triggered a fierce backlash against the Court, including the introduction of constitutional amendments to override them.[106] Efforts to amend the Constitution failed, however. President John F. Kennedy's judicious response to the 1962 ruling helped tamp down the furor.[107]

In the early 1990s, the Supreme Court returned to this topic. The Court decided *Lee v. Weisman* in 1992, a case involving a public middle school's decision to include a nonsectarian prayer in its graduation program.[108] The Rhode Island middle school's principal, Robert E. Lee, invited a rabbi, Rabbi Leslie Gutterman, to deliver prayers at the school's graduation exercises. Prior to the event, Principal Lee gave Rabbi Gutterman a pamphlet entitled "Guidelines for Civic Occasions," prepared by the National Conference of Christians and Jews, and he advised Gutterman to make his prayers nonsectarian.[109]

In an opinion written by Justice Kennedy, the Court struck down the school's prayer practice. The Court said: "It is beyond dispute that, at a minimum, the Constitution guarantees that government may not coerce anyone to support or participate in religion or its exercise . . . ."[110] The school decided that prayers should be part of the program, invited a rabbi to give them, and provided guidance on the nature of the prayers, the Court noted. Further, while the public school did not require that students attend graduation and participate in the prayers, "their attendance and participation in the state-sponsored religious activity are in a fair and real sense obligatory . . . ."[111] Citing its earlier decisions prohibiting public schools from organizing classroom prayers and Bible readings, the Court held that the school could not conduct a religious exercise at a graduation ceremony where "young graduates who object are induced to conform."[112]

Once again, a Supreme Court decision triggered proposals to amend the Constitution. In the wake of the *Lee v. Weisman* decision, some members of Congress called for an amendment to the First Amendment to permit state-sponsored prayer and other religious exercises at public schools.[113] Even some who disagreed with the Court's decision, however, opposed such a constitutional amendment, fearing it could do more harm than good. Eventually, a group of church-state lawyers who approved of the *Lee* decision as well as those who disapproved of it joined together to draft a joint statement describing current law regarding religious expression in American public schools. This diverse group could not agree about what the law *should be*, but the group could agree in many cases on what the law *was*.[114] The drafters of the statement also agreed that current law provides a range of opportunities for students to express their faith in public schools.

This diverse coalition released their joint statement in April 1995, and it drew the attention of the Clinton White House. In July 1995, President Clinton signed a memorandum[115] that, as he said, "borrow[ed] heavily and gratefully from [the coalition's] wise and thoughtful statement."[116] In remarks made at the time of the memorandum's release, Clinton emphasized that the First Amendment "does not convert our schools into religion-free zones."[117] He described a wealth of opportunities for religious expression in public schools and noted that the statement would be sent to school districts nationwide.[118]

The Clinton administration statement notes that school-sponsored prayers and other religious exercises are prohibited, but it also emphasizes that students generally are free to pray individually or in groups, read scriptures, and discuss their faith at public schools.[119] Students cannot disrupt the school day or violate time, place, and manner restrictions that are placed on all student speech; and they may not violate others' rights, but their rights to religious expression are protected.[120] Under the Equal Access Act, middle and high school students may form religious clubs that meet on school property during noninstructional time if other extracurricular student clubs are permitted to do so.[121] Students may discuss their religious beliefs in schoolwork where other personal views can be expressed. Such assignments should be evaluated based on academic standards.[122] To the extent that students are permitted to share items at school with other students, students may distribute religious items on the same basis.[123]

The Clinton administration's memorandum also affirmed that public school teachers may teach about religion. The document quoted a 1963 case holding that public schools may not organize and conduct classroom prayer and devotional Bible readings, in which the Court said:

> [I]t might well be said that one's education is not complete without a study
> of comparative religion or the history of religion and its relationship to the
> advancement of civilization. It certainly may be said that the Bible is worthy
> of study for its literary and historic qualities. Nothing we have said here indi-
> cates that such study of the Bible or of religion, when presented objectively

as part of a secular program of education, may not be effected consistently with the First Amendment.[124]

A guide endorsed by a range of educational and religious groups summarizes some crucial differences between the teaching of religion and teaching about religion. The school's approach must be *"academic*, not *devotional."* The goal is to create "student *awareness* of religions," not to "press for student *acceptance* of any religion." And schools are to sponsor *study* about religion, not the *practice* of religion."[125]

A study has found that teaching about religion, when done properly, not only boosts students' understanding of religion but also increases their respect for religious liberty.[126] At the same time, learning about religion "did not contribute to religious relativism or encourage students to change their religious beliefs." In other words, "[s]tudents who held firm views about their religion prior to the course maintained their views about the rightness of their religious tradition compared to others after taking the course."[127]

There is widespread agreement that teaching about religion in public schools is permitted but sometimes disagreement about the curricula used to do so. Complaints were understandably raised, for example, when public school teachers used a textbook that instructed students to write an Islamic statement of faith as a way of becoming familiar with Arabic calligraphy.[128] An important guideline for teaching about religion is not to involve students in participating in religious expression or ritual, which can make them feel as if they are violating their faith or beliefs.[129]

Curricula for teaching about the Bible in public schools have also drawn fire.[130] A Bible course created by a nongovernmental organization called the National Council on Bible Curriculum in Public Schools (NCBCPS) has triggered lawsuits for allegedly promoting religion generally as well as particular religious viewpoints that are not shared by Jews, Catholics, Orthodox Christians, and some Protestants.[131] Guidelines produced by the Society for Biblical Literature and the First Amendment Center, on the other hand, have drawn strong support.[132]

An important advance for teaching about religion occurred in 2017, when the National Council for the Social Studies (NCSS) added a supplement to its framework for the academic study of religion in social studies instruction.[133] This framework is used by state and school district curriculum experts for social studies standards and curriculum development. NCSS has rightly noted that study about religion is essential and strengthens citizenship, cross-cultural understanding, and religious liberty.[134] Especially at a time when confusion and conflict over these issues are prevalent, this resource is timely.[135]

RECOMMENDATIONS: PROVIDING SPACE FOR FAITH TO FLOURISH, WITHOUT GOVERNMENTAL SUPPORT OR INTERFERENCE

The Constitution places some firm limits on government's involvement with religion. The government can endorse many causes, for example, but it cannot endorse religion. At the same time, the Constitution generally cannot interfere with religious expression attributable to nongovernmental organizations and individuals. Instead, the government must protect such expression just as it protects nonreligious expression.

While the government cannot promote or denigrate faith, the state must welcome nongovernmental speech about religion to government property and other government forums in accordance with the equal access principle. In addition to recognizing the right of nongovernmental speakers to use public parks and squares, governmental leaders sometimes have the latitude to open equal access forums in other settings. Using that power to allow both nonreligious and religious voices to speak is one way for government to promote a healthy role for religion in the public square.

In short, the Supreme Court's decisions identify numerous ways for religious individuals and organizations to express themselves on government property. Government officials and civil society leaders, including religious leaders, do well when they understand such rights and facilitate protected expression, including by taking the following steps.

(1) Ensure that the equal access principle is understood and applied.

Government officials should ensure that they and their staff understand the equal access principle and the ways in which it applies to religious speakers. If property traditionally has been open to the public, or if the government opens up another piece of property for expression by nongovernmental organizations and individuals, religious as well as nonreligious voices generally should be welcome.

Policymakers should also ensure that nongovernmental organizations and individuals, including religious organizations and individuals, understand equal access policies. Officials may do so by posting plain language versions of these policies on websites and discussing them in town hall meetings and webinars, for example. Religious leaders can do likewise by hosting workshops of their own.

(2) Hew closely to Supreme Court guidance on any governmental monuments, displays, or acknowledgments that include religious elements.

Supreme Court precedent provides some examples of governmental acknowledgments of religion and governmental monuments and displays including religious elements that fall on the right and wrong side of the constitutional lines. Government officials who wish to engage in such expression should hew closely to those decisions.

Civil society leaders, including religious leaders, can play crucial roles here. In the wake of the Supreme Court's 2019 decision in *American Legion v. American Humanist Association*, for example, civil society leaders can and should insist that government monuments and memorials respect the country's great religious diversity.

As the Court noted in its opinion, it is understandable and unobjectionable for governmental Holocaust memorials to contain Jewish symbols. And individual gravestones in burial grounds like Arlington Cemetery appropriately display symbols, religious or otherwise, that are chosen by the deceased service member or his or her family.

But collective governmental memorials for Americans of different faiths and beliefs are different. Such memorials certainly should not use the specific symbol of one faith, and generally should avoid using specific religious symbols. Instead, such memorials should employ symbolism that is open to a variety of interpretations, both religious and nonreligious. Examples of memorials that take this approach include the Vietnam Veterans Memorial on the Mall in Washington, D.C.; 9/11 memorials in New York City, Washington, D.C., and Shanksville, Pennsylvania; and the memorial to the victims of the 1995 bombing of the Alfred P. Murrah Federal Building in Oklahoma City, Oklahoma.

(3) Remember that bright-line rules on governmental displays, monuments, and acknowledgments are not necessarily better rules.

Admittedly, the Supreme Court's rules on governmental displays, monuments and acknowledgments containing religious elements are not a model of clarity. But rules that would create brighter lines are not necessarily better ones. Consider the fact that some are urging the Court to uphold all such governmental expression so long as the government does not require Americans to take religious action or refrain from doing so. This approach might allow states to establish official religions and cities to place Latin crosses on the tops of municipal buildings, so long as the government did not require citizens to attend or give tithes and offerings to a church, for example. But the Establishment Clause properly requires the government to be neutral on religion. The country has benefited enormously from rules generally barring the government from sending the message that some Americans are more welcome based on their religion or otherwise making religion relevant to an American's standing in the civic community. In a nation that is increasingly diverse, these principles will only become more important in the future.

Bright-line rules that reject or undermine core Establishment Clause principles are not improvements.

> *(4) Public schools should train administrators and teachers on consensus rules and proactively draft school policy on religious expression in consultation with the full range of stakeholders.*

Further education is needed regarding consensus rules on religious expression in public schools. Administrators and teachers should be required to attend trainings on these rules, and optional trainings should be offered for students and parents.[136] The materials used for these trainings must be ones that are endorsed by organizations with varying perspectives on church-state issues to ensure that they represent consensus views.[137] Religious communities can and should encourage such trainings and consider conducting similar trainings of their own.

Also, as Dr. Charles Haynes, founding director of the Religious Freedom Center of the Freedom Forum Institute, has suggested, public schools should use common-ground guidelines to develop specific policies on these issues at the outset of the school year as a part of a consultation with teachers, administrators, parents, and students.[138] Such policies should include as many "yeses" as "noes" to religious expression in public schools, as Haynes says.

Sometimes, public schools are reluctant to take a proactive approach on religion-related issues. Such reluctance is a mistake. Taking a proactive approach that welcomes all stakeholders helps enormously to manage conflicts when they inevitably arise.

> *(5) Teach about religion.*

We simply cannot understand our nation or our world without understanding religion. One cannot comprehend the struggle against Jim Crow segregation, for example, without understanding how religious communities both supported and opposed racial equality. A proper education includes academic study about religion, both in elementary and secondary schools and beyond. Public schools can do so without running afoul of the First Amendment's Establishment Clause. Other components of government should also teach about religion. The U.S. State Department, for example, should ensure that diplomats understand the religious aspects of the landscape in which they work. A diplomat who works in Iraq needs to know the difference between Sunni and Shiite Muslims, for example. Policymakers, administrators, and teachers should avail themselves of resources designed to help them teach about religion in ways that are educationally sound and constitutionally compliant.

6

GOVERNMENT PARTNERSHIPS
WITH FAITH-BASED ORGANIZATIONS

Creating Partnerships to Serve People in Need

The government and religious organizations have long worked together to serve people in need. In the nineteenth century, for example, the federal government provided funds to a variety of orphanages and hospitals, some of which had religious origins and affiliations. In 1899, the U.S. Supreme Court held that the District of Columbia did not violate the Establishment Clause when it contracted with Providence Hospital, run by the Sisters of Charity, an order of Catholic nuns, to provide health care to D.C. residents.

Partnerships between the government and nongovernmental organizations, including faith-based groups, can be nonfinancial or financial. Nonfinancial partnerships are ones in which no money passes hands from the government to the religious organization, but the two parties nonetheless work together toward a common goal.

President George W. Bush implemented new rules for financial partnerships between the federal government and religious organizations. President Obama retained many of these rules, while reforming some of them based on common-ground recommendations from a diverse Advisory Council on Faith-Based and Neighborhood Partnerships. A key rule is that the government must permit faith-based organizations to compete on an equal footing for federal social service aid, while retaining their religious character. At the same time, organizations may not use direct aid to subsidize activities with explicit religious content, like worship and religious instruction, and must separate religious activities, in either time or location, from government-funded activities. Protections for beneficiaries of federal social service aid include a prohibition on discrimination against beneficiaries or potential beneficiaries of the social services programs on the basis of religion.

When partnerships supported by indirect government aid are involved, such as vouchers or certificates, some of the rules are significantly different. In that context, according to U.S. Supreme Court precedent, explicitly religious content need not be separated from government-funded activities, and government aid may subsidize programs with both religious and nonreligious elements. Put simply, the reasoning here is that, in a voucher-type program, the beneficiary will always have the choice of at least one adequate secular provider. Thus, if he or she selects a religious program, then the choice is deemed to have been independently and freely made.

The law allows government and faith-based organizations to form financial partnerships to serve people in need, and such partnerships are now widely accepted. At the same time, certain issues connected to such partnerships are unsettled and hotly contested. Contentious issues include those involving religious objections to certain conditions that follow government funds.

President George W. Bush established the White House Office of Faith-Based and Community Initiatives in January 2001. With the opening of this office, Bush triggered a nationwide discussion about the relationship between religion and government.[1] Americans debated whether having such an office was consistent with the principle of church-state separation. They asked about the nature, aims, and constitutionality of governmental partnerships with religious organizations. As with all discussions about the White House, the conversation had at least a partisan tinge.

The office broke new ground, but not as much as critics feared or supporters claimed. For the first time, a White House office had the word "faith" in it. It was certainly not the first time, however, that the job description of some White House staff included outreach to the religious community or work on religion-related issues. During the Clinton administration, for example, the Office of Public Liaison included staff whose job was to engage with religious leaders and organizations, the portfolio of the deputy of the Domestic Policy

Council included policy issues touching on religion, and the White House Counsel's Office included scholars on church-state issues.[2]

Having a White House office with the word "faith" was unprecedented, but it was not unconstitutional. The Constitution prohibits the government from advancing or denigrating religion, preferring one faith over another, or becoming excessively entangled with religion. As long as a governmental office respects limits like these, there is nothing unconstitutional about having an office of faith-based and neighborhood partnerships, even in the White House.

President Bush proposed new rules for partnerships between the federal government and religious organizations, declaring, for example, that congregations as well as religiously affiliated groups could receive government aid. But the government and religious organizations had long worked together to serve people in need.[3] In the nineteenth century, for example, the federal government provided funds to a variety of orphanages and hospitals, some of which had religious origins and affiliations. In 1899, the U.S. Supreme Court held that the District of Columbia did not violate the Establishment Clause when it contracted with Providence Hospital, run by the Sisters of Charity, an order of Catholic nuns, to provide health care to D.C. residents.[4]

In 2008, the White House faith-based office got bipartisan buy-in.[5] Then-presidential-candidate-and-senator Barack Obama announced that, if elected, he would keep this White House office, while making some changes to its name, mission, practices, and policies.

People who were familiar with President Obama's biography were not surprised. His first job after college was serving as a community organizer on the South Side of Chicago, where he worked closely with leaders of religious as well as secular groups.[6] The Campaign for Human Development, an antipoverty initiative of the Catholic Church, provided funding for Barack Obama's work, and his office was at Holy Rosary Church.[7] President Obama has long recognized that bringing religious as well as other civil society leaders to the table is not only the right thing to do; it is also the smart thing to do.

Additionally, then-senator Obama promised that, if elected, he would establish an Advisory Council on Faith-Based and Neighborhood Partnerships, a group comprised of religious and community leaders. He said he would ask the Advisory Council to make recommendations for strengthening the partnerships the government forms with faith-based and community organizations.[8]

At his maiden speech at the National Prayer Breakfast in 2009, President Obama announced the establishment of the White House Office of Faith-Based and Neighborhood Partnerships, saying:

> The goal of this office will not be to favor one religious group over another—or even religious groups over secular groups. It will simply be to work on behalf

of those organizations that want to work on behalf of our communities, and to do so without blurring the line that our founders wisely drew between church and state. This work is important, because whether it's a secular group advising families facing foreclosure or faith-based groups providing job-training to those who need work, few are closer to what's happening on our streets and in our neighborhoods than these organizations.[9]

President Obama signed an executive order opening the White House Office of Faith-Based and Neighborhood Partnerships and creating the Advisory Council.[10] He appointed Joshua DuBois to lead the office and named leaders to the council who were diverse in many ways, including in their politics, ideology, and theology.[11] Working groups within the Advisory Council captured even more diversity. For example, the working group tasked with examining church-state issues included a former staff member of President Bush's Office of Faith-Based and Community Initiatives and the head of Americans United for Separation of Church and State as well as leaders falling somewhere in between.[12] The Advisory Council made a slate of recommendations to the White House, a number of which were subsequently adopted.[13]

Working with faith-based and community organizations is good governance. The government often has a difficult time reaching people who most need help. Faith-based and community groups usually do not. Faith and community leaders are the middlemen (and women) who can effectively reach vulnerable people and also know how to work with government. Religious organizations frequently serve as anchors of their communities due to their knowledge of neighborhoods, the services they provide, and the trust and respect they command.[14] There is power in partnerships between the government and nonprofits, including religious organizations.

At the same time, it is also true that controversy surrounds some of these partnerships, including when awardees raise religious objections to certain conditions on government funds. This chapter provides examples of both financial and nonfinancial partnerships and discusses some of the legal rules governing those partnerships. It also examines certain controversies that arise in this area.

Nonfinancial Partnerships

Partnerships between the government and nongovernmental organizations, including faith-based groups, can be financial or nonfinancial. Nonfinancial partnerships are ones in which no money passes hands from the government to the religious organization, but the two parties nonetheless work together toward a common goal.

For example, some congregations and community groups sponsor jobs clubs.[15] Jobs clubs help unemployed or underemployed people develop interview and résumé-writing skills, make connections for new job opportunities, and receive support for their job search. As a 2014 White House report noted: "These employment support groups, which are typically run by volunteers and led by peers in familiar community settings, are well-positioned to engage long-term unemployed individuals and other hard-to-reach populations."[16] During the Obama administration, the federal government did not provide money to nongovernmental organizations to start or grow jobs clubs, but it did provide information about how to do so, materials on best practices and governmental resources for job seekers, as well as information about how to connect with other congregations and community organizations that are doing similar work.[17] In this way, the government and faith-based and community groups are able to work together to promote economic opportunity for all.

Efforts to treat diseases and prevent their spread is another area where faith and government join hands. Sometimes the work that nongovernmental entities do in this area is supported by federal dollars, but it also includes nonfinancial partnerships.

In 2014, the terrible Ebola virus emerged in West Africa. From the start, it was clear that a vigorous response would be required from medical professionals and government officials, including the military posted in that area. To President Obama, it was also clear that the response from faith-based and humanitarian organizations and leaders would be crucial.

During this period, President Obama invited Dr. Kent Brantly and his wife, Amber, to the White House. Brantly is one of the courageous doctors who treated Ebola patients as part of his work with a faith-based organization. Tragically, while caring for his patients, Dr. Brantly contracted Ebola himself. He was airlifted to the United States, was treated, and made a full recovery. Shortly after Kent and Amber arrived at the White House, President Obama welcomed them to the Oval Office, shook their hands, and listened to their stories and observations, while a photographer captured the moment.[18]

At the time, there was great fear and some hysteria about the disease. Many were scared about any interaction with Ebola survivors. President Obama's meeting with Kent, and the pictures and media stories that came out of it, were a teaching tool. As the *Washington Post* said at the time, "That [President] Obama is willing to sit in a room with Brantly demonstrates that the leader of the free world believes [concerns about interaction with Ebola survivors] have no basis."[19]

Leaders from diverse medical, faith, and humanitarian communities partnered with the Obama administration to counter misinformation about the Ebola virus and the stigma attached to Ebola survivors. Working across lines of faith and government, teams created trainings on safe burial practices for use on the ground in West Africa, practices that respected religious practices and helped to contain the disease.[20] As President Obama later said, "When Ebola ravaged West Africa, Jewish, Christian, [and] Muslim groups responded to the outbreak to save lives. And as the news fanned the flames of fear, churches and mosques responded with a powerful rebuke, welcoming survivors into their pews."[21]

Financial Partnerships with the Federal Government

The government also forms financial partnerships with civil society organizations, including faith-based groups. Today, there are countless forms of such partnerships, including those aimed at disaster relief, refugee resettlement, combatting human trafficking, supporting maternal and child health around the world, and promoting sustainable development.

Refugee resettlement partnerships are among the longstanding public-private financial collaborations in which religious organizations have played a leading role. Refugees are individuals who are outside their home country and are unable or unwilling to return because of persecution or a well-founded fear of persecution on account of their race, religion, nationality, membership in a particular social group, or political opinions.[22] For more than fifty years, the United States has contracted with nongovernmental bodies to care for refugees who enter the country.[23] These nongovernmental organizations include several faith-based organizations: Church World Service, Episcopal Migration Ministries, Hebrew Immigrant Aid Society (HIAS), Lutheran Immigration and Refugee Services (LIRS), United States Conference of Catholic Bishops' Migration and Refugee Services, and World Relief, an evangelical body.[24]

After refugees undergo rigorous screening and are admitted to the United States, refugee resettlement organizations, along with the large volunteer networks they are able to tap, assist refugees in getting acclimated. Resettlement organizations connect refugees with employment help and language services. They provide refugees with access to education and to health services and teach them how to accomplish countless other tasks they need to manage their new lives. Congregations often partner with refugee groups to adopt refugee families. Congregation members take on tasks like stocking refrigerators with food, providing clothes for families as well as books and toys for children, taking family members to doctor appointments or job interviews, bringing hot meals, and providing listening ears.[25] In 2016, for example, a New Jersey church continued its longstanding tradition of adopting refugee families when it accepted a Syrian family with special needs. The father of the family was blind due to wounds he had suffered in the Syrian war. One of the many tasks the church tackled to prepare for the family's arrival was to ask a blind person to test an apartment they had rented for the Syrian family to ensure that it had been adequately modified for the father's use.[26]

Such donations of time and resources from congregations and other volunteer groups supplement the federal aid that nongovernmental refugee resettlement organizations receive.[27] A 2008 study by Lutheran Immigration and Refugee Services found, for example, that the State Department funded only 39 percent of the actual cost of resettling a refugee. Nongovernmental organizations covered the remaining 61 percent with their own funds.[28]

Supreme Court Speaks to Financial Partnerships

The Supreme Court considered the constitutionality of financial partnerships between the government and religious bodies as early as 1899 in *Bradfield v. Roberts*, a case involving an agreement between the District of Columbia and Providence Hospital, a hospital organized by an order of Catholic nuns.[29] Congress appropriated money to the district for the construction of buildings that would be used for the treatment of minor contagious diseases. The district then contracted with Providence Hospital for those buildings to be erected on its grounds and for treatment of patients there. Taxpayers complained that such an arrangement violated the First Amendment's Establishment Clause, but the Court rejected the claim. The purpose of the arrangement was "the opening and keeping a hospital in the city of Washington for the care of such sick and invalid persons as may place themselves under the treatment and care" of Providence Hospital, the Court said. "There is no allegation that its hospital work is confined to members of that church,"[30] and the hospital would be held to the terms of the agreement.[31]

Almost a hundred years later, the Court considered another financial partnership between the government and faith-based organizations to provide social services. *Bowen v. Kendrick* involved a federal statute called the Adolescent Family Life Act (AFLA) that authorized grants to governmental and nongovernmental organizations to provide services regarding adolescent sexual relations and pregnancy.[32] Congress specified that grant applicants should demonstrate how they would involve private sector organizations, including faith-based groups, in this work, and religious organizations were among the organizations that received AFLA grants from the Department of Health and Human Services (HHS).[33]

A group of taxpayers alleged that the program violated the Establishment Clause.[34] The Supreme Court held that the statute as a whole did not violate the Establishment Clause, although the Court remanded the case for consideration of whether particular AFLA grants were invalid.[35] In an opinion written by Chief Justice Rehnquist, the Court said: "Nothing in our previous cases prevents Congress . . . from recognizing the important part that religion or religious organizations may play in resolving certain secular problems."[36] Citing *Bradfield v. Roberts*, the Court emphasized that it had "never held that religious organizations are disabled by the First Amendment from participating in publicly sponsored social welfare programs."[37] AFLA lacked an express provision prohibiting the use of federal funds for religious purposes, but the legislative history of the statute counseled against such use, and HHS had the authority to ensure that the grants were carried out in a manner consistent with this constitutional requirement, the Court said. The Court also noted that it saw "no reason to conclude that the AFLA serves an impermissible religious purpose simply because some of the goals of the statute coincide with the beliefs of certain religious organizations."[38]

Justices Blackmun, Brennan, Marshall, and Stevens dissented, saying AFLA "facilitated and, indeed, encouraged the use of public funds for [religious instruction], by giving religious groups a central pedagogical and counseling role without imposing any restraints on the sectarian quality of the participation."[39] The Court majority was wrong to downplay the dangers of government-subsidized and government-sponsored religious indoctrination here, the dissenters said, citing numerous examples from the record of misuse of government funds by some religious organizations. Instead of upholding the statute, the Court should have struck it down, the dissenters said.[40]

Rules for Financial Partnerships with Faith-Based Organizations: Direct Aid

The Bush administration relied on these and other court decisions to develop a set of rules that apply to government social service aid that is open to nongovernmental organizations, including religious organizations.[41] The Obama administration retained the Bush rules, while making some reforms.[42] The rules seek to balance an openness to the participation of religious providers and protections for the religious identity of those providers on the one hand, with protections for social service beneficiaries and a stance of governmental neutrality toward religion.

The rules include a variety of protections for the religious identity of faith-based organizations. A key protection is the command that the government must permit faith-based organizations to compete on an equal footing for federal social service aid. Government may not favor or disfavor faith-based organizations in the competition for aid. What matters is what you can do, not who you are, as former president George W. Bush said.[43]

Also, the government must ensure that decisions about awards of federal financial assistance are made on the basis of merit, not political or religious ties or lack of such ties. The organization that receives the award should be the one most qualified to do the work, not the one with the most political cronies. Government officials who make awards must also ensure that they do not allow bias for or against religion, or for or against particular faiths, to creep into the process.

The rules assure faith-based organizations that receive federal aid that they may retain their religious character by maintaining facilities without removing or altering religious art, icons, scriptures, or other symbols; by retaining religious terms in their organizational names; by selecting board members on a religious basis; and by including religious references in organizational mission statements and other governing documents, for example.[44] As Professor John DiIulio, the director of the first White House Office of Faith-Based and Community Initiatives, has said, the St. Vincent DePaul Center should not have to change its name to the Mr. Vincent DePaul Center in order to receive government social service aid.[45]

At the same time, other rules guard against the use of government aid to promote religion or to discriminate against beneficiaries of such aid. Organizations may not use direct aid to subsidize activities involving explicit religious content, like worship and religious instruction. This rule not only helps to safeguard the neutrality of the state and the consciences of taxpayers; it also protects religion. If the government were to fund religious activities, it would have to regulate those activities, something neither church nor state wants.

Organizations receiving direct aid also must separate religious activities, in either time or location, from government-funded activities. Religious activities must be privately funded and purely voluntary for social service beneficiaries. If a faith-based organization offers a government-funded job retraining program and a privately funded Bible study at the same location, for example, it must offer that Bible study either before or after the government-funded program. And if the Bible study follows the government-funded program, the job retraining program must be dismissed before the Bible study begins. Rules like these protect liberty of conscience and shield religious activities from government regulation.

Protections for beneficiaries of federal social service aid include a prohibition on discrimination against beneficiaries or potential beneficiaries of the social services programs on the basis of religion. Discrimination based on religious beliefs or lack thereof, or on attendance at or participation in religious activities or refusal to do so, also is prohibited. In short, beneficiaries cannot be turned away from a government-funded program because they are the "wrong" religion, because they are religious or not religious, or because they attend and participate in religious activities or decline to do so.

Thus, while President George W. Bush popularized the principle that faith-based providers should be able to retain their religious identity *and* receive government aid to serve people in need, even President Bush recognized that this principle was not absolute. Under the Bush administration, for example, religious contractors were prohibited from discriminating against employees on a variety of bases, even if they claimed they had religious reasons for doing so. Faith-based grantees were not permitted to pay female employees less than male employees due to any religious convictions about the nature and roles of men and women. Religious contractors were not allowed to deny services to beneficiaries based on the beneficiary's faith, or lack thereof. Faith-based organizations were not permitted to weave religious content and activities into programs funded by direct government aid. Protections for the religious character of faith-based organizations are significant, but they have never been absolute.

On the recommendation of President Obama's diverse Advisory Council on Faith-Based and Neighborhood Partnerships, existing protections for the religious liberty of social service beneficiaries were strengthened, and new ones were added.[46] Under the council-recommended rules, if a beneficiary objects to an organization's religious character, the religious organization is required to make reasonable efforts to refer the beneficiary to a provider to which the beneficiary does not object. This protection applies to religious organizations receiving direct federal aid for domestic programs and is known as the "alternative-provider requirement." Available evidence indicates that beneficiary requests of this kind are exceedingly rare, and religious organizations are usually among the first to say such requests should be honored. Such organizations are also required to provide beneficiaries with written notice of this and other beneficiary protections as well as specific contact information beneficiaries may use to report any violations of the rules.[47]

The notice requirement ensures that beneficiaries knew about these protections. Distributing such notices also provides a helpful reminder for the staff of faith-based organizations about applicable rules.

The following hypothetical cases help to explain the difference the council-recommended rules make:

- An Orthodox Jewish man is assigned to a federally funded employment training program that meets in a church. He asks to be referred to an alternative provider because his religious beliefs prevent him from entering a church. The rules require that reasonable efforts be made to find alternative providers in such a case.

- A Catholic woman who is a victim of human trafficking is served by a federal grantee that is an evangelical organization. The woman would prefer not to attend the privately funded Bible study program that the evangelical provider separately offers because it conflicts with some of her religious beliefs, yet she fears that doing so might jeopardize her access to government benefits. Under the council-recommended rules, this woman would be informed that she need not participate in privately funded religious activities in order to receive federally funded social services.

- A couple participates in a foster care and adoption program that is funded by a federal grant, but they are bothered by the fact that the program leader proselytizes. Under the council-recommended rules, the couple would learn that providers receiving direct federal aid must separate any privately funded religious content from the government-funded program. The couple would also be given specific information about how to report any violations of the rules to the relevant government entity.

The incorporation of these protections in federal regulations reduced opposition to financial partnerships between the government and faith-based organizations. To be sure, some progressives still oppose certain rules President George W. Bush put in place with his faith-based initiative, but both progressives and conservatives supported these new protections.

In May 2018, however, President Trump signed an executive order that strikes the alternative-provider requirements from President Obama's executive order. Trump's order also struck the requirement that beneficiaries receive a written notice outlining protections for their religious liberty.[48]

The White House offered no explanation for its actions, but supporters of the initiative described several possible justifications. Requiring religious providers to make reasonable efforts to identify alternative providers and offer referrals simply is not a good use of providers' time, they said. If any referrals are required, governmental bodies should do it.[49]

Under a few longstanding federal programs, religious providers have had to make referrals to alternative providers, with no reported problems.[50] Deciding to place this responsibility on government instead could prove to be a respectable choice, but striking these religious liberty protections, as President Trump did, is not.

Another justification that has been offered for rescinding the protections is that some prolife religious providers fear that they would have to make referrals to providers that also offer abortions.[51] According to the available data, referrals are rarely requested, and this specific kind of referral request seems even more unlikely. In such a case, however, the religious provider could request and receive an accommodation under the federal Religious Freedom Restoration Act (RFRA), one that would recognize the objection and identify another way to make the referral.[52] The federal government should not, however, remove protections for the religious liberties of countless social service beneficiaries due to the remote possibility that a religious provider might have to successfully raise an objection to a referral.

Some have also said that the separation requirements—ones requiring privately funded religious activities to be separated from government grant-funded activities—make the alternative-provider requirements unnecessary.[53] One cannot assume, however, that the separation requirements will always be perfectly observed. Also, even when those requirements are fully respected, some beneficiaries may nonetheless object to receiving federally funded services in a religious context or a particular religious context. If the consciences of beneficiaries are to be honored, then these additional protections must be included. That is exactly what the diverse Advisory Council recommended.

Others have suggested that, because referrals are rarely requested, eliminating the protection will not make a significant difference.[54] Requests for referrals do seem to be rare, but they are extremely important to those who request them. Such protections are designed for the minority, not the majority. Further, the fact that referrals are rarely requested means that the entities charged with making them should not be substantially burdened by the alternative provider requirements.

Rules for Financial Partnerships with Faith-Based Organizations: Indirect Aid

When partnerships supported by indirect government aid are involved, such as vouchers or certificates, some of the constitutional rules are significantly different. Aid is indirect when the aid first goes to the beneficiary and then the beneficiary chooses where to "spend" that aid. In that context, according to U.S. Supreme Court precedent, explicitly religious content need not be separated from government-funded activities, and government aid may subsidize programs with both religious and nonreligious elements. Put simply, the reasoning here is that, in a voucher-type program, the beneficiary will always have the choice of at least one adequate secular provider. Thus, if he or she selects a religious program, then the choice is deemed to have been independently and freely made.

When the program involves "true private choice," the Court has said, "the circuit between government and religion [is] broken, and the Establishment Clause [is] not implicated."[55] Thus, there is no need in such cases to ensure that the aid does not subsidize religious activities, according to the Court.[56]

FINANCIAL PARTNERSHIPS: EMERGING ISSUES

The law allows government and faith-based organizations to form financial partnerships to serve people in need, and such partnerships are now widely accepted. At the same time, certain issues connected to partnerships are unsettled and hotly contested. Contentious issues include those involving religious objections to certain conditions that follow government funds. Here are two examples of such issues.

Religious Objections to Certain Nondiscrimination Conditions

There have long been battles about religious organizations' latitude to make religion-based employment decisions regarding government-funded jobs. Some of the most controversial current battles involve conditions on government funds that bar awardees, including religious organizations, from engaging in employment discrimination on the basis of sexual orientation or gender identity.

This debate demands some historical context.[57] Federal civil rights laws generally prohibit employers from making employment decisions on the basis of religion, but they allow religious organizations to hire and fire employees on the basis of faith.[58] Thus, Jewish synagogues may prefer rabbis over Baptist preachers. This protection applies to more than simply ministers, however. Federal civil rights laws allow religious organizations to insist that *all* of their employees meet religious standards. For example, the U.S. Supreme Court upheld this protection in a case involving the dismissal of a janitor from an organization affiliated with the Church of Jesus Christ of Latter-day Saints (LDS Church) because the janitor did not have a "temple recommend," a certificate stating that he was a member of the LDS Church in good standing.[59]

Religious bodies also retain full freedom to make employment decisions regarding their ministers. This "ministerial exception" flows from the First Amendment's protection for the independence of religious bodies from the state. The U.S. Supreme Court, therefore, has held that a former employee could not sue her employer, a religious school, for alleged discrimination against her due to a disability because she had been serving in a ministerial position.[60] In this case, the Court said:

> The interest of society in the enforcement of employment discrimination statutes is undoubtedly important. But so too is the interest of religious groups in choosing who will preach their beliefs, teach their faith, and carry out their mission. When a minister who has been fired sues her church alleging that her termination was discriminatory, the First Amendment has struck the balance for us. The church must be free to choose those who will guide it on its way.[61]

Religious organizations do not forfeit their exemptions when they accept government financial awards, but they may be subject to separate rules that apply to entities receiving government funds.[62] For example, President Lyndon B. Johnson signed and later amended Executive Order 11246 (EO 11246) to bar organizations that contract with the federal government from discriminating in employment on the basis of race, color, religion, sex, or national origin throughout their organizations.[63]

The federal government contracts with nongovernmental entities, both nonprofit and for-profit, when its goal is to acquire certain goods or services for use by or the direct benefit of the U.S. government.[64] By virtue of contracts with the federal government, nongovernmental organizations provide a wide range of services—they build airplanes for the military, serve food in national parks, run homeless shelters, provide disaster relief services, and perform research for federal agencies, for example. Federal grants, on the other hand, are "much more flexible"[65] agreements "to carry out a public purpose . . . for the direct benefit or use of the United States Government."[66]

When the federal government forms a financial partnership with a religious entity, it usually does so through a grant, not a contract. And while there is one executive order setting forth the employment nondiscrimination rules for all federal contractors, there is no such order governing all federal grantees.

In 2014, the Obama administration announced it would add prohibitions on discrimination on the basis of sexual orientation and gender identity to the federal contracting executive order.[67] This announcement triggered a discussion about the order's exemptions and whether any new exemptions should be added.

As originally issued by President Johnson in 1965, EO 11246 contained some exemptions. For example, the order permits the secretary of labor to exempt a contracting agency from any or all of the order's nondiscrimination provisions when the secretary "deems that special circumstances in the national interest so require" it.[68] But the order contained no exemptions specifically for religious bodies. In other words, EO 11246 did not say that religious organizations that served as federal contractors could prefer job applicants of their same faith.

In 2002, however, President George W. Bush added a religious exemption to this executive order, stating that religious organizations that serve as federal contractors could do so, although the order also states that religious organizations must still comply with the order's other requirements, including the requirements prohibiting discrimination on the basis of race, color, sex, and national origin.[69] The George W. Bush administration implemented a similar policy across partnerships with religious organizations that were supported by other forms of federal funding.[70] This policy was hailed by some as long-overdue protection for faith-based providers and was vigorously opposed by others as a form of government-funded religious discrimination.

President Obama's announcement that he would add prohibitions against LGBT discrimination to the federal contracting order sparked a debate about whether its existing religious exemption should be rescinded, retained, or expanded. Some insisted that federal contractors should be exempted from the new requirements to allow them to make employment decisions based on certain religious codes of conduct regarding sexual behavior, including prohibitions on sex outside of heterosexual marriage.[71] Ultimately, the new nondiscrimination conditions were added to the executive order, and the religious exemption in EO 11246 was left intact, neither expanded nor rescinded.

Even though the existing religious exemption of the order was not expanded, some argue that the existing exemption as well as other law, such as RFRA, requires the government to allow contractors to make employment decisions according to their sexual codes of conduct, if those codes are faith-based.[72] Thus, they say, a religious contractor must be permitted to refuse to hire an individual because she or he is married to a person of the same gender, despite the new LGBT nondiscrimination conditions. Religious entities must be permitted to retain their religious character in this way, while partnering with government, they argue. Advocates of this position cite certain Supreme Court decisions, including the one recognizing marriage equality as a constitutional right—*Obergefell v. Hodges*[73]—but also noting that religious organizations should be able to continue to maintain their religious beliefs and practices. In the *Obergefell* decision, the Court said:

> [I]t must be emphasized that religions, and those who adhere to religious doctrines, may continue to advocate with utmost, sincere conviction that, by divine precepts, same-sex marriage should not be condoned. The First Amendment ensures that religious organizations and persons are given proper protection as they seek to teach the principles that are so fulfilling and so central to their lives and faiths, and to their own deep aspirations to continue the family structure they have long revered. The same is true of those who oppose same-sex marriage for other reasons. In turn, those who believe allowing same-sex marriage is proper or indeed essential, whether as a matter of religious conviction or secular belief, may engage those who disagree with their view in an open and searching debate.[74]

Others argue that religious organizations that accept government contracts prohibiting contractors from discriminating on the basis of sexual orientation or gender identity should not be categorically exempt from such nondiscrimination rules, just as they are not categorically exempt from rules prohibiting discrimination on the basis of race, national origin, or sex. Religious organizations that accept government contracts with nondiscrimination conditions like these generally should not be able to turn away people from government-funded jobs due simply to religious objections to their marriage, for example. The U.S. Supreme Court's decision recognizing the right to civil marriage for all couples, whether gay or straight, is relevant here, and language in that decision regarding religious dissenters does not apply to federal contractors, they say. If organizations cannot abide by such restrictions, they are free not to seek or accept the contract.[75]

In August 2019, the Trump administration's Department of Labor (DOL) proposed a major expansion of the religious exemption of Executive Order 11246.[76] The agency referenced two of President Trump's executive orders[77] and recent Supreme Court decisions, although it conceded that the decisions "are not specific to the federal government's regulation of contractors . . . ."[78]

The rule would allow federal contractors to invoke the exemption so long as they could point to a religious purpose that is a public part of their mission and demonstrate that they exercise their religion to further that purpose. If so, the rule permits federal contractors to make employment decisions based on sincere expressions of religious tenets, which could include certain religious codes of conduct regarding sexual behavior such as prohibitions on sex outside of heterosexual marriage. According to DOL, the rule is to be construed in favor of the broadest possible protection for religious interests.

If adopted, this rule would greatly expand the types of federal contractors and the kinds of employment decisions that could be shielded from nondiscrimination obligations. To qualify for the exemption, entities would no longer have to be deemed primarily religious, which is a much higher bar. Closely held businesses, some of which are quite large, for example, could invoke the exemption if they meet relevant requirements, and the rule would allow exempt entities wide latitude to disregard nondiscrimination obligations.[79] The debate over religious objections to certain nondiscrimination policies continues, including through litigation in the courts.[80]

Religious Objections to Certain Service Requirements

Other conflicts involve a religious organization's refusal to provide certain services that a grant or contract says should or must be offered. One such case involved the Trafficking Victims Protection Act (TVPA).[81]

In an effort to tackle the problem of human trafficking, Congress passed the TVPA in 2000.[82] "Trafficking in persons is a modern form of slavery, and it is the largest manifestation of slavery today," Congress said, with at least 700,000 persons annually, "primarily women and children," being trafficked "within or across international borders."[83] Around "50,000 women and children are trafficked into the United States each year."[84] The TVPA directed the Department of Health and Human Services (HHS) to expand the benefits and services it offered to trafficking victims in the United States,[85] and it appropriated funds toward this end.[86]

In response, HHS developed the Trafficking Victims Assistance Program (TVAP) to provide comprehensive victim services to foreign trafficking victims within the United States.[87] Under some iterations of this program, HHS grantees have been required to provide victims with the full range of gynecological and obstetric services, including contraception and lawful abortion services or referrals for such services. Many victims of human trafficking have been raped and subjected to other forms of sexual assault.[88]

Certain religious organizations, however, refuse to provide some of these services to anyone. At the same time, some of these same objectors have long records of achievement in providing other services to victims of human trafficking.

The Department of Health and Human Services sought to develop a way that would allow it to work with organizations that have religious objections to providing certain services but otherwise strong records of achievement in assisting victims of trafficking. Without taking the position that objecting organizations had any legal claim to grants or contracts in these situations,[89] HHS announced that an organization should not be disqualified simply because it would not provide all the services required by the grant or contract due to religious objections, so long as the services to which it objected could be effectively delivered to beneficiaries by either the government or other awardees.[90]

In 2015, HHS made grants to three organizations, one of which had such religious objections.[91] If a trafficking victim were to ask an objecting awardee for an abortion or contraception, the awardee would notify HHS, and HHS would then ensure that the victim got the requested treatment.[92]

The American Civil Liberties Union sued HHS, charging that this arrangement violated the Establishment Clause.[93] In October 2018, a federal district court in California found there was no evidence that this system had caused any trafficking victim who had asked for abortion or contraception to be unable to obtain them due to the religious objections of an awardee or subawardee.[94] The court also ruled that the TVAP program had a secular purpose that did not endorse religion, that HHS did not delegate state functions to the objecting awardee, that no grant money had been used for religious activities, and that the relationship between the awardee and HHS did not foster unconstitutional entanglement.[95] Accordingly, the court rejected the ACLU's motion for summary judgment in this case.[96]

RECOMMENDATIONS: MOVING FORWARD ON FAITH-BASED PARTNERSHIPS

Partnerships with faith-based organizations to serve people in need are part of the way the U.S. government does business. Policymakers should consider taking the following steps when administering such partnerships. A few pieces of advice are offered to religious leaders and organizations too. The next three chapters also cover issues that are relevant to these partnerships.

> *(1) Task staff with forming partnerships with faith-based and community organizations that are consistent with the Constitution and other applicable legal rules.*

Government can accomplish great things in collaboration with faith-based and community partners. Government officials should affirmatively task staff with forming such partnerships and ensure that both staff and partners understand the legal rules governing them. While difficult questions remain, the rules regarding financial partnerships between the federal government and faith-based organizations have become more uniform in recent years, providing greater predictability and continuity.

> *(2) Emphasize nonfinancial partnerships as much as financial partnerships.*

A relatively small group of nonprofits, both religious and nonreligious, will seek and receive financial awards from government. Many more, including many religious organizations, will not do so yet will still want to work with government to accomplish shared goals. Nonfinancial partnerships provide an alternative way for religious organizations to work with government on shared aims, with no special strings attached. Faith-based groups of any size can participate in nonfinancial partnerships, and such partnerships are a welcome alternative for religious organizations who are open to collaboration but have reservations about working with government in more formalized ways. Government at all levels should take nonfinancial partnerships as seriously as they do financial partnerships.

> *(3) Share partnership information and invitations widely, and take affirmative steps to reach out to minorities, including religious minorities.*

Do not fall into the trap of sharing partnership information and invitations only with political allies. Instead, share such information widely. In addition to helping people in need, partnerships between the government and faith-based organizations can reduce political and religious polarization. Religious leaders usually can find at least one aim they share with government in this area, even with administrations for whom they did not vote. When religious leaders and government officials of different political or ideological views work together on issues of shared concern, those bonds can help diminish the alienation, bitterness, and distrust that is all too common in American civic life today. Even leaders with serious differences can find common ground in serving their neighbors.

Also, government officials should not wait for minority groups to come to them for partnership opportunities. Instead, officials should reach out to them for conversation and collaboration. Religious minorities, for example, may not have the longstanding and prominent array of religiously affiliated social service entities that groups associated with the religious majority do. Even when that is true, minority communities can still be excellent partners. Government officials should contact leaders of minority groups to ensure that they are fully included in partnerships work.

(4) Make partnerships two-way streets.

Government and civil society have overlapping concerns and can learn a great deal from one another. Government can share information about programs, trends, and data, for example. Religious communities and neighborhood leaders can offer feedback on how those programs are actually working on the ground, for both beneficiaries and providers, and also offer other insights, including their sense of key needs the government has not yet spotted or has failed to address adequately. Discussions between civil society groups and government can lead to complementary or even joint efforts that improve people's lives.

(5) Use the government's convening power to promote partnerships, including by organizing forums where faith-based and other community-serving groups can share best practices.

One of the most effective partnership practices that government officials can employ is to convene forums where faith-based and community partners, as well as the people they serve, can connect with government and one another. The government has strong convening power, meaning that a wide variety of organizations and individuals are likely to attend a meeting organized by government officials. Officials can use that power to bring people together who may have never met and to encourage the sharing of best practices and discussions of new forms of collaboration. Making such gatherings regular practices has the potential to strengthen government responsiveness, community relationships, and services for people in need.

⊬   *(6) Protect the religious liberty of both faith-based providers and social
      service beneficiaries.*

The government should protect the religious liberty of *both* faith-based providers and social service beneficiaries in these partnerships. Faith-based organizations should be able to compete on an equal footing for federal social service aid. Religious organizations that receive federal aid should be able to retain their religious character by maintaining facilities without removing or altering religious art, icons, scriptures, or other symbols; by retaining religious terms in its organizational name; by selecting board members on a religious basis; and by including religious references in the organization's mission statements and other governing documents, for example. Prospective and current beneficiaries and clients should not be discriminated against or pressured to participate in religious activities, and programs supported by government grants and contracts should not contain religious content or activities. When beneficiaries object to the religious character of their assigned provider, best efforts should be made to refer them to an alternative provider of similar value and accessibility. Beneficiaries should also receive written notice of these and other religious liberty protections as well as details about how to contact the government if the rules are not observed.

(7) Practice transparency in partnerships.

Government agencies should post online documents needed by nongovernmental organizations to apply for, receive, and maintain government social service aid, such as requests for proposals and sample grants, contracts, and assurances. That way, potential partners and interested members of the public can gain a better understanding of how such partnerships work. The government should also post a list of entities that receive state aid in a timely manner. Some of this information may be publicly available through actions like Freedom of Information Act (FOIA) requests, but the public will be much better served by making it automatically available online.

(8) Ensure that awards are made based on merit, not political ties.

Awards of government aid should never be rewards for political cronies. As the relevant federal rules state: "Decisions about awards of Federal financial assistance must be free from political interference or even the appearance of such interference and must be made on the basis of merit, not on the basis of the religious affiliation of a recipient organization or lack thereof."[97] Peer reviews of award applications should be done without political bias, preferably through processes that separate applications from applicants' names.

(9) When awardees object to conditions on government funds for religious reasons, government officials should consider several questions.

Awardees or potential awardees sometimes object to conditions on government funds for religious reasons. When they do so, government officials should consider several questions. Is the government legally required to exempt the organization from the conditions to which it objects? Alternatively, is the government legally prohibited from doing so? If the state is neither required to recognize such exemptions nor prohibited from doing so, policymakers have a decision to make: Does accommodating the religious objection serve the government's interests? Litigation continues over the first two questions, so interested parties should track the law's development.

(10) Note differences between cases involving religious objections to conditions on government funds.

Cases involving prospective or current government awardees' religious objections (hereinafter "objecting awardees") to conditions on funds include cases in which awardees object to conditions requiring them to provide certain services and cases in which awardees object to conditions requiring them to comply with certain nondiscrimination principles. These cases share certain similarities, but they also may have different impacts on some of the equities at stake.

In both types of cases, it may be possible to ensure that clients or job seekers promptly receive the services or nondiscriminatory treatment from another awardee. A religious organization that will not provide certain foster care or adoption services to couples of the same sex, for example, may agree to refer the couple to another awardee that is easily accessible and fully complies with a grant's conditions prohibiting discrimination on the basis of sexual orientation.[98]

Even assuming such referrals can be made successfully, there appear to be important differences between these two types of cases. In one set of cases, an objecting awardee denies a client a government-subsidized service due to the client's protected personal characteristics, such as his or her religious affiliation or sexual orientation. In another set of cases, an objecting awardee denies a client a government-subsidized service because the objecting awardee does not offer such services to anyone. It seems reasonable to assume that clients experience greater harm to their sense of equality and dignity in the former cases than the latter. This factor, therefore, counsels in favor of requiring uniform compliance with nondiscrimination conditions binding the use of award funds.

    (11) Before seeking and accepting government aid, faith-based organizations should carefully consider the impact such aid might have on its activities.

Financial partnerships between government and faith-based and community organizations are often desirable on both ends, but they are not without risk. Faith-based organizations, for example, can become dependent on government money or shift priorities based simply on what the government will fund. Before seeking or accepting government financial aid, religious organizations should carefully consider whether they will be able to avoid developing a dependence on government, whether the aid is consistent with their sense of mission, and whether they will be able to comply with the restrictions that follow the funds.[99] If a religious body decides to accept government aid, it should segregate such aid from private funds.

    (12) Rebuild the U.S. refugee resettlement system.

Refugees are individuals who are fleeing persecution, including persecution for their faith or beliefs. Every year, the president, in consultation with Congress, sets the ceiling for the number of refugees who can be admitted to our country. Once refugees undergo a rigorous series of security checks, they are resettled by nongovernmental groups, including many faith-based groups.

Until a few years ago, the refugee admissions and resettlement programs had been treasured and strengthened by presidents of both parties.[100] Participating in a robust, global system of refugee resettlement has helped the United States to fulfill its promise to protect human rights and to prevent crises and conflicts around the world.[101] The refugee resettlement program has also been an excellent example of the good work government can do with faith-based and humanitarian organizations.

Since 2017, however, the resettlement program has been dismantled, and the ceiling for refugees has been driven to a historic low.[102] Leaders from across the political and religious spectrum have called for the refugee admissions and resettlement programs to be restored, noting that the United States can be both secure *and* compassionate. The refugee resettlement system must be rebuilt.

    (13) Train government officials and nongovernmental organizations, including religious institutions, on how to partner with government.

Government officials should host internal and external trainings about how nongovernmental organizations may partner with the state to serve people in need. Such trainings should cover both nonfinancial and financial partnerships and include information about church-state rules.

FAITH AND FEDERAL FUNDS

Supporting Secular, Not Religious, Activities

The Supreme Court has ruled that exempting religious as well as charitable and educational entities from property taxes does not violate the constitutional prohibition on governmental establishment of religion. The purpose of such exemptions is neither to advance nor to inhibit religion. Instead, the purpose is to allow certain community nonprofit organizations to be free from the burden of taxation. Also, rather than creating entanglement between religion and government, tax exemption tends to help the state avoid it.

In 1983, the Supreme Court upheld the Internal Revenue Service's revocation of certain private religious schools' tax exemptions because they had racially discriminatory policies. The Court emphasized that all three branches of the federal government had long expressed a fundamental interest in eradicating racial discrimination in education, which outweighed any burden on religious exercise. The Supreme Court has not extended this decision beyond racial discrimination in education.

In the late 1980s, the Supreme Court began to move from a posture of close scrutiny of government aid that flowed to religious entities and relatively minimal allowance of it toward one of broad approval for many forms of government aid and a pattern of treating religious institutions the same as nonreligious institutions in terms of their ability to receive government aid. Accompanying, and largely explaining, this shift are significant changes in Court personnel.

Constitutional standards may differ depending on the form of the aid. These standards include a general prohibition on the use of direct government aid, including government grant funds, for religious items, expression, and activities. A somewhat different set of rules applies to indirect aid programs, like school vouchers. In 2002, the Court upheld an Ohio school voucher program that included religious schools. When vouchers are provided to a wide group of individuals who make "genuine and independent private choice[s]" about the destination of such aid, any advancement of religion is properly attributable to the individuals, not to the government, the Court has said.

In 2017, the Court found that a state violated the First Amendment's Free Exercise Clause when it prohibited a church school from competing for a grant under a playground resurfacing program. The state's exclusion of the church due solely to its religious character was unconstitutional. Several justices who agreed with this judgment were careful to note, however, that the grant funds in this case would be used for a secular task.

In 1784, Patrick Henry, who was serving as a Virginia delegate at the time, proposed a bill that would have imposed a tax to support "teachers of the Christian religion." Such a tax was justified, the bill said, because

> the general diffusion of Christian knowledge hath a natural tendency to correct the morals of men, restrain their vices, and preserve the peace of society; which cannot be effected without a competent provision for learned teachers, who may be thereby enabled to devote their time and attention to the duty of instructing such citizens, as from their circumstances and want of education, cannot otherwise attain such knowledge.[1]

The bill would have allowed each Virginian to specify the Christian community that should receive their share of taxes, with the money being given to Christian leaders to support "a Minister or Teacher of the Gospel of their denomination . . . ."[2] Quakers and Mennonites, who did not necessarily have formal ministers, could place the money in their general fund "to promote their particular mode of worship."[3] Money that was not directed to any particular Christian group would support "seminaries of learning . . . ."[4]

James Madison was among the Virginians who was deeply concerned about Patrick Henry's proposal. Madison drafted a petition to the Virginia General Assembly, called *A Memorial and Remonstrance against Religious Assessments*, outlining a series of arguments against the proposal.[5] In the petition, Madison argued that the state had no jurisdiction over religion and that creating a dependence on government for the propagation of Christianity—or any faith—was dangerous, both for the government and for religion. Madison also asked:

> Who does not see that the same authority which can establish Christianity, in exclusion of all other Religions, may establish with the same ease any particular sect of Christians, in exclusion of all other Sects? That the same authority which can force a citizen to contribute three pence only of his property for the support of any one establishment, may force him to conform to any other establishment in all cases whatsoever?[6]

Henry's proposal was ultimately defeated. In 1786, Virginia enacted its *Statute for Religious Freedom*, which was written by Thomas Jefferson and served as a precursor to the religion clauses of the First Amendment.[7] Since that time, Americans have continued to ask what kind of government aid constitutes a religious establishment. At times, answering that question has been challenging.

Some matters are clear. The Supreme Court, for example, has ruled that exempting religious organizations, along with other charitable and educational institutions, from property taxes does not violate the Establishment Clause.[8] And, as early as 1899, the Supreme Court held that not all government funding that flows to religiously affiliated organizations constitutes an establishment of religion.[9] At the same time, a tax for the support of one or all religions would clearly be unconstitutional, the Court has said.[10]

In between those poles, however, the Supreme Court has sometimes struggled to establish clear guidance for when government aid that flows to religious organizations and activities crosses a constitutional line. In recent years, however, the Court has moved toward brighter and more permissive lines regarding government aid and religious institutions. The most notable trend has been the Court's move, beginning in the late 1980s, from a posture of close scrutiny of such aid and relatively minimal allowance of it toward one of broad approval for many forms of government aid and a pattern of treating religious institutions the same as nonreligious institutions in terms of their ability to receive government aid. Accompanying, and largely explaining, this shift are significant changes in Court personnel. Considering a few key decisions helps to chart the Court's judgments and journey.

TAX EXEMPTIONS FOR RELIGIOUS, CHARITABLE, AND EDUCATIONAL ENTITIES

In 1970, the Supreme Court ruled that exempting religious as well as charitable and educational entities from taxation did not violate the constitutional prohibition on governmental promotion of religion. The Court did so in a case involving a claim by a New York real estate owner, Frederick Walz.[11] Walz sought to stop the New York City Tax Commission from granting property tax exemptions to religious organizations for properties used solely for religious worship. Walz said the law recognizing such exemptions forced him to make contributions to religious bodies in violation of the Establishment Clause.

The U.S. Supreme Court rejected Walz' claim.[12] The purpose of the exemption was neither to advance nor to inhibit religion, the Court said. Instead, it was to allow certain community nonprofit organizations to be free from the burden of taxation. Rather than creating excessive entanglement between religion and government, tax exemption helped the state avoid it. "Elimination of [the] exemption would tend to expand the involvement of government by giving rise to tax valuation of church property, tax liens, tax foreclosures, and the direct confrontations and conflicts that follow in the train of those legal processes," the Court said.[13]

Exemption from federal income taxes "is an 'aid' to churches no more and no less in principle than the real estate tax exemption granted by States," the Court said. "Few concepts are more deeply embedded in the fabric of our national life, beginning with pre-Revolutionary colonial times, than for the government to exercise at the very least this kind of benevolent neutrality toward churches and religious exercise generally so long as none was favored over others and none suffered interference."[14]

The Supreme Court tackled the issue of tax exemption for religious institutions again in the 1980s in a case known as *Bob Jones University v. United States.*[15] Bob Jones University (BJU) was founded in Florida in 1927 and moved to its current location in Greenville, South Carolina, in the late 1940s. BJU is not affiliated with any religious denomination. Instead, the school offers education according to its understanding of the Bible.

BJU students are required to agree to certain rules of conduct. As described by a court in 1978, BJU's code of conduct prohibited students from engaging in activities such as dancing, card playing, using tobacco, moviegoing, and listening to rock and jazz music. Also, a male student could not walk with a female student on campus "unless both of them have a legitimate reason for going in the same direction."[16] Based on a belief that the Bible forbade interracial dating and marriage, BJU did not accept student applications from unmarried black students, unless the applicant had been a BJU staff member for four years or longer. Later, in response to a Supreme Court decision that racially discriminatory policies of private schools were unlawful, BJU changed its admissions policy to admit unmarried black students. The BJU policy also stated, however, that students would be expelled if they dated or married someone "outside their own race"; were members of any organization advocating for interracial marriage; or encouraged others to violate BJU policy.[17]

Until 1970, the Internal Revenue Service granted tax-exempt status under 501(c)(3) of the Internal Revenue Code to private schools without regard to their admissions policies.[18] The IRS subsequently changed its practice in response to court decisions prohibiting it from granting tax-exempt status to private schools in Mississippi because the schools discriminated on the basis of race in admissions.[19] The new IRS policy declared that private schools that discriminate against students based on race would no longer qualify for tax-exempt status under Section 501(c)(3) of the Internal Revenue Code.[20] According to the IRS, 501(c)(3) organizations could not have a purpose that was "illegal or contrary to public policy."[21] Developments over recent decades in courts and legislatures had established "a national policy to discourage racial discrimination in education, whether public or private."[22] Racial discrimination in education is contrary to public policy. Thus, the IRS said, if a school had a racially discriminatory policy, it was not "charitable" and would not qualify as a tax-exempt organization.[23]

Accordingly, the IRS revoked BJU's tax-exempt status in 1976. BJU sued, claiming the IRS had violated its right to religious liberty under the First Amendment.[24] A trial court agreed with BJU, but an appellate court reversed that decision.[25] The Supreme Court subsequently agreed to hear the case and consolidated it with a case involving Goldsboro Christian Schools (GCS), a North Carolina school system. The IRS had denied tax-exempt status to GCS because it "maintained a racially discriminatory admissions policy based upon its interpretation of the Bible."[26]

Considering the BJU and Goldsboro cases together, the Court noted that granting tax exemptions to institutions and allowing deductions to their donors indirectly enlists taxpayers in supporting tax-exempt institutions. Exemptions of this kind are justified because of the public benefits charitable organizations provide. "The institution's purpose," however, "must not be so at odds with the common community conscience as to undermine any public benefit that might otherwise be conferred," the Court said.[27]

Religious organizations usually must be free to disagree with the U.S. government, while keeping their tax-exempt status, the Court said. "We are bound to approach these questions with full awareness that determinations of public benefit and public policy are sensitive matters with serious implications for the institutions affected; a declaration that a given institution is not 'charitable' should be made only where there can be no doubt that the activity involved is contrary to a fundamental public policy."[28] Here, "there can no longer be any doubt that racial discrimination in education violates deeply and widely accepted views of elementary justice."[29]

The Supreme Court upheld the revocations of BJU's and GCS's tax-exempt status on this basis. "An unbroken line of cases following *Brown v. Board of Education* establishes beyond doubt this Court's view that racial discrimination in education violates a most fundamental national public policy, as well as rights of individuals."[30] All three branches of the federal government had condemned racial discrimination in education, the Court noted.[31]

The Supreme Court also rejected the schools' argument that the IRS could not revoke the tax exemptions of private religious schools without violating the Free Exercise Clause. The "fundamental, overriding interest in eradicating racial discrimination from education,"[32] the Court said, "substantially outweighs whatever burden denial of tax benefits places on petitioners' exercise of their religious beliefs,"[33] and there was no less restrictive means for the government to achieve its aim. The IRS action also did not violate the Establishment Clause, the Court held. The government was not preferring religions that did not discriminate on racial grounds. The IRS ruling had a secular basis that simply happened to coincide with the tenets of certain faiths.[34]

Finally, the Supreme Court rejected BJU's argument that its policies did not discriminate on the basis of religion because it allowed all races to enroll, "subject only to its restrictions on the conduct of all students, including its prohibitions of association between men and women of different races, and of interracial marriage."[35] Even though the dating ban applied to all students, the policy discriminated on the basis of race.[36]

The Court noted that the religious institutions involved in the case were schools, not churches. "We deal here only with religious *schools*—not with churches or other purely religious institutions; here, the governmental interest is in denying public support to racial discrimination in education."[37]

In 2015, Justice Alito raised the *Bob Jones University* case during oral argument in *Obergefell v. Hodges*, the case in which the Court found that it was unconstitutional for the government to deny couples the right to marry based on their sex.[38] In *Obergefell*, Solicitor General Don Verrilli argued on behalf of the United States as a friend of the court in support of James Obergefell and other representatives of couples of the same sex. By defining marriage as a union between one woman and one man, Obergefell said, the states of Michigan, Kentucky, Ohio, and Tennessee violated the Fourteenth Amendment. In other words, the states violated couples' constitutional rights when they denied them the right to marry or to have their marriages, which were lawfully performed in other states, fully recognized.

During oral argument in the case, Justice Alito asked General Verrilli if the federal government would deny tax-exempt status to a university or college that opposed marriage between couples of the same sex, assuming the Court ruled in favor of marriage equality. Verrilli responded:

> You know, I—I don't think I can answer that question without knowing more specifics, but it's certainly going to be an issue. I—I don't deny that. I don't deny that, Justice Alito. It is—it is going to be an issue.[39]

The response did not point out key aspects of the Court's decision in the *Bob Jones University* case. In that case, the Court was careful to note that all three branches of the federal government had forcefully condemned racial discrimination for decades before the IRS acted. The Court said that racial nondiscrimination in the context of education was a "fundamental, overriding interest"[40] and that "[f]ew social or political issues in our history have been more vigorously debated and more extensively ventilated than the issue of racial discrimination, particularly in education."[41] The response also did not recognize that the Supreme Court, in the more than thirty years since the *Bob Jones* case was decided, has not extended this decision beyond racial discrimination in education.

The Alito-Verrilli exchange drew the attention of religious traditions and some legislators that oppose marriage between couples of the same sex. In a Senate oversight hearing of the IRS in July 2015, Senator Mike Lee (R-Utah) referenced the exchange and asked IRS Commissioner John Koskinen: "Will you commit to me that as long as you remain on as the commissioner of the IRS, you will not, in the absence of a directive by Congress or by the courts, a subsequent directive, one not in place right now, that you will not take any action to remove the tax exempt status from religious colleges or universities based on their belie[f] that the marriage is between a man and a woman?" Koskinen answered: "I can make that commitment."[42]

When the Supreme Court handed down its decision in the *Obergefell* case in June 2015, the Court extended an olive branch to religious individuals and institutions that oppose marriage between couples of the same sex. "Many who deem same-sex marriage to be wrong reach that conclusion based on decent and honorable religious or philosophical premises, and neither they nor their beliefs are disparaged here," the Court said.[43] Further, the Court emphasized that religious institutions and individuals that disagreed with the ruling should be accorded First Amendment protections:

> [I]t must be emphasized that religions, and those who adhere to religious doctrines, may continue to advocate with utmost, sincere conviction that, by divine precepts, same-sex marriage should not be condoned. The First

Amendment ensures that religious organizations and persons are given proper protection as they seek to teach the principles that are so fulfilling and so central to their lives and faiths, and to their own deep aspirations to continue the family structure they have long revered. The same is true of those who oppose same-sex marriage for other reasons. In turn, those who believe allowing same-sex marriage is proper or indeed essential, whether as a matter of religious conviction or secular belief, may engage those who disagree with their view in an open and searching debate.[44]

President Obama struck some similar notes in his statement praising the *Obergefell* decision:

I know change for many of our LGBT brothers and sisters must have seemed so slow for so long. But compared to so many other issues, America's shift has been so quick. I know that Americans of goodwill continue to hold a wide range of views on this issue. Opposition in some cases has been based on sincere and deeply held beliefs. All of us who welcome today's news should be mindful of that fact; recognize different viewpoints; revere our deep commitment to religious freedom.[45]

Courts and policymakers are wrestling now with exactly how religious dissenters should be protected. One thing that seems quite clear, however, is that the tax-exempt statuses of religious bodies are not at risk because they differ with the state on the definition of marriage.

"Only Dimly Perceiv[ing] the Lines of Demarcation" between Permissible and Impermissible Aid

The Supreme Court battle over government aid and religious institutions has been long, complicated, and tedious, and it is far from over. In 1971, the Court confessed: "Candor compels acknowledgment . . . that we can only dimly perceive the lines of demarcation in this extraordinarily sensitive area of constitutional law."[46] Because battles of this kind have often involved religious schools, they have been further complicated by the debate over the place of religious elementary and secondary education generally, and often the place of Catholic education and Catholicism specifically, in American public life. Anti-Catholic views have unfortunately sometimes played a role.[47]

At the dawn of this debate, some justices insisted that church-state separation basically meant that the government simply could not allow any aid to flow to religious institutions. These justices lost the battle from the outset. The debate quickly shifted to which kinds of aid could flow to faith-based organizations, and under what circumstances. The Court engaged in complex and sometimes confusing line-drawing exercises that disallowed a variety of forms of aid.

Senator Daniel Patrick Moynihan poked at some of the Court's distinctions. Moynihan said the Supreme Court had held that the government could fund books that flow to religious schools but not maps. So what about atlases, Moynihan wondered, which are, of course, books of maps.[48]

During the 1970s, the Court majority emphasized relatively strict separationism. The Court's posture began to change in the late 1980s, due largely to changes in Court personnel. Rather rapidly, the Court moved toward bright lines that allowed more forms of aid to flow to more types of religious bodies. While welcome to some, the shift raised concerns for others.

"A WALL OF SEPARATION" BETWEEN CHURCH AND STATE?

The Court handed down its first major decision on government aid and religious institutions in 1947 in the case of *Everson v. Board of Education.*[49] Taxpayers challenged a township's decision to authorize reimbursements to parents of money spent on public bus transportation for their children to school, including parents who sent their children to Catholic schools. Challengers claimed the reimbursements violated the First Amendment's Establishment Clause because it forced them to support church schools.

In an opinion written by Justice Black, a closely divided Court rejected the taxpayers' challenge. Justice Black famously wrote:

> The "establishment of religion" clause of the First Amendment means at least this: Neither a state nor the Federal Government can set up a church. Neither can pass laws which aid one religion, aid all religions, or prefer one religion over another. Neither can force nor influence a person to go to or to remain away from church against his will or force him to profess a belief or disbelief in any religion. No person can be punished for entertaining or professing religious beliefs or disbeliefs, for church attendance or non-attendance. No tax in any amount, large or small, can be levied to support any religious activities or institutions, whatever they may be called, or whatever form they may adopt to teach or practice religion. Neither a state nor the Federal Government can, openly or secretly, participate in the affairs of any religious organizations or groups and vice versa. In the words of Jefferson, the clause against establishment of religion by law was intended to erect "a wall of separation between church and State."[50]

The aid at issue did not violate such principles, the Court said. The money did not flow to the schools, nor did it support them. Instead, the township's policy did "no more than provide a general program to help parents get their children, regardless of their religion, safely and expeditiously to and from accredited schools."[51] The benefits were akin to government services like "ordinary police and fire protection, connections for sewage disposal, public highways and sidewalks," aid that also had long been provided to religious as well as secular schools.[52] Denying religious schools services of this nature, which are "so separate and so indisputably marked off from the religious function, would make it far more difficult for the schools to operate."[53] That was not the aim of the First Amendment, the Court said. "That Amendment requires the state to be neutral in its relations with groups of religious believers and nonbelievers; it does not require the state to be their adversary. State power is no more to be used so as to handicap religions than it is to favor them."[54]

Justice Black's opinion drew forceful rebukes from some of his colleagues. Justice Rutledge wrote a dissenting opinion, which Justices Frankfurter, Jackson, and Burton joined, saying there was no "pretense that [the aid] relate[d] only to the secular instruction given in religious schools or that any attempt is or could be made toward allocating proportional shares as between the secular and religious instruction."[55] Further, the aid was not aimed at securing safe and expeditious travel for children, Rutledge said. The aid was for public transportation and thus "subject to all the hazards and delays of the highway and the streets incurred by the public generally . . . ."[56] Rutledge attached James Madison's *Memorial and Remonstrance against Religious Assessments* to his opinion, saying, "New Jersey's action therefore exactly fits the type of exaction and the kind of evil at which Madison and Jefferson struck."[57] The First Amendment's purpose, according to Rutledge, "was to create a complete and permanent separation of the spheres of religious activity and civil authority by comprehensively forbidding every form of public aid or support for religion."[58]

In another dissenting opinion, Justice Jackson took it upon himself to offer his personal assessment of the nature of Catholic education, saying the church "relie[d] on early and indelible indoctrination in the faith . . . ."[59] Jackson even went so far as to associate the nation's public schools with one faith, Protestantism, and distinguish them from another, Catholicism. "Our public school," Jackson said, "if not a product of Protestantism, at least is more consistent with it than with the Catholic culture and scheme of values."[60] Justice Jackson's rhetoric was neither religiously neutral nor consistent with church-state separation, properly understood.

The *Lemon* Test

Only Justices Black and Douglas were still on the Court when it ruled in 1971 by a margin of eight to one against other forms of aid that flowed to religious schools and when it announced a test for evaluating whether aid was consistent with the Establishment Clause, a test the Court still sometimes uses today.[61] In *Lemon v. Kurtzman*, the Court considered Rhode Island and Pennsylvania statutes that provided government aid to religious elementary and secondary schools, among other private schools.

The quality of education in Rhode Island nonpublic elementary schools had fallen, according to legislators, because schools could not pay enough to attract qualified teachers. Thus, the state authorized supplements for the salaries of teachers of secular subjects in such schools. The state would pay a teacher an amount not to exceed 15 percent of the teacher's current annual salary. Only teaching materials that were used in public schools could be included in such classes, and any teacher who received a supplement had to agree not to teach a religion course for so long as he or she received the aid.[62]

Around the same time, Pennsylvania legislators passed the Nonpublic Elementary and Secondary Education Act due to their concern that the costs of an education at the state's nonpublic schools were rapidly rising. The statute authorized the state to reimburse nonpublic schools, including religious schools, for their expenditures on teachers' salaries, textbooks, and instructional materials in specific nonreligious subjects. Reimbursement of any course containing religious material was forbidden.[63]

Considering the Rhode Island and Pennsylvania policies in one consolidated case, the Court said: "In the absence of precisely stated constitutional prohibitions, we must draw lines with reference to the three main evils against which the Establishment Clause was intended to afford protection: 'sponsorship, financial support, and active involvement of the sovereign in religious activity.'"[64] The Court continued:

> Every analysis in this area must begin with consideration of the cumulative criteria developed by the Court over many years. Three such tests may be gleaned from our cases. First, the statute must have a secular legislative purpose; second, its principal or primary effect must be one that neither advances nor inhibits religion; finally, the statute must not foster "an excessive government entanglement with religion."[65]

If government action failed any one of these tests, the Court said, it violated the Establishment Clause.

The Rhode Island and Pennsylvania policies had a secular purpose—improving secular education in all schools—so it passed the first part of the *Lemon* test.[66] The Court found that it need not decide whether the policies passed the second step of the *Lemon* test—whether the primary effect of the aid was to advance religion—because the policies violated *Lemon's* third and final step: the policies fostered excessive entanglement between church and state.[67]

Such entanglement was revealed by examining the character and purposes of the institutions that would receive benefits, the nature of the government aid, and the resulting relationship between government and religion. The schools were closely tied to churches and inculcated religious doctrine. Thus, the Court said, the legislature had provided for "careful governmental controls and surveillance by state authorities in order to ensure that state aid supports only secular education."[68]

Permitting state aid programs that allow "secular, neutral, or nonideological services, facilities or materials" to flow to religious as well as other private and public schools was one thing, the Court said; allowing aid programs that subsidized teachers' salaries was another. The Court did not assume teachers would violate applicable rules by inculcating religion, but one could not inspect a teacher like a book—"comprehensive, discriminating, and continuing state surveillance will inevitably be required to ensure that these restrictions are obeyed and the First Amendment otherwise respected."[69] Religious schools make a valuable contribution to society, the Court said, but the government was to be "entirely excluded from the area of religious instruction and churches from the affairs of government."[70]

In a concurring opinion, Justice Brennan identified a host of ills he believed would result if aid of this nature was not invalidated. Brennan focused in part on the harm government aid could do to the religious sphere, saying:

> [G]overnment and religion have discrete interests which are mutually best served when each avoids too close a proximity to the other. It is not only the nonbeliever who fears the injection of sectarian doctrines and controversies into the civil polity, but in as high degree it is the devout believer who fears the secularization of a creed which becomes too deeply involved with and dependent upon the government.[71]

Brennan warned, for example, that a religious school would become obligated not to discriminate in admissions or faculty selection if it accepted state aid.[72]

Justice White was the lone dissenter from the Court's holding on excessive entanglement, saying it created an "insoluble paradox" for church and state. "The State cannot finance secular instruction if it permits religion to be taught in the same classroom; but if it exacts a promise that religion not be so taught—a promise the school and its teachers are quite willing and on this record able to give—and enforces it, it is then entangled in the 'no entanglement' aspect of the Court's Establishment Clause jurisprudence," White said.

"Our Establishment Clause Law Has 'Significant[ly] Changed'"

Two decades later, the Court's makeup had changed significantly, and the perspective articulated by Justice White had moved from the margins to the mainstream. Chief Justice Burger had been replaced by Chief Justice Rehnquist, who had little patience for the relatively strict and complex line-drawing exercises the Court had used in some previous church-state cases. Justice Anthony Kennedy had replaced Justice Lewis Powell, thus exchanging a defender of the Court's Establishment Clause precedent for a frequent critic of it.[73] Justice Scalia, who had filled Justice Rehnquist's seat, not only lacked tolerance for much of the Court's Establishment Clause precedent; he belittled it and became the leading opponent of the *Lemon* test. Justice Clarence Thomas, who had replaced liberal lion Justice Thurgood Marshall, would soon reveal that he did not even believe that the Establishment Clause applied to states and localities.[74]

This newly constituted Supreme Court heard the *Agostini v. Felton* case, in which the Court reversed a decision it had made in 1985 to bar the city of New York from sending public school teachers into parochial schools to provide remedial education pursuant to Title I of the Elementary and Secondary Act (ESEA).

Under the ESEA, federal funds went to local educational agencies (LEAs) that could spend the funds on remedial education, guidance, and job counseling for students who needed them. Eligible students included students who were failing, or at risk of failing, and who lived in low-income areas, whether the students attended public or private schools. If the funds flowed to nonpublic schools, the LEAs were charged with ensuring that they retained control over the funds and title to all educational materials used to provide the services, and that public employees (or others not employed by the nonpublic school) would offer the services. The services themselves had to be "secular, neutral, and nonideological," and they had to "supplement, and in no case supplant, the level of services" the private school already provided.[75]

The New York City Board of Education determined that 10 percent of the students who were entitled to Title I aid were private school students and that over 90 percent of the private schools within the board's jurisdiction were religious. Thus, the board sent public employees to religious schools to offer Title I services. Only volunteers were given such duties, and they were informed of the limits on Title I aid. Also, a publicly employed supervisor was supposed to visit each teacher's classroom at least once monthly.[76]

Taxpayers sued the New York Board of Education, claiming that the arrangement violated the Establishment Clause. In a 1985 ruling, *Aguilar v. Felton*, the Supreme Court agreed, concluding that the scheme created excessive entanglement between church and state.[77] Accordingly, the lower courts ordered the LEAs to find a way to provide the aid that did not involve public employees teaching on the premises of religious schools. The board decided to provide instruction at public schools and at mobile instructional units, much like vans, that were parked near religious schools. This method of complying with the *Aguilar* decision proved costly and actually reduced the amount of

Title I funds that could be used for education, leading to cuts in the number of students who could take advantage of the program. In 1995, the New York City Board of Education asked the Court to revisit its 1985 decision. The board said Supreme Court doctrine had changed so dramatically since 1985 that the Court's current doctrine would allow the exact arrangement the Court had struck down ten years ago. The Supreme Court agreed to hear the case and reversed its decision in *Aguilar*.

Justice O'Connor wrote the opinion for the Court. As a former legislator and dogged pragmatist, O'Connor was appalled by the fact that this arrangement reduced the amount of Title I aid that was available to needy students and did so for no legitimate reason, in her view. In short, the New York City Board of Education had her sympathies. O'Connor also had shown both an interest in revamping aspects of Establishment Clause doctrine that she believed to be outdated, or even wrongheaded from the start, while still retaining certain core Establishment Clause principles. Justice O'Connor seized such an opportunity in the *Agostini* case. O'Connor said:

> Distilled to essentials, the Court's conclusion [in an earlier decision that a school-aid program] had the impermissible effect of advancing religion rested on three assumptions: (i) any public employee who works on the premises of a religious school is presumed to inculcate religion in her work; (ii) the presence of public employees on private school premises creates a symbolic union between church and state; and (iii) any and all public aid that directly aids the educational function of religious schools impermissibly finances religious indoctrination, even if the aid reaches such schools as a consequence of private decisionmaking. Additionally, in *Aguilar* there was a fourth assumption: that New York City's Title I program necessitated an excessive government entanglement with religion because public employees who teach on the premises of religious schools must be closely monitored to ensure that they do not inculcate religion.[78]

The Court's more recent decisions had undermined such assumptions, O'Connor said.[79] Led by Justice O'Connor, the Court took the opportunity to downsize the *Lemon* test, saying that entanglement should be considered "as an aspect of [the Court's inquiry] into a statute's [primary] effect," rather than as a freestanding consideration, thus reducing the test from three steps to two.[80] Under this new understanding of Court doctrine, New York City's Title I program did not violate the Establishment Clause. "[O]ur Establishment Clause law has 'significantly changed' since we decided *Aguilar*," the Court announced.[81]

Justices Souter, Ginsburg, Stevens, and Breyer dissented, saying the Court's reading of current Establishment Clause doctrine and applicable procedural rules was wrong. On the contrary, they said, the repudiated Establishment

Clause doctrine drew "a very reasonable line."[82] In contrast, the Court's new position "authorize[d] direct state aid to religious institutions on an unparalleled scale, in violation of the Establishment Clause's central prohibition against religious subsidies by the government."[83]

A COURT PLURALITY PUSHES FOR MORE CHANGE

Four justices on the Court were not content to stop with these revisions to Establishment Clause doctrine. In 2000, Chief Justice Rehnquist and Justices Thomas, Scalia, and Kennedy engaged in a failed attempt to rewrite Establishment Clause doctrine further in another case involving government aid and religious schools. In *Mitchell v. Helms*, the Court considered a federal program known as Chapter 2 whereby the federal government distributed funds to state and local governments, which then lent educational materials and equipment to public and private schools, with the amount of aid being determined by the school's enrollment.[84] The question at issue in the case was whether the application of the aid program to schools in Jefferson Parish, Louisiana, was constitutional. Many of the schools that received the aid were religiously affiliated.[85]

Six justices agreed that the aid was constitutional, but four of them took the opportunity to attempt to weaken Establishment Clause doctrine in new ways. Their attempt failed because an opinion is not controlling if it does not draw the support of five justices. Nonetheless, the four justices' views—called a "plurality"—are noteworthy.[86]

In an opinion written by Justice Thomas, the plurality said the aid had a secular purpose, and "it neither result[ed] in religious indoctrination by the government nor define[d] its recipients by reference to religion."[87] That was all that was necessary for the aid to pass muster under the Establishment Clause here, according to the plurality. "If the religious, irreligious, and areligious are all alike eligible for government aid, no one would conclude that any indoctrination that any particular recipient conducts has been done at the behest of the government."[88] The plurality went further to say that even direct aid that flowed to religious entities and was used to support religious activities did not violate the Constitution.

The plurality rebuked what was known as the "pervasively sectarian" doctrine. According to the "pervasively sectarian" doctrine, some institutions are so pervaded with religion that funding any part of them amounts to governmental promotion of religion. A religious body that incorporates evangelism in all of its activities would meet this definition, for example. The pervasively sectarian doctrine, the plurality said, is "not only unnecessary but also offensive."[89] The government should not "troll[] through a person's or institution's religious beliefs."[90] The religious nature of the aid recipient should be irrelevant, the plurality insisted, so long as that recipient was advancing the government's secular purpose. Also, the pervasively sectarian test was tainted by anti-Catholicism, these justices argued. The plurality thundered: "The pervasively sectarian recipient has not received any special favor, and it is most bizarre that the Court would, as the dissent seemingly does, reserve special hostility for those who take their religion seriously, who think that their religion should affect the whole of their lives, or who make the mistake of being effective in transmitting their views to children."[91] The pervasively sectarian doctrine, "born of bigotry, should be buried now," they said.[92]

Justices O'Connor and Breyer concurred only in the Court's judgment that the aid at issue in the *Mitchell* case did not violate the Establishment Clause. Otherwise, Justices O'Connor and Breyer strongly disagreed with the plurality's approach. Justice O'Connor explained that she wrote separately because, "in my view, the plurality announces a rule of unprecedented breadth for the evaluation of Establishment Clause challenges to government school aid programs." O'Connor continued:

> Reduced to its essentials, the plurality's rule states that government aid to religious schools does not have the effect of advancing religion so long as the aid is offered on a neutral basis and the aid is secular in content. The plurality also rejects the distinction between direct and indirect aid, and holds that the actual diversion of secular aid by a religious school to the advancement of its religious mission is permissible.[93]

In an attempt to demonstrate the radical nature of the plurality's opinion, Justice O'Connor noted that "there is no reason that, under the plurality's reasoning, the government should be precluded from providing direct money payments to religious organizations (including churches) based on the number of persons belonging to each organization. And, because actual diversion is permissible under the plurality's holding, the participating religious organizations (including churches) could use that aid to support religious indoctrination."[94] Rather than taking a restrained approach, often lauded as the conservative ideal, the plurality also decided much more than needed to dispose of the case, O'Connor noted.

Justice Souter wrote a dissenting opinion *Mitchell v. Helms*, which Justices Stevens and Ginsburg joined. The dissenters cited three concerns that animate the First Amendment: forcing an individual to support religion violates freedom of conscience; government support corrupts faith; and religious establishments are inevitably linked to conflict. "The plurality's mistaken assumptions explain and underscore its sharp break with the Framers' understanding of establishment and this Court's consistent interpretative course," the dissenters said:

> Under the plurality's regime, little would be left of the right of conscience against compelled support for religion; the more massive the aid the more potent would be the influence of the government on the teaching mission; the more generous the support, the more divisive would be the resentments of those resisting religious support, and those religions without school systems ready to claim their fair share.[95]

Justice Souter rejected the notion that the pervasively sectarian test was rooted in bigotry or that opposition to government aid for a school's religious mission was based in hostility to faith. The pervasively sectarian test applied to all faiths, Souter emphasized, and it simply made common sense: "[W]here religious indoctrination pervades school activities of children and adolescents, it takes great care to be able to aid the school without supporting the doctrinal effort."[96] If opposition to government aid for religious activities demonstrated hostility to faith, then the founders were at fault as well.[97]

DISCRIMINATION OR SEPARATION?

Until 2017, the typical issue in an aid case had been whether the extension of the aid to religious bodies would violate the First Amendment's Establishment Clause. In 2017, the Court considered the question of whether excluding certain entities from the opportunity to compete for government aid due to their religious character violated the First Amendment's Free Exercise Clause.

By that time, the Court's makeup had shifted further. Justice Alito, another critic of the Supreme Court's traditional approach to Establishment Clause issues, had replaced the more centrist and measured Justice O'Connor. After Justice Antonin Scalia passed away on February 13, 2016, President Obama nominated Judge Merrick Garland to take his place, but a Republican-led Senate blocked any consideration of this nomination.[98] After President Trump took office, he nominated—and the Senate confirmed—Justice Neil Gorsuch to take this seat. Early indications suggest that, if Justice Gorsuch differs from Justice Scalia on such issues, he is likely even less tolerant of a wide swath of Establishment Clause precedent.[99]

In 2017 the Court considered the case of *Trinity Lutheran Church v. Comer*, involving the state of Missouri's program of offering reimbursement grants to nonprofits for playground resurfacing. Trinity Lutheran Church applied for the aid for its school, and the church placed highly enough in the competition to receive such a grant. The Missouri Department of Natural Resources denied the church the grant, however, because Trinity Lutheran was a church. Missouri officials cited a state constitutional provision barring the flow of aid to churches and other houses of worship. The Court found the state prohibition to be unconstitutional under the federal Constitution because the state was discriminating against religion without any compelling interest to support such discrimination.[100] "The express discrimination against religious exercise here is not the denial of a grant, but rather the refusal to allow [a church]—solely because it is a church—to compete with secular organizations for a grant."[101] While Missouri defended its policy on the basis of its interest in avoiding any possible concerns about religious establishments, the parties agreed that it would not violate the First Amendment's Establishment Clause for the aid to flow to a church.

The Court found that this interest was not compelling in the face of the Free Exercise Clause violation presented by the case. There was no constitutional issue with regard to the use of the funds—the aid would be used for the secular task of resurfacing a playground. The state had excluded the church due to its religious character, and that was unconstitutional.

The Court's opinion in *Trinity Lutheran v. Comer* closed with a reference to a Maryland legislator's advocacy almost two hundred years ago for a bill that would end the state's disqualification of Jewish individuals from public office. The legislator called the disqualification "[a]n odious exclusion from any of the benefits common to the rest of my fellow-citizens," saying it was "persecution, differing only in degree, but of a nature equally unjustifiable with that, whose instruments are chains and torture." The Court concluded:

> The Missouri Department of Natural Resources has not subjected anyone to chains or torture on account of religion. And the result of the State's policy is nothing so dramatic as the denial of political office. The consequence is, in all likelihood, a few extra scraped knees. But the exclusion of Trinity Lutheran from a public benefit for which it is otherwise qualified, solely because it is a church, is odious to our Constitution all the same, and cannot stand.[102]

Justices Sotomayor and Ginsburg filed a stiff dissent: "The Court today profoundly changes [the relationship between church and state] by holding, for the first time, that the Constitution requires the government to provide public funds directly to a church." The Court erred by simply relying on the fact that the parties agreed that the aid could be extended without violating the First Amendment's Establishment Clause. Instead, the Court should have confronted that issue and ruled that the aid was impermissible because it would flow to a church, the playground was part of the church's religious mission, and there were no assurances that the aid would not be used for religious activities. "The Church's playground surface—like a Sunday School room's walls or the sanctuary's pews—are integrated with and integral to its religious mission."[103] Providing aid and monitoring in this context would create entanglement between church and state. The state was not discriminating against religion by refusing to provide direct aid to a church. Missouri was simply making "a valid choice to remain secular in the face of serious establishment and free exercise concerns."[104] The Court, the dissenters said, "leads us to a place where separation of church and state is a constitutional slogan, not a constitutional commitment."[105]

The *Trinity Lutheran Church* case left a number of open questions. In a footnote that split the majority, the Court said:

> This case involves express discrimination based on religious identity with respect to playground resurfacing. We do not address religious uses of funding or other forms of discrimination.[106]

With this statement, four of the justices who joined the majority opinion signaled that the decision was quite narrow.[107] Justice Breyer wrote a separate opinion concurring only in the Court's judgment. In his opinion, Justice Breyer analogized the case to *Everson*: "Here, the [s]tate would cut Trinity Lutheran off from participation in a general program designed to secure or to improve the health and safety of children."[108] Therefore, Breyer said, "I would leave the application of the Free Exercise Clause to other kinds of public benefits for another day."[109] Lower courts and commentators continue to debate the scope of the *Trinity Lutheran* decision.[110]

SUPREME COURT VOUCHES FOR VOUCHERS

The Supreme Court treats indirect aid, like school vouchers, quite differently from direct aid. Unlike direct aid programs, such as ones involving government grants, indirect aid programs are ones in which government aid reaches religious entities "only as a result of genuine and independent choices of private individuals."[111] Usually, the aid is given to citizens who then "spend" the aid at the institution of their choice.

In 2002, the Court upheld an Ohio school voucher program that included religious schools. The Ohio legislature enacted the Pilot Project Scholarship Program to provide financial assistance to families in any state school district that is or had been under a federal court order requiring supervision by the state superintendent. The Cleveland school district was the only Ohio school district that had been under such an order. The program offered two basic forms of assistance for parents of students in a covered district. Parents could seek tuition aid for students wishing to attend a public or private school of their choice. Alternatively, if students wished to remain in public schools, parents could receive aid that could be used for tutoring. The law prohibited participating private schools from discriminating on the basis of race, religion, or ethnic background. Private schools also had to agree not to "advocate or foster unlawful behavior or teach hatred of any person or group based on race, ethnicity, national origin, or religion."[112] Parents received tuition aid according to financial need. When parents chose schools, checks were made payable to the parents who then endorsed the checks over to the school of their choosing. The program, the Court said, was part of a broader effort to increase educational options for Cleveland schoolchildren. For example, Cleveland families could also choose "community schools," schools that the state funds but are run under their own school boards, not by local school districts. Magnet schools—public schools operated by a local school board that stress a specific subject, student service, or teaching method—are another option.[113]

In an opinion written by Chief Justice Rehnquist, the Court said that an indirect aid program must be neutral with regard to religion and provide assistance directly to a wide group of individuals who made "genuine and independent private choice[s]" about the destination of such aid.[114] In such cases, any advancement of religion is properly attributable to the individuals, not the government. The Ohio scholarship program passed this test and thus did not violate the Establishment Clause, the Court held. Justice O'Connor joined the Court's majority opinion, but she wrote separately to stress that she did not believe the decision constituted "a major departure from this Court's prior Establishment Clause jurisprudence."[115] O'Connor also added: "For nonreligious schools to qualify as genuine options for parents, they need not be superior to religious schools in every respect." Instead, "they need only be adequate substitutes for religious schools in the eyes of parents."[116]

Acknowledging the poor condition of Cleveland public schools, the dissenting justices—Justices Souter, Stevens, Ginsburg, and Breyer—said: "If there were an excuse for giving short shrift to the Establishment Clause, it would probably apply here," but "there is no excuse."[117] To protect constitutional values, constitutional prohibitions must be observed in "hard cases" as well as easy ones.[118]

The dissenting justices argued that the Court's decision overruled the prohibition on levying taxes to support religious activities or institutions, which was first adopted in the *Everson* case. The aid would pay for instruction in religious as well as secular subjects. "[T]he majority makes no pretense that substantial amounts of tax money are not systematically underwriting religious practice and indoctrination."[119] The Court no longer cared about Madison's "three pence," the dissenters said. It would be difficult, if not impossible, to avoid divisive fights over some of the religious content of the curriculum that was not government-funded. "True, the majority has not approved vouchers for religious schools alone, or aid earmarked for religious instruction," but "no scheme so clumsy will ever get before us, and in the cases that we may see, like these, the Establishment Clause is largely silenced."[120]

Also, there was not a genuine choice between religious and secular schools. The vouchers were not enough to cover private nonreligious schools, leaving failing public schools as the only secular option. "There is . . . no way to interpret the 96.6% of current voucher money going to religious schools as reflecting a free and genuine choice by the families that apply for vouchers."[121] A future Court should "reconsider today's dramatic departure from basic Establishment Clause principle," the dissenters said.[122]

Under the *Zelman* decision, faith-based organizations are permitted to use indirect aid for religious purposes, so long as there are adequate secular alternatives and the program allows genuine choice among religious and secular alternatives. The rationale for treating direct and indirect aid differently is that, in a permissible voucher-type program, the beneficiary will always have choices. Thus, if he or she selects a religious program, then that was a choice the beneficiary freely made, according to the Court. The use of government funds for religious activities is irrelevant here, the Court has said, because the fact that the program involves "true private choice" nullifies the need to ensure that the aid does not subsidize religious activities.[123]

Looking Backward and Forward

Decades ago, the Supreme Court decided against adopting a position that would have stopped the flow of many forms of government aid to religious organizations. While the channel for such aid remained relatively narrow for decades, it began to widen significantly in the late 1980s.

Changes in Court personnel were a key factor in the shift. Another factor is the prevalence of state aid when compared to the founding era. When aid flows widely to nongovernmental (including nonprofit) entities, refusing to allow religious nonprofits to receive such aid raises more questions. Also, the crisis in public education in certain parts of the country has created a sympathetic context for including religious schools in government aid programs, including school voucher programs.

As the Supreme Court widened the channel for government aid to flow to religious institutions, it began to chip away at some principles that had been fundamental. The Court moved from generally barring the use of government aid for the religious activities of private elementary and secondary schools, for example, to generally allowing such uses in the context of a school voucher program. When citizens make genuine and independent choices about the institutions that receive the aid, the chain that connects the aid to the government is broken, the Court held. Even so, taxpayer contributions still support indirect aid, governmental conditions still follow the aid, and the danger of religious institutions becoming dependent on such aid has not disappeared.

It is highly unlikely that the Court will roll back decisions permitting more kinds of religious institutions to receive more types of government aid. The government rarely retracts eligibility for aid, due in part to the blowback that would result. Meanwhile, some justices will continue to try to remove long-standing safeguards in this area, including the general bar on the use of direct aid for religious expression, items, and activities.

RECOMMENDATIONS: ADVICE ON AID-RELATED ISSUES

The suggestions offered to governmental and religious leaders in the previous chapter also apply here. Here are a few additional suggestions for such leaders as they seek to navigate issues related to government aid.

> (1) *Recognize that the Internal Revenue Service can rescind educational institutions' tax-exempt status under Section 501(c)(3) of the Internal Revenue Code, including the tax-exempt status of religiously affiliated educational institutions, for racial discrimination. Also recognize that, while the Supreme Court upheld the Service's judgment in that case, it has not extended its ruling to any other forms of discrimination.*

When the Supreme Court upheld the rescission of Bob Jones University's tax-exempt status due to its racially discriminatory policies, the Court was careful to note that racial nondiscrimination in the context of education was a "fundamental, overriding interest"[124] and that "[f]ew social or political issues in our history have been more vigorously debated and more extensively ventilated than the issue of racial discrimination, particularly in education."[125] The Court also underscored the fact that the IRS was revoking the tax-exempt status not of a house of worship but rather of a religiously affiliated educational institution. The Supreme Court has not extended the *Bob Jones University* ruling to any other forms of discrimination.

> (2) *Condemn bigotry and discrimination against Catholics. Preserve the separation of church and state.*

Bigotry and discrimination against Catholics has played a role in the American debate about religious freedom, including the debate about religious institutions and government aid. Americans should roundly condemn such prejudice and practice vigilance against it today. At the same time, the separation of church and state should never be dismissed as simply a form of anti-Catholicism. Valid concerns animate a cautious approach regarding government aid and religious institutions and activities, ones having no basis in anti-Catholic or anti-religious animus. Such concerns are found, for example, in seminal documents such as James Madison's *Memorial and Remonstrance against Religious Assessments*. Americans who share these concerns should vigorously argue their cases, while also forcefully condemning anti-Catholic bigotry and discrimination.

(3) Mind the general bar on the use of direct government aid for religious expression, items, and activities.

When the government makes financial aid available to nonprofit organizations, religious organizations generally are permitted to apply for the aid. Such aid, however, must be configured in a way that does not violate the prohibition on government support for religion.

A faith-based organization that receives a government grant to assist victims of opioid abuse, for example, cannot use grant funds to pay for Bibles, Torahs, or Qur'ans or for devotional studies of these texts. Any religious activities must be privately funded, voluntarily attended, and clearly separated from social service activities funded by government grants. Government officials should spell out these kinds of conditions in authorizing statutes and awards. Doing so will serve as a helpful teaching tool for both government and religious recipients of the aid.

(4) When the government observes limits on its involvement with religion, do not assume that such treatment constitutes unjust discrimination or hostility to faith.

Both the Establishment and Free Exercise Clauses place special limits on government that pertain to religion. The Establishment Clause, for example, generally bars the use of direct government aid to subsidize religious expression, items, or activities. Nonetheless, some have wrongly argued that not only is this prohibition *not required* by the Constitution but the prohibition *is actually itself barred* by the First Amendment because it is a form of discrimination against religion.[126]

This bar is not unjust discrimination or hostility to faith. It is the benevolent neutrality toward religion that the Constitution requires. In his *Memorial and Remonstrance against Religious Assessments*, James Madison recognized sound and religion-friendly reasons to support bars on government subsidies for religion. Many of those reasons apply just as much to aid that flows to both religious and nonreligious entities.

What the government funds, it regulates, even if what it funds is religious. And, depending on the city or town, direct government subsidies for certain sacred texts will surely generate fierce political opposition. It is difficult enough to ensure that minority faiths are not discriminated against in the awards process when it is clear that direct aid can be used only for secular content. It would be impossible to do so if direct aid could also be used for religious content. Allowing direct state aid to subsidize religious messages and activities would result in governmental promotion and regulation of religion as well as de facto preferences for some faiths over others, given differing levels of public support for particular religious traditions. The mere fact that the government observes certain limits on state aid and religious activities does not mean the government is engaging in unjust discrimination against religion or demonstrating hostility toward faith.

(5) Recognize the limits of the Trinity Lutheran Church *decision.*

In the wake of the *Trinity Lutheran Church* case, some are basically arguing that the government violates the Free Exercise Clause whenever it denies religious bodies almost any form of government aid or whenever it refuses to recognize religious exemptions from conditions following government aid. But the *Trinity Lutheran Church* decision does not mandate or support such a stand. In a footnote that split the majority, the Supreme Court said:

> This case involves express discrimination based on religious identity with respect to playground resurfacing. We do not address religious uses of funding or other forms of discrimination.

Note that the decision did not disturb the general prohibition on the use of direct government aid for religious expression, items, and activities. It also did not speak to issues of discrimination beyond those of "express discrimination based on religious identity . . . ."

(6) Guard against implicit bias in the distribution of government aid.

One danger is that governmental aid will not be truly available to institutions that are affiliated with minority faith traditions, not due to express prohibitions but rather due to implicit bias within the awards process. Government officials should seek to root out all forms of bias in the awards process. One way to do so is to remove the name of the applicant in the peer review process in order to assist reviewers in ensuring that their decisions are made on the basis of merit, not religious affiliation or lack thereof.

(7)   Remember that vouchers or other indirect aid programs are
constitutionally invalid if they fail to provide "genuine choice."

Programs that provide indirect aid (like vouchers or certificates) to nongovernmental organizations (including religious organizations) and allow religious organizations to use the aid for religious content must provide genuine choice between religious and nonreligious alternatives. As Justice O'Connor said in her opinion in the Ohio school voucher case: "For nonreligious schools to qualify as genuine options for parents, they need not be superior to religious schools in every respect." Instead, "they need only be adequate substitutes for religious schools in the eyes of parents." If beneficiaries lack such a choice, then the program is unconstitutional.

(8)   Before seeking and accepting government aid, religious organizations
should carefully consider the impact such aid might have on their
activities.

As noted in chapter 6, religious organizations can become dependent on government money or shift priorities based simply on what the government will fund. Before seeking or accepting government financial aid, faith-based organizations should carefully consider whether they will be able to avoid developing a dependence on that aid, whether the aid is consistent with their sense of mission, and whether they will be able to accept the restrictions that follow the aid. If a religious body decides to accept government aid, it should segregate such aid from private funds.

(9)   Train government officials and nongovernmental organizations,
including religious institutions, on the rules that apply to government
aid.

Government officials should host internal and external trainings regarding the rules that apply to the aid it distributes. Governmental leadership is needed to ensure that these matters are understood.

8

RELIGIOUS EXEMPTIONS AND ACCOMMODATIONS

Balancing Claims of Conscience with Other Interests

From the early 1960s to 1990, the Supreme Court applied the "compelling interest test" to a range of claims brought under the First Amendment's Free Exercise Clause. When it substantially burdened religious exercise, the state had to justify that burden with a compelling interest. The government also usually had to show that it was advancing that interest by the means that is least restrictive of religious exercise.

In its 1990 decision in Employment Division v. Smith, *however, the Supreme Court abruptly ended this practice.* The Constitution's Free Exercise Clause does not require application of the compelling interest test when laws and policies are neutral toward religion and generally applicable, the Court said. To be neutral, a law must not target faith, either overtly or covertly. To be generally applicable, a law must not restrict only conduct that is religiously motivated. Also, a law is not generally applicable if religiously motivated conduct is restricted because it endangers the state's interests, yet a similar amount of nonreligious conduct that endangers the state's interest in the same way is not.

When the Supreme Court announced the Smith *decision, a coalition of religious freedom advocates of different religious and political stripes condemned the ruling for significantly reducing protections for free exercise.* This group decided that a legislative response was needed, and it coalesced around the federal Religious Freedom Restoration Act (RFRA). RFRA, which was enacted in 1993, restored the compelling interest test the Court had used pre-*Smith*.

When the Supreme Court said in 1997 that RFRA was unconstitutional as applied to states and localities, the coalition came together again to support the Religious Land Use and Institutionalized Persons Act (RLUIPA). RLUIPA, which was enacted in 2000, binds government at all levels—federal, state, and local—and applies the compelling interest test and other free exercise protections in two specific areas: land use matters and situations in which the government institutionalizes persons, like prisons, state hospitals, and immigrant detention centers.

Requests for religious exemptions are requests to be freed from obligations that conflict with one's religious beliefs or practices. The terms "exemptions" and "accommodations" are often used interchangeably. But the term "accommodation" may also refer to a modification to a law or policy that is not an exemption, such as an allowance for workplace shift switches that permit employees to keep their Sabbath and their job. Religious exemptions or accommodations can take one of three forms. Mandatory exemptions or accommodations are required by law. Permissible exemptions or accommodations are not compelled by law, but they also are not forbidden by it. Impermissible exemptions or accommodations are legally prohibited.

The Establishment Clause places certain limits on religious exemptions. The state's aim must be to lift burdens on religious exercise, and it must ensure that exemptions or accommodations do not privilege any particular religion or single out any faith for disadvantageous treatment. Also, the government has to "take adequate account" of the burdens a requested religious accommodation may impose on individuals who do not benefit from the accommodation. "[A]n accommodation must be measured so that it does not override other significant interests," the Supreme Court has said. The Court's pre-*Smith* free-exercise precedent also recognized certain limits on religious exemptions. When religious accommodations have failed to strike an appropriate balance, the Court has invalidated them.

In her nightly prayers, Eleanor Roosevelt asked God to "[k]eep us at tasks too hard for us that we may be driven to Thee for strength."[1] Protecting human rights was one of the hard tasks Roosevelt tackled.

The Commission on Human Rights of the newly established United Nations unanimously elected Eleanor Roosevelt to serve as its chair in January 1947,[2] and it asked her to lead representatives from around the world in drafting the first "international bill of rights."³ On December 10, 1948, after painstaking labor and debate, the General Assembly of the United Nations adopted the Universal Declaration of Human Rights (UDHR) without a dissenting vote.⁴

The declaration challenged the common view that a country's treatment of its own citizens was no other nation's concern.⁵ The framers of the declaration sought to articulate a set of principles that were "so basic that no nation would wish openly to disavow them."⁶ The UDHR "quickly displaced all antecedents as the principal model for the rights instruments in force in the world."⁷ Historians and Eleanor Roosevelt herself considered her role in this work to be her greatest achievement.⁸

The UDHR recognizes that "[a]ll humans beings are born free and equal in dignity and rights."⁹ It asserts that "the inherent dignity" and "the equal and inalienable rights of all members of the human family is the foundation of freedom, justice and peace in the world."¹⁰ The declaration sets forth a series of basic human rights and calls on nations to protect those rights. Article 18 of the UDHR states: "Everyone has the right to freedom of thought, conscience and religion; this right includes freedom to change his religion or belief, and freedom, either alone or in community with others and in public or private, to manifest his religion or belief in teaching, practice, worship and observance."¹¹

The United States protects such rights through the Constitution and other laws. These rights are not absolute, but the United States has a tradition of seeking to avoid instances in which Americans are forced to choose between obeying the law and keeping their faith.

Exempting or accommodating religious individuals and institutions from laws or policies that conflict with their faith is one way the country has sought to honor this tradition. The terms "exemptions" and "accommodations" are often used interchangeably. But the term "accommodation" may also refer to some other modification to law or policy that is not an exemption, such as an allowance for workplace shift switches that permit employees to keep their Sabbath and their job.

The government is sometimes legally required to grant requests for exemptions or accommodations. Permissible exemptions or accommodations are not compelled by law, but they also are not forbidden by it. Other requests for exemptions or accommodations must be denied because they are legally prohibited.¹²

The range of requests for exemptions or accommodations from laws and policies reflects the diversity of religion in the United States. The following requests are illustrative:

- Sikhs who wish to serve in the military have requested religious accommodations to wear modified beards and turbans.[13]

- Public school students who are Jehovah's Witnesses have sought exemptions from rules requiring them to salute the American flag and recite the Pledge of Allegiance.[14]

- Individuals have said that their religious motivations should shield them from criminal charges based on their provision of humanitarian and medical aid to undocumented immigrants in deserts at the Southwest border.[15]

- Muslim and Orthodox Jewish girls have sought permission to wear more modest athletic gear than the uniforms public schools generally require.[16]

- Pharmacists or pharmacies that refuse for religious reasons to fill prescriptions for RU-486 or suicide drugs have requested exemptions from laws or policies generally requiring them to dispense such drugs.[17]

- In the face of deportation orders, churches have asserted free exercise rights to shelter undocumented immigrants in their sanctuaries.[18]

- Citing religious beliefs, some employers have sought exemptions from laws requiring them to provide cost-free contraception coverage as part of their employee health benefit plans.[19]

- Native Americans and Catholic nuns who oppose oil pipelines because of their faith have sought to block the government from empowering oil companies to run such pipelines across their land or sacred sites.[20]

- A bakery that refused for religious reasons to make and sell a wedding cake to a couple of the same sex sought an exemption from a state public accommodations law banning discrimination on the basis of sexual orientation.[21]

- A Catholic diocese in Texas that opposes a border wall for religious reasons has tried to stop the federal government from taking a parcel of its land for the wall.[22]

Government officials must decide whether to grant or deny requests like these. Decision-makers will be better equipped to make such judgments when they understand how free exercise doctrine has developed, including the ongoing dialogue between Congress and the Supreme Court on these issues. This chapter picks up the story in 1990, when the Court handed down its decision in the landmark case of *Employment Division v. Smith*.

Supreme Court Deems Robust Free Exercise Rights
a "Luxury" We "Cannot Afford"

From the early 1960s until 1990, the U.S. Supreme Court applied the compelling interest test to a range of claims brought under the First Amendment's Free Exercise Clause.[23] If the religious claimants could prove that the government had substantially burdened their sincere faith practices, then the government had to demonstrate that such a burden was justified by a compelling state interest. The religious claimants won the case if the government lacked such an interest. If, however, the government made such a showing, then it had one more hurdle to clear. The government had to demonstrate that it was advancing its compelling interest in a manner that places only the lightest possible burden on religious exercise. If the government could not do so, the religious claimant won the case.

Considering a hypothetical case helps to illustrate how the compelling interest test works. Assume a public school adopts a policy prohibiting students from wearing hats at school. The school defines "hats" as anything covering a student's head. Assume also that a Jewish boy asks to be exempt from that rule in order to wear his yarmulke to school. In such a case, the school would have to ask itself if failing to exempt the Jewish boy would substantially burden the boy's religious exercise. Assuming the answer to that question would be "yes," the school would next consider whether it had a compelling interest to justify its refusal to exempt the boy from the rule. If the school wants to ban hats because some hats are being used as gang signifiers and thus have resulted in fights at school, the school may have a compelling interest in generally prohibiting the wearing of hats at school. The school still does not have a compelling interest in prohibiting a boy from wearing a yarmulke for religious reasons, however. Thus, if the school imposes a "no hat" rule, the school must provide an exemption for the Jewish boy and anyone else in similar circumstances.

The Supreme Court has traditionally recognized some limits on religious exemptions or accommodations, both under the Establishment and Free Exercise Clauses. The state's aim must be to lift burdens on religious exercise, and it must ensure that exemptions or accommodations do not "differentiate among bona fide faiths," by privileging any particular religion or singling out any faith for disadvantageous treatment, for example.[24] Additionally, the First Amendment's Establishment Clause requires the government to "take adequate account of the burdens a requested [religious] accommodation may impose on" people who do not benefit from the accommodation.[25] This command is consistent with James Madison's vision. Madison said free exercise rights should be protected unless they "trespass on private rights or the public peace."[26] The Court has said: "Our decisions indicate that an accommodation must be measured so that it does not override other significant interests."[27] When religious exemptions have failed to strike an appropriate balance, the Court has invalidated them.[28]

One such case involved a Connecticut law that "decreed that those who observe a Sabbath any day of the week as a matter of religious conviction must be relieved of the duty to work on that day, no matter what burden or inconvenience this imposes on the employer or fellow workers."[29] The law was invalid under the Establishment Clause, the Court said, because it "unyielding[ly] weigh[ted]" the interests of Sabbatarians "over all other interests . . . ."[30]

The Court has also refused to recognize an exemption in a 1982 free-exercise case involving an Amish man who employed several workers on his farm and in his carpentry shop.[31] The Amish employer refused to withhold social security taxes from his employees or to pay the employer's share of such taxes because he believed participating in public insurance systems violated his faith.[32] The IRS assessed the employer the unpaid taxes, prompting the owner to assert a free exercise defense—a defense the Supreme Court rejected.

In this case, *United States v. Lee*, the Court first noted that Congress had granted an exemption from social security taxes to self-employed individuals who are part of a religious community that has its own "welfare" system.[33] But the Court distinguished that practice from an employer's refusal to withhold social security taxes from employees or to pay the employer's share of such taxes. The Court said:

> Congress and the courts have been sensitive to the needs flowing from the Free Exercise Clause, but every person cannot be shielded from all the burdens incident to exercising every aspect of the right to practice religious beliefs. When followers of a particular sect enter into commercial activity as a matter of choice, the limits they accept on their own conduct as a matter of conscience and faith are not to be superimposed on the statutory schemes which are binding on others in that activity. Granting an exemption from social security taxes to an employer operates to impose the employer's religious faith on the employees. Congress drew a line in § 1402(g), exempting the self-employed Amish but not all persons working for an Amish employer. The tax imposed on employers to support the social security system must be uniformly applicable to all, except as Congress provides explicitly otherwise.[34]

The Supreme Court used these standards when evaluating a range of claims made under the Free Exercise Clause prior to 1990. As constitutional scholars have noted, however, the compelling interest test that the Court applied to free exercise issues was not as strong as the compelling interest test it applied to issues of racial discrimination, and the Court did not apply the compelling interest test to all free exercise claims, including ones that would constrain government's "internal operations" and ones against prisons and the military, areas where the state is often given great deference.[35] Even so, a closely divided Supreme Court announced in 1990 that the First Amendment required much less protection for free exercise.[36]

The Court made this announcement in a case involving two Native Americans—Alfred Smith and Galen Black—who had been fired from their jobs at a private drug-rehabilitation organization because they had ingested peyote for religious purposes at a service of the Native American Church.[37] Smith and Black subsequently applied for unemployment compensation, but the state of Oregon denied them these benefits because they had been fired for job-related "misconduct"—using a drug that was criminally prohibited by the state, even though Smith and Black had a religious reason for doing so.[38] The issue in the case was whether the Free Exercise Clause allowed the state to include religious use of peyote within a general criminal prohibition on ingestion of that drug and to deny unemployment benefits to individuals who were fired from their jobs due to such use.[39] In their briefs, Smith and Black cited Supreme Court precedent requiring or allowing such exemptions, although those rules did not speak to violations of criminal drug laws.[40]

Justice Antonin Scalia wrote the opinion for the Court majority in *Smith*. Smith and Black lost, which did not shock Court-watchers. The state of Oregon had argued that uniform application of its criminal prohibition on the use of peyote was "essential to accomplish" the compelling state interests of health and safety. What did surprise Court-watchers, however, was the fact that the Court majority used the *Smith* case to announce a new interpretation of the First Exercise Clause that would apply to all such claims, even though that question had not been formally presented by the case or briefed by the parties.[41]

If a law is neutral toward religion and generally applicable, the Court said, it "need not be justified by a compelling governmental interest even if the law has the incidental effect of burdening a particular religious practice."[42] Applying the compelling interest test to all free exercise claims would "court[] anarchy," the Court said.[43] "[P]recisely because we value and protect . . . religious divergence, we cannot afford the luxury of deeming *presumptively invalid*, as applied to the religious objector, every regulation of conduct that does not protect an interest of the highest order."[44]

A law is not neutral toward religion if it targets faith, either overtly or covertly.[45] A law is not generally applicable if it restricts only conduct that is religiously motivated or if it fails to prohibit a similar amount of nonreligious conduct that endangers the state's interests in the same way the religiously motivated conduct does.[46] Such a shift in constitutional doctrine had costs, but those costs were justified, the Court said:

It may fairly be said that leaving accommodation to the political process will place at a relative disadvantage those religious practices that are not widely engaged in; but that unavoidable consequence of democratic government must be preferred to a system in which each conscience is a law unto itself or in which judges weigh the social importance of all laws against the centrality of all religious beliefs.[47]

In an opinion concurring only in the judgment that Smith and Black should lose their case, Justice O'Connor said the Court's ruling "dramatically departs from well settled First Amendment jurisprudence, appears unnecessary to resolve the question presented, and is incompatible with our Nation's fundamental commitment to individual religious liberty."[48] The compelling interest test should have been applied, O'Connor insisted:

> To say that a person's right to free exercise has been burdened, of course, does not mean that he has an absolute right to engage in the conduct. Under our established First Amendment jurisprudence, we have recognized that the freedom to act, unlike the freedom to believe, cannot be absolute. Instead, we have respected both the First Amendment's express textual mandate and the governmental interest in regulation of conduct by requiring the Government to justify any substantial burden on religiously motivated conduct by a compelling state interest and by means narrowly tailored to achieve that interest.[49]

In another passionate opinion, Justices Blackmun, Brennan, and Marshall dissented from the judgment and also from the interpretation of the Free Exercise Clause the Court majority announced in *Smith*. Justice Blackmun said:

> [The majority's] distorted view of our precedents leads [it] to conclude that strict scrutiny of a state law burdening the free exercise of religion is a "luxury" that a well-ordered society cannot afford, and that the repression of minority religions is an "unavoidable consequence of democratic government." I do not believe the Founders thought their dearly bought freedom from religious persecution a "luxury," but an essential element of liberty— and they could not have thought religious intolerance "unavoidable," for they drafted the Religion Clauses precisely in order to avoid that intolerance.[50]

When the Court announced the *Smith* decision, a coalition of religious freedom advocates of different religious and political stripes condemned the ruling.[51] The coalition included representatives of religious communities as well as advocacy groups spanning the political spectrum, from the American Civil Liberties Union to Pat Robertson's American Center for Law and Justice. The Baptist Joint Committee for Religious Liberty (BJC) chaired the association, which became known as the Coalition for the Free Exercise of Religion.[52]

Coalition members often disagreed about which party should prevail in free exercise cases. But they agreed on the standard by which such cases should be evaluated—the compelling interest test. This group of advocates was shocked that the Court had abandoned the compelling interest standard and done so abruptly. The coalition believed the Court's ruling would undermine the right to free exercise generally and religious minorities' free exercise rights particularly. When the Court denied their request to rehear the case, coalition members began to discuss federal and state legislation that might respond to the *Smith* ruling.[53]

Congress Seeks to Fill the Gap: The Religious Freedom Restoration Act and the Religious Land Use and Institutionalized Persons Act

The coalition that was outraged by the Supreme Court's decision in *Smith* ultimately came together around amendments to the American Indian Religious Freedom Act (AIRFA)[54] and the federal Religious Freedom Restoration Act (RFRA). AIRFA, which Congress approved by a voice vote, declared that Native Americans' use, possession, or transportation of peyote for "bona fide traditional ceremonial purposes in connection with the practice of a traditional Indian religion is lawful, and shall not be prohibited by the United States or any State."[55]

RFRA also brought together a bipartisan group of leaders in Congress, including Senators Orrin Hatch (R-UT) and Edward Kennedy (D-MA) and Representatives Lamar Smith (R-TX) and Jerrold Nadler (D-NY). The act passed by a nearly unanimous margin, and President Clinton signed the bill into law in a Rose Garden ceremony on November 16, 1993. RFRA required the government—whether federal, state, or local—to justify any substantial burden it placed on a person's religious exercise with a narrowly tailored compelling government interest.[56] In other words, it required application of the compelling interest test through statutory law without "creat[ing] . . . new rights for any religious practice or for any potential litigant."[57] Congress noted that it expected courts considering RFRA claims to "look to free exercise cases decided prior to *Smith* for guidance."[58]

Four years later, however, the Supreme Court struck back. In an opinion written by Justice Anthony Kennedy, the Court found that Congress lacked the power to apply RFRA to states and localities.[59] RFRA still applied to the actions of the federal government, but there was no longer any federal law that would subject states and localities to the compelling interest test when their neutral and generally applicable actions substantially burdened religious exercise. Some states had their own state RFRAs, or they interpreted their state constitutions in ways that provided a high degree of protection for free exercise rights, but other states lacked both.[60]

The Court's ruling in *City of Boerne v. Flores* prompted the RFRA coalition to reconvene to see if it could come together around successor legislation. The coalition found it could not. Since the *Smith* decision, part of the coalition had become increasingly concerned that laws like RFRA would be used to undermine other civil rights protections. This subset of the coalition was initially concerned that RFRA would be used to seek exceptions from laws prohibiting discrimination on the basis of marital status, and they feared that this pattern would eventually undermine emerging civil rights protections for gays, lesbians, bisexuals, and transgender individuals.

To these civil rights advocates, a case decided in 1994, *Swanner v. Anchorage Equal Rights Commission*, served as a warning sign. The *Swanner* case involved a business that managed certain rental properties in Alaska. The owner of the business, Tom Swanner, refused to rent property to unmarried cohabitating couples due to his religious beliefs. The state of Alaska sued the business for violating a state law prohibiting housing discrimination on the basis of marital status. Swanner responded by asserting a RFRA defense. RFRA required that he be exempted from the state prohibition on marital status discrimination, Swanner said. The Alaska Supreme Court held that RFRA did not affect the outcome of the case because compelling state interests supported the prohibition on marital status discrimination.[61] According to the court,

> The most effective tool the state has for combatting discrimination is to prohibit discrimination; these laws do exactly that. Consequently, the means are narrowly tailored and there is no less restrictive alternative.[62]

Swanner asked the U.S. Supreme Court to hear the case, but the Court declined to do so.

Justice Thomas, however, wrote an opinion dissenting from the Court's decision not to hear the case.[63] In his dissent, Thomas said he was "quite skeptical that Alaska's asserted interest in preventing discrimination on the basis of marital status is 'compelling' enough" to meet the RFRA test.[64] Justice Thomas cited the Court's decision in the *Bob Jones University* case, where the Court said there was a compelling interest in eradicating racial discrimination in education due to a firm national policy against such discrimination. "[T]here is surely no 'firm national policy' against marital status discrimination in housing decisions," Thomas said.[65] The state of Alaska treated married couples more favorably than unmarried couples in several instances, and the federal Fair Housing Act does not prohibit marital status discrimination, he noted. Thomas concluded:

> If, despite affirmative discrimination by Alaska on the basis of marital status and a complete absence of any national policy against such discrimination, the State's asserted interest in this case is allowed to qualify as a "compelling" interest—that is, a "paramount" interest, an interest "of the highest order"—then I am at a loss to know what asserted governmental interests are not compelling. The decision of the Alaska Supreme Court drains the word *compelling* of any meaning and seriously undermines the protection for exercise of religion that Congress so emphatically mandated in RFRA.[66]

Some members of the RFRA coalition welcomed Justice Thomas' opinion. For others, Justice Thomas' opinion caused concern: when they backed RFRA, they did not intend for a rental business to be able to claim RFRA's protections, much less that RFRA might require an exemption from civil rights laws. The *Swanner* case, and others like it, suggested that religious objectors to marriage between individuals of the same sex would soon make similar RFRA claims when they were charged with violating laws against discrimination on the basis of sexual orientation.

Under these circumstances, it became impossible for the coalition to unite behind broad successor legislation to RFRA. The coalition was able to come together, however, around more modest legislation known as the Religious Land Use and Institutionalized Persons Act (RLUIPA).[67] RLUIPA binds government at all levels—federal, state, and local—and applies the compelling interest test and other free exercise protections in two specific areas: land use matters and situations in which the government institutionalizes persons, like prisons, state hospitals, and immigrant detention centers. In such cases, the act says, the government cannot place a substantial burden on religious exercise without justifying that burden by a narrowly tailored compelling governmental interest.

RLUIPA also prohibits the government from imposing land use requirements in ways that treat religious assemblies on less than equal terms than nonreligious assemblies. Additionally, totally excluding or unreasonably limiting religious bodies from a jurisdiction is prohibited. The act continues to provide robust protections for congregations that are zoned out of particular jurisdictions or subjected to onerous regulation in order to expand their worship sites. RLUIPA also has helped to ensure that prisoners can practice their faith in ways that do not undermine prison safety and security.[68]

Some states have enacted their own state RFRAs in the wake of the *City of Boerne* decision. Efforts to do so in recent years have become fraught, however, especially when the language of such measures differs from the language used in the federal RFRA or when advances in protecting LGBT equality seem to have been the trigger for such measures.

The RFRA coalition also splintered over the issue of whether for-profit corporations could invoke RFRA's protections. That issue became front-page news years later when for-profit corporations asserted RFRA claims to support their refusals to comply with the Affordable Care Act's requirement that most employers' health plans offer cost-free contraception coverage, often called the "contraception mandate." Challenges to the contraception mandate ultimately made their way to the U.S. Supreme Court. Given the importance and complexity of these cases, some historical background is required.

Burwell v. Hobby Lobby Stores, Inc.—and Beyond

As passed by Congress in 2010, the Affordable Care Act (ACA) generally requires employer-sponsored health plans to cover preventive services without cost sharing.[69] The ACA provision mandates coverage of women's preventive services as defined by the Health Resources and Services Administration (HRSA), a division of the Department of Health and Human Services (HHS). HRSA asked the Institute of Medicine (IOM), a division of the National Academy of Sciences, to recommend the kinds of women's preventive services that should be covered.[70] Based on IOM's recommendation, such services include comprehensive breastfeeding support and counseling; well-woman visits; folic acid supplements; mammograms; anemia and osteoporosis screenings; and all contraceptives approved by the FDA. Preventive services do not include, however, any drugs the FDA has determined to be abortifacients.[71]

In 2011, three federal agencies adopted an exceedingly narrow definition of the religious organizations that would be exempt from the ACA's requirement that most employers provide their employees with cost-free contraception coverage. To be exempt, religious organizations had to meet *all* of the following criteria: (1) have the inculcation of religious values as their purpose; (2) primarily employ persons who shared their religious tenets; (3) primarily serve persons who shared their religious tenets; and (4) be a house of worship or closely associated body, a convention or association of churches, or a religious order.[72] These requirements could have had the effect of pressuring religious groups to violate a basic tenet of their faith—serving all people, no matter their faith, background, or beliefs. Also, this policy ignored the fact that religious organizations that were not houses of worship or closely associated bodies—like religiously affiliated schools and charities—had the same sincere religious objections to the contraception mandate.

At President Barack Obama's direction, the agencies subsequently broadened this exemption. Revised regulations exempted all houses of worship and other closely affiliated entities from these obligations and also "effectively exempted" other religiously affiliated nonprofits.[73] Religiously affiliated entities that raised religious objections to contraception coverage did not have to contract, arrange, pay, or refer for contraception coverage for their employees. At the same time, the federal government required insurers or third-party administrators (TPAs) for plans of objecting religiously affiliated organizations to provide such coverage to their female employees. The rules required objecting entities either to submit a form to their insurers or TPAs or to register their objections with HHS. HHS would then notify the relevant insurer or TPA of its obligations under federal law to provide cost-free contraception coverage to women working for objecting employers. This arrangement became known as the "accommodation."[74]

For-profit corporations were ineligible for these exemptions, prompting some businesses to sue. Hobby Lobby Stores and Conestoga Wood Specialties, two such businesses, objected to the contraception mandate because certain forms of contraception may prevent the implantation of a fertilized egg, which they believe constitutes abortion. Both are closely held corporations that are owned by families who oppose abortion and emphasize the religious character of their work. Conestoga has 950 employees, and Hobby Lobby has more than 13,000 employees across five hundred stores.[75] When these businesses were denied an exemption from the mandate, they sued the federal government under RFRA and the Free Exercise Clause. Lower courts came to conflicting conclusions about whether for-profit corporations could claim RFRA's protections, and the Supreme Court agreed to hear the case to resolve that conflict, among others.

In 2014, the Supreme Court ruled in favor of the businesses under RFRA by a vote of 5-4. Writing for the Court, Justice Alito first found that the businesses were persons under RFRA and that their religious exercise had been substantially burdened by the mandate. Assuming that the government had a compelling interest in requiring businesses to comply with the mandate, the Court nonetheless found that the government could advance that interest in a way that was less restrictive of the business owners' religious beliefs and practices. The government could make the accommodation it offered religiously affiliated nonprofits available to closely held businesses that had religious objections to the mandate. That way, the objecting businesses also would not have to contract, arrange, pay, or refer for contraception coverage for their employees. At the same time, insurers or TPAs for plans of objecting businesses would provide such coverage to their female employees.

Beyond its decision on the merits, the Court drew some broad and controversial conclusions about RFRA. Even though the Court said these conclusions
were not essential to its ruling, it is worth quoting some relevant passages from
the majority and dissenting opinions at length.[76]

Rather than *restoring* the compelling interest test as it was used prior to the
Smith decision, the Act *remade* that test, according to Justice Alito. The Court
pointed, for example, to an amendment to RFRA made in 2000, describing
it as "an obvious effort to effect a complete separation from First Amendment
case law . . . ."[77] The Court majority said:

> That amendment deleted the prior reference to the First Amendment, and
> neither HHS nor the principal dissent can explain why Congress did this
> if it wanted to tie RFRA coverage tightly to the specific holdings of our
> pre-*Smith* free-exercise cases. Moreover, . . . the amendment went further,
> providing that the exercise of religion "shall be construed in favor of a broad
> protection of religious exercise, to the maximum extent permitted by the
> terms of this chapter and the Constitution." It is simply not possible to read
> these provisions as restricting the concept of the "exercise of religion" to
> those practices specifically addressed in our pre-*Smith* decisions.[78]

The dissenters provided a vigorous response to these arguments. "Congress
intended only to restore, not to scrap or alter, the balancing test as this Court
had applied it pre-*Smith*."[79] Justice Ginsburg explained:

> RFRA's purpose is specific and written into the statute itself. The Act was
> crafted to "restore the compelling interest test as set forth in *Sherbert v.
> Verner*, 374 U. S. 398 (1963) and *Wisconsin v. Yoder*, 406 U. S. 205 (1972)
> and to guarantee its application in all cases where free exercise of religion is
> substantially burdened." The legislative history is correspondingly emphatic
> on RFRA's aim. In line with this restorative purpose, Congress expected
> courts considering RFRA claims to "look to free exercise cases decided
> prior to *Smith* for guidance." In short, the Act reinstates the law as it was
> prior to *Smith*, without "creat[ing] . . . new rights for any religious practice
> or for any potential litigant." Given the Act's moderate purpose, it is hardly
> surprising that RFRA's enactment in 1993 provoked little controversy.[80]

On behalf of the dissenters, Justice Ginsburg also recounted and rebutted
other arguments the Court majority had made:

> Despite these authoritative indications, the Court sees RFRA as a bold
> initiative departing from, rather than restoring, pre-*Smith* jurisprudence.
> To support its conception of RFRA as a measure detached from this Court's
> decisions, one that sets a new course, the Court points first to the Religious
> Land Use and Institutionalized Persons Act of 2000 (RLUIPA), which

altered RFRA's definition of the term "exercise of religion." RFRA, as originally enacted, defined that term to mean "the exercise of religion under the First Amendment to the Constitution." As amended by RLUIPA, RFRA's definition now includes "any exercise of religion, whether or not compelled by, or central to, a system of religious belief." That definitional change, according to the Court, reflects "an obvious effort to effect a complete separation from First Amendment case law."

The Court's reading is not plausible. RLUIPA's alteration clarifies that courts should not question the centrality of a particular religious exercise. But the amendment in no way suggests that Congress meant to expand the class of entities qualified to mount religious accommodation claims, nor does it relieve courts of the obligation to inquire whether a government action substantially burdens a religious exercise.

Next, the Court highlights RFRA's requirement that the government, if its action substantially burdens a person's religious observance, must demonstrate that it chose the least restrictive means for furthering a compelling interest. "[B]y imposing a least-restrictive-means test," the Court suggests, RFRA "went beyond what was required by our pre-*Smith* decisions." But as RFRA's statements of purpose and legislative history make clear, Congress intended only to restore, not to scrap or alter, the balancing test as this Court had applied it pre-*Smith*. And the view that the pre-*Smith* test included a "least restrictive means" requirement had been aired in testimony before the Senate Judiciary Committee by experts on religious freedom. Our decision in *City of Boerne*, it is true, states that the least restrictive means requirement "was not used in the pre-Smith jurisprudence RFRA purported to codify." As just indicated, however, that statement does not accurately convey the Court's pre-*Smith* jurisprudence.[81]

The majority and dissenters also debated whether *United States v. Lee* was relevant and whether requiring the government to pay the costs of providing the contraceptives to which the businesses objected was a less restrictive alternative.[82] They sparred over the majority's pointed refusal to say whether the accommodation that was extended to these businesses was valid in other contexts.[83] Soon enough, the Court agreed to entertain challenges by certain nonprofit religious entities to the accommodation under RFRA.

After oral argument of these nonprofit cases in 2016, the Court asked the parties for supplemental briefing. The Court wanted to know whether contraception coverage could be provided to female employees of objecting employers through their insurers without those employers having to submit any notice of their objections, whether to the government, their insurers, or

TPAs.[84] After receiving those briefs, the Supreme Court expressed no views on the merits of the case but remanded it to the lower courts for further consideration, noting that the parties should have "an opportunity to arrive at an approach going forward that accommodates petitioners' religious exercise while at the same time ensuring that women covered by petitioners' health plans 'receive full and equal health coverage, including contraceptive coverage.'"[85] The cases returned to the lower courts, where the litigants explored potential avenues for settlement. In January 2017, the Obama administration noted that it could not find a resolution of the issues at that time that would satisfy the various interests at stake.[86]

On May 4, 2017, President Trump signed an executive order directing the Departments of Health and Human Services, Labor, and Treasury to "consider issuing amended regulations, consistent with applicable law, to address conscience-based objections to the preventive care mandate" of the ACA.[87] In November 2018, the agencies published final regulations that were responsive to that executive order.[88] The regulations retain the exemption and accommodation described above as an option for objecting employers, but they also create broad new exemptions. Any nongovernmental employer that objects to providing contraception coverage for *religious* reasons is exempted. And any nongovernmental employer, other than publicly traded for-profit companies, that objects to providing contraception coverage for *moral* reasons is exempted. In sum, the new regulations allow all nonprofit and closely held for-profit employers to refuse to offer contraceptive coverage due to objections based on religious beliefs or moral convictions, while publicly traded for-profit companies can also refuse to provide such coverage due to objections based on religious beliefs.[89]

The new federal policy differs from previous policy, therefore, in four key ways. First, the new rules greatly expand the types of employers that are excused from the contraception coverage requirements. Under the previous policy, houses of worship, religiously affiliated nonprofits, and closely held businesses did not have to contract, arrange, pay, or refer for contraception coverage for their employees. Under the new rules, virtually any employer can exempt themselves from the requirements, including publicly traded businesses that assert a religious objection to providing contraception coverage. Second, while the previous policy only recognized *religious* objections to providing contraception coverage, the new rule states that *moral* objections are equally valid in many cases. Third, employers can invoke the exemptions without filling out any form, undergoing any government scrutiny, or making any special notification of their employees. Finally, while the previous policy ensured that almost all women working for objecting employers would get cost-free contraception coverage from either an insurer or a TPA, the government does not do so under the new rules. A variety of parties challenged these new rules in court, and that litigation continues.[90]

Religious Freedom and LGBT Rights: *Masterpiece Cakeshop v. Colorado Civil Rights Commission*

When the U.S. Supreme Court agreed to hear *Masterpiece Cakeshop v. Colorado Civil Rights Commission*, the Court appeared to be poised to tackle another prominent conflict regarding religious objections to legal requirements.[91] Ultimately, however, the Court sidestepped most of those issues.

In July 2012, Charlie Craig, David Mullins, and Deborah Munn (Craig's mother) visited Masterpiece Cakeshop in Lakewood, Colorado, and met with Jack Phillips, the owner of the bakery. Craig and Mullins asked Phillips to create a wedding cake that they could use at their wedding reception. At the time, the state of Colorado did not recognize same-sex marriages, so the couple planned to marry in Massachusetts and then host a reception for friends and family in Denver. Phillips told Charlie Craig and David Mullins that he did not create wedding cakes for same-sex weddings. Phillips did offer, however, to sell the couple any other baked goods from his store.

Mullins and Craig promptly left the bakery without discussing any details regarding the cake they requested. The next day, Deborah Munn called Phillips to ask why he had refused to make a wedding cake for her son and his fiancé. Phillips informed Munn that the refusal was based on his religious beliefs and the fact that Colorado did not (at the time) recognize same-sex marriages.

Craig and Mullins subsequently filed charges with the Colorado Civil Rights Division, alleging discrimination on the basis of sexual orientation in violation of the Colorado Anti-Discrimination Act (CADA).[92] CADA prohibits places of public accommodation, including business like Masterpiece that are open to the public, from denying "the full and equal enjoyment" of the "goods, services, facilities, privileges, advantages or accommodations" they provide to individuals or groups because of their race, creed, color, sex, sexual orientation, marital status, national origin, or ancestry. CADA specifically states that "a church, synagogue, mosque, or other place that is principally used for religious purposes" is not a public accommodation.

The Colorado Civil Rights Division found probable cause that Masterpiece had violated CADA, and an administrative law judge subsequently ruled in favor of Craig and Mullins. The Colorado Civil Rights Commission then held public hearings to consider the case. Phillips told the commission that he did not violate CADA. If the commission nonetheless found that he did, Phillips argued he was entitled to an exemption from CADA under the First

Amendment's Free Speech and Free Exercise Clauses. The commission found that Masterpiece had violated CADA and that Phillips had no valid First Amendment claims. The business needed to alter the company's policies in order to comply with the law and train staff accordingly, the commission said. Masterpiece must also file compliance reports describing measures taken to comply with CADA and document all instances in which patrons are denied service and the reasons such denials.

The Colorado Court of Appeals reviewed the case *de novo*, meaning the court heard the case as if none of the prior proceedings or determinations had taken place.[93] Phillips reiterated his position that he refused to create the wedding cake due to his opposition to same-sex marriage, not due to any opposition to individuals based on their sexual orientation. Masterpiece was drawing a line at conduct, not status, Phillips asserted. The court did not find that claim persuasive, citing the Supreme Court's earlier rejection of such a conduct-status distinction.[94] The Colorado court also noted that Masterpiece's willingness to provide other baked goods to Craig and Mullins "does not permit it to refuse services to Craig and Mullins that it otherwise offers to the general public."[95]

In a footnote, the court discussed the fact that three other bakeries had refused to make and sell two Bible-shaped cakes to a customer, William Jack, with inscriptions such as "Homosexuality is a detestable sin. Leviticus 18:2."[96] The court cited the Civil Rights Division's finding that the bakeries' refusal to do so was not based on the customer's religion. "The Division found that the bakeries did not refuse the patron's request because of his creed, but rather because of the offensive nature of the requested message."[97]

Masterpiece violated CADA, the Colorado Court of Appeals concluded, and neither the First Amendment nor state law exempted the bakery from CADA. "We conclude that the Commission's order merely requires that Masterpiece not discriminate against potential customers in violation of CADA and that such conduct, even if compelled by the government, is not sufficiently expressive to warrant First Amendment protections," the court said.[98] The court assumed without deciding that a business can make a free exercise claim under the First Amendment. Still, the court also found that CADA was a neutral law of general applicability and thus did not violate the First Amendment's Free Exercise Clause. The Colorado court, therefore, affirmed the commission's decision.

By a margin of seven to two, the U.S. Supreme Court reversed the Colorado court's judgment in a narrowly written opinion. The Colorado Civil Rights Commission did not consider Masterpiece's claims "with the religious neutrality that the Constitution requires," the Court said.[99] In an opinion written by Justice Anthony Kennedy, the Court majority criticized comments made by certain Colorado commissioners, comments that were never retracted or censured during the proceedings.[100] In particular, the Court focused on the following comments by one commissioner during a public hearing. The commissioner said:

> I would also like to reiterate what we said in the hearing or the last meeting. Freedom of religion and religion has been used to justify all kinds of discrimination throughout history, whether it be slavery, whether it be the holocaust, whether it be—I mean, we—we can list hundreds of situations where freedom of religion has been used to justify discrimination. And to me it is one of the most despicable pieces of rhetoric that people can use to—to use their religion to hurt others.[101]

Justice Kennedy responded:

> To describe a man's faith as "one of the most despicable pieces of rhetoric that people can use" is to disparage his religion in at least two distinct ways: by describing it as despicable, and also by characterizing it as merely rhetorical—something insubstantial and even insincere. The commissioner even went so far as to compare Phillips' invocation of his sincerely held religious beliefs to defenses of slavery and the Holocaust. This sentiment is inappropriate for a Commission charged with the solemn responsibility of fair and neutral enforcement of Colorado's antidiscrimination law—a law that protects against discrimination on the basis of religion as well as sexual orientation.[102]

The Court also contrasted the treatment of Jack Phillips by the Colorado Civil Rights Division with the division's treatment of the other bakers who refused to create cakes with images and religious text that opposed marriage between individuals of the same sex. In Phillips' case, the division found that any message the cake would communicate would be attributed to the customer, not to the baker, while saying the reverse would be true in the other cases. Also, the division found that the bakers' willingness to create and sell other baked products to the client who opposed same-sex marriage was legally significant, while Phillips' statement that he would sell the gay couple other baked goods did not matter. The commission, therefore, did not carry out its constitutional duty under the Free Exercise Clause "to proceed in a manner neutral toward and tolerant of Phillips' religious beliefs," the Court found.[103]

At the same time, the Court repeatedly reaffirmed the rights of gay and lesbian people. While "religious and philosophical objections are protected," the Court said, "it is a general rule that such objections do not allow business owners and other actors in the economy and in society to deny protected persons equal access to goods and services under a neutral and generally applicable public accommodations law."[104] To justify this proposition, the Court cited a 1968 decision in which it rejected religious justifications for a business' refusal to serve African Americans. In briefs submitted to the Court, the parties had hotly contested whether this Court precedent was relevant. The Court concluded its opinion by stating:

> The outcome of cases like this in other circumstances must await further elaboration in the courts, all in the context of recognizing that these disputes must be resolved with tolerance, without undue disrespect to sincere religious beliefs, and without subjecting gay persons to indignities when they seek goods and services in an open market.[105]

While the Court majority did not consider some of the key issues presented by the case, other justices did so in their separate opinions. A debate between Justices Kagan and Gorsuch demonstrates how differently some justices see certain relevant issues.

In her concurring opinion, which Justice Breyer joined, Justice Kagan focused on the Court's concern about discrepancies between the government's treatment of Masterpiece and its treatment of the other bakeries. "What ma[de] the state agencies' [differing standards for the bakers' cases] yet more disquieting is that a proper basis for distinguishing the cases was available—in fact, was obvious," Kagan said.[106] The bakers who refused to decorate cakes with images and text that opposed same-sex marriage did not violate CADA because they would not have made such cakes for *anyone*. In other words, they did not refuse their customer's requests because of his religion, "but instead treated him in the same way they would have treated anyone else—just as CADA requires."[107] In contrast, Kagan wrote, Masterpiece denied the request of Craig and Mullins for a wedding cake, even though it would have made such a cake for an opposite-sex couple. "A vendor can choose the product he sells, but not the customers he serves—no matter the reason."[108]

Justice Gorsuch's concurring opinion, in which Justice Alito joined, saw these matters quite differently. Gorsuch noted that Phillips said "he would have refused to create a cake celebrating a same-sex marriage for any customer, regardless of his or her sexual orientation."[109] Justice Gorsuch cited the fact, for example, that Phillips would have refused to sell a wedding cake to Charlie Craig's mother, if the cake was to be used to celebrate a marriage between individuals of the same sex.[110] Thus, Phillips and the bakeries that would not make and sell cakes with anti-same-sex marriage messages did the same thing—they "refused service to persons who bore a statutorily protected trait (religious faith or sexual orientation). But in both cases the bakers refused service intending only to honor a personal conviction[,]" not because of the customers' protected characteristic. Thus, Justice Gorsuch concluded, "[i]n both cases, it was the kind of cake, not the kind of customer, that mattered to the bakers."[111] Even without words on it, a wedding cake conveys a message, Gorsuch said. That is what Phillips believes, and the government must take him at his word. The government erred, Gorsuch said, by not treating these two types of cases the same way.

Dividing wedding cakes into "same-sex wedding cakes" and other wedding cakes was wrong, Justice Kagan retorted. The cake that Craig and Mullins requested from Masterpiece "was simply a wedding cake—one that (like other standard wedding cakes) is suitable for use at same-sex and opposite-sex weddings alike."[112] The cake does not become something different because Phillips views its sale to certain customers as religiously significant. "As this Court has long held, and reaffirms today," Justice Kagan wrote, "a vendor cannot escape a public accommodations law because his religion disapproves selling a product to a group of customers, whether defined by sexual orientation, race, sex, or other protected trait."[113]

Justice Clarence Thomas, with whom Justice Gorsuch joined, wrote a separate opinion concurring in part and concurring in the Court's judgment. Thomas took issue with the lower court's conclusion that Phillips was not engaged in expressive conduct and thus was not protected by the First Amendment's Free Speech clause. Justice Thomas closed his opinion with the following warning about the Court's decision in *Obergefell v. Hodges*, where the Court ruled that the Constitution protected marriage equality:

> In *Obergefell*, I warned that the Court's decision would "inevitabl[y] . . . come into conflict" with religious liberty, "as individuals . . . are confronted with demands to participate in and endorse civil marriages between same-sex couples." This case proves that the conflict has already emerged. Because the Court's decision vindicates Phillips' right to free exercise, it seems that religious liberty has lived to fight another day. But, in future cases, the freedom of speech could be essential to preventing *Obergefell* from being used to "stamp out every vestige of dissent" and "vilify Americans who are unwilling to assent to the new orthodoxy." If that freedom is to maintain its vitality, reasoning like the Colorado Court of Appeals' must be rejected.[114]

Two justices dissented from the ruling: Justices Ginsburg and Sotomayor. Justice Ginsburg, with Justice Sotomayor joining, argued that the Supreme Court should have affirmed the lower court's decision in favor of the same-sex couple. Regarding the comments of the Colorado commissioners, Ginsburg said:

Whatever one may think of the statements in historical context, I see no reason why the comments of one or two Commissioners should be taken to overcome Phillips' refusal to sell a wedding cake to Craig and Mullins. The proceedings involved several layers of independent decisionmaking, of which the Commission was but one. First, the Division had to find probable cause that Phillips violated CADA. Second, the [administrative law judge] entertained the parties' cross-motions for summary judgment. Third, the Commission heard Phillips' appeal. Fourth, after the Commission's ruling, the Colorado Court of Appeals considered the case *de novo*. What prejudice infected the determinations of the adjudicators in the case before and after the Commission? The Court does not say. Phillips' case is thus far removed from the only precedent upon which the Court relies, *Church of Lukumi Babalu Aye, Inc. v. Hialeah*, 508 U.S. 520 (1993), where the government action that violated a principle of religious neutrality implicated a sole decisionmaking body, the city council.[115]

Justice Ginsburg agreed with Justice Kagan that Justice Gorsuch was wrong to say that Phillips and the other bakers should be treated the same way. "[W]hat critically differentiates" these cases, Ginsburg said, was "the role the customer's 'statutorily protected trait' played in the denial of service."[116] Justice Ginsburg explained: "Change Craig and Mullins' sexual orientation (or sex), and [Jack] Phillips would have provided the cake. Change [William] Jack's religion, and the bakers would have been no more willing to comply with his request."[117] Phillips discriminated "*because of* sexual orientation," whereas the other bakers "did not discriminate *because of* religious belief."[118] Thus, Ginsburg said, the commission properly found discrimination in one case but not the other.

A final note on the *Masterpiece Cakeshop* case. In the first two sentences of his concurring opinion in the case, Justice Gorsuch went out of his way to flag the fact that the *Employment Division v. Smith* decision "remains controversial in many quarters."[119] This statement and another like it suggest that Justices Thomas, Alito, Gorsuch, and Kavanaugh may be inclined to vote in favor of overruling *Smith* in an appropriate case. Moreover, with Justice Anthony Kennedy's retirement from the Court in July 2018, no justice who sat on the Court when *Smith* was decided remains on the bench.[120] Thus, the Court may be poised to reassess *Smith*.

RECOMMENDATIONS: THE FUTURE OF FREE EXERCISE

The Supreme Court's decision in *Employment Division v. Smith* failed to reckon adequately with the fact that free exercise can be badly damaged even by neutral and generally applicable laws and policies. Garb and grooming rules for military service members that are neutral and generally applicable, for example, can still have the effect of preventing Sikhs from being able to serve, depriving these Americans of the ability to exercise their faith and the United States of outstanding soldiers. Even if public school rules do not target students for their faith, rules that exclude students from athletic events if they refuse to wear a school uniform harm students who would like to play while wearing more modest attire for religious reasons.

A nation that claims to honor free exercise can and should do better. Stronger protections for free exercise shield the rights of conscience and also redound to the nation's benefit by ensuring that it can draw on the strengths of all of its citizens. At the same time, free exercise interests must be carefully balanced with other compelling concerns.

Especially in the current climate, getting these issues right is a formidable challenge. Navigating constitutional tensions is part of that challenge.[121] Weathering intense partisan and ideological headwinds is another. To safeguard free exercise rights, both in this perilous moment and far into the future, an approach must be sought that manages risks on all sides. The following suggestions are aimed at encouraging such an approach.

(1) Maintain religious neutrality when considering religious exemptions or accommodations.

When making decisions about exemptions or accommodations, the government must not "differentiate among bona fide faiths" by privileging any particular religion or singling out any faith for disadvantageous treatment.[122] Also, when considering whether to create a religious exemption, government officials should carefully avoid offering their opinions on the rightness or wrongness of the religious beliefs of individuals and institutions. Further, officials should never assume that religious beliefs and practices are insincere or simply a cloak for discrimination or hatred.[123] That does not mean the government must always grant requested religious exemptions or accommodations. It also does not mean that government officials cannot express their beliefs about what is right and wrong as a matter of secular policy. There is a difference between saying religious beliefs are wrong or merely a mask for bigotry and advocating for the application of certain civic values to policymaking or denying certain claims for religious exemptions pursuant to the requirements of applicable law.

(2) Take account of burdens a requested exemption or accommodation may impose on third parties.

The Supreme Court has said that the government must "take adequate account of the burdens a requested [religious] accommodation may impose on" people who do not benefit from the accommodation:[124] "Our decisions indicate that an accommodation must be measured so that it does not override other significant interests."[125] When religious exemptions have failed to strike an appropriate balance, the Supreme Court has invalidated them.[126]

It is important to note that the Supreme Court has upheld certain religious exemptions even when they negatively impact others. Conscientious objectors to combat have been excused from such duties, even though other Americans had to fight in their place, for example.[127] And the Court has upheld the ability of religious bodies to prefer employees of their own faith, no matter how much individuals of other faiths believe they are harmed by such decisions.[128]

In the Supreme Court's rulings on such employment matters, the Court took into account the weighty burden its decisions would place on the employees who were fired from their jobs for religious reasons, but it concluded that the strong countervailing interests at stake—the free exercise, autonomy, and self-definition of houses of worship and other religious affiliated entities—were core religious freedom concerns that outweighed those burdens.[129] Notably, these employment positions were within religious nonprofits, not commercial entities, and the positions were not supported by government aid. The nature of the entity requesting the exemption and the presence (or absence) of government aid are factors that should be considered when evaluating harm to third parties. As scholars have suggested, other factors that should be considered are the degree to which the third parties who would be harmed are specific and identifiable, the gravity of the harm, and whether there are secular exemptions from the relevant law or policy.[130]

Also, if an exemption would have the effect of depriving a third party of a government entitlement, that fact must be considered, even if the entitlement has only recently been established.[131] In the contraception mandate cases, some objecting employers argued that an exemption that would deprive their female employees of cost-free contraception coverage could not constitute an impermissible burden on those women because they would simply be back in the same place they would have been had the Affordable Care Act never been enacted. Such arguments should be rejected.[132]

(3) When determining what constitutes a "substantial burden" on religious exercise, leave room for legal judgment.

The first step of the RFRA test asks whether the government has substantially burdened the sincere exercise of faith.[133] Some argue that religious practices are substantially burdened whenever a sincere claimant suffers "substantial *religious* costs" if she or he does what the government requires and "substantial *secular* costs" if she or he does not.[134] Because courts are prohibited from answering religious questions, this approach limits them to addressing the sincerity of the believer and the legal penalties for noncompliance with a law or policy. As Professor Fred Gedicks has explained, determining sincerity and whether penalties for exercising faith are substantial seem like important tasks, but courts are understandably reluctant to question a religious person's sincerity, and laws and policies usually provide significant punishment for those who do not comply, meaning that they usually have "substantial secular costs." Therefore, "[a]s a practical matter," Gedicks says, "limiting review to sincerity and secular costs leaves the question of substantiality wholly to RFRA claimants."[135] Taking this approach basically means laws and policies are presumptively unconstitutional based solely on religious claimants' assertions.[136]

This approach is inconsistent with pre-*Smith* precedent and Congress' intent when it passed RFRA.[137] Congress added the modifier "substantial" to the word "burden" so that the government could make an objective evaluation of the substantiality of any burden on religious exercise as a legal matter.[138] As Professor Doug Laycock, the leading constitutional scholar who advocated for RFRA's passage, and the Baptist Joint Committee for Religious Liberty (BJC), the chair of the RFRA Coalition, have noted, the Supreme Court has found at times that there is "no legally cognizable burden on religion even though claimants sincerely believed there was such a burden."[139] Regarding congressional intent on this point, Professor Laycock and the BJC have observed:

> Congress did not discuss the meaning of substantial burden in any detail. But Congress clearly rejected absolute judicial deference to religious claimants. Congress intended the substantial-burden requirement to be a meaningful part of RFRA's "workable test for striking sensible balances between religious liberty and competing prior governmental interests." Absolute deference on substantial burden would effectively repeal half of RFRA's statutory design.[140]

Instead, courts can and must determine whether the law imposes a substantial burden on religious exercise as a legal matter.[141] Courts may do so by relying on secular law, including Supreme Court precedent.[142]

Courts cannot decide theological issues, but they can decide cases involving theological issues by relying on secular law.[143] Courts take a similar approach in cases involving the ministerial exception—they reserve a role for legal judgment in determining whether a person is a "minister" under the law.[144] Retaining a role for legal judgment on these issues is essential to safeguard both the rule of law and the political viability of laws like RFRA.[145]

(4) Clarify RFRA.

When it passed RFRA, Congress intended to restore the compelling interest test the Court had used prior to *Employment Division v. Smith*, not invent a new, more demanding compelling interest test.[146] All of the free exercise cases where the compelling interest test was employed, including *United States v. Lee*, are relevant when interpreting the Act.[147]

While the government has no proper role in determining theological issues, Congress inserted the word "substantial" before burden for a reason—to allow governmental decision-makers to use legal judgment in evaluating this standard.[148] Also, as outlined in Supreme Court precedent, the burden a religious exemption or accommodation may place on third parties (parties who are not the beneficiaries of religious exemptions) is a factor that must be considered.[149] Further, interpretation of RFRA's "least restrictive means" requirement[150] needs to closely track relevant pre-*Smith* precedent.[151]

When Congress passed RFRA, it noted that "the compelling interest test as set forth in prior Federal court rulings is a workable test for striking sensible balances between religious liberty and competing prior governmental interests."[152] Clarifications like these are needed to ensure that the same can be said of RFRA.[153]

(5) When Supreme Court precedent is cited to justify proposed expansions of religious exemptions, consider all relevant aspects of those decisions.

The Trump administration has recently proposed several expansions of religious exemptions and cited Supreme Court precedent to justify them. Take the example of the Department of Labor's (DOL) proposal for a major expansion of a religious exemption from federal contractors' nondiscrimination obligations.[154] To support this expansion, DOL points to Supreme Court precedent, including *Burwell v. Hobby Lobby*, *Trinity Lutheran Church v. Comer*, and *Masterpiece Cakeshop, Ltd. v. Colorado Civil Rights Commission*. These cases, however, neither mandate nor support DOL's proposed rule.

In *Trinity Lutheran*, for example, the Court held that a state policy that categorically disqualified churches and other religious organizations from receiving grants under its playground resurfacing program was invalid under the Free Exercise Clause. In other words, the Court addressed a policy that singled out religious bodies for special restrictions. It did not speak to policies that apply to both religious and nonreligious entities alike, such as the federal contracting executive order. In *Hobby Lobby*, the

Court held that the government had to make a religious accommodation available to a closely held for-profit entity that objected to the Affordable Care Act's contraception mandate. At the same time, however, the Court was careful to note that the impact on Hobby Lobby's employees would be "precisely zero" because others would extend cost-free contraception coverage to those employees.[155] If businesses like Hobby Lobby could make religion-based decisions to refuse to hire or fire individuals due to their faith or marriage to a person of the same sex, for example, the impact on prospective and current employees would not be "precisely zero." Further, the *Hobby Lobby* case did not involve federal funds, whereas DOL's religious exemption is for federal contractors. And unlike the *Masterpiece Cakeshop* case, there is no evidence that the prohibitions on employment discrimination in federal contracting stem from any bias against religion. These matters deserve attention, but DOL does not address any of them in its proposed rule.

(6) When evaluating requests for religious exemptions, recognize distinctions between businesses and nonprofits.

Exemptions for businesses can impact a much larger population than exemptions for nonprofits. Professor Tom Berg has calculated that "the religious non-profit sector covers perhaps 6–7 percent of jobs and wages, but the for-profit sector probably covers ten times that."[156] As Professor Berg also notes, the government has a stronger interest in ensuring that businesses do not get unfair commercial advantages over their competitors, and the state is justified in more readily presuming the sincerity of free-exercise claims by religious bodies over against commercial entities. Further, customers, and perhaps employees, are more apt to be surprised by businesses' religiously informed policies than they are by religiously informed policies of a house of worship, religious denomination or association, or religiously affiliated nonprofit.[157]

For all these reasons, businesses should be subject to careful analysis to determine if they are entitled to a religious exemption. When engaging in such a review, a range of factors should be considered. Such factors include whether the business has sincere religious objections; whether it is closely held or publicly traded;[158] whether it is large or small;[159] and whether, if granted, the requested exemption would have the effect of significantly burdening its employees or other third parties.

(7) In cases such as Masterpiece Cakeshop, *follow Justice Kagan's lead.*

In the *Masterpiece Cakeshop* case, Jack Phillips wanted to avoid making and selling cakes that he believes violate his religious convictions. Charlie Craig and David Mullins wanted to be able to buy a cake for their wedding without regard to their sexual orientation. Common-ground policy solutions certainly should be sought regarding such conflicts, and litigation should be carefully considered and sometimes avoided for prudential reasons.

Having said that, Justice Kagan took the right approach in the *Masterpiece Cakeshop* case. Kagan joined the Court majority in concluding that the Colorado Civil Rights Commission did not satisfy its obligation to maintain religious neutrality in this case. But Kagan also said there was a legitimate basis for distinguishing between *Masterpiece Cakeshop* and cases in which bakers refused to make cakes with messages on them that denounced marriage between individuals of the same sex. In the latter cases, the bakers would have turned away anyone who asked them to apply such messages to their goods. In the *Masterpiece Cakeshop* case, however, while Jack Phillips immediately turned away Craig and Mullins when they asked for a cake for their wedding, he would not have done so had a heterosexual couple made the same request. Thus, Justice Kagan said:

> Colorado can treat a baker who discriminates based on sexual orientation differently from a baker who does not discriminate on that or any other prohibited ground. But only, as the Court rightly says, if the State's decisions are not infected by religious hostility or bias.[160]

It is also worth noting that this approach protects bans on other forms of discrimination in public accommodations, such as bans on discrimination on the basis of race, religion, gender, and national origin. At Supreme Court oral argument in this case, a lawyer for Masterpiece Cakeshop conceded that allowing the business to refuse to provide some goods and services to couples of the same-sex would also allow businesses to refuse certain goods and services to potential customers based on their religion, gender, or national origin.[161]

Cases like these are fact-sensitive, and the *Masterpiece Cakeshop* case presents simply one of many fact patterns that may arise.[162] Further, the law on these issues is developing. Interested parties should continue to monitor cases in this area.

(8) Whenever feasible and appropriate, craft specific exemptions or accommodations from particular laws and policies rather than simply relying on RFRA's general standards.

Whenever feasible and appropriate, policymakers should insert specific religious exemptions within the particular laws or policies containing requirements that are objectionable to some for religious reasons. Religious exemptions from laws and policies on garb and grooming requirements that are applicable to military service members should be included in those laws and policies, for example. Such exemptions would spell out the latitude service members have to differ from those requirements due to their religious beliefs and practices. This approach will create much more certainty about how laws and policies will actually work rather than simply relying on RFRA's general standards.

(9) Seek win-win solutions.

Sometimes a free exercise interest is so strong that it must be upheld even when doing so is costly for other interests. The Supreme Court has held, for example, that synagogues must be permitted to hire rabbis, not Baptist preachers, no matter how upstanding those Baptists may be or how much they need a job. In other cases, however, both sides must be accommodated, even when it cannot be done to everyone's complete satisfaction. In still other cases, accommodating competing interests may be possible although not required. In such cases, win-win solutions should be sought. And in every case involving competing human rights claims, all claims should be evaluated rather than dismissed. Respect for the equal dignity of every individual requires such an approach.[163]

(10) Demand a fair hearing for free exercise claims.

Governmental decisions regarding free exercise do not, or should not, turn on whether Americans believe another person or entity's religious practices are praiseworthy, whether they align with a denomination's teachings, or whether they are in sync with a decision-maker's policy preferences. Such decisions should instead turn on whether applicable standards shield particular acts of conscience. Even Americans who disagree with a religious practice, or do not believe a free exercise claim should ultimately prevail, ought to support a fair and neutral hearing for sincere religious claims.

9

FAITH AND THE WORKPLACE

Respecting Religious Freedom in Employment

Title VII of the 1964 Civil Rights Act prohibits employers with fifteen or more employees from discriminating against any individual on the basis of race, color, religion, sex, or national origin. Employers cannot discriminate on these grounds in any aspect of employment, including hiring, compensation, promoting, or firing. Under Title VII, therefore, employers generally may not make employment decisions based on an employee's, or prospective employee's, faith or lack thereof. Employers also have an affirmative obligation to accommodate employees' religious beliefs, observance, and practice, unless they can demonstrate that doing so would impose an undue hardship on their businesses. The Supreme Court has defined "undue hardship" as anything that creates more than a *de minimis* cost for the employer.

The original draft of the 1964 Civil Rights Act would have exempted religious employers from all of Title VII's nondiscrimination requirements. The legislation was revised "to apply the bulk of Title VII's provisions to religious employers but still permit[] [religious employers] to employ individuals of a particular religion." Title VII's religious exemption basically allows religious organizations (including, but not limited to, houses of worship) to prefer employees (including, but not limited to, ministers) of their own faith. Title VII also contains a separate exemption for religiously affiliated educational institutions.

The First Amendment affords religious bodies full freedom to make employment decisions regarding their ministers. This "ministerial exception" flows from the First Amendment's protection for the independence of religious bodies from the state.

Because the First Amendment also applies to the governmental workplace, additional concerns are relevant in that context. Thus, the government must respect both the Free Exercise and the Establishment Clauses in the workplace. Governmental employers must ensure, for example, that they neither promote nor denigrate religion.

For the past few years, around 71 percent of Americans have said they support legislation that would protect LGBT individuals from discrimination in the workplace. Nonetheless, at the federal level and in some states, efforts to pass such legislation have not yet borne fruit. A key reason for this failure is the inability of the various sides to come to agreement on whether there should be religious exemptions in this kind of legislation and, if so, what such exemptions should look like.

Samantha Elauf applied for a job at an Abercrombie & Fitch store in Oklahoma when she was seventeen years old.[1] Ms. Elauf, a practicing Muslim, wore a head scarf to her job interview with the store's assistant manager, Heather Cooke.[2]

At the time Elauf applied for the job, she was unaware of Abercrombie & Fitch's "Look Policy." This policy requires employees to dress "in clothing and merchandise consistent with that sold in the store" and "prohibits 'caps' but does not mention any other head wear."[3]

Cooke, the assistant manager, believed Samantha Elauf was a good job candidate, but she was unsure whether Elauf could wear her head scarf while at work. Cooke told her superior, Randall Johnson, that Ms. Elauf wore the scarf for religious reasons and asked whether Elauf should be hired. Johnson said Cooke should not hire Elauf because her head scarf conflicted with the store's Look Policy.[4]

Based on this guidance, Cooke did not hire Ms. Elauf. Samantha later learned through a friend who worked at the store that she did not get the job because of her head covering.[5]

Elauf subsequently contacted the Equal Employment Opportunity Commission (EEOC), and the agency sued Abercrombie & Fitch on her behalf, alleging that the company had violated Title VII of the 1964 Civil Rights Act.

Title VII is a landmark civil rights law prohibiting religious discrimination in employment and requiring employers to provide reasonable accommodations for employees' religious practices.[6] The EEOC and Elauf won their case at the trial court level, only to see an appellate court reverse. They asked the Supreme Court to hear the case, and the Court agreed.

When the late Justice Scalia announced the Supreme Court's eight-to-one decision in favor of the EEOC and Elauf, he described it as a "really easy" case.[7] "An employer may not make an applicant's religious practice, confirmed or otherwise, a factor in employment decisions," the Court said.[8] The company's claim that a job applicant must demonstrate that the employer has "actual knowledge" of the applicant's need for a religious accommodation in order to prove intentional discrimination under Title VII was wrong. Instead, an applicant "need only show that h[er] need for an accommodation was a motivating factor in the employer's decision."[9] The Court also rejected Abercrombie's argument that its Look Policy did not treat religious practices any worse than similar secular practices. "Title VII does not demand mere neutrality with regard to religious practices," the Court explained.[10] "Rather, it gives them favored treatment, affirmatively obligating employers not 'to fail or refuse to hire or discharge any individual . . . because of such individual's' 'religious observance and practice.' "[11]

Contrast the approach of the United States to such issues with that of the European Union. Samira Achbita, a Muslim, was employed by a Belgium-based private business as a receptionist. When Achbita informed her employer that she intended to wear a head scarf during working hours, management said doing so would violate company policy. A company rule prohibited employees from "wearing visible signs of their political, philosophical or religious beliefs [in the workplace] and/or from engaging in any observance of such beliefs."[12]

Achbita nevertheless wore a head scarf to work. The company fired her. Achbita then sued, claiming violations of the E.U.'s Employment Equality Directive requiring all E.U. member states to bar employers from discriminating on the basis of religion or belief.

In its ruling on the case, the E.U. Court of Justice said the company did not engage in direct discrimination against Achbita. The company's rule was "appropriate for the purpose of ensuring that a policy of neutrality is properly applied, provided that that policy is genuinely pursued in a consistent and systematic manner."[13] If an ostensibly neutral rule nevertheless puts individuals of certain faiths at a disadvantage, the rule may constitute indirect discrimination, the Court of Justice said. Even policies like these can be justified, however, "by a legitimate aim, such as the pursuit by the employer, in its relations with its customers, of a policy of political, philosophical and religious neutrality, and the means of achieving that aim are appropriate and necessary . . . ."[14]

In the United States, company rules cannot make workplaces religion-free zones or treat people of faith, or of certain faiths, like second-class employees. A U.S. employer generally cannot refuse to hire, or fire, someone because they wear religious garb, while an E.U. employer may do so.

Workplace protections for religious freedom in the United States are not perfect, nor have they been perfectly interpreted and applied. Nonetheless, workplace protections rightly seek to ensure that people of all faiths, and of none, can compete for jobs on a level playing field and that employees do not have to choose between their professions and their religious identities and practices. Federal employment law also recognizes that the government must respect the autonomy of religious communities. The state must not interfere with a religious body's selection of its ministers, and religious employers must have the freedom to prefer members of their own faith throughout their operations.

Considering the ways in which Congress and the courts have vindicated, or sometimes failed to vindicate, such values fosters a deeper understanding of these rights and protections. An evaluation of how the federal legislative and judicial branches are managing tensions between competing goods in this area, including the tension between the autonomy of religious organizations and the applicability of various civil rights protections, sheds light on key issues confronting our country today.

Prohibiting Religious Discrimination

Title VII of the 1964 Civil Rights Act prohibits employers with fifteen or more employees from discriminating against any individual on the basis of race, color, religion, sex, or national origin.[15] Employers cannot discriminate on these grounds in any aspect of employment, including hiring, compensation, promoting, or firing. Under Title VII, therefore, employers generally cannot make employment decisions based on an employee's, or prospective employee's, faith or lack thereof. An employer may not treat employees, or applicants for employment, more or less favorably, for example, because they are or are not religious or because they participate or do not participate in religious activities.

An employer cannot assign an employee who wears a head scarf or a yarmulke or a necklace with a cross to a job that does not entail customer contact, due to actual or assumed customer preference.[16] Title VII prohibits employers from segregating employees in the workplace based on religion, including because of their religious garb and grooming practices.[17]

If the employer permits workers to keep personal books at their desk to read during breaks, the employer must permit employees to keep a Bible or Qur'an. If an employer allows employees to discuss non-work-related issues at the water cooler, the employer must allow employees to discuss religious issues. The employer generally must give employees access to a conference room for lunchtime Bible study if the employer allows employees to use that room at lunchtime for other non-work-related purposes.[18]

Employees can attempt to persuade their fellow employees to embrace their beliefs, including their religious beliefs, but employees must halt such attempts if a fellow employee asks them to stop or demonstrates in other ways that such overtures are unwanted.[19] Employees have the right to be free from a hostile work environment, including a workplace where religious discrimination, intimidation, or insults occur. Mere exposure to expression with which the employee disagrees, however, does not constitute exposure to a hostile work environment.[20] Supervisors have special responsibilities to ensure that employees' rights are respected.[21]

These basic rules apply to both governmental and nongovernmental workplaces. Because the First Amendment also applies to the governmental workplace, additional concerns are relevant in that context. The government must respect both the Free Exercise and the Establishment Clauses in the workplace. Governmental employers must ensure, for example, that they neither promote nor denigrate religion.

REQUIRING REASONABLE ACCOMMODATION OF RELIGIOUS PRACTICES

Title VII defines the term "religion" broadly to include "all aspects of religious observance and practice, as well as belief, unless an employer demonstrates that he is unable to reasonably accommodate an employee's or prospective employee's religious observance or practice without undue hardship on the conduct of the employer's business."[22] Thus, employers have an affirmative obligation to accommodate employees' religious beliefs, observance, and practice, so long as doing so would not impose an undue hardship on their operations.[23]

In 1977, the Supreme Court said neither Congress nor the EEOC had offered guidance on how the term "undue hardship" should be defined.[24] The Court, therefore, offered its own definition of the term, one that has proved to be controversial.

The case, known as *Trans World Airlines v. Hardison*, involved Larry Hardison, an employee of Trans World Airlines (TWA), who had begun to study the teachings of the Worldwide Church of God. One of the tenets of the faith is to observe the Sabbath by ceasing work from sunset Friday until sunset on Saturday. Hardison, therefore, began seeking time off from work in order to honor the Sabbath in this way. When Hardison and TWA could not come to agreement about his work schedule, Hardison was discharged for refusing to work his shift.[25]

The Court found that TWA's conduct did not violate Title VII's religious accommodation standard. The Court defined "undue hardship" as anything that places more than a *de minimis* cost on the employer,[26] and it applied an equality standard. "[T]o require TWA to bear additional costs when no such costs are incurred to give other employees the days off that they want would involve unequal treatment of employees on the basis of their religion," the Court said.[27]

Justice Thurgood Marshall, joined by Justice Brennan, filed a vigorous dissent. Such a weak definition of the term "undue hardship" flouted congressional intent, Marshall said:

> Today's decision deals a fatal blow to all efforts under Title VII to accommodate work requirements to religious practices. The Court holds, in essence, that although the EEOC regulations and the Act state that an employer must make reasonable adjustments in his work demands to take account of religious observances, the regulation and Act do not really mean what they say. An employer, the Court concludes, need not grant even the most minor special privilege to religious observers to enable them to follow their faith. As a question of social policy, this result is deeply troubling, for a society that truly values religious pluralism cannot compel adherents of minority religions to make the cruel choice of surrendering their religion or their job. And as a matter of law today's result is intolerable, for the Court adopts the very position that Congress expressly rejected in 1972, as if we were free to disregard congressional choices that a majority of this Court thinks unwise.[28]

Recognizing exemptions from general workplace rules "will always result in a privilege being 'allocated according to religious beliefs,'" but Title VII requires such accommodations unless they would place an undue hardship on the employer, the dissenters said.[29] Justices Marshall and Brennan emphatically rejected the Court's philosophy in interpreting Title VII's accommodation requirements:

> With respect to each of the proposed accommodations to respondent Hardison's religious observances that the Court discusses, it ultimately notes that the accommodation would have required "unequal treatment," in favor of the religious observer. That is quite true. But if an accommodation can be rejected simply because it involves preferential treatment, then the regulation and the statute, while brimming with "sound and fury," ultimately "signif[y] nothing."[30]

The dissenters left the decision of exactly how much cost would constitute an "undue hardship" for another day. But, in addition to taking issue with the Court's general interpretation of Title VII's standards, the dissenters said TWA should have been required to consider other options to accommodate Hardison's religious observances.[31]

In 1997, the Clinton administration summarized Title VII's accommodation requirements in guidance on religious exercise and expression in the federal workplace.[32] Regarding the duty of religious accommodation, the guidance said:

> Though an employer need not incur more than *de minimis* costs in providing an accommodation, the employer hardship nevertheless must be real rather than speculative or hypothetical. Religious accommodation cannot be disfavored relative to other, nonreligious, accommodations. If an employer regularly permits accommodation for nonreligious purposes, it cannot deny comparable religious accommodation: "Such an arrangement would display a discrimination against religious practices that is the antithesis of reasonableness."[33]

If there is more than one reasonable accommodation that would not create an undue hardship for the employer, the employer is not required to provide the accommodation the employee prefers. But an employer's suggested accommodation will not be deemed reasonable if an accommodation is provided to other employees for nonreligious purposes that is more favorable, for example. The reasonableness of an accommodation is a factual determination that must be made on a case-by-case basis.[34]

If a religious accommodation for one employee would require another employee to give up a job benefit guaranteed by a bona fide seniority system or collective bargaining agreement, that would be an undue hardship for the employer. Allowing employees to make voluntary swaps does not constitute an undue hardship for the employer, however, if those arrangements do not violate a bona fide seniority system or collective bargaining agreement.[35]

In the wake of the *Trans World Airlines v. Hardison* decision, bills aimed at strengthening the Title VII religious accommodation standard have been introduced. The Workplace Religious Freedom Act (WRFA) of 2013, for example, would amend Title VII to require an employer to engage in sincere and affirmative efforts to reasonably accommodate religious practices in the workplace.[36] WRFA also says an employer must accommodate an employee's religious grooming, clothing, and scheduling needs (taking time off for religious reasons) unless doing so would create a significant difficulty or expense for the employer. Further, the legislation would codify the conclusion that segregating employees from customers or the general public due to their religious practices is not a reasonable accommodation under Title VII.

Treating Religious Employers Differently

Federal law recognizes that religious employers must be treated somewhat differently from nonreligious employers. A synagogue has to be able to hire a rabbi, not a Baptist pastor, for example.

While Title VII generally prohibits religious discrimination in the workplace, the act also contains two exemptions for religious employers. Title VII does not apply to "a religious corporation, association, educational institution or society" when it makes employment decisions regarding "individuals of a particular religion to perform work connected with the carrying on [of such entities] of its activities."[37] This exemption, often called the "702 exemption," basically allows religious organizations (including, but not limited to, houses of worship) to prefer employees (including, but not limited to, ministers) of their own faith throughout their organizations.

Title VII also contains a separate exemption for religiously affiliated educational institutions.[38] Education institutions are also permitted to make employment decisions on the basis of religion, if they are "in whole or in substantial part, owned, supported, controlled, or managed by a particular religion or by a particular religious corporation, association, or society, or if the[ir] curriculum . . . is directed toward the propagation of a particular religion."[39]

The legislative history of these exemptions helps to explain their nature and significance. As originally proposed in the House of Representatives, Title VII exempted religious employers entirely from the law's antidiscrimination provisions. When Title VII was enacted in 1964, however, that exemption had been scaled back considerably. As passed, the 702 exemption only permitted religious employers to prefer employees of a particular religion in jobs related to the organizations' "religious activities." Educational institutions, including religiously affiliated educational institutions, were entirely exempt from the 1964 act.[40]

In 1972, however, Congress brought educational institutions within the ambit of Title VII. At the same time, Congress added religious educational institutions to the 702 exemption and also created a separate exemption for such institutions. Congress broadened the 702 exemption in another way in 1972. When Congress initially passed Title VII in 1964, the 702 exemption was limited to job positions within religious organizations handling "religious activities."[41] In 1972, however, Congress struck the word "religious," allowing religious organizations to make employment decisions on the basis of religion in all employee positions.[42]

These moves were concessions to senators, chiefly Sam Ervin and James Allen, who had argued for complete exemptions for religious organizations and educational institutions from Title VII. Senators Ervin and Allen were particularly concerned that one of the effects of making educational institutions subject to the act would be that religious schools would no longer be able to make faith-based decisions regarding jobs that did not necessarily perform religious activities. For example, Senator Allen said: "Under the provisions of the bill, there would be nothing to prevent an atheist being forced upon a religious school to teach some subject other than theology."[43] To remove this concern, Congress deleted the word "religious" from the 702 exemption, thus allowing religious employers, including religious educational institutions, to prefer members of their own faith throughout their institutions.

The Supreme Court considered the constitutionality of this broadened 702 exemption in a 1987 case, *Corporation of Presiding Bishop v. Amos.*[44] The case involved a building engineer, Arthur Frank Mayson, who worked at a gymnasium owned by the Church of Jesus Christ of Latter-day Saints (LDS Church).[45] Mayson's duties included maintaining the physical facility of the gym and its equipment as well as the grounds outside.[46] The church discharged the engineer after sixteen years of service because he failed to qualify for a "temple recommend," a certificate demonstrating that he was a church member in good standing and thus eligible to attend LDS temples. According to the Court, temple recommends are issued "only to individuals who observe the Church's standards in such matters as regular church attendance, tithing, and abstinence from coffee, tea, alcohol, and tobacco."[47] To the extent that the Title VII exemption allowed the LDS Church to fire him for this reason, it violated the First Amendment's Establishment Clause, Mayson argued, because his job consisted of nonreligious activities.

A unanimous Court ruled in favor of the LDS Church, finding that the exemption did not violate the First Amendment's Establishment Clause:[48] "This Court has long recognized that the government may (and sometimes must) accommodate religious practices, and that it may do so without violating the Establishment Clause."[49] The First Amendment did not necessarily require Congress to write the religious exemption so broadly, but the Constitution also did not prohibit it from doing so.

Applying the *Lemon v. Kurtzman* test, the Court first found that the exemption had a bona fide secular purpose. "Under the *Lemon* analysis, it is a permissible legislative purpose to alleviate significant governmental interference with the ability of religious organizations to define and carry out their religious missions," the Court said. Religious organizations would be "significant[ly] burden[ed]" if they were required to predict which of their jobs a court would find to be engaged in religious activities and which were not.[50] The exemption spared a religious organization this concern, thus freeing it to define and advance its mission as it saw fit, rather than as the government saw fit. The exemption also did not have the forbidden primary effect of advancing religion. The Court said, "A law is not unconstitutional simply because it *allows* churches to advance religion, which is their very purpose. For a law to have forbidden 'effects' under *Lemon* [*v. Kurtzman*], it must be fair to say that the *government itself* has advanced religion through its own activities and influence."[51] Finally, the Court found that rather than impermissibly entangling the governmental and religious sectors, the exemption had "effectuate[d] a more complete separation of the two" by avoiding intrusive inquiries into religious belief and practice.[52] The Court explicitly declined, however, to consider whether the Constitution mandated the Title VII religious exemption.[53] The Court also left open "the question of the constitutionality of the [Section] 702 exemption as applied to for-profit activities of religious organizations . . . ."[54]

Frank Mayson did not contest the LDS gymnasium's assertion that it was a religious employer for the purposes of Title VII, but litigants in other cases have argued that particular institutions do not fit within the act's religious exemptions. The act itself does not provide a definition of religious corporations, associations, educational institutions, or societies, so courts have had to define such terms through case law. To claim these religious exemptions, an institution's "purpose and character" must be "primarily religious," with such a determination being based on "[a]ll significant religious and secular characteristics" of the organization, courts have said.[55]

Applying these standards, lower courts have found that religious colleges and universities and nonprofit social service organizations qualify for Title VII's religious exemptions when they are organized for religious purposes, are engaged in activities consistent with those purposes, and hold themselves out as religious.[56] On the other hand, courts have also held that elementary and secondary schools and a social service organization that had religious roots but had nonetheless become primarily secular over time did not qualify for Title VII's religious exemptions.[57] Also, a court has held that a closely held for-profit company that manufactured mining equipment did not qualify for a Title VII religious exemption, even though the business owners were sincerely religious and included some religious activities into the company's work.[58] In this case, *EEOC v. Townley Engineering and Manufacturing Company*, a federal appellate court said:

> On the secular side, the company is for profit. It produces mining equipment, an admittedly secular product. It is not affiliated with or supported by a church. Its articles of incorporation do not mention any religious purpose.

Against these elements are the facts that Townley encloses Gospel tracts in its outgoing mail, prints Bible verses on its commercial documents (such as invoices and purchase orders), financially supports churches, missionaries, a prison ministry, and Christian radio broadcasts, and, of course, conducts a weekly devotional service. Underlying these facts, of course, is "the discipleship Jake and Helen Townley have for the Lord Jesus Christ."

When viewed together, we have no difficulty in holding that these characteristics indicate that Townley is primarily secular. We do not question the sincerity of the religious beliefs of the owners of Townley. Nor do we question that they regard the conduct of their company as subject to a compact with God. We merely hold that the beliefs of the owners and operators of a corporation are simply not enough in themselves to make the corporation "religious" within the meaning of section 702.[59]

Because Title VII also does not define what it means for a religious organization to be able to prefer employees "of a particular religion," courts have had to interpret that phrase as well. Again, the original draft of the 1964 Civil Rights Act would have exempted religious employers from all of Title VII's nondiscrimination requirements, but the legislation was revised "to apply the bulk of Title VII's provisions to religious employers but still permit[] [religious employers] to employ individuals of a particular religion."[60] The religious exemptions of Title VII have been interpreted to permit religious organizations to make employment decisions based not only on whether an individual is formally Baptist, Jewish, or Muslim, for example, but also on whether individuals comply with religious doctrine, such as standards on alcohol consumption and tithing (the *Amos* case) or divorce.[61]

A federal appellate court has held that a Catholic school could refuse to renew the contract of a Protestant teacher, Susan Little, who was married at the time she was hired but who later divorced and remarried a Catholic man.[62] The school considered Little's remarriage to a Catholic "without proper validation" to be a serious public rejection of the church's teaching on marriage.[63] While Little cited the fact that she had been hired as a Protestant, and thus the school should not be able to dismiss her subsequently due to other differences with the church, the school responded that the 702 exemption gave the school the right to make employment decisions regarding conduct it believed to have religious significance. Title VII's "permission to employ persons 'of a particular religion' includes permission to employ only persons whose beliefs and conduct are consistent with the employer's religious precepts," the court said.[64] The court ruled, therefore, that the school had the right to fire Little because it believed her conduct violated church teaching and because the court had no appropriate role in second-guessing that determination. Prohibiting the school from making such decisions, or parsing them, would raise serious constitutional questions. Doing so would require the court to determine, for example, what constitutes the official teaching of the church and whether Little had rejected such teachings with her conduct. That would also create excessive entanglement between church and state.[65]

Of course, Title VII provides no protection to employees based on the fact that they divorce and remarry, consume alcohol, or fail to tithe. Other cases, however, involve claims against religious employers that involve forms of discrimination prohibited under the act and applicable to such employers, such as sex discrimination claims. Various courts and the EEOC have said Title VII's religious exemption does not allow religious employers to escape liability for discrimination on the basis of race, sex, or national origin by asserting a faith-based reason for such discrimination.[66] Thus, a religious organization cannot immunize its practice of paying female employees less by citing religious beliefs that men and women must be treated differently, for example.[67]

One appellate court has noted, however, "there are circumstances in which Congress' intention to apply Title VII to religious employers is less clear."[68] A case involving a teacher, Michele Curay-Cramer, at a Delaware Catholic school provides one example. While she was a teacher at Ursuline Academy in Wilmington, Delaware, Curay-Cramer signed a prochoice advertisement that ran in the local newspaper on the thirtieth anniversary of the Supreme Court's decision in *Roe v. Wade*. Ursuline Academy fired Curay-Cramer for taking such a public position against church teaching. Curay-Cramer sued, claiming that her discharge violated the gender nondiscrimination requirements of Title VII, among other claims.[69] The teacher argued that the school had treated her more harshly than it had treated male teachers who had taken other actions that were allegedly inconsistent with church teaching.[70]

The appellate court found it could not inquire into whether Ursuline Academy had treated certain doctrinal violations by a female employee more harshly than different alleged doctrinal violations by male employees of the school:

> [A]bsent an allegation that a male employee publicly attacked the Church's position on abortion, evaluating the comparators would require an analysis of Catholic doctrine to determine whether the decision to employ a teacher of a different religious background constitutes an affront to the Catholic faith and, if so, whether it is an affront of at least the same seriousness as the Plaintiff's repudiation of Catholic doctrine on when life begins and the responsibility to preserve life *in utero*.[71]

Engaging in that analysis would inevitably involve the court in making theological determinations, which is forbidden by the First Amendment. In this case, therefore, it was not clear that Congress intended "to have Title VII apply when its application would involve the court in evaluating violations of Church doctrine."[72] The court rejected Curay-Cramer's claim. At the same time, the court warned against overreading its decision: "It is by no means the case that all claims of gender discrimination against religious employers are impermissible."[73]

THE SACRED TASK OF SELECTING MINISTERS

Another major protection for religious organizations in employment is the First Amendment's "ministerial exception." The First Amendment recognizes that religious bodies retain full freedom to make employment decisions regarding their ministers.[74] This doctrine flows from the First Amendment's protection for the independence of religious bodies from the state.

The ministerial exception is both narrower and broader that Title VII's religious exemptions. The ministerial exception applies only to ministers, not to other employees of religious organizations. But the ministerial exception allows a religious organization to make employment decisions for any reason, whereas Title VII's religious exemptions allow religious organizations to prefer employees only on the basis of religion, not on the basis of race, color, sex, or national origin.

The Supreme Court decided a ministerial exception case for the first time in 2012. The Court considered a case brought by a former teacher, Cheryl Perich, at Hosanna-Tabor Evangelical Lutheran Church and School, a member of the Lutheran Church–Missouri Synod. The school classified teachers as either "called teachers" or "lay teachers." Lay teachers were appointed without a vote of the congregation to one-year renewable terms. "Called teachers" were considered to have been called by God to their positions through confirmation by the synod. To qualify as a "called teacher," a teacher had to complete a colloquy program at a Lutheran college or university, a program that involved theological study; pass an oral exam by a faculty committee; and receive the endorsement of their local synod. If a teacher met these requirements, he or she could be called by a congregation. When a teacher was called, the teacher's formal title became "Minister of Religion, Commissioned," and the teacher served an open-ended term. Such a teacher could not be removed unless the congregation rescinded the call for cause by a supermajority vote.[75]

Cheryl Perich first served at Hosanna-Tabor as a lay teacher. She later became a called teacher. Perich taught a range of subjects, including religion, and led her students in prayers and devotional exercises. She also attended, and sometimes led, the weekly school-wide chapel services. Perich got sick while serving as a called teacher and ultimately had to take a disability leave. She was diagnosed with narcolepsy and said she wished to return to teaching after settling on a course of medication. The school had reservations about whether Perich was ready to return, however. A complicated set of interactions ensued, including Perich's return to school and refusal to leave the premises without documentation that she had willingly returned. The congregation ultimately rescinded Perich's call and sent her a letter of termination.

The EEOC subsequently filed suit on Perich's behalf, alleging that her termination violated the Americans with Disabilities Act (ADA). The ADA prohibits employers from discriminating against qualified individuals based on disability. The act also bars employers from retaliating against an individual because he or she makes an ADA claim. The school asserted that Perich was a minister and thus her lawsuit was barred by the First Amendment's ministerial exception.

The U.S. Supreme Court unanimously held that Perich could not sue her employer, a religious school, for alleged discrimination, because Perich had been serving in a ministerial position. "Both Religion Clauses [of the First Amendment] bar the government from interfering with the decision of a religious group to fire one of its ministers."[76] Requiring a church to accept a minister it does not want would not only interfere with the church's internal governance; it would also allow the government to dictate who will embody the church's beliefs. The Court determined that Perich was a minister because the school (and Perich) held her out as a minister and Perich had a role in spreading the church's teachings and advancing its mission.[77]

The Court did not offer a precise definition of the term "minister," but it did offer some guidance. A person can be a minister even though he or she is not the head of a congregation. Yet the mere fact that the religious community calls a person a minister does not necessarily mean the ministerial exception applies. The legal definition of the term "minister" is not always the same as the theological definition. Courts should not simply defer to a religious organization's determination of who is a minister for purposes of the ministerial exception. Instead, they should consider all the relevant facts and circumstances.

Employees do not have to have exclusively religious duties to be considered ministers for purposes of the ministerial exception. Also, courts should not decide who is a minister merely by applying "stopwatch" tests—counting the number of minutes a person spends on religious and secular activities each day. "The amount of time an employee spends on particular activities is relevant in assessing that employee's status, but that factor cannot be considered in isolation, without regard to the religious functions performed and []other considerations," the Court said.[78]

The Court expressed no view on whether the ministerial exception "bars other types of suits, including actions by employees alleging breach of contract or tortious conduct by their religious employers."[79] It stressed that the ministerial exception applies only to employment lawsuits by *ministers* against the bodies they serve. When nonministerial employees, like a church janitor, sue their employer for discrimination on the basis of disability or age, for example, the church will not be able to claim the protections of the ministerial exception. Also, one should not assume the exception will block criminal prosecutions or lawsuits brought by congregants and other third parties against a religious institution based on alleged wrongdoing by a minister, like sexual abuse or sexual harassment. In the *Hosanna-Tabor* case, the Lutheran Church took the position that the exception did not bar such lawsuits. "There will be time enough to address the applicability of the exception to other circumstances if and when they arise," the Court said.[80]

In the *Hosanna-Tabor* case, the Court concluded:

> The interest of society in the enforcement of employment discrimination statutes is undoubtedly important. But so too is the interest of religious groups in choosing who will preach their beliefs, teach their faith, and carry out their mission. When a minister who has been fired sues her church alleging that her termination was discriminatory, the First Amendment has struck the balance for us. The church must be free to choose those who will guide it on its way.[81]

Exactly who is and is not a minister for purposes of the ministerial exception is a matter that is now being litigated in the lower courts. Some such cases are likely to reach the Supreme Court eventually.

Protecting LGBT Rights and Religious Liberty

For the past few years, around 71 percent of Americans have said they support legislation that would protect LGBT individuals from discrimination in the workplace.[82] Nonetheless, at the federal level and in some states, efforts to pass such legislation have not yet borne fruit. A key reason for this failure is the inability of the various sides to come to agreement on whether there should be religious exemptions in this kind of legislation and, if so, what such exemptions should look like. Considering the demise of the federal Employment Non-Discrimination Act (ENDA) provides one window into this ongoing debate.

ENDA was legislation modeled on the landmark federal employment nondiscrimination law, Title VII of the 1964 Civil Rights Act. The act would have prohibited employers from engaging in discrimination on the basis of sexual orientation or gender identity.[83] ENDA differed from Title VII in another important way, however. Title VII permits religious organizations to prefer people of their faith in employment decisions but does not exempt religious organizations from the law's prohibitions on discrimination on the basis of race, color, sex, or national origin.[84] ENDA, on the other hand, would have exempted religious organizations entirely from the obligation to refrain from discrimination on the basis of sexual orientation or gender identity.

In 2013, the Senate passed ENDA, but the measure later died in the House of Representatives.[85] ENDA initially had the support of a variety of civil rights organizations. These organizations disliked ENDA's religious exemption, but they believed at the time that such an exemption was necessary in order to gain federal protection for LGBT workers.

In the spring of 2013, however, several leading civil rights organizations pulled their support for the bill due to its religious exemption. The American Civil Liberties Union said, for example, that it could no longer support a bill that gave religious organizations a "blank check" to engage in employment discrimination against LGBT individuals.[86] Calling attention to the way in which ENDA differed from Title VII, the ACLU said: "ENDA's religious exemption also gives a stamp of legitimacy to LGBT discrimination that our civil rights laws have never given to discrimination based on an individual's race, sex, national origin, age or disability."[87]

Meanwhile, some religious advocates found even the religious exemption of ENDA to be insufficient. These advocates pressed for an exemption that would clearly shield at least some entities that are not primarily religious, including for-profit entities whose owners object for religious reasons to marriages between individuals of the same sex.[88]

Divides of this kind continue to play a central role in preventing the passage of legislation that protects the civil rights of LGBT people at the federal level as well as at some state and local levels. Some advocates insist that laws should not treat LGBT discrimination any differently than discrimination on the basis of race, gender, or national origin, for example. There is no exemption in Title VII for religious employers from the prohibitions on these forms of discrimination. Treating LGBT discrimination differently would create a troubling precedent, they say. On the other side, advocates insist that any religious exemptions must immunize at least religious organizations from prohibitions on LGBT discrimination, no matter if that requires treating LGBT discrimination differently than others form of discrimination.[89] Without such an exemption, they say, religious institutions that oppose marriage between individuals of the same sex would have to close. These advocates point to the fact that the Supreme Court only recently recognized marriage equality and that the Court specifically called for tolerance of competing views in its opinion.[90] In the wake of ENDA's demise, various proposals have been introduced in Congress or simply floated in Washington, D.C., that would address these issues in the workplace and beyond, and do so in strikingly different ways.[91]

Where sexual orientation and gender identity have been explicitly added to the list of prohibited bases of discrimination in particular state or local employment laws or policies, there is obviously no question about whether such discrimination is prohibited, but there may still be some questions about how those prohibitions interact with any exemptions for religious organizations. In other cases, however, sexual orientation and gender identity have not been explicitly added to the list of prohibited bases of discrimination, but courts have nonetheless determined that existing bans on sex or gender discrimination include bans on discrimination on the basis of sexual orientation or gender identity. The Supreme Court may weigh in on this matter soon. The Court has agreed to hear several consolidated cases during its 2019–2020 term that consider whether Title VII's prohibition on sex discrimination includes bars on discrimination based on sexual orientation or gender identity.[92] Debate continues about whether there must or should be religious exemptions from civil rights laws protecting LGBT workers and, if so, what those exemptions should look like.

RECOMMENDATIONS: PROTECTING RELIGIOUS LIBERTY AND AUTONOMY

Federal law regarding faith in the workplace is protective of both individuals' religious liberty and the freedom of religious institutions. The American concept of religious freedom includes the notion that a worker's faith, or lack thereof, should not qualify or disqualify him or her from a job with a secular employer. Further, workers should be able to express their faith on the job in ways that respect their coworkers, and the religious needs of workers must be taken seriously by their employers.

The First Amendment's ministerial exception and Title VII's religious exemptions play key roles in protecting the independence of religious institutions. Religious communities define themselves in large part by the ministers they select and the other people they employ. At the same time, such laws seek to balance the right to religious liberty with other important rights, including the right of prospective and current employees to be free from unlawful discrimination.

Government officials have a duty to protect equal employment opportunity and the autonomy of religious organizations. Secular employers have specific duties of nondiscrimination and religious accommodation regarding their employees. Religious employers need to understand their rights and responsibilities too. Leaders can further those aims by taking the following steps.

(1) Augment training on religion in the workplace.

Government officials should augment training and resource development on religion in the workplace, both governmental and nongovernmental, secular and religious. Americans will not necessarily agree on all of the balances the Supreme Court and Congress have struck on religion and the workplace, but learning more about them will help to avoid surprises and spark needed conversations about the role of faith in public life.

(2) Secular employers should have written policies on religious nondiscrimination, harassment, and accommodation and share them with both prospective and current employees.

Secular employers should spell out their policies on religious nondiscrimination, harassment, and accommodation in writing. These policies should be shared with both prospective and current employees. To the extent that religious accommodation policies allow for mechanisms like shift swaps, employers should facilitate employees' efforts to find matches.

(3) Religious employers should inform prospective and current employees about which jobs are religiously qualified and the standards that apply to such jobs.

The Court's decisions say a great deal about the freedom religious institutions enjoy from governmental oversight under the First Amendment, but they say nothing about the ethical and moral responsibilities of religious institutions, and properly so. That is not the Court's job—it is the job of religious communities. One way in which religious communities should discharge their ethical and moral responsibilities is by being transparent about which job positions are subject to religious qualifications.

So, for example, when prospective employees apply for jobs that are considered ministerial, religious organizations should inform applicants of that fact and the ramifications of that designation. A religious employer should also inform prospective employees whether the position they hope to fill is religiously qualified (although not ministerial) and, if so, what religious qualifications are required in order to attain and retain such a position.[93]

(4) Consider legislation that would strengthen protections for religious practices in the workplace.

The Supreme Court weakened the religious accommodation obligations of Title VII in 1977 when it said that an "undue hardship" for an employer is anything more than a minor burden. Under this standard, an employer can deny an employee's request for a religious accommodation if the accommodation would create anything more than a trivial cost for the business. There is evidence that Congress intended to put a higher standard in place.[94]

Congress, therefore, should consider passing legislation like the Workplace Religious Freedom Act (WRFA) that would amend Title VII. This legislation would require an employer to engage in sincere and affirmative efforts to reasonably accommodate religious practices in the workplace.[95] WRFA says an employer should be required to accommodate an employee's religious grooming, clothing, and scheduling needs (taking time off for religious reasons) unless doing so would create a significant difficulty or expense for the employer, which would include any significant burdens that these accommodations would place on other employees. The legislation also makes clear that segregating employees from customers or the general public due to their religious practices is not a reasonable accommodation under Title VII.

(5) Protect LGBT equality and religious liberty in the workplace and beyond.

Debates over the treatment of religious entities have been a stumbling block, if not *the* stumbling block, that has prevented passage of workplace protections for LGBT people at the federal level and also in some states and cities. Advocates of LGBT rights and religious liberty should redouble their efforts to seek common ground on protections for these rights and liberties, in the workplace, in housing, public accommodations, and beyond.

RELIGIOUS DISCRIMINATION AND HATE CRIMES

Fighting Hatred and Bias—
Protecting Freedom and Pluralism

Both the First Amendment's Establishment and Free Exercise Clauses address governmental discrimination against religion generally and against particular faiths. "In our Establishment Clause cases," the Court has said, "we have often stated the principle that the First Amendment forbids an official purpose to disapprove of a particular religion or religion in general." The Free Exercise Clause, which protects the ability of members of all faiths to practice their religion, also bars government from acting based on animus toward religion or particular faiths. "At a minimum, the protections of the Free Exercise Clause pertain if the law at issue discriminates against some or all religious beliefs or regulates or prohibits conduct because it is undertaken for religious reasons," the Court has noted.

The fact that a law or policy is neutral on its face does not mean that it does not target religious conduct or is not based in animus toward religion or specific faiths. The First Amendment "protects against governmental hostility which is masked as well as overt."

The Supreme Court has struck down laws and policies that were based in hostility toward Jehovah's Witnesses and members of the Santeria faith. In June 2018, the Court set aside a judgment against a bakery that refused to make and sell a wedding cake for a same-sex couple due to religious beliefs because the Court found that bias had tainted the process. Later that month, despite a pattern of anti-Muslim statements by President Trump, the Supreme Court held by a vote of five to four that it had to accept the Trump administration's justification of a policy banning the entry of certain foreign nationals into the United States "because the entry suspension ha[d] a legitimate grounding in national security concerns, quite apart from any religious hostility."

The 1964 Civil Rights Act guards against discrimination based on religious beliefs or affiliations, or lack thereof, in employment; educational institutions; public accommodations, such as hotels, restaurants, nightclubs, and theaters; and state-operated facilities. The Fair Housing Act prohibits such discrimination by entities such as landlords, real estate companies, municipalities, lending institutions, and homeowners insurance companies. The Equal Credit Opportunity Act prohibits creditors from discriminating against credit applicants on the basis of religion. The federal Religious Land Use and Institutionalized Persons Act (RLUIPA) bars the government from discriminating on the basis of religion in the context of land use matters and state institutionalization.

A range of federal statutes penalizes violent and intimidating acts that are motivated by animus based on several personal characteristics, including a person's actual or perceived religion. The most well-known provision is called the Matthew Shepard and James Byrd Jr. Hate Crimes Prevention Act of 2009, making it a federal crime to willfully cause bodily injury, or attempt to do so, based on a person's actual or perceived race, color, religion, national origin, gender, sexual orientation, gender identity, or disability. The Church Arson Prevention Act states that damage to religious property due to its religious, racial, or ethnic character constitutes a violation of federal law.

In August 1790, President George Washington arrived in Newport, Rhode Island, for a visit.[1] Washington had toured several northeastern states during the previous year, but he had not stopped in Rhode Island, because the state had yet to ratify the Constitution.[2] On May 29, 1790, Rhode Island ratified the Constitution, becoming the last of the original thirteen colonies to do so.[3] With this act, Rhode Island cleared the way for a presidential visit.[4]

Among President Washington's stops in Newport was Touro Synagogue.[5] While the presidential delegation was at Touro, Moses Seixas, a synagogue leader, read a letter to President Washington that was dated August 17. Seixas, born in 1744, was a first-generation American whose parents had left Lisbon, Portugal, to settle in Newport. The letter said in part:

Deprived as we heretofore have been of the invaluable rights of Citizens, we now with a deep sense of gratitude to the Almighty disposer of all events behold a Government, erected by the Majesty of the People—a Government, which to bigotry gives no sanction, to persecution no assistance—but generously affording to all Liberty of conscience, and immunities of Citizenship: deeming every one, of whatever Nation, tongue, or language equal parts of the great governmental Machine.[6]

President Washington penned a reply on August 18. Washington's letter made use of Seixas' reference to government that gave to bigotry no sanction, to persecution no assistance. As Supreme Court Justice Elena Kagan has noted, "Like any successful politician," Washington "appreciated a great line when he saw one—and knew to borrow it too."[7] President Washington wrote:

The Citizens of the United States of America have a right to applaud themselves for having given to mankind examples of an enlarged and liberal policy: a policy worthy of imitation. All possess alike liberty of conscience and immunities of citizenship. It is now no more that toleration is spoken of, as if it was by the indulgence of one class of people, that another enjoyed the exercise of their inherent natural rights. For happily the Government of the United States, which gives to bigotry no sanction, to persecution no assistance requires only that they who live under its protection should demean themselves as good citizens, in giving it on all occasions their effectual support.

It would be inconsistent with the frankness of my character not to avow that I am pleased with your favorable opinion of my Administration, and fervent wishes for my felicity. May the Children of the Stock of Abraham, who dwell in this land, continue to merit and enjoy the good will of the other Inhabitants; while every one shall sit in safety under his own vine and figtree, and there shall be none to make him afraid.[8]

Tolerance was not enough, President Washington said. Rights such as liberty of conscience are inalienable and possessed by all citizens alike, not doled out by one privileged group to others. Rather than giving prejudice and persecution any breathing room, the U.S. government must firmly reject them.

The Constitution embodies these ideals. Individuals of all faiths and none are equally American. There are no second-class faiths under the Constitution—the government must not prefer one faith over another or discriminate against any faith. The Constitution also prohibits the government from discriminating on the basis of religion generally. The United States has at times been a shining example of adherence to such principles, while at other times it has turned its back on them.

During the mid-nineteenth century, for example, government officials brutally forced thousands of American Indians from their lands.[9] On the Trail of Tears, members of the Cherokee Nation were driven from their remaining land in Georgia and Alabama to Oklahoma.[10] While on this forced winter march, half of the sixteen thousand Cherokee men, women, and children died.[11] Other Indian tribes experienced similar death rates when they were "removed" from their home lands.[12] Heaping egregious insult upon these injuries, some white Americans, including some government officials, sought to justify such practices by appealing to the Bible.[13] The record of atrocities committed by federal and state government against American Indians and Indian tribes is long and varied.[14] Acts of governmental discrimination and injustice are a continuing problem.[15]

In nineteenth-century America, certain government officials described the Church of Jesus Christ of Latter-day Saints (LDS Church) as a "community of traitors, murderers, fanatics and whores"[16] and targeted its members with special restrictions.[17] Members of the LDS Church were viewed as "potentially dangerous outsiders" and were frequently the subjects of hostility.[18]

Some colonial charters prohibited Catholics from holding public office.[19] In nineteenth-century America, the majority of schools required students to listen to and read from the Protestant King James Version of the Bible.[20] When Catholics sought to open schools of their own in response to this treatment, they were often met with resistance. In 1922, for example, a campaign started in Oregon by the Ku Klux Klan aimed at closing Catholic schools.[21] The campaign resulted in the passage of a state constitutional amendment requiring children to attend public schools.[22] The U.S. Supreme Court invalidated the amendment, although that certainly did not end anti-Catholicism.[23]

To redress discrimination against Native Americans and to protect their free exercise, Congress passed a number of laws, including the American Indian Religious Freedom Act.[24] To combat religious discrimination generally, Congress passed certain laws prohibiting both governmental and nongovernmental entities from treating Americans differently based on their religion, or lack thereof. Religion is one of a number of protected bases—like race, gender, or national origin—that are typically enumerated in federal civil rights laws and policies.[25] Policymakers recognize that individuals' faith or beliefs generally should not prevent them from getting a job, an education, housing, or credit or from having access to public accommodations like retail stores and other businesses.

Congress has also decided that crimes based on hatred of a religion deserve special penalties. With these laws, the United States has signaled that it will not tolerate efforts to intimidate or terrorize individuals due to their faith. Rather than living in fear, every individual should be able to "sit in safety under his own vine and figtree," with "none to make him afraid," as President Washington said, quoting scripture.[26]

Protections like these advance human rights, religious pluralism, and peace. Welcoming people of all faiths and of none also helps to foster a stable and productive society, one that is able to benefit from the talents of all citizens. This chapter considers several cases in which the Supreme Court struck down discriminatory acts by government. It also explores certain laws passed by Congress that target religious bias and hate crimes as well as steps civil society has taken to support such laws and to build bridges of understanding across different faiths and beliefs.

STRIKING DOWN ACTS OF RELIGIOUS DISCRIMINATION AND DENIGRATION

Both the First Amendment's Establishment and Free Exercise Clauses bar governmental discrimination against religion generally and against particular faiths.[27] "In our Establishment Clause cases," the Court has said, "we have often stated the principle that the First Amendment forbids an official purpose to disapprove of a particular religion or religion in general."[28] The Free Exercise Clause, which protects the ability of members of all faiths to practice their religion, also bars government from acting based on animus toward religion or particular faiths. "At a minimum, the protections of the Free Exercise Clause pertain if the law at issue discriminates against some or all religious beliefs or regulates or prohibits conduct because it is undertaken for religious reasons," the Court has said.[29]

There are few Supreme Court cases that rest on these principles because they are usually well understood by government officials.[30] Understanding has sometimes been lacking, including in cases involving Jehovah's Witnesses and members of the Santeria faith.

Less than 1 percent of Christians living in the United States are Jehovah's Witnesses. Due to their religious beliefs, Jehovah's Witnesses do not salute the flag of their country or stand for the singing of a national anthem.[31] Jehovah's Witnesses believe that doing so gives reverence to the state, when reverence belongs only to God.[32] Beliefs of this kind have sometimes brought Jehovah's Witnesses into conflict with governments and drawn harsh criticism from some of their fellow citizens.[33]

The most prominent Supreme Court cases involving Jehovah's Witnesses are the so-called "flag-salute" cases. The Supreme Court decided these cases under the First Amendment generally, not the religious clauses specifically, but they help explain some of the hostility that has been directed toward members of this faith and the appropriate response to such hostility.

In 1940, the Court considered the case of Lillian Gobitis (age twelve) and her brother William (ten), who were expelled from a Minersville, Pennsylvania, public school for refusing to salute the American flag as part of a daily exercise at school.[34] The Gobitis family were Jehovah's Witnesses, and Lillian and William "had been brought up conscientiously to believe that such a gesture of respect for the flag was forbidden by command of Scripture."[35] Due to the flag-salute requirements, the Gobitis children were denied a free public education and had to enroll in private schools.

Appealing to the First Amendment, the Gobitis family asked the Supreme Court to stop the public schools from requiring their children to participate in the flag-salute ceremony as a condition of their attendance. In an opinion written by Justice Felix Frankfurter, the Court denied the request. If the Pennsylvania legislature had not exempted children whose scruples prevented them from saluting the flag from this requirement, the Court had no role in doing so, Justice Frankfurter said.[36]

Three years later, the Supreme Court reversed course in *West Virginia State Board of Education v. Barnette.*[37] The Court held that the First Amendment required public schools to exempt students who, for reasons of conscience, object to rules requiring them to salute the flag. In an opinion written by Justice Jackson, the Court said:

> The very purpose of a Bill of Rights was to withdraw certain subjects from the vicissitudes of political controversy, to place them beyond the reach of majorities and officials and to establish them as legal principles to be applied by the courts. One's right to life, liberty, and property, to free speech, a free press, freedom of worship and assembly, and other fundamental rights may not be submitted to vote; they depend on the outcome of no elections.[38]

The Supreme Court protected the constitutional rights of Jehovah's Witnesses in the *Barnette* case, but the decision did not necessarily make Witnesses more popular, nor did it stop certain governmental officials from discriminating against them.

In 1951, for example, the Court considered a case involving a group of Jehovah's Witnesses who wished to use a public park in Havre de Grace, Maryland, for their talks on the Bible.[39] Although it was customary for organizations to seek permits before using the park, no ordinance required them to do so. The Jehovah's Witnesses sought permission to use the park for four consecutive Sundays in the summer of 1949. The city refused their requests. Believing that "any prohibition against such use was in violation of the decisions of the Supreme Court of the United States,"[40] the Jehovah's Witnesses informed the city council that they would nevertheless use the park. When

Daniel Niemotko, a minister for the Jehovah's Witnesses, arrived at the park, he found members of the police there. The chief of police warned Niemotko that he would be arrested if he spoke to the crowd. Mr. Niemotko began speaking anyway. After about ten or fifteen minutes, Niemotko was arrested and charged with disorderly conduct. When Mr. Niemotko was found guilty as charged and fined fifty dollars, he appealed his conviction to the Maryland Court of Appeals, asking the court to consider whether the verdict and judgment abridged his "right to freedom of speech, freedom of assembly, freedom of worship and freedom of conscience, contrary to the First and Fourteenth Amendments to the United States Constitution and the Declaration of Rights of Maryland[.]"[41] The Maryland Court of Appeals denied his petition.

The Supreme Court reversed these decisions, finding no evidence of disorder or threats of violence.[42] Indeed, the Court said, "rarely has any case been before this Court which shows so clearly an unwarranted discrimination in a refusal to issue such a license." The Court continued:

> The only questions asked of the Witnesses at the hearing pertained to their alleged refusal to salute the flag, their views on the Bible, and other issues irrelevant to unencumbered use of the public parks. The conclusion is inescapable that the use of the park was denied because of the City Council's dislike for or disagreement with the Witnesses or their views. The right to equal protection of the laws, in the exercise of those freedoms of speech and religion protected by the First and Fourteenth Amendments, has a firmer foundation than the whims or personal opinions of a local governing body.[43]

The city argued it should be permitted to exclude religious groups from public parks, but the Court said: "[W]hatever force this contention could possibly have is lost in light of the testimony of the Mayor at the trial that within his memory permits had always been issued for religious organizations and Sunday-school picnics."[44] The utter lack of standards meant that the city's practice was a prior restraint that violated the Fourteenth Amendment. Also, "the completely arbitrary and discriminatory refusal to grant the permits was a denial of equal protection," the Court ruled.[45]

Americans who practice the Santeria faith comprise another religious community that has sometimes been targeted by government. Santeria, which means "the way of the saints,"[46] is a blend of a traditional religion practiced in Africa, often called the Yoba or Yoruba faith, with elements of Roman Catholicism.[47] During the sixteenth, seventeenth, and eighteenth centuries, Yoba practitioners were enslaved and brought to Cuba, where the practice of their faith was forbidden.[48] "[T]o escape the severe penalties and social stigma, [this community] began to express the Yoba faith through the use of Catholic saints and symbolism."[49] Members of the Santeria community were among the Cubans who fled the Castro regime in the 1950s and 1960s for the United States.[50]

Animal sacrifice is part of Santeria practices:

> Sacrifices are performed at birth, marriage, and death rites, for the cure of the sick, for the initiation of new members and priests, and during an annual celebration. Animals sacrificed in Santeria rituals include chickens, pigeons, doves, ducks, guinea pigs, goats, sheep, and turtles. The animals are killed by the cutting of the carotid arteries in the neck. The sacrificed animal is cooked and eaten, except after healing and death rituals.[51]

Due to the persecution that members of the Santeria faith have faced, it is not uncommon for them to exercise their faith in secret.[52]

The Church of Lukumi Babalu Aye is a Florida nonprofit that practices Santeria. As part of the congregation's aim of claiming their faith openly, the church leased land in Hialeah, Florida, in April 1987 and announced plans to establish a church, school, cultural center, and museum there.[53] Some members of the Hialeah community raised concerns about these plans, prompting the Hialeah City Council to convene an "emergency" public session and pass various resolutions and ordinances relating to animal sacrifice. Concerns about animal cruelty laws and "public morals, peace or safety" were cited.[54] The city council later adopted additional ordinances generally prohibiting animal sacrifice within city limits, although exemptions were made for practices such as the slaughter of animals for food.[55]

Transcripts from a June 1987 hearing where the council adopted these ordinances included the following remarks:

> When Councilman Martinez, a supporter of the ordinances, stated that in prerevolution Cuba "people were put in jail for practicing this religion," the audience applauded . . . .
>
> [A]fter noting his belief that Santeria was outlawed in Cuba, [Councilman Martinez] questioned: "If we could not practice this [religion] in our home-land [Cuba], why bring it to this country?" Councilman Cardoso said that Santeria devotees at the Church "are in violation of everything this country stands for." Councilman Mejides indicated that he was "totally against the sacrificing of animals" and distinguished kosher slaughter because it had a "real purpose." The "Bible says we are allowed to sacrifice an animal for consumption," he continued, "but for any other purposes, I don't believe that the Bible allows that." The president of the city council, Councilman Echevarria, asked: "What can we do to prevent the Church from opening?"
>
> Various Hialeah city officials made comparable comments.

The chaplain of the Hialeah Police Department told the city council that Santeria was a sin, "foolishness," "an abomination to the Lord," and the worship of "demons." He advised the city council: "We need to be helping people and sharing with them the truth that is found in Jesus Christ." He concluded: "I would exhort you . . . not to permit this Church to exist." The city attorney commented that Resolution 87–66 indicated: "This community will not tolerate religious practices which are abhorrent to its citizens . . . ."[56]

The church filed suit against the City of Hialeah, alleging that the ordinances violated the First Amendment's Free Exercise Clause. The trial court found no constitutional violations, saying that the purpose of the ordinances was to promote public health and welfare and that any effect on the church's religious practices were merely incidental to those legitimate secular purposes. A court of appeals affirmed the lower court's judgment in a one-paragraph opinion.[57]

The Supreme Court unanimously reversed the judgments of the courts below. Even though the ordinances did not necessarily discriminate on their face, the city had nonetheless targeted the Santeria practice of animal sacrifice in an effort to suppress it:

Official action that targets religious conduct for distinctive treatment cannot be shielded by mere compliance with the requirement of facial neutrality. The Free Exercise Clause protects against governmental hostility which is masked as well as overt.

According to the Court, "The legitimate governmental interests in protecting the public health and preventing cruelty to animals could be addressed by restrictions stopping far short of a flat prohibition of all Santeria sacrificial practice."[58] The ordinances did not prohibit nonreligious conduct that jeopardized the same governmental interests of protecting public health and preventing cruelty to animals in ways similar to or greater than the ways Santeria sacrifice did.[59] The ordinances did not forbid, for example, fishing, hunting, or destruction of animals for humanitarian reasons. The measures also did not prohibit other possible health risks associated with the disposal of animal carcasses and the consumption of uninspected meat. "We conclude, in sum," the Court ruled, "that each of Hialeah's ordinances pursues the city's governmental interests only against conduct motivated by religious belief."[60] The ordinances, therefore, failed to pass the compelling interest test. Indeed, the city's regulations "f[e]ll well below the minimum standard necessary to protect First Amendment rights," the Court said.[61] "The Free Exercise Clause commits government itself to religious tolerance, and upon even slight suspicion that proposals for state intervention stem from animosity to religion or distrust of its practices, all officials must pause to remember their own high duty to the Constitution and to the rights it secures."[62]

In the *Lukumi* case, the Court noted that the First Amendment's Establishment Clause also forbade the government from disapproving of a particular faith or of religion in general. Because the church and its members "allege[d] an attempt to disfavor their religion because of the religious ceremonies it commands," the Court said, "the Free Exercise [was] dispositive" in the *Lukumi* case.

TRUMP V. HAWAII

Like Jehovah's Witnesses and members of the Santeria faith, Muslims too have sometimes been targeted for discrimination, especially since the attacks on the United States on September 11, 2001.[63] In 2018, the Supreme Court considered whether certain executive actions by President Donald Trump were based in anti-Muslim animus and thus prohibited by the Establishment Clause. A chronological summary of some of Trump's comments on Islam and Muslims and the relevant portions of his executive actions lays the foundation for a discussion of the Supreme Court's opinion in this case.

In October 2015, then-candidate Donald Trump said he would "certainly look at" the idea of closing mosques in the United States.[64] Trump reiterated that sentiment in November and also suggested that he was open to the notion of creating a database of all American Muslims.[65]

On December 7, 2015, in the wake of an ISIS-inspired terrorist attack in San Bernardino, California,[66] Trump's campaign issued a press release entitled *Donald J. Trump Statement on Preventing Muslim Immigration.*[67] The statement said Trump was "calling for a total and complete shutdown of Muslims entering the United States until our country's representatives can figure out what is going on."[68]

On March 9, 2016, Donald Trump said: "I think Islam hates us. There's something there that—there's a tremendous hatred there. There's a tremendous hatred. We have to get to the bottom of it. There's an unbelievable hatred of us."[69] Later in March, candidate Trump called again for surveillance of mosques and said, "We're having problems with the Muslims, and we're having problems with Muslims coming into the country."[70]

Donald Trump also defended his proposed Muslim ban in July 2016, saying:

> People were so upset when I used the word Muslim. "Oh, you can't use the word Muslim[.]" . . . But just remember this: Our Constitution is great, but it doesn't necessarily give us the right to commit suicide, okay? Now, we

have a religious—you know, everybody wants to be protected. And that's great. And that's the wonderful part of our Constitution. I view it differently. Why are we committing suicide? Why are we doing that?[71]

Seven days after his inauguration, President Trump issued an executive order (EO-1) barring the entry of aliens from seven Muslim-majority countries (Iran, Iraq, Libya, Somalia, Sudan, Syria, and Yemen) for ninety days and barring the entry of refugees for 120 days, while refugees from Syria were banned indefinitely.[72] When the U.S. Refugee Program resumed, the secretary of state and the secretary of homeland security were directed "to prioritize refugee claims made by individuals on the basis of religious-based persecution, provided that the religion of the individual is a minority religion in the individual's country of nationality."[73] In the meantime, individuals could be admitted to the United States as refugees on a case-by-case basis "but only so long as they determine that the admission of such individuals as refugees is in the national interest—including when the person is a religious minority in his country of nationality facing religious persecution . . .—and it would not pose a risk to the security or welfare of the United States."[74] The executive order also said the United States "should not admit those who engage in acts of bigotry or hatred (including 'honor' killings, other forms of violence against women, or the persecution of those who practice religions different from their own) or those who would oppress Americans of any race, gender, or sexual orientation."[75] The order required the secretary of homeland security to collect and make available "information regarding the number and types of acts of gender-based violence against women, including honor killings, in the United States by foreign nationals . . . ."[76]

As members of the media gathered in the Oval Office to document the signing of the order, President Trump read the order's title aloud, "the 'Protection of the Nation from Foreign Terrorist Entry into the United States,'" and he said, "We all know what that means."[77] On the same day President Trump signed the order, he gave an interview to the Christian Broadcasting Network and said Christian refugees would be preferred.[78]

One day after the White House issued EO-1, former New York mayor Rudy Giuliani, an advisor to the president, was asked about the genesis of the order. After the Trump campaign issued its December 7, 2015, press release, Giuliani said, Trump told Giuliani that he wanted a "Muslim ban" and requested that Giuliani assemble a commission to show him "the right way to do it legally."[79]

A variety of individuals, organizations, and states immediately challenged EO-1 on statutory and constitutional grounds, including on the ground that the order violated the First Amendment's Establishment Clause.[80] Two federal district courts temporarily enjoined enforcement of the order.[81] The Ninth Circuit Court of Appeals subsequently denied the federal government's request to stay such an injunction.[82] The Ninth Circuit said the challengers' Establishment Clause claims "raise[d] serious allegations and present[ed] significant constitutional questions," but the court declined to rule on those issues at the time because it had already found that the challengers were likely to succeed on their due process claims.[83]

In the wake of these rulings against the Trump administration, President Trump signed a second executive order (EO-2) on March 6, 2017, revoking the January executive order and replacing it with a new order that responded to some of the issues that had been raised in the litigation.[84] The order reimposed the ninety-day ban on entry to the country from selected countries but removed Iraq from the list of such countries. Syrian refugees were placed within the 120-day bar on refugees, and references to refugee claims by adherents of minority faiths were removed. Provisions regarding "honor killings" were retained, however. President Trump's advisors characterized EO-2 as being substantially similar to EO-1, although the president described EO-2 as "a watered-down version" of the first order.[85]

Various courts found that EO-2 had the improper purpose of banning Muslims from the United States.[86] In addition to finding an improper purpose, one federal appellate court found that the order "identifie[d] and discriminate[d] against Muslims on its face." The court said that the order

> identifies only Muslim majority nations, thus banning approximately 10% of the world's Muslim population from entering the United States. It discusses only Islamic terrorism. And, it seeks information on honor killings—a stereotype affiliated with Muslims—even though honor killings have no connection whatsoever to the stated purpose of the Order.[87]

The court also noted that "[n]umerous amici explain that invoking the specter of 'honor killings' is a well-worn tactic for stigmatizing and demeaning Islam and painting the religion, and its men, as violent and barbaric."[88] The text's references to "honor killings" was "yet another marker that its national security purpose is secondary to its religious purpose."[89]

On May 8, 2017, after a reporter asked the White House whether President Trump's call for a Muslim ban was still on his campaign's website, the statement was removed without comment.[90]

On August 17, 2017, President Trump tweeted a horrific story of doubtful authenticity involving General Pershing and a purported massacre of Muslims with bullets dipped in a pig's blood.[91] President Trump urged people to "[s]tudy what General Pershing . . . did to terrorists when caught. There was no more

Radical Islamic Terror for 35 years!"[92] On September 15, 2017, President Trump tweeted, "The travel ban into the United States should be far larger, tougher and more specific—but stupidly, that would not be politically correct!"[93]

On September 24, 2017, President Trump signed a proclamation that indefinitely extended entry restrictions on all the countries listed in EO-2 except Sudan and that added North Korea, Chad, and Venezuela to the list.[94] There were no references to honor killings in the proclamation. The White House handled refugee issues separately in an executive order, which was issued on October 24, 2017.[95]

On November 29, 2017, President Trump retweeted three videos entitled: "Muslim Destroys a Statue of Virgin Mary!"; "Islamist mob pushes teenage boy off roof and beats him to death!"; and "Muslim migrant beats up Dutch boy on crutches!"[96] The source of the tweets was an extreme political party whose mission is to oppose "all alien and destructive politic or religious doctrines, including . . . Islam."[97] When White House Deputy Press Secretary Raj Shah was asked about the three videos, Shah said: The "President has been talking about these security issues for years now, from the campaign trail to the White House."[98]

On February 15, 2018, the Fourth Circuit Court of Appeals temporarily enjoined President Trump's proclamation as having an improper purpose under the Establishment Clause.[99] The court first asked whether the proffered reason for the proclamation was "facially legitimate and bona fide."[100] The stated purpose of the proclamation is to protect U.S. citizens from terrorist attacks and to encourage other governments to share information for immigration screening and vetting systems. Assuming without deciding that the purpose of the proclamation was facially legitimate, the court nonetheless found that its aim was not bona fide:

> Plaintiffs here do not just plausibly allege with particularity that the Proc-lamation's purpose is driven by anti-Muslim bias, they offer undisputed evidence of such bias: the words of the President. This evidence includes President Trump's disparaging comments and tweets regarding Muslims; his repeated proposals to ban Muslims from entering the United States; his subsequent explanation that he would effectuate this "Muslim" ban by targeting "territories" instead of Muslims directly; the issuance of EO-1 and EO-2, addressed only to majority-Muslim nations; and finally the issuance of the Proclamation, which not only closely tracks EO-1 and EO-2, but which President Trump and his advisors described as having the same goal as EO-1 and EO-2.[101]

The court found that the proclamation violated the Constitution because its primary purpose was not secular. The proclamation was facially neutral, but that was not dispositive. Even setting aside President Trump's pre-inaugural statements, the court determined that the primary purpose of the proclamation was based in anti-Muslim animus. The addition of two nonmajority Muslim countries did not rid the proclamation of a clear antireligious objective.

When the government argued that President Trump's past actions should not "forever taint" his future actions, the court noted that "President Trump could have removed the taint of his prior troubling statements; for a start he could have ceased publicly disparaging Muslims." Instead, "President Trump continued to disparage Muslims and the Islamic faith."[102] The court concluded:

> Our constitutional system creates a strong presumption of legitimacy for presidential action and we often defer to the political branches on issues related to immigration and national security. But the disposition in this case is compelled by the highly unusual facts here. Plaintiffs offer undisputed evidence that the President of the United States has openly and often expressed his desire to ban those of Islamic faith from entering the United States. The Proclamation is thus not only a likely Establishment Clause violation, but also strikes at the basic notion that the government may not act based on "religious animosity." *Church of the Lukumi Babalu Aye, Inc. v. City of Hialeah*, 508 U.S. 520, 532, 535 (1993).[103]

In 2017, the U.S. Supreme Court agreed to hear the case against presidential proclamation. Among other questions, the Court asked the parties to submit arguments regarding whether the proclamation violates the First Amendment's Establishment Clause.[104]

The standard of review, the Court said, was "whether the entry policy is plausibly related to the Government's stated objective to protect the country and improve vetting processes."[105] On June 26, 2018, the Supreme Court held by a vote of five to four that it had to accept the Trump administration's justification of its policy because "the entry suspension has a legitimate grounding in national security concerns, quite apart from any religious hostility . . . ."[106] The text of the proclamation said nothing about religion and was premised on the need to prevent the entry of nationals who were not adequately vetted, the Court said. Even though five of the seven nations currently covered by the proclamation have Muslim-majority populations, "that fact alone does not support an inference of religious hostility, given that the policy covers just 8% of the world's Muslim population and is limited to countries that were previously designated by Congress or prior administrations as security risks."[107] We "cannot substitute our own assessment for the Executive's predictive judgments on [national security] matters," the Court majority said.[108] Thus, the Court reversed the grant of preliminary injunction in favor of the state of Hawaii as an abuse of discretion and remanded the case for "further proceedings as may be appropriate."[109]

Justice Kennedy joined the Court's opinion in full, but he also wrote a brief separate opinion. Kennedy seemed to leave room for the lower court to address any religious animus in this case, so long as the court could do so without "intrud[ing] on the foreign affairs power of the Executive."[110] Justice Kennedy said that the Establishment Clause applied to the government's actions "even in the sphere of foreign affairs," a matter the opinion of the Court had mostly dodged. Kennedy also said:

> There are numerous instances in which the statements and actions of Government officials are not subject to judicial scrutiny or intervention. That does not mean those officials are free to disregard the Constitution and the rights it proclaims and protects. The oath that all officials take to adhere to the Constitution is not confined to those spheres in which the Judiciary can correct or even comment upon what those officials say or do.[111]

While the import of Justice Kennedy's comments is not entirely clear, the comments seem to suggest that lower courts and governmental officials could and should correct or even retract the policy, if they view it to be unconstitutional.[112]

Justice Breyer, joined by Justice Kagan, wrote a dissenting opinion, saying further proceedings were needed to determine whether the waiver system included in the ban was in effect a "Muslim ban."[113] If forced to decide the question without further litigation, Justice Breyer said he would, "on balance, find the evidence of anti-religious bias . . . a sufficient basis to set the Proclamation aside."[114]

Justice Sotomayor, with whom Justice Ginsburg joined, wrote a separate dissenting opinion attacking the Court majority's reasoning and conclusion. A reasonable observer, one who was aware of the context of the proclamation, would find that its primary purpose was to discriminate against Muslims by banning them from the United States, Justice Sotomayor said. Sotomayor also took issue with an assertion the solicitor general of the United States, Noel Francisco, had made at oral argument to defend President Trump. General Francisco asserted that President Trump "made crystal-clear on September 25 that he had no intention of imposing the Muslim ban" and "has praised Islam as one of the great countries [*sic*] of the world." Justice Sotomayor responded:

> Because the record contained no evidence of any such statement made on September 25th, . . . the Solicitor General clarified after oral argument that he actually intended to refer to President Trump's statement during a television interview on January 25, 2017. During that interview, the President

was asked whether EO–1 was "the Muslim ban," and answered, "no it's not the Muslim ban." But that lone assertion hardly qualifies as a disavowal of the President's comments about Islam—some of which were spoken after January 25, 2017. Moreover, it strains credulity to say that President Trump's January 25th statement makes "crystal-clear" that he never intended to impose a Muslim ban given that, until May 2017, the President's website displayed the statement regarding his campaign promise to ban Muslims from entering the country.[115]

The government had not cleared the low bar of demonstrating that the proclamation was "genuinely and primarily rooted in a legitimate national-security interest."[116]

Justice Sotomayor also noted the inconsistency in the Court's handling of the *Masterpiece Cakeshop* case and the Court's approach here.[117] In *Masterpiece*, the Court majority found that one-time derogatory statements by some commissioners of the Colorado Civil Rights Commission about the faith of the Christian baker constituted unconstitutional hostility toward religion. The majority should apply the same principles in this case, Justice Sotomayor said:

> In both instances, the question is whether a government actor exhibited tolerance and neutrality in reaching a decision that affects individuals' fundamental religious freedom. But unlike in *Masterpiece*, where a state civil rights commission was found to have acted without "the neutrality that the Free Exercise Clause requires," the government actors in this case will not be held accountable for breaching the First Amendment's guarantee of religious neutrality and tolerance. Unlike in *Masterpiece*, where the majority considered the state commissioners' statements about religion to be persuasive evidence of unconstitutional government action, the majority here completely sets aside the President's charged statements about Muslims as irrelevant. That holding erodes the foundational principles of religious tolerance that the Court elsewhere has so emphatically protected, and it tells members of minority religions in our country "that they are outsiders, not full members of the political community."[118]

The challengers of the ban were likely to succeed on the merits of their Establishment Clause claim, in the view of Justices Sotomayor and Ginsburg. Justice Sotomayor concluded:

> Our Constitution demands, and our country deserves, a Judiciary willing to hold the coordinate branches to account when they defy our most sacred legal commitments. Because the Court's decision today has failed in that respect, with profound regret, I dissent.[119]

Targeting Hate and Discrimination with Legislation

In April 2014, a former leader of the Ku Klux Klan fatally shot a boy and his grandfather outside a Jewish community center (JCC) near Kansas City, Kansas, as well as a woman at a nearby Jewish assisted living facility.[120] After his arrest, the gunman said: "I wanted to make damned sure I killed some Jews or attacked the Jews before I died." Admitting that he was an anti-Semite, Cross asked police officers, "How many did I get?"[121]

The murderer went to Jewish institutions with the heinous intent of killing Jews. As it turns out, he slaughtered Christians.

The murderer killed a fourteen-year-old boy, Reat Griffin Underwood, and his grandfather, William Lewis Corporan, in the parking lot of the JCC. Reat planned to practice at the JCC for tryouts for KC Superstar, a singing contest. Corporan, his grandfather, took Reat to the practice. Corporan was a longtime member of United Methodist Church of the Resurrection. Cross also murdered Terri LaManno, an occupational therapist who was making her regular Sunday visit to her mother, who lived at Village Shalom. LaManno was a member of St. Peter's Parish, a local Catholic church.[122]

The murderer could not imagine that Jewish institutions would open their arms to people of all faiths and of none, and that people of different religions would happily live and interact there. The lesson is plain: hate must be stopped, or it will harm us all.

The problem has become more dire, with data from the FBI showing that hate crimes in the United States rose 17 percent in 2017.[123] Religion-based hate crimes rose by 23 percent, with a 37 percent increase in crimes targeting Jews and Jewish institutions.[124] According to the Anti-Defamation League (ADL), the 1,564 religion-based hate crimes that were reported in 2017 is the second-highest number of such hate crimes ever, with more being reported only in 2001 in the wake of the 9/11 terrorist attacks.[125]

On October 27, 2018, a gunman entered the Tree of Life synagogue in Pittsburgh, Pennsylvania, and killed eleven worshippers.[126] The attack is believed to be the deadliest one on American Jews in U.S. history.[127] The gunman was an anti-Semite, and one of his latest fixations appears to have been the Jewish community's compassionate response to immigrants and refugees.[128] In August 2018, the Senate Judiciary Committee noted that there were 161 bomb threats made on Jewish community centers in 2017, which is an increase of 127 percent from the previous year.[129]

The Sikh Coalition has estimated that American Sikhs are experiencing an average of one hate crime per week in 2018.[130] A study of anti-Muslim activities—including attacks on mosques and Islamic centers, statements by local government officials denouncing Islam, and state legislatures debating anti-Muslim laws—found that there were 757 unique incidents of such activities from 2012 to August 2018 and that anti-Muslim activities have increased dramatically since late 2015.[131] Some officeholders have even argued that Islam is not a religion in order to seek to deny it First Amendment protections.[132]

It is no defense to cite the fact that groups like ISIS, and those it inspires, have committed heinous attacks around the world and in the United States, including the 2015 attack at a San Bernardino, California, community center and the 2016 attack at an Orlando, Florida, nightclub.[133] The appropriate response to these attacks is to combat terrorism, not to discriminate against Muslims. Just as it is wrong to blame the Christian community when murderers cite the Bible and Jesus Christ to try to justify their evil acts, as the man who attacked the Tree of Life synagogue did, it is wrong to blame the Muslim community when murderers cite the Qur'an and Allah to do the same.[134]

Researchers have also documented cases in which predominantly African American churches in the United States have been targeted for violent attacks. In November 2018, a gunman tried to enter a historically black church, First Baptist Church of Jeffersontown, Kentucky, shortly after a noon-day Bible study concluded.[135] The doors of the church were locked, a precaution taken in the wake of the attack on Mother Emanuel African Methodist Episcopal Church in 2015 in Charleston, South Carolina, so the gunman was thwarted. The administrator of the church, Billy Williams, "still shudders to think what might have happened if he had heard" the gunman knocking. "I would have welcomed him in," Williams said.[136] The killer left the church and went to a nearby grocery store, where he brutally gunned down two African American shoppers, sparing some white customers because, he said, "Whites don't shoot whites."[137]

There have been at least ninety-four attacks on predominantly African American churches since the 1950s.[138] After a series of arsons of these churches in the 1990s, Congress passed the Church Arson Prevention Act (CAPA).[139] The act strengthened an existing law that made it a crime to damage real property because of its religious nature or to use violence or threats of violence to interfere with free exercise. CAPA made it easier to prosecute incidents where the value of the damage to religious property is relatively small. The law also states that if religious property is damaged due to its racial or ethnic character, not simply its religious character, that also constitutes a violation of federal law.[140]

Similarly, federal statutes prohibit violent and intimidating acts against individuals that are motivated by animus based on personal characteristics, including a person's actual or perceived religion.[141] The most well-known provision is called the Matthew Shepard and James Byrd Jr. Hate Crimes Prevention

Act of 2009, making it a federal crime to willfully cause bodily injury, or attempt to do so, based on a person's actual or perceived race, color, religion, national origin, gender, sexual orientation, gender identity, or disability.[142]

Law enforcement officials used the Church Arson Prevention Act, along with the Shepard-Byrd Act, against a man who murdered nine African Americans who had gathered for Wednesday-night prayer and Bible study at an African Methodist Episcopal Church in Charleston, South Carolina, on June 17, 2015.[143] In a statement on the judgment against the murderer, Attorney General Loretta Lynch said:

> On June 17, 2015, Dylann Storm Roof sought out and opened fire on African-American parishioners engaged in worship and bible study at Emanuel African Methodist Episcopal Church in Charleston, South Carolina. He did so because of their race. And he did so to interfere with their peaceful exercise of religion. The victims in the case led lives as compassionate civic and religious leaders; devoted public servants and teachers; and beloved family members and friends. They include a young man in the bloom of youth and an 87-year-old grandmother who still sang in the church choir. We remember those who have suffered, and especially those that lost their lives: Cynthia Graham Hurd, 54; Susie Jackson, 87; Ethel Lance, 70; Rev. DePayne Middleton Doctor, 49; Rev. Clementa Pinckney, 41; Tywanza Sanders, 26; Rev. Daniel Simmons Sr., 74; Sharonda Coleman-Singleton, 45; and Myra Thompson, 59.[144]

Federal authorities also used the Church Arson Prevention Act to convict a man who sought to convince others to help him attack Islamberg, New York, a town founded by a group of African American Muslims. The FBI thwarted the would-be attacker's plans, which included bombing the city's mosque and shooting members of the community. In 2017, the man was convicted and sentenced to nearly twenty years in prison for his crimes.[145]

Other statutes passed by Congress guard against religious discrimination by governmental and nongovernmental bodies. The landmark 1964 Civil Rights Act, for example, prohibits discrimination based on religious beliefs or affiliations, or lack thereof, in a variety of ways. In addition to Title VII's prohibition on religious discrimination in employment, other provisions of the act bar religious discrimination, among other forms of discrimination, in educational institutions;[146] public accommodations, such as hotels, restaurants, nightclubs, and theaters;[147] and state-operated facilities.[148] The Fair Housing Act prohibits such discrimination by entities such as landlords, real estate companies, municipalities, lending institutions, and homeowners insurance companies.[149] The Equal Credit Opportunity Act prohibits creditors from discriminating against credit applicants on the basis of religion.[150]

The federal Religious Land Use and Institutionalized Persons Act (RLUIPA) bars governmental discrimination in the context of land use matters "against any assembly or institution on the basis of religion or religious denomination."[151] Civil rights and religious groups have been active in defending this law. In 2016, for example, almost twenty civil rights and religious groups filed a friend-of-the-court brief in a RLUIPA case to support a Muslim community in New Jersey that had been trying to build a house of worship there for almost a decade.[152] The groups agreed with the U.S. Department of Justice, which alleged that a New Jersey township had discriminated against the Islamic Society based on its religion when it denied the society's zoning application. The president of the Islamic Society said at the time:

> I came to America almost fifty years ago with a firm belief in the values that America represents, including freedom of religion and equality before the law. This mosque is part of my American dream. We are overwhelmed by this extraordinary support from so many diverse groups all supporting our position and affirming that Muslims too have the right to worship in Bernards Township.[153]

In May 2017, the township ultimately settled the case, agreeing to permit the Islamic Society to build their mosque.[154]

The Department of Justice has also enforced RLUIPA against localities that have discriminated against or improperly burdened the religious exercise of synagogues and churches.[155] In April 2011, DOJ filed a friend-of-the-court brief with a federal district court to support a small Orthodox Jewish congregation seeking to hold services at a home within a residential neighborhood. The city had permitted nonreligious assemblies and institutions to operate in this neighborhood, but not the Jewish congregation. The Jewish members of the community needed to be able to walk to their place of worship on their Sabbath, making services in the area essential. In July 2011, the court ruled that the city's refusal to allow the congregation to hold services at the home violated RLUIPA.[156]

DOJ also came to the aid of a small church in Schodack, New York. The city denied the church's request to rent space in a building that had previously been the site of a business training center. The building was in a commercial zone that allowed various nonreligious assemblies to rent property there. In 2011, the town amended its zoning code to treat places of worship the same as other assemblies.[157]

Creating a "World Without Hate"

Government officials are not the only ones who have taken action to combat hate. Civil society has also played an essential role, including by advocating for laws and policies and building bridges of understanding across differences of faith and belief.

One such civil society leader is Rais Bhuiyan. On September 21, 2001, Bhuiyan, a former pilot who was born in Bangladesh, was working in a friend's service station in Dallas, Texas, when Mark Anthony Stroman entered with a gun.[158] Stroman was enraged by the 9/11 terrorist attacks and aimed to kill "Arabs."[159] Stroman had already killed two people: Vasudev Patel (an Indian immigrant who was Hindu) and Waqar Hasan (a Muslim born in Pakistan). When he entered the store, Stroman asked Bhuiyan where he was from. Before Bhuiyan could answer, Stroman shot him at close range. The attack partly blinded Bhuiyan in one eye.

Citing his Islamic faith, Bhuiyan forgave Stroman and argued that he be spared the death penalty, which had been imposed on Stroman for murdering Vasudev Patel. Stroman called Bhuiyan "an inspiring soul" and expressed his gratitude for "Bhuiyan's [e]fforts to save my life after I tried to end [h]is."[160] Despite Bhuiyan's campaign, Stroman was executed in July 2011.[161]

Bhuiyan subsequently founded a World Without Hate to "shar[e] the transformational power of forgiveness, embrac[e] compassion and mercy, and teach[] others the beauty of acceptance and empathy."[162] A World Without Hate trains young people to be "empathy ambassadors," leaders who are skilled in conflict resolution. The project also sponsors a filmmaking program for teens to tell stories about the ability to overcome bias through empathy and compassion.[163] A World Without Hate is "a movement, stemming from one man's journey of survival to hope and healing, cultivating a world that we all want, inspiring a world without hate, a world without violence, a world without victims."[164]

Other efforts to bring people together across faiths and beliefs include the *Know Your Neighbor* initiative. In December 2015, the White House Office of Faith-Based and Neighborhood Partnerships helped launch *Know Your Neighbor*, an alliance of diverse religious and secular leaders dedicated to creating greater understanding among individuals with religious differences.[165] The coalition invites people of different beliefs and backgrounds to get to know one another through informal meetings and events.[166] A similar initiative launched by Christian, Muslim, and Jewish ministers aims to foster dialogue and build relationships based on mutual trust.[167] And the ADL has a wealth of resources to combat hate and bullying, including its *A World of Difference* curriculum.[168]

An important function these projects carry out is relationship-building. Surveys have found that "the more likely a person is to know a Muslim," for example, "the more likely she is to express positive feelings toward Muslims as a group."[169] The hope and expectation is that, through such projects, individuals not only form positive relationships and gain empathetic understanding but also become invested in defending each other's rights.[170]

A distinguished group of American civil society leaders did so in 2014 by traveling to Berlin for a conference sponsored by the Organization for Security and Co-operation in Europe (OSCE) to commemorate the tenth anniversary of the Berlin Conference on Anti-Semitism and the accompanying Berlin Declaration.[171] The 2004 declaration reaffirmed the Universal Declaration of Human Rights—including its promise that everyone has the right to freedom of thought, conscience, and religion—and it specifically committed participants to intensify efforts "to combat anti-Semitism in all its manifestations and to promote and strengthen tolerance and non-discrimination."[172] The various delegations from around the world vowed to take steps to address anti-Semitism, including by promoting "education about the tragedy of the Holocaust, and the importance of respect for all ethnic and religious groups"; combating hate crimes; and supporting the work of nongovernmental organizations on these issues."[173]

The delegation of American civil society leaders, led by the Leadership Conference on Civil and Human Rights, included current or former representatives of the American Islamic Congress, the ADL, the Human Rights Campaign, Asian Americans Advancing Justice, the Sikh American Legal Defense and Education Fund, the League of United Latin American Citizens, American Jewish World Service, and Human Rights First.[174] This delegation stated:

> We have come together to demonstrate that Jewish communities must not face these threats alone. Working together, [coalitions of nongovernmental organizations] can help create political space for more effective government action against anti-Semitism and all forms of bigotry and hate crime which are also rising in the region.[175]

This diverse American coalition of civil society leaders drew notice at the Berlin conferences. Delegations from other countries appreciated the fact that American citizens of so many different faiths, beliefs, and racial and ethnic backgrounds not only worked together closely on a range of human rights issues but also traveled across the Atlantic Ocean to stand together against anti-Semitism. Wade Henderson, the leader of the civil society delegation, who had also led a similar delegation to the 2004 Berlin conference, described the coalition's impact:

> There was no other group like us. We brought diversity to the conference and made an impact simply by being there. There is still much work to be done in the United States, but our lessons learned over centuries of struggle to be a more inclusive democracy—from emancipation, women's suffrage, Jim Crow, Japanese internment, immigration reform, protecting

religious minorities and LGBT equality—can resonate in the global struggle for human rights for all.[176]

RECOMMENDATIONS: A PROMISE TO KEEP

Combatting hate and discrimination and protecting religious freedom for all is wise as well as just. Every religion is a minority faith somewhere in the world. When the United States protects religious minorities at home, such as Muslims, it strengthens the government's hand in asking other countries, such as Muslim-majority countries, to protect religious minorities abroad. President Obama made this point when he visited a mosque in Baltimore, Maryland, in February 2016. President Obama said:

> [I]f we're serious about freedom of religion—and I'm speaking now to my fellow Christians who remain the majority in this country—we have to understand an attack on one faith is an attack on all our faiths. And when any religious group is targeted, we all have a responsibility to speak up. And we have to reject a politics that seeks to manipulate prejudice or bias, and targets people because of religion.
>
> We've got to make sure that hate crimes are punished, and that the civil rights of all Americans are upheld. And just as faith leaders, including Muslims, must speak out when Christians are persecuted around the world—or when anti-Semitism is on the rise—because the fact is, is that there are Christians who are targeted now in the Middle East, despite having been there for centuries, and there are Jews who've lived in places like France for centuries who now feel obliged to leave because they feel themselves under assault—sometimes by Muslims. We have to be consistent in condemning hateful rhetoric and violence against everyone. And that includes against Muslims here in the United States of America.
>
> So none of us can be silent. We can't be bystanders to bigotry. And together, we've got to show that America truly protects all faiths.[177]

President Obama made these remarks before a large group in the main gathering area of the Baltimore mosque. After the speech was over, he made a surprise visit to the overflow room next door, where a large group of students who attended the mosque's school were gathered. When the president walked in, the students got excited. Some of them had two flags in their hands—a U.S. flag and the flag of their Islamic school. As President Obama entered the room, the students' hands shot up with these two flags in their fists—one flag representing a religious identity and another representing their identity as U.S. citizens.

The students' gesture serves as a reminder of a principle that has united Americans in the past and can unite us moving forward. People of all religious beliefs want to be able to claim both their religious and American identities publicly and proudly—and to have our nation respect and protect them in equal measure. That is part of the promise of religious freedom, a promise Americans must continue to strive to keep. Taking the following steps will help Americans to do so.

(1) Augment initiatives to combat discrimination, hate crimes, and violent extremism.

Policymakers must take a range of steps to combat discrimination, hate crimes, and violent extremism. Helpful suggestions can be readily found. In 2016, for example, DOJ catalogued a series of recommendations for addressing religious discrimination, including calls for increased education and training about existing law and building more and stronger relationships between government and civil society.[178] Nongovernmental organizations such as the ADL, the Leadership Conference on Civil and Human Rights, and Human Rights First also have offered a variety of resources for getting these issues right.[179] After the neo-Nazis, the KKK, and other white supremacists marched in Charlottesville, Virginia, in the summer of 2017, a coalition of more than eighty civil rights, religious, education, and professional organizations recommended specific actions that governmental bodies can take to improve hate crimes reporting.[180] Also, projects aimed at countering violent extremism must address rising violence by white supremacists.[181]

(2) Eschew dehumanizing language and avoid violent expression that whips up fears based on factors like faith.

Leaders have a responsibility to eschew dehumanizing language, such as calling human beings "animals" and referring to the migration of people as "infestations." They must also avoid violent speech and imagery. People who are on the edge may be encouraged to act violently when they hear such charged language. And leaders should never demonize religions or seek to turn people against one other based on faith affiliations or beliefs, or lack thereof.

(3) Consistently condemn attacks against religious communities.

President Trump has sometimes failed to condemn terrorist attacks on Muslims, and at other times he has been slow to do so.[182] One staff member in the Trump White House even dismissed reports of hate crimes against Muslim communities as false claims stirred up by political opponents.[183] These approaches could not be more wrong. Government officials should ensure that they consistently condemn attacks against religious communities rather than take a selective approach. Also, government officials should never dismiss attacks or spread rumors about them.

(4) Consistently condemn governmental failures to demonstrate religious neutrality.

When two cases involving official religious bias came before the U.S. Supreme Court during its 2017–2018 term, the Court ruled inconsistently. The Court forcefully condemned a lack of religious neutrality on the part of certain government officials in the *Masterpiece Cakeshop* case, yet it upheld a policy in *Trump v. Hawaii* where the evidence of official religious bigotry was far stronger.

There are some distinctions between the cases, but those distinctions cut both ways. Unlike the *Masterpiece Cakeshop* case, the *Trump v. Hawaii* case involved issues of immigration and national security, where the courts generally demonstrate great deference to the executive branch. Also, the *Masterpiece Cakeshop* case involved governmental adjudicatory bodies rather than lawmaking bodies, a context in which more members of the Court have been willing to consider statements reflecting the motivations of decision-makers.[184] At the same time, the evidence of official hostility toward a faith was much stronger in *Trump v. Hawaii*, and President Trump played a much larger role in the development of the travel ban policy than certain government decision-makers did in the resolution of the *Masterpiece Cakeshop* case.[185]

Also, in *Masterpiece Cakeshop*, the Court majority faulted governmental officials for not disavowing some problematic statements made by members of the Colorado Civil Rights Commission.[186] But the Court majority in *Trump v. Hawaii* did not even mention the fact that President Trump has never apologized for, much less retracted, his call for Muslims to be banned from the United States.

In *Trump v. Hawaii*, the Supreme Court could and should have written a narrow but forceful opinion recognizing the differences between the cases and also noting that President Trump's proclamation would not have been issued but for his obvious hostility to Islam. Especially given Justice Anthony Kennedy's previous record of vigilance against governmental hostility toward religion, the fact that he did not take such a position in the *Trump v. Hawaii* case is deeply disappointing.[187] The inconsistency in these rulings leaves a stain on the Court's reputation, one the Court must seek to remove.

(5) Government officials should visit houses of worship in their jurisdiction to promote religious freedom for all and inclusion.

Government officials should visit diverse houses of worship in their jurisdictions to promote religious freedom and pluralism, if congregations are interested in hosting such visits. Officials should plan such visits outside of election season so that the visits will not be misunderstood or misused. Officials should ensure that these visits are nonpartisan and that they include a wide variety of religious traditions overall. Religious communities can and should play an active role in planning these events.

(6) Do not "securitize" relationships with the American Muslim or any other religious community.

Sometimes government officials tend to reach out to American Muslims only when they want to discuss issues like combating violent extremism. This approach falsely suggests that the American Muslim community is responsible for terrorism, and that Muslims do not have the full range of interests and concerns or do not make the same kinds of contributions to their country that other Americans do. Instead, government officials should invite Muslims and members of other religious communities to briefings and discussions on a range of other issues, including health care, the environment, education, veterans, and business development. Government officials must ensure that they are not putting unnecessary and unhelpful limits on their relationships with religious communities.

(7) Support projects that encourage Americans to get to know their neighbors.

Studies demonstrate that the most important factor in creating positive views of people of other faiths and beliefs is actually knowing individuals of other religions and beliefs. Several existing projects are aimed at connecting diverse people and building relationships. *Know Your Neighbor,* for example, is an alliance of diverse religious and secular leaders dedicated to creating greater understanding across religious differences. The coalition brings together people of different beliefs and backgrounds to get to know one another through informal meetings and events. A similar initiative launched by Christian, Muslim, and Jewish ministers aims to foster dialogue and build relationships based on mutual trust. Also, the ADL has a wealth of resources to combat hate and bullying, including its *A World of Difference* curriculum.[188] Government officials can and should highlight efforts of this kind and participate in their work. Individuals of all faiths, beliefs, and political perspectives should also consider participating in efforts like these.[189]

CONCLUSION

A Crossroads for Faith in American Public Life

President Barack Obama addressed three different religiously inflected gatherings during the space of one week in the final year of his presidency. On January 28, 2016, President Obama offered remarks at a ceremony at the Israeli embassy to honor individuals who were not Jewish but who risked their lives during the Holocaust to save Jews from extermination by Nazis.[1] Six days later, President Obama spoke at a Baltimore mosque and hosted a small roundtable with Muslim leaders.[2] The next day, February 4, he addressed attendees of the National Prayer Breakfast for the final time as president.

In his remarks at the prayer breakfast, President Obama offered reflections on a verse from Second Timothy: "For God has not given us a spirit of fear, but of power and of love and of a sound mind."[3] The president wove stories he had learned during the previous two events into his remarks. President Obama said:

> A week ago, I spoke at a ceremony held at the Israeli Embassy for the first time, honoring the courage of people who saved Jews during the Holocaust. And one of the recipients was the grandson—or the son of an American soldier who had been captured by the Nazis. So a group of American soldiers are captured, and their captors ordered Jewish POWs to identify themselves. And one sergeant, a Christian named Roddie Edmonds, from Tennessee, ordered all American troops to report alongside them. They lined up in formation, approximately 200 of them, and the Nazi colonel said, "I asked only for the Jewish POWs," and said, "These can't all be Jewish." And

225

Master Sergeant Edmonds stood there and said, "We are all Jews." And the colonel took out his pistol and held it to the Master Sergeant's head and said, "Tell me who the Jews are." And he repeated, "We are all Jews." And faced with the choice of shooting all those soldiers, the Nazis relented. And so, through his moral clarity, through an act of faith, Sergeant Edmonds saved the lives of his Jewish brothers-in-arms.

A second story. Just yesterday, some of you may be aware I visited a mosque in Baltimore to let our Muslim-American brothers and sisters know that they, too, are Americans and welcome here. And there I met a Muslim-American named Rami Nashashibi, who runs a nonprofit working for social change in Chicago. And he forms coalitions with churches and Latino groups and African Americans in this poor neighborhood in Chicago. And he told me how the day after the tragedy in San Bernardino happened, he took his three young children to a playground in the Marquette Park neighborhood, and while they were out, the time came for one of the five daily prayers that are essential to the Muslim tradition. And on any other day, he told me, he would have immediately put his rug out on the grass right there and prayed.

But that day, he paused. He feared any unwelcome attention he might attract to himself and his children. And his seven-year-old daughter asked him, "What are you doing, Dad? Isn't it time to pray?" And he thought of all the times he had told her the story of the day that Dr. Martin Luther King Jr., and Rabbi Robert Marx, and 700 other people marched to that very same park, enduring hatred and bigotry, dodging rocks and bottles, and hateful words, in order to challenge Chicago housing segregation, and to ask America to live up to our highest ideals.

And so, at that moment, drawing from the courage of men of different religions, of a different time, Rami refused to teach his children to be afraid. Instead, he taught them to be a part of that legacy of faith and good conscience. "I want them to understand that sometimes faith will be tested," he told me, "and that we will be asked to show immense courage, like others have before us, to make our city, our country, and our world a better reflection of all our ideals." And he put down his rug and he prayed.

Now, those two stories, they give me courage and they give me hope. And they instruct me in my own Christian faith. I can't imagine a moment in which that young American sergeant expressed his Christianity more profoundly than when, confronted by his own death, he said "We are all Jews." I can't imagine a clearer expression of Jesus's teachings. I can't imagine a better expression of the peaceful spirit of Islam than when a Muslim father, filled with fear, drew from the example of a Baptist preacher and a Jewish rabbi to teach his children what God demands.[4]

These stories reflect some of the best of the human spirit. Individuals rising to counter the worst kinds of hatred and bigotry—even risking their lives to do so. People drawing inspiration from the heroism of others, including leaders of other faiths.

The president of the United States wove these threads together to celebrate spiritual courage, interfaith solidarity, and the American traditions of religious pluralism and freedom. President Obama certainly was not the first president to take this approach. President George W. Bush demonstrated the same kind of leadership when he visited a mosque just six days after the 9/11 attacks.[5] Standing beside Muslim leaders, President Bush said:

> America counts millions of Muslims amongst our citizens, and Muslims make an incredibly valuable contribution to our country. Muslims are doctors, lawyers, law professors, members of the military, entrepreneurs, shopkeepers, moms and dads. And they need to be treated with respect. In our anger and emotion, our fellow Americans must treat each other with respect.
>
> Women who cover their heads in this country must feel comfortable going outside their homes. Moms who wear cover must be not intimidated in America. That's not the America I know. That's not the America I value.
>
> I've been told that some fear to leave; some don't want to go shopping for their families; some don't want to go about their ordinary daily routines because, by wearing cover, they're afraid they'll be intimidated. That should not and that will not stand in America.
>
> Those who feel like they can intimidate our fellow citizens to take out their anger don't represent the best of America, they represent the worst of humankind, and they should be ashamed of that kind of behavior.
>
> This is a great country. It's a great country because we share the same values of respect and dignity and human worth. And it is my honor to be meeting with leaders who feel just the same way I do. They're outraged, they're sad. They love America just as much as I do.
>
> I want to thank you all for giving me a chance to come by. And may God bless us all.[6]

President Bush's words and actions sent a message the nation needed to hear.

CHOOSING RELIGIOUS FREEDOM FOR ALL

This kind of leadership must be restored in the White House and reflected throughout public service and civil society. The choices Americans make now will help to determine our course.

"We make our own history," Eleanor Roosevelt said.[7] "The course of history is directed by the choices we make and our choices grow out of the ideas, the beliefs, the values, the dreams of the people. It is not so much the powerful leaders that determine our destiny as the much more powerful influence of the combined voice of the people themselves."[8]

With hate crimes and hostility toward certain faiths soaring, Americans have to decide whether we will tolerate this state of affairs or act to change it. If we truly believe all are created with equal dignity and worth, the answer is clear: every human being deserves safety, security, and religious liberty. And an attack on any faith must be treated as an attack against our own.

Especially under current circumstances, there should be no more tolerance for violent rhetoric or fearmongering by candidates or government officials. To be sure, government cannot stop every hate crime or heal all of our divisions. But leaders have a solemn obligation to do everything in their power to keep us safe and bring us together. Let us reaffirm that the United States of America should give "to bigotry no sanction, to persecution no assistance . . . ."[9]

These are among the values embodied in the First Amendment's religion clauses, which serve as "co-guarantor[s]" of religious liberty.[10] In the face of efforts to dismantle or diminish it, Americans should register their support for a robust understanding of the Establishment Clause, one that applies to both the federal government and the governments of all fifty states. State support for religion violates liberty of conscience and leads to religious discrimination. It also warps and weakens the faith the state backs. In an America that is rapidly becoming more diverse, it is perhaps more important than ever that the government maintain neutrality toward religion, neither promoting nor denigrating faith, nor preferring one or more religions over others.

Strong support is also needed for robust protections for religious exercise, including appropriate religious exemptions. Exempting or accommodating religious individuals and institutions from laws and policies that conflict with their consciences is a time-honored American tradition, one that plays a key role in recognizing human dignity and protecting inalienable rights. This same tradition, however, has also taken seriously the burdens that religious exemptions place on individuals who do not benefit them, and coexisted with robust protections for other human and civil rights. It has also acknowledged distinctions between the commercial and nonprofit spheres.[11]

Making lasting progress on issues like these will require renewed efforts to bring diverse Americans of good faith together to listen to one another and seek common ground. That will not resolve all of our differences, but it will make our conversations and our country better.

In the recent past, presidents have called on Americans of vastly different political and theological stripes to seek common ground, and those efforts have borne fruit. Such initiatives have produced consensus guidance on current law regarding religious expression in public schools and the federal workplace. Another initiative produced consensus recommendations for strengthening the partnerships the government forms with faith-based and other community organizations to serve people in need. This common-ground tradition needs to be revived.

Another piece of common-ground work should be rebuilding the U.S. refugee admissions and resettlement system. Refugees are individuals who are fleeing persecution, including persecution for their faith or beliefs. Every year, the president, in consultation with Congress, sets the ceiling for the number of refugees who can be admitted to our country. Once refugees undergo a rigorous series of security checks, they are resettled by nongovernmental groups, including many faith-based groups. Until a few years ago, the refugee admissions and resettlement programs had been treasured and strengthened by presidents of both parties. Participating in a robust, global system of refugee resettlement has helped the United States to make good on its promise to protect human rights and to prevent crises and conflicts around the world.[12] Since 2017, however, the resettlement program has been dismantled, and the ceiling for refugees has been driven to a historic low. Leaders from across the political and religious spectrum have called for the refugee admissions and resettlement programs to be restored, noting that the United States can be both secure *and* compassionate.[13]

Restoration of the refugee resettlement program should be part of a larger plan for renewed cooperation between government and a wide range of religious and humanitarian leaders. The Constitution *permits* governmental and willing religious leaders to work together to promote the common good. Common sense *requires* it. To conquer scourges like the Ebola and Zika viruses, end global poverty, promote racial justice, advance maternal and child health, counter violent extremism, make peace around the world, and slow the climate change that threatens especially the poorest among us, government should collaborate with civil society organizations, including interested religious organizations. Such collaboration ought to be prioritized and always conducted in a manner consistent with the Constitution.

Lift Every Voice and Sing

The independence of faith and its capacity to call our nation to heed "the better angels of its nature," as President Abraham Lincoln so eloquently put it, also must be protected. Religion should never become a creature of the state, whether through government action or faith's own quest for power.

One of the times when African American religious communities served as the conscience of the state was when they challenged Jim Crow segregation and discrimination. Their protests featured not only slogans but songs. *Lift Every Voice and Sing* was one of those songs. James Weldon Johnson wrote the lyrics, and his brother, John Rosamond Johnson, composed the music.

In 1900, James Weldon Johnson was preparing for a school assembly celebrating Abraham Lincoln's birthday. Johnson, a black lawyer, served as the principle of Stanton School in Jacksonville, Florida.[14] At the time, racial segregation was required in the public schools of all Southern states, and 90 percent of African Americans lived in the South.[15]

Principal Johnson's initial intention was to draft a speech for the school assembly. He later considered writing a poem instead. In a conversation with his brother, John, however, the idea of composing a song for the schoolchildren to sing began to take shape.[16]

The song's title was *Lift Every Voice and Sing*. Here are its three verses:

> Lift every voice and sing,
> Till earth and heaven ring,
> Ring with the harmonies of Liberty;
> Let our rejoicing rise
> High as the list'ning skies,
> Let it resound loud as the rolling sea.
> Sing a song full of the faith that the dark past has taught us,
> Sing a song full of the hope that the present has brought us;
> Facing the rising sun of our new day begun,
> Let us march on till victory is won.
>
> Stony the road we trod,
> Bitter the chast'ning rod,
> Felt in the days when hope unborn had died;
> Yet with a steady beat,
> Have not our weary feet
> Come to the place for which our fathers sighed?
> We have come over a way that with tears has been watered.
> We have come, treading our path through the blood of the slaughtered,
> Out from the gloomy past,
> Till now we stand at last
> Where the white gleam of our bright star is cast.
>
> God of our weary years,
> God of our silent tears,
> Thou who hast brought us thus far on the way;
> Thou who hast by Thy might,
> Led us into the light,

Keep us forever in the path, we pray.
Lest our feet stray from the places, our God, where we met Thee,
Lest, our hearts, drunk with the wine of the world, we forget Thee;
Shadowed beneath Thy hand,
May we forever stand,
True to our God,
True to our native land.[17]

As Professor Imani Perry has explained, "The song proved to be, both then and soon thereafter, much bigger than an ode to any one leader or icon. It was a lament and encomium to the story and struggle of black people."[18] The song's three verses have often been described as "praise, lament, and prayer."[19] James Weldon Johnson called it "a hymn for Negro people."[20]

The song soon spread far beyond Stanton School. It became the official song of the National Association for the Advancement of Colored People (NAACP),[21] then the national Negro hymn,[22] and eventually the National Negro Anthem.[23] James Weldon Johnson said: "I have commonly found printed or typewritten copies of the words [of the anthem] pasted in the back of hymnals and the song books used in Sunday schools, [YMCAs,] and similar institutions and I think that is the manner by which it gets its widest circulation . . . ."[24]

The hymn drew ecumenical appreciation. In 1928, for example, Rabbi Stephen S. Wise wrote to Johnson after hearing the song performed at Morehouse College. Rabbi Wise called it the "noblest anthem I have ever heard. It is a great upwelling of prayer from the soul of a race long wronged but with faith unbroken."[25]

Beginning with the first public speech he delivered in April 1944, Rev. Dr. Martin Luther King Jr. often wove verses from the hymn in his remarks.[26] As King spoke to Americans in 1968—including leaders of different races, denominations, and faiths who had come from across the nation to protest in Selma, Alabama—King drew on the song's lyrics to remember the martyrs of the civil rights struggle.[27]

In 2009, *Lift Every Voice and Sing* became part of the ceremony inaugurating the first black American to serve as president of the United States. Rev. Joseph Lowery, a longtime leader of the civil rights movement, incorporated the final verse of the hymn into the benediction he offered from the podium of the U.S. Capitol.[28]

Lift Every Voice is full of hope, yet it is also a painful reminder that at times the United States has not even considered non-white people to be deserving of the blessings of liberty. "We have come over a way that with tears has been watered," the hymn says. "We have come, treading our path through the blood of the slaughtered." And even as the nation has made progress in achieving justice and liberty for all, the battle is far from over. "Let us march on till victory is won."

The nation's record on religious freedom specifically is similarly stained. The country has sometimes turned a blind eye to violence, oppression, and discrimination against religious minorities and even perpetrated it. Some of the same government officials who claim to be champions of religious freedom actually foment fear about certain faiths and condone, or even call for, discrimination against them. At times it has been argued that a right to religious freedom should block other human rights, like the equal right of same-sex couples to have their marriages recognized by the state.

At its best, however, the United States has made it possible for individuals to reconcile conflicts between their faith and the law, while also giving due respect to other human rights. The American system of religious freedom has created space for people to draw on religious as well as civic ideals to push the country to new heights. Our government has recognized people of all religions and no religion as equal citizens, and individuals with a stunning array of faiths and beliefs have coexisted peacefully and productively. And, despite deep differences, leaders have often sought and found common ground.

Getting these issues right is rarely easy, and the current moment is certainly no exception to this general rule. Yet there is reason for hope today. Recent events have laid bare certain injustices and blind spots, spurring new conversations, alliances, and action. And while some of the principles that have produced remarkable religious freedom and cooperation are threatened today, there is still much that can be done to preserve and perfect those principles. In sum, at this juncture in our nation's history, Americans have an opportunity to make significant progress in our quest to extend religious freedom to all and to strengthen the best traditions of religious engagement in American public life. May we seize it.

NOTES

Introduction

1. In addition to heading the Catholic Church, the pope is the head of Vatican City, making him "a civil chief of state like any other monarch of a small state recognized under international law." Thomas J. Reese, *Inside the Vatican: The Politics and Organization of the Catholic Church* (Cambridge, Mass.: Harvard University Press 1996) 5.

2. *See Conference Call on Upcoming Visit of Pope Francis*, CSPAN (September 18, 2015).

3. *See* His Holiness Pope Francis, *Laudato Si', mi' Signore* (Praise be to you, My Lord: On Care for our Common Home), The Holy See (May 24, 2015).

4. *See below* chap. 6.

5. *Fact Sheet: Advancing Shared Values for a Better World*, The White House (September 23, 2015), https://obamawhitehouse.archives.gov/the-press-office/2015/09/23/fact-sheet -advancing-shared-values-better-world.

6. *Papal Visits to the White House*, White House Historical Association, https://www .whitehousehistory.org/papal-visits-to-the-white-house.

7. *See, e.g.,* Alanna Durkin, *Cross-Section of Religious Life to Greet Pope Francis in the United States*, Associated Press (September 10, 2015). Both the White House and the Vatican regretted that the visit took place on Yom Kippur. *See Conference Call on Upcoming Visit.*

8. *See Remarks by President Obama and His Holiness Pope Francis at Arrival Ceremony*, The White House (September 23, 2015), https://obamawhitehouse.archives.gov/the-press-office/ 2015/09/23/remarks-president-obama-and-his-holiness-pope-francis-arrival-ceremony.

9. Amber Phillips, *An Insider's Look at the Pope's Visit to the White House*, The Washington Post (September 23, 2015).

10. Dalia Fahmy, *Americans Are Far More Religious than Adults in Other Nations*, Pew Research Center (July 31, 2018), http://www.pewresearch.org/fact-tank/2018/07/31/americans-are -far-more-religious-than-adults-in-other-wealthy-nations/.

For instance, more than half of American adults (55 percent) say they pray daily, compared with 25 percent in Canada, 18 percent in Australia and 6 percent in Great Britain. (The average European country stands at 22 percent.) Actually, when it comes to their prayer habits, Americans are more like people in many poorer, developing nations—including South Africa (52 percent), Bangladesh (57 percent) and Bolivia (56 percent)—than people in richer countries.

Id.

11 *See below* chap. 1.

12 *See id.*

13 *See id.*

14 *Walz v. Tax Commission*, 397 U.S. 664, 669 (1970).

15 *See below* chap. 2.

16 *Abington Township v. Schempp*, 374 U.S. 203, 256 (1963) (Brennan, J., concurring).

17 In *Church of Lukumi Babalu Aye, Inc. v. Hialeah*, the U.S. Supreme Court found that the city's regulations on animal sacrifice prohibited religiously motivated conduct related to public health and preventing cruelty to animals but did not "prohibit nonreligious conduct that endangers these interests in a similar or greater degree than Santeria sacrifice does." 508 U.S. 520, 543 (1993). The underinclusion of nonreligious conduct by the city in this case was "substantial, not inconsequential." *Id.* Indeed, the Court said, the city acted only against conduct motivated by religious beliefs. Thus, the city's regulations "f[e]ll well below the minimum standard necessary to protect First Amendment rights." *Id. See below* chaps. 8 and 10.

18 *See below* chaps. 2 and 8.

19 *West Virginia State Bd. of Educ. v. Barnette*, 319 U.S. 624, 638 (1943).

20 *See* Stephen Asma, *Religiously Unaffiliated "Nones" Are Pursuing Spirituality but Not Community*, Los Angeles Times (June 7, 2018).

21 Circle of Protection, http://circleofprotection.us/.

22 Refugee Council USA, http://www.rcusa.org/.

23 *Id.*

24 Interaction, https://www.interaction.org/about.

25 *Id.*

26 *See below* chap. 10.

27 *See* Isabel Fattal, *A Brief History of Anti-Semitic Violence in America*, The Atlantic (October 28, 2018).

28 *Id.*

29 *See* Yonat Shimron and Jack Jenkins, *Pittsburgh Suspect's Hatred of Jews, HIAS Part of Larger Anti-immigrant Surge*, Religion News Service (October 29, 2018); Stoyan Zaimov, *Robert Bowers, Shooter Who Killed 11 at Synagogue, Quoted the Bible, Talked About Jesus Christ*, The Christian Post (October 29, 2018); Adam Serwer, *Trump's Caravan Hysteria Led to This*, The Atlantic (October 28, 2018).

30 *See below* chap. 10.

31 Sheera Frenkel, Mike Isaac, and Kate Conger, *On Instagram, 11,696 Examples of How Hate Thrives on Social Media*, The New York Times (October 29, 2018).

32 *See below* chap. 10.

33 *See below id.*

34 Matthew Haag and Jacey Fortin, *Two Killed in Portland While Trying to Stop Anti-Muslim Rants, Police Say*, New York Times (May 27, 2017).

35 *See below* chap. 10.

36 New America Foundation, *Anti-Muslim Activities in the United States*, https://www
    .newamerica.org/in-depth/anti-muslim-activity/.

37 Asma T. Uddin, *The Latest Attack on Islam: It's Not a Religion*, The New York Times
    (September 26, 2018); Asma Uddin, *When Islam Is Not a Religion: Inside America's Fight
    for Religious Freedom* (New York: Pegasus Books, 2019).

38 *See below* chap. 10.

39 *See* Federal Bureau of Investigation, *FBI Releases 2017 Hate Crime Statistics* (November
    13, 2018), https://ucr.fbi.gov/hate-crime/2017/resource-pages/hate-crime-summary.

40 Anti-Defamation League, *ADL Calls on Leaders to Redouble Efforts to Counter Hate after
    FBI Reports Hate Crimes Jumped 17%* (November 13, 2018), https://www.adl.org/news/
    press-releases/adl-calls-on-leaders-to-redouble-efforts-to-counter-hate-after-fbi-reports
    -hate.

41 *See* Sikh Coalition, *New Wave of Hate Crimes Demand Vigilance* (March 9, 2018), https://
    www.sikhcoalition.org/blog/2018/new-wave-hate-crimes-demands-vigilance/. *See also*
    chap. 10.

42 Rosie Gray, *Trump Defends White-Nationalist Protesters: "Some Very Fine People on Both
    Sides,"* The Atlantic (August 15, 2017); *Trump Says Both Sides to Blame amid Char-
    lottesville Backlash*, CNN Transcript (August 15, 2017), http://transcripts.cnn.com/
    TRANSCRIPTS/1708/15/cg.01.html.

43 *See, e.g.*, Serwer, *Trump's Caravan Hysteria Led to This*; Brian Resnick, *Donald Trump
    and the Disturbing Power of Dehumanizing Language*, Vox (August 14, 2018).

44 *See below* chap. 10.

45 *Id.*

46 Aliza Nadi and Ken Dilanian, *In Closed-Door Meeting, Trump Told Christian Leaders He
    Got Rid of a Law: He Didn't*, NBC News (August 28, 2018).

47 *Id.*

48 *See* Nick Gass, *Ben Carson: American President Can't Be Muslim*, Politico (September 20,
    2015).

49 *See* Jon Greenberg, *Flake: Roy Moore said Muslims Shouldn't Serve in Public Office*, Politifact
    (November 9, 2017). Moore failed in his Senate race, but only by a narrow margin.

50 Joby Warrick and Abigail Hauslohner, *Trump's Security Picks Deepen Worries about an
    Anti-Muslim White House*, The Washington Post (November 16, 2017).

51 Maggie Haberman and Matt Stevens, *Sebastian Gorka Is Forced Out as White House
    advisor, Officials Say*, The New York Times (August 25, 2017); Spencer Ackerman,
    FBI Fired Sebastian Gorka for Anti-Muslim Diatribes, The Daily Beast (June 21,
    2017).

52 *See below* chap. 10.

53 Rev. Dr. Martin Luther King Jr., *Letter from a Birmingham Jail* (April 16, 1963), https://
    www.africa.upenn.edu/Articles_Gen/Letter_Birmingham.html.

54 *See, e.g.*, Robert Jones, *The End of White Christian America* (New York: Simon & Schuster
    2016).

55 *See below* chap. 10.

56 *See* Department of Labor, *Implementing Legal Requirements Regarding the Equal Oppor-
    tunity Clause's Religious Exemption*, Notice of Proposed Rulemaking, 84 Fed. Reg. 41677
    (August 15, 2019). *See also below* chaps. 6, 7, and 8.

57 Letter from Health and Human Services to Governor Henry McMaster regarding request
    for deviation or exception from HHS Regulation 45 C.F.R. Section 75.300(c) (Janu-
    ary 23, 2019), https://governor.sc.gov/sites/default/files/Documents/newsroom/HHS

%20Response%20Letter%20to%20McMaster.pdf. *See also Maddonna v. United States Department of Health and Human Services*, https://www.au.org/sites/default/files/2019-02/Maddonna%20v.%20HHS%20Complaint%202.15.19.pdf. HHS requires subgrantees to refer prospective foster parents that they refuse to serve to the government or to other subgrantees that will serve them. For further discussion of these issues, *see below* chap. 6.

58 *See, e.g., Masterpiece Cakeshop, Ltd. v. Colorado Civil Rights Comm'n*, Brief of the United States as Amicus Curiae in Support of Respondents, Department of Justice (September 2017), http://www.scotusblog.com/wp-content/uploads/2017/09/16-111-tsac-USA.pdf; Thomas Howell Jr., *DOJ Says It Has Settled "Contraception Mandate" Cases: Trump's Move to Broaden Exemption Paved Way for Resolution*, The Washington Times (October 23, 2017).

59 Katherine Franke, *Religious Freedom for Me, but Not for Thee*, The Washington Post (September 28, 2018).

60 *See below* chap. 8.

61 *See, e.g., below* chaps. 6, 7, 8, and 9 for a few examples of times when President Obama and his administration sought to demonstrate respect for differing views.

62 *See* Office of the Attorney General, *Federal Law Protections for Religious Liberty*, Department of Justice (October 6, 2017), https://www.justice.gov/opa/press-release/file/1001891/download. The guidance states:

> [The Establishment Clause] prohibits government from establishing *a religion* and coercing Americans to follow it . . . . And it prohibits government from officially favoring or disfavoring particular religious groups as such or officially advocating particular religious points of view.

Id. at 4a (emphasis added) (citations omitted). The guidance does not say that the government is prohibited from promoting religion generally. *Compare with Epperson v. Arkansas*, 393 U.S. 97, 104 (1968) ("The First Amendment mandates governmental neutrality between religion and religion, and between religion and nonreligion.").

63 *See American Legion v. American Humanist Association*, 139 S. Ct. 2067, 2095 (2019) (Thomas, J., concurring in the judgment). *See also below* chap. 5.

64 *See id.* at 2098–2103 (Gorsuch, J., concurring in the judgment).

65 *Id.* at 2102 (Gorsuch, J., concurring in the judgment).

66 *See below* chap. 5. Justice Kavanaugh may be less concerned than Justice Kennedy was about certain forms of government-sponsored prayers in public schools, for example. *See, e.g.,* Brief of Amici Curiae Congressmen Steve Largent and Congressman J. C. Watts in support of Petitioner Santa Fe Indep. Sch. Dist., Brett Kavanaugh, Counsel of Record (December 30, 1999), https://www.au.org/sites/default/files/2018-07/Santa%20Fe%20Independent%20School%20Dist%20v%20Doe%20amicus%20brief.pdf; excerpt of Kavanaugh confirmation hearing transcript containing exchange with Senator Cornyn regarding *Santa Fe v. Doe*, CNN (September 15, 2018), http://transcripts.cnn.com/TRANSCRIPTS/1809/05/wolf.01.html.

67 *Santa Fe Indep. Sch. Dist. v. Doe*, 530 U.S. 290, 302 (2000) (quoting *Board of Ed. of Westside Community Schools v. Mergens*, 496 U.S. 226, 250 (1990)) (opinion of O'Connor, J.). *See below* chap. 5.

68 *See, e.g., Mitchell v. Helms*, 530 U.S. 793, 801-835 (2000) (plurality opinion). *See also* Brett M. Kavanaugh, *From the Bench: The Constitutional Statesmanship of Chief Justice William Rehnquist*, The Heritage Foundation (December 12, 2017) (hailing Chief Justice Rehnquist's views on government funding and religious institutions, which included the belief that religious bodies should be able to use government grant money to buy Bibles

and subsidize religious activities, so long as the government grant program has a secular purpose and is open to religious and nonreligious entities alike), https://www.aei.org/publication/from-the-bench-the-constitutional-statesmanship-of-chief-justice-william-rehnquist/. *See also below* chap. 7.

69 *See Trinity Lutheran Church v. Comer*, 582 U.S. ___ 137 S. Ct. 2012 (2017) (Gorsuch, J., concurring); Email from Brett Kavanaugh to White House colleagues regarding "Faith based bill changes" (June 27, 2001), https://www.scribd.com/document/388017956/Booker-Confidential-4-Kavanaugh-Hearing; *Morris County v. Freedom From Religion Foundation*, Nos. 18-364 and 18-365, 586 U.S. ___ (2019) (Statement of Justice Kavanaugh with whom Justice Alito and Justice Gorsuch join, respecting the denial of certiorari); *Morris County v. Freedom From Religion Foundation*, 232 N.J. 543 (N.J. 2018).

70 *Group Health Plans and Health Insurance Issuers Relating to Coverage of Preventive Services under the Patient Protection and Affordable Care Act*, 76 Federal Register 46626 (August 3, 2011).

71 *See* E. J. Dionne, *Obama's Breach of Faith over Contraception Ruling*, The Washington Post (January 29, 2012).

72 *See above* n.61.

73 Here is the full statement of USCRC Chairman Martin R. Castro in this 2016 report:

> "The government of the United States is not, in any sense, founded on the Christian religion."—*John Adams*
>
> The phrases "religious liberty" and "religious freedom" will stand for nothing except hypocrisy so long as they remain code words for discrimination, intolerance, racism, sexism, homophobia, Islamophobia, Christian supremacy or any form of intolerance.
>
> Religious liberty was never intended to give one religion dominion over other religions, or a veto power over the civil rights and civil liberties of others. However, today, as in the past, religion is being used as both a weapon and a shield by those seeking to deny others equality. In our nation's past religion has been used to justify slavery and later, Jim Crow laws. We now see "religious liberty" arguments sneaking their way back into our political and constitutional discourse (just like the concept of "state rights") in an effort to undermine the rights of some Americans. This generation of Americans must stand up and speak out to ensure that religion never again be twisted to deny others the full promise of America.

United States Commission on Civil Rights, *Peaceful Coexistence: Reconciling Nondiscrimination Principles with Civil Liberties* (September 2016) 29, https://www.usccr.gov/pubs/docs/Peaceful-Coexistence-09-07-16.PDF. *See also* Joe Davidson, *Civil Rights or Religious Liberty—What's on Top?* The Washington Post (September 9, 2016).

74 Hillary Clinton, Keynote Speech at 2015 Women in the World Summit, https://womenintheworld.com/videos/hillary-clintons-keynote-address-at-the-2015-women-in-the-world-summit/.

75 *See below* chap. 6.

76 Sarah Eekhoff Zylstra, *Trump's "Greatest Contribution to Christianity": Pastors Preaching Politics*, Christianity Today (July 22, 2016).

77 *See, e.g., Branch Ministries v. Rossotti*, 211 F.3d 137 (D. C. Cir. 2000). *See also* David Saperstein and Amanda Tyler, *Trump Vowed to Destroy the Johnson Amendment: Thankfully, He Has Failed*, The Washington Post (February 7, 2018).

78 *Id.*

79 *See below* chap. 4.

80   *See* Trevor Potter, *Churches Cannot Be Allowed to Become Political Dark Money Shops*, The Hill (May 4, 2017).

81   *McCreary County v. American Civil Liberties Union*, 545 U.S. 844, 882 (2005) (O'Connor, J., concurring) (citations omitted).

82   *See Religious Expression in American Public Life: A Joint Statement of Current Law*, Wake Forest University Center for Religion and Public Affairs (January 2010), https://www .brookings.edu/wp-content/uploads/2012/04/0112_religious_expression_statement.pdf (hereinafter: Wake Forest, *Religious Expression*).

83   *Id.*

Chapter 1: Religion and the Constitution: Historical Origins

1   Ron B. Flowers, Melissa Rogers, and Steven K. Green, *Religious Freedom and the Supreme Court* (Waco, Tex.: Baylor University Press 2008) 29. "Originalists attempt to use sources such as the notes from the Constitutional Convention and the ratifying conventions of the various states as well as other contemporaneous writings by the framers and ratifiers to determine the 'original meaning' of various constitutional provisions." *Id.*

2   As Professor Michael W. McConnell has said, "Even opponents of originalism generally agree that the historical understanding is relevant, even if not dispositive." McConnell, *The Origins and Historical Understanding of Free Exercise of Religion*, 103 Harv. L. Rev. 1409, 1415 (1990) (hereinafter *Origins*). Professor Kent Greenawalt, who is not an originalist, has expressed a similar view: "I do not think that the original understanding, either of those who enacted the constitutional provisions or of those who then read the provisions, should be the final determinant in constitutional adjudication. Nevertheless, I agree that original understanding, in some form, should be an important consideration in Supreme Court decisions." Flowers, Rogers, and Green, *Religious Freedom and the Supreme Court* at 30. *See id.* at 29–34 for alternative ways to interpret the Constitution.

3   Kurt T. Lash, *The Second Adoption of the Establishment Clause: The Rise of the Non-Establishment Principle*, 27 Ariz. St. L. Jnl. 1085 (1995).

4   Other books and articles provide more detailed accounts of the emergence of these constitutional guarantees and explorations of their meaning. *See, e.g.*, Flowers, Rogers, and Green, *Religious Freedom and the Supreme Court*; John Witte Jr., *Religion and the American Constitutional Experiment: Essential Rights and Liberties* (Boulder, Colo.: Westview 2000); Noah Feldman, *The Three Lives of James Madison: Genius, Partisan, President* (New York: Random House 2017).

5   Catherine Drinker Bowen, *Miracle at Philadelphia: The Story of the Constitutional Convention May to September 1787* (Boston: Little, Brown 1966) 214. The Harvard Law Review notes:

> Like England, many American states imposed religious tests to limit the ability of individuals of certain denominations to hold public office. As of 1789, five states (Delaware, Maryland, Massachusetts, North Carolina, and Pennsylvania) had constitutional provisions requiring individuals holding public office to swear a belief in Christianity—specifically, for instance, a belief in the Holy Trinity or a belief that the New Testament was divinely inspired. And New York required officeholders to take an oath disavowing allegiance to a foreign prince—in other words, the Pope—in all ecclesiastical and civil matters, thereby "exclud[ing] Catholics from state office" because of their "ecclesiastical ties to Rome." The oath was an unmistakable component of each of these tests. Only if individuals passed

such a test—that is, only if they bound themselves through such an oath—could they hold office.

An Originalist Analysis of the No Religious Test Clause, 120 Harv. L. Rev. 1649, 1651–52 (2007) (citations and footnotes omitted).

6   Alexander Leitch, *A Princeton Companion* (Princeton, N.J.: Princeton University Press 1978); https://etcweb.princeton.edu/CampusWWW/Companion/ellsworth_oliver.html.

7   Gerard V. Bradley, *The No Religious Test Clause and the Constitution of Religious Liberty: A Machine That Has Gone of Itself,* 37 Case W. L. Rev 674, 714 (1987) (citation omitted).

8   *Originalist Analysis of the No Religious Test Clause*, 120 Harv. L. Rev. at 1651.

9   *Id.*

10   McConnell, *Origins*, 103 Harv. L. Rev. at 1474 (quoting Bradley, *No Religions Test Clause*, 37 Case W. L. Rev. at 681–83).

11   Bowen, *Miracle at Philadelphia* at 216; *Oaths Affirmations and Religious Tests*, website of National Historic Park Pennsylvania, National Park Service, https://www.nps.gov/inde/learn/historyculture/oaths-affirmations-and-religious-tests.htm.

12   Bowen, *Miracle at Philadelphia* at 216.

13   *Id.*

14   *A Letter of Jonas Phillips to the Federal Convention*, Publications of the American Jewish Historical Society, no. 2 (Baltimore: Johns Hopkins University Press 1894) 109.

15   Bradley, *No Religious Test Clause*, 37 Case W. L. Rev. at 688.

16   *Id.* at 688–89. *Originalist Analysis of the No Religious Test Clause*, 120 Harv. L. Rev. at 1652.

17   *Id.* at 1652–53.

18   The final clause of Article VI states:

> The Senators and Representatives before mentioned, and the members of the several state legislatures, and all executive and judicial officers, both of the United States and of the several states, shall be bound by oath or affirmation, to support this Constitution; but no religious test shall ever be required as a qualification to any office or public trust under the United States.

U.S. Const. art VI, cl. 3. A federal court has said: "whether Article VI applies to the states through the Fourteenth Amendment is an unsettled question under the law." *Habecker v. Town of Estes Park*, 452 F. Supp. 2d 1113, 1129 (D. Colo. 2006) (cited in 120 Harv. L. Rev. at n.61).

19   Bradley, *No Religious Test Clause*, 37 Case W. L. Rev. at 688 (quoting C. Antineau, A. Downey, and E. Roberts, *Freedom from Federal Establishment: Formation and Early History of the First Amendment Religion Clauses* (Milwaukee: Bruce 1964) 95, 100).

20   *Originalist Analysis of the No Religious Test Clause*, 120 Harv. L. Rev. at 1653–54.

21   *Id.* at 1654.

22   McConnell, *Origins*, 103 Harv. L. Rev. at 1474 (citation omitted). Ellsworth also said:

> [T]est-laws are utterly ineffectual: they are no security at all; because men of loose principles will, by an external compliance, evade them. If they exclude any persons, it will be honest men, men of principle, who will rather suffer an injury, than act contrary to the dictates of their consciences. If we mean to have those appointed to public offices, who are sincere friends to religion, we, the people who appoint them, must take care to choose such characters; and not rely upon such cob-web barriers as test-laws are.

An Originalist Analysis, 120 Harv. L. Rev. at 1653–54 (citation omitted). Professor McConnell says: "Oddly, Ellsworth supported a strict religious test for office in his own state." McConnell, *Origins*, 103 Harv. L. Rev. at 1474–75 n.327 (citation omitted).

Professor Bradley argues that we may "confidently conclude that the rejection of religious tests did *not* stem from the delegates' condemnation of them as a matter of principle," citing the fact that several delegates who supported state religious tests voted in favor of the federal test ban. Bradley, *No Religious Test Clause*, 37 Case W. L. Rev. at 689. Yet some of the delegates—most prominently, James Madison—did oppose tests as a matter of principle. *See below* at chap. 4.

Madison and other founders considered oaths to be "inherently religious." *Originalist Analysis of the No Religious Test Clause*, 120 Harv. L. Rev. at 1656. "The essence of an oath was an appeal to God to witness the truth of what one said," Professor Robert Natelson explained. *Id.* (citation omitted). President Lincoln said oaths are "registered in heaven." *Id.* (citation omitted). "Even if the Oath Clause itself contained an implicit religious test, the affirmation option made that test voluntary and thus not '*required* as a Qualification to any Office or public Trust under the United States.'" *Id.* at 1658 n.47 (quoting Art. VI of the Constitution, emphasis added).

23 *Id.* at 1657. According to Professor Gerard Bradley, the provision was billed, therefore, "as a constitutionalized Golden Rule with a Machiavellian spin to it: 'Constrain yourself as you would constrain others.'" Bradley, *No Religious Test Clause*, 37 Case W. Res. L. Rev. at 703.

24 *Originalist Analysis of the No Religious Test Clause*, 120 Harv. L. Rev. at 1657 (citing McConnell, *Origins*, 103 Harv. L. Rev. at 1475). Objectors cited the following Bible verses from Matt 5:33-37 (RSV):

> "Again you have heard that it was said to the men of old, 'You shall not swear falsely, but shall perform to the Lord what you have sworn.' But I say to you, Do not swear at all, either by heaven, for it is the throne of God, or by the earth, for it is his footstool, or by Jerusalem, for it is the city of the great King. And do not swear by your head, for you cannot make one hair white or black. Let what you say be simply 'Yes' or 'No'; anything more than this comes from evil."

25 *Id.*

26 This same permission to substitute an affirmation for an oath also appears in Articles I (sec. 3) and II (sec. 1) of the Constitution.

27 James Madison, *The Federalist No. 52*, in *James Madison: Writings* (New York: The Library of America, 1999) 300.

28 John Leland, *The Rights of Conscience Inalienable in the Writings of the Late Elder John Leland: Including Some Events in His Life*, ed. L. F. Greene (New York: G. W. Wood 1845) 191.

29 James Madison, *Debates on the Adoption of the Federal Constitution*, ed. Jonathan Elliot (Washington, D.C.: 1845) 538, https://oll.libertyfund.org/titles/madison-the-debates -on-the-adoption-of-the-federal-constitution-vol-5; George Mason and the Constitution, Gunston Hall, Home of George Mason website, http://www.gunstonhall.org/ georgemason/essays/constitution.html.

30 Madison, *Debates* at 538.

31 *Id.*

32 *Id.*

33 The National Constitution Center provided the following commentary on these matters:

Some delegates reasoned that a federal bill of rights was unnecessary because most state constitutions already included some form of guaranteed rights; others said that outlining certain rights would imply that those were the only rights reserved to the people. However, historian Richard Beeman, a Trustee of the National Constitution Center, has pointed out a much more prosaic reason the delegates were so skeptical: They had spent four arduous months of contentious debate in a hot, stuffy room, and were anxious to avoid anything that would prolong the convention. They wanted to go home, so they took a pass. A bill of rights was overruled.

Holly Munson, *FAQ: Basic Facts about the Bill of Rights*, Constitution Daily, National Constitution Center (May 22, 2013), https://constitutioncenter.org/blog/everything-you -ever-wanted-to-know-about-the-bill-of-rights.

34　James Madison, General Defense of the Constitution 1788, https://founders.archives .gov/documents/Madison/01-11-02-0077; Robert S. Alley, *James Madison on Religious Liberty* (New York: Prometheus Books 1985) 71 (citation omitted);

35　McConnell, *Origins*, 103 Harv. L. Rev. at 1478–79 (footnotes omitted).

36　Jeff Broadwater, *George Mason: Forgotten Founder* (Chapel Hill: University of North Carolina Press 2006) 202.

37　McConnell, *Origins*, 103 Harv. L. Rev. at 1479 (footnote omitted).

38　*Id.* at 1480.

39　*Writings of the Late Elder John Leland* at 52–54.

40　*Id.* at 53.

41　*Id.* at 54–55.

42　McConnell, *Origins*, 103 Harv. L. Rev. at 1476–77.

43　*Id. See also* Noah Feldman, *The Three Lives of James Madison: Genius, Partisan, President* (New York: Random House 2017) 251–57. Some states agreed to ratify the Constitution only if a bill of rights would be swiftly added. Munson, *FAQ*.

44　Noah Feldman, *The Three Lives of James Madison: Genius, Partisan, President* (New York: Random House 2017) 267–85.

45　Munson, *FAQ*. "The first two amendments in the 12 that Congress proposed to the states were rejected: The first dealt with apportioning representation in the House of Representatives; the second prevented members of Congress from voting to change their pay until the next session of Congress. This original 'Second Amendment' was finally added to the Constitution as the 27th Amendment, more than 200 years later." *Id. See also The Bill of Rights: A Transcription*, National Archives, America's Founding Documents, https://www.archives.gov/founding-docs/bill-of-rights-transcript.

46　McConnell, *Origins*, 103 Harv. L. Rev. at 1476–77.

47　*Wallace v. Jaffree*, 472 U.S. 38, 106 (1985) (Rehnquist, J., dissenting) (citations omitted). *See also* Robert L. Cord, *Church-State Separation: Restoring the "No Preference" Doctrine of the First Amendment*, 9 Harv. Jnl. Law & Pub. Pol'y 129 (1986).

48　*See* Douglas Laycock, *"Nonpreferential" Aid to Religion: A False Claim about Original Intent*, 27 Wm and Mary L. Rev. 875 (1986). Professor Doug Laycock, a leading constitutional scholar, has said that while "[n]either [the Establishment Clause's] history nor its text offers us a single unambiguous meaning," the historical evidence indicates that the framers "certainly did not consciously intend to permit nonpreferential aid [for religion], and those of them who thought about the question probably intended to forbid it." *Id.* at 877, 878. Laycock notes that "the First Congress considered and rejected at least four drafts of the [E]stablishment [C]lause that explicitly stated the 'no preference' view." *Id.* at 879. The version of the Establishment Clause that was adopted, Laycock observes, "is one of the broadest versions considered by either House." *Id.* at 881. Unlike other drafts, Laycock explains, the Establishment Clause that was adopted "forbids not only establishments, but also any law respecting or relating to an establishment of 'religion.' It does not say '*a* religion,' 'a national religion,' 'one sect or society' or 'any particular denomination of religion.'" Instead, the Establishment Clause says "religion generically . . . may not be established." *Id.* at 881.

49   *Id.* at 879.

50   *Id.* at 881.

51   *Lee v. Weisman*, 505 U.S. 577, 615–16 (1992) (Souter, J., concurring) (footnote and citations omitted) (quoting Laycock, *"Nonpreferential" Aid to Religion*, 27 Wm and Mary L. Rev. at 882–883).

52   Professor Laycock explains:

> With respect to money, religion was to be wholly voluntary. Churches either would support themselves or they would not, but the government would neither help nor interfere.
>
> This is what disestablishment meant to the Framers in the context in which they thought about it. They applied the principle only in that context—only to tax support. Their society was so homogeneous that they had no occasion to think about other kinds of support. Now that we have thought about it, we are not unfaithful to the Framers' intent when we apply their principle to analogous problems. Congress cannot impose civil disabilities on non-Protestants or ban blasphemy against the Trinity just because the Framers did it. It is no more able to endorse the predominant religion just because the Framers did it. Our task is not to perpetuate the Framers' blind spots, but to implement their vision.

"Nonpreferential" Aid to Religion, 27 Wm and Mary L. Rev. at 923.

53   *See below* chap. 2.

54   McConnell, *Origins*, 103 Harv. L. Rev. at 1481–85.

55   *Id.* at 1491–1503.

56   Professor McConnell has noted that the final version of the First Amendment omitted any reference to the "rights of conscience," only referencing religion (*Id.* at 1488–1500). "If 'the rights of conscience' were dropped because they were redundant, 'conscience' must have been used in its narrow, religious, sense," Professor McConnell says. But "[i]f the omission was a substantive change, then the framers deliberately confined the clause to religious claims," he argues. "Neither explanation supports the view that free exercise exemptions must be extended to secular moral conflicts." *Id.* at 1496. Justice Rutledge made a related point in his dissenting opinion in the *Everson v. Board of Educ.* case:

> "Religion" appears only once in the Amendment. But the word governs two prohibitions, and governs them alike. It does not have two meanings, one narrow, to forbid "an establishment," and another much broader, for securing "the free exercise thereof." "Thereof" brings down "religion" with its entire and exact content, no more and no less, from the first into the second guaranty, so that Congress, and now the states, are as broadly restricted concerning the one as they are regarding the other.

Everson v. Board of Educ., 330 U.S. 1, 32 (1947) (Rutledge, J., dissenting).

57   Professor McConnell has said that "[w]hile the historical evidence may not be unequivocal (it seldom is), it does, on balance, support [an] interpretation of the free exercise clause" that requires the government "in the absence of a sufficiently compelling need,

to grant exemptions from legal duties that conflict with religious obligations[.]" *Id.* at 1415, 1411.

Professor Philip A. Hamburger, on the other hand, has concluded that "late eighteenth-century Americans tended to assume that the Free Exercise Clause did not provide a constitutional right of religious exemption from civil laws." Hamburger, *A Constitutional Right of Religious Exemption: An Historical Perspective*, 60 Geo. Wash. L. Rev. 915, 916 (1992).

58 Alan Brownstein, ed., *The Establishment of Religion Clause: Its Constitutional History and the Contemporary Debate* (Amherst, N.Y.: Prometheus Books 2008) 13.

Madison proposed a separate amendment stating that "no State shall infringe the equal rights of conscience, nor the freedom of speech or of the press, nor the right of trial by jury in criminal cases." Noah Feldman, *The Intellectual Origins of the Establishment Clause*, 77 N. Y. U. L. Rev. 346, 411 (May 2002) (quoting *Annals of Congress*, vol. 1, ed. Joseph Gales (1789) 783). As Professor Michael McConnell notes:

> Madison said that he conceived this to be "the most valuable amendment in the whole list. If there were any reason to restrain the Government of the United States from infringing upon these essential rights, it was equally necessary that they should be secured against the State Governments." Significantly, Madison did not propose that the establishment clause be made applicable to the states; this reflects the prevailing view at the time that states should be permitted to set their own course with respect to establishment, but that liberty of conscience was an unalienable right.

McConnell, *Origins*, 103 Harv. L. Rev. at 1484. The House of Representatives approved the proposal, but the Senate rebuffed it. *Id.* Thomas Tucker offered "the sole recorded objection" to Madison's proposal, saying, "[I]t [went] only to the alteration of the constitutions of particular States. It will be much better, I apprehend, to leave the State Governments to themselves, and not to interfere with them more than we already do; and that is thought by many to be rather too much." Lash, *Second Adoption of the Establishment Clause*, 27 Ariz. St. L. Jnl. at 1091 and Feldman, *Intellectual Origins of the Establishment Clause*, 77 New York Univ. L. Rev. at 411 (quoting *Annals of Congress*, vol. 1, ed. Gales, at 783).

59 Steven K. Green, *The Second Disestablishment: Church and State in Nineteenth-Century America* (New York: Oxford University Press 2010) 143.

60 Brownstein, *Establishment of Religion Clause* at 13.

61 *See* Kent Greenawalt, *Common Sense about Original and Subsequent Understandings of the Religion Clauses*, 8 Pa. J. Const. L. 479, 506–10 (2006).

62 *Cantwell v. Connecticut*, 310 U.S. 296, 303 (1940) (holding that the Free Exercise Clause applies to states and localities through the Fourteenth Amendment). *See also Everson v. Board of Education*, 330 U.S. 1 (1947) (holding that the Establishment Clause applies to states and localities through the Fourteenth Amendment).

63 At least one prominent scholar argues, however, that the Fourteenth Amendment changed the meaning of the Free Exercise Clause. While "the available evidence supports the view that the Founders did not anticipate the need for religious exemptions from generally applicable laws," Professor Kurt Lash argues, the "second adoption" of the Free Exercise Clause enlarged its scope. Lash, *The Second Adoption of the Free Exercise Clause: Religious Exemptions under the Fourteenth Amendment*, 88 Northwestern Univ. L. Rev. 1106, 1108–9, 1134–56 (1994) (citing Southern laws prohibiting the writing, publication, and dissemination of abolitionist literature, including those by religious people; heavy

regulation of black assemblies, including black religious assemblies; bans on teaching slaves how to read and write, which prevented slaves from reading the Bible as well as all other literature; and the fact that the framers of the Fourteenth Amendment specifically spoke against these and related measures, emphasizing the impact they had on former slaves' ability to exercise their faith). Professor Lash concludes: "Under the amended Free Exercise Clause, religious minorities can invoke the original intent of the framers of the Fourteenth Amendment and claim a religious liberty that requires exemption from the unjustified impact of generally applicable law." *Id.* at 1156.

64   In *Everson v. Board of Education*, the Court said:

> The meaning and scope of the First Amendment, preventing establishment of religion or prohibiting the free exercise thereof, in the light of its history and the evils it was designed forever to suppress, have been several times elaborated by the decisions of this Court prior to the application of the First Amendment to the states by the Fourteenth. The broad meaning given the Amendment by these earlier cases has been accepted by this Court in its decisions concerning an individual's religious freedom rendered since the Fourteenth Amendment was interpreted to make the prohibitions of the First applicable to state action abridging religious freedom. There is every reason to give the same application and broad interpretation to the "establishment of religion" clause. The interrelation of these complementary clauses was well summarized in a statement of the Court of Appeals of South Carolina, quoted with approval by this Court in *Watson v. Jones*, 13 Wall. 679, 80 U. S. 730: "The structure of our government has, for the preservation of civil liberty, rescued the temporal institutions from religious interference. On the other hand, it has secured religious liberty from the invasion of the civil authority."

330 U. S. at 14–15 (footnotes omitted).

65   Professor Fred Gedicks calls out the Court's "casual incorporation" of the Establishment Clause:

> The Supreme Court gave little thought to how or why the First Amendment might limit state action before actually deciding that it did. In 1925, the Court "assumed" without explanation that the rights guaranteed by the Speech and Press Clauses bind the states through the Fourteenth Amendment, just three years after it had rejected the identical proposition. Fifteen years later it held the same for the Free Exercise Clause in *Cantwell v. Connecticut*, apparently because of its congruence with the Speech Clause. Though Establishment Clause incorporation was not before the Court in *Cantwell*, the Justices acted as if the Clause had already been incorporated when the question was squarely presented in *Everson v. Board of Education*. The basis for incorporation remained just as opaque when the Court used the Clause to invalidate a state religious education program the next term.

Frederick Mark Gedicks, *Incorporation of the Establishment Clause against the States: A Logical, Textual, and Historical Account*, 88 Indiana L. Jnl. 669, 677–78 (2013) (footnotes omitted).

66   *Abington Township v. Schempp*, 374 U.S. at 308 (Stewart, J., dissenting). Justice Stewart argued that the cases should be remanded to a lower court to allow them to gather more factual evidence.

67   *Id.* at 309–10.

68   *Id.* at 310 (citation omitted).

69   *Id.*

70   *Id.* at 254–55 (Brennan, J., concurring).

71   *Id.*

72   *Id.* at 256.

73   *Id.* Quoting an earlier Court decision, Justice Brennan said, "The Free Exercise Clause 'was not to be the full extent of the Amendment's guarantee of freedom from govern-mental intrusion in matters of faith.'" *Id.* (citing *McGowan v. Maryland*, 366 U.S. 420, 464 (1961) (opinion of Frankfurter, J.)).

74   *Elk Grove Unified School District v. Newdow*, 542 U.S. 1, 45–54 (2004) (Thomas, J., concurring in the judgment).

75   *Id.* at 45.

76   *Id.* at 49 (citations omitted). *See also Van Orden v. Perry*, 545 U.S. 677, 692–93 (2005) (Thomas, J., concurring); *Zelman v. Simmons-Harris*, 536 U.S. 639, 677–80 (2002) (Thomas, J., concurring); *Town of Greece v. Galloway*, 572 U.S. 565, 604–10 (2014) (Thomas, J., concurring in part and concurring in the judgment). In his concurring opinion in *Town of Greece v. Galloway*, Justice Thomas said:

> This Court has never squarely addressed these barriers to the incorporation of the Establishment Clause. When the issue was first presented in *Everson v. Board of Ed. of Ewing*, 330 U.S. 1 (1947), the Court casually asserted that "the Fourteenth Amendment [has been] interpreted to make the prohibitions of the First applicable to state action abridging religious freedom. There is every reason to give the same application and broad interpretation to the 'establishment of religion' clause." *Id.* at 15 (footnote omitted). The cases the Court cited in support of that proposition involved the Free Exercise Clause—which had been incorporated seven years earlier, in *Cantwell v. Connecticut*, 310 U.S. 296, 303 (1940)—not the Establishment Clause. 330 U. S., at 15, n. 22 (collecting cases). Thus, in the space of a single paragraph and a nonresponsive string citation, the Court glibly effected a sea change in constitutional law. The Court's inattention to these doctrinal questions might be explained, although not excused, by the rise of popular conceptions about "separation of church and state" as an "American" constitutional right. *See generally* P. Hamburger, *Separation of Church and State* 454–63 (2002); *see also* at 391–454 (discussing the role of nativist sentiment in the campaign for "separation" as an American ideal).

Id. at n.1.

It is important to note that some religious Americans have argued since before the founding that establishments of religion rob individuals of religious freedom and that disestablishment promotes that liberty. *See, e.g.,* William McLoughlin, ed., *Isaac Backus on Church, State and Calvinism, Pamphlets, 1754–1789* (Cambridge, Mass.: Harvard University Press 1968); and John Leland, *The Rights of Conscience Inalienable*, in *Writings of the Late Elder John Leland*.

77   *Elk Grove Unified School District v. Newdow*, 542 U.S. at 50–51 (Thomas, J., concurring in the judgment).

78   *Id.* at 51.

79   *Id.*

80   *See, e.g.,* Douglas Laycock, *Two Problems in the Original Understanding of the Estab-lishment Clause: Religious Exemptions, and the Claim that the Clause Was Really about Federalism* (working draft) (2005), https://law.utexas.edu/faculty/dlaycock/TwoProblems .pdf; Greenawalt, *Common Sense*, 8 Pa. J. Const. L. 479; Green, *Second Disestablishment*; Gedicks, *Incorporation of the Establishment Clause against the States*, 88 Indiana L. Jnl. 668. The conversation post-*Newdow* also drew on earlier articles that had both questioned

and supported the incorporation of the Establishment Clause. *See, e.g.,* Gerard V. Bradley, *Church-State Relationships in America* (Westport, Conn.: Greenwood 1987); Daniel O. Conkle, *The Establishment Clause as a Federalism Mandate,* 82 Northwestern L. Rev. 1129 (1988); Steven D. Smith, *Foreordained Failure: The Quest for a Constitutional Principle of Religious Freedom* (New York: Oxford University Press 1995); Lash, *Second Adoption of the Establishment Clause,* 27 Ariz. St. L. J. 1085; Akhil Reed Amar, *The Bill of Rights: Creation and Reconstruction* (New Haven: Yale University Press 1998); and Feldman, *Intellectual Origins of the Establishment Clause,* 77 N.Y.U. L. Rev. at 373–98, 405–12.

81   *See* Green, *Second Disestablishment* at 67–72. Professor Green says:

> The historical basis for a federalism interpretation of the establishment clause is grossly overstated. The argument takes an issue of undeniable importance to the drafters and ratifiers of the Bill of Rights and gives it meaning that the framers likely did not intend. That the drafters of the First Amendment were interested in limiting federal power is hardly profound; the overarching purpose of the Bill of Rights was to limit potential federal authority in relation to individual and states' rights. That consensus on limiting federal power, however, does not lead to the conclusion that the framers thought the establishment clause had no independent, substantive meaning other than federalism nor that they intended the clause to *protect* and *preserve* the existing state establishments, rather than have them die on their own accord . . . .
>
> [W]hen the First Congress convened in 1789 to consider proposed amendments to the Constitution, there was little reason for the representatives to be concerned about *preserving* state religious establishments against federal meddling. This is particularly true since most observers acknowledged the inconsistency between establishments and liberty of conscience and believed that religious establishments would soon vanish from the American scene.

Id. at 67–68, 72. *See also* Lash, *Second Adoption of the Establishment Clause,* 27 Ariz. St. L. J. at 1091–92 ("Under the federal Establishment Clause [as originally adopted], religious establishments were neither good nor bad—they were simply a matter left to the states. On this issue, the federal government was to remain agnostic."); *see* Laycock, *Two Problems* at 36 ("The political demand for the Establishment Clause did not come from supporters of the surviving establishments in New England, but rather from the dissenting churches who were successfully pursuing disestablishment in the states.").

82   Gedicks, *Incorporation of the Establishment Clause against the States,* 88 Indiana L. Jnl. 670. *See also* Greenawalt, *Common Sense,* 8 Pa. J. Const. L. at 506; Feldman, *Intellectual Origins of the Establishment Clause,* 77 N.Y.U. L. Rev. at 373–98.

83   Professor Kurt Lash has said: "To the extent that incorporation of *any* right [under the Fourteenth Amendment] can be justified as a matter of historical intent, there is *no less reason* to incorporate the Establishment Clause than any other provision in the First Amendment." *See* Lash, *Second Adoption of the Establishment Clause,* 27 Ariz. State L Jnl. at 1088 (1995). Professor Lash qualifies his argument in the following way:

> Whether those who framed and adopted the Fourteenth Amendment specifically intended to incorporate any of the rights contained in the first eight amendments is beyond the scope of this article. My purpose is simply to determine whether the Establishment Clause would have been considered an appropriate candidate for incorporation *if there was* any such intention.

Id. at 1141.

84 *Id.* at 1136–53. Professor Douglas Laycock agrees:

> No southern state had a formal establishment of a *church* in the nineteenth century, but all southern states effectively established a particular religious *teaching*. They supported a pro-slavery version of Christianity and vigorously suppressed any contrary teaching. They narrowly restricted and closely monitored religion among the slaves, especially emphasizing Paul's teaching that "slaves be subject to your masters." Republicans charged the South with violating both Religion Clauses, and listed both among the rights to be incorporated. The Republican objection was not to federal interference with state establishments, but rather to state support for a religious teaching and state suppression of competing religious teachings. Incorporation of a ban on state establishment of religion is thus entirely consistent with the goals of those who sponsored the Amendment. Congress was given express power to enforce this ban on state establishments by appropriate legislation. If once there had been a proscription on federal interference with state establishments, that proscription is inconsistent with the Fourteenth Amendment, and necessarily repealed.

Laycock, *Two Problems* at 37 (footnotes omitted). *See also* Gedicks, *Incorporation of the Establishment Clause against the States*, 88 Indiana L. Jnl. 670.

85 *See* Lash, *Second Adoption of the Establishment Clause*, 27 Ariz. State L Jnl. at 1136–45 (1995). As Professor Lash explains, the rules were understood by the framers of the Fourteenth Amendment as violating both the Establishment and Free Exercise Clauses. *Id.* at 1140–45.

86 *Id.* at 1137. Professor Lash quotes the following passage written by William Goodell in 1853:

> The slave master *may* withhold education and the Bible; he *may* forbid religious instruction, and access to public worship. He *may* enforce upon the slave and his family a religious worship and a religious teaching which he disapproves. In all this, as completely as in secular matters, he is "entirely subject to the will of a master, *to whom he belongs.*" The claim of chattelhood extends to the soul as well as to the body, for the body cannot be otherwise held and controlled. There is no other religious despotism on the face of the earth so absolute, so irresponsible, so soul-crushing as this.

Id. (quoting William Goodell, *The American Slave Code in Theory and Practice: Its Distinctive Features Shown by Its Statutes, Judicial Decisions and Illustrative Facts* (New York: American and Foreign Anti-Slavery Society 1853) 254–55).

87 In his argument against incorporation of the Establishment Clause, Professor Dan Conkle cites the fact that in 1876, the U.S. Senate rejected a provision known as the Blaine Amendment that would have applied the Establishment and Free Exercise Clauses to the states. Conkle, *Establishment Clause as a Federalism Mandate*, 82 Northwestern L. Rev. 1129. *See also* Steven K. Green, *Blaming Blaine: Understanding the Blaine Amendment and the No-Funding Principle*, 2 UNC First Amendment L. Rev. 107 (2003). As passed by the House of Representatives, the Blaine Amendment stated:

> No State shall make any law respecting an establishment of religion, or prohibiting the free exercise thereof; and no religious test shall ever be required as a qualification to any office or public trust under any State. No public property, and no public revenue of, nor any loan of credit by or under the authority of, the United States, or any State, Territory, District, or municipal corporation, shall be appropriated to, or made or used for, the support of any school, educational or other institution,

under the control of any religious or anti-religious sect, organization, or denomination, or wherein the particular creed or tenets of any religious or anti-religious sect, organization, or denomination shall be taught. And no such particular creed or tenets shall be read or taught in any school or institution supported in whole or in part by such revenue or loan of credit; and no such appropriation or loan of credit shall be made to any religious or anti-religious sect, organization, or denomination, or to promote its interests or tenets. This article shall not be construed to prohibit the reading of the Bible in any school or institution; and it shall not have the effect to impair rights of property already vested . . . .

McCollum v. Board of Educ., 333 U.S. 203, 218 n.6 (1948) (Frankfurter, J., separate opinion).

As both Professors Lash and Green note, however, the rejection of the Blaine Amendment cannot fairly be said to represent a simple rejection of the notion that the Establishment Clause should apply to the states. The Blaine Amendment would have applied both the Establishment and Free Exercise Clauses to the states, so "it is a hollow victory to prove that both rights were equally rejected." Lash, *Second Adoption of the Establishment Clause*, 27 Ariz. L. Rev. at 1146. *See also Abington Township v. Schempp*, 374 U.S. at 257 (Brennan, J., concurring) ("the Fourteenth Amendment's protection of the free exercise of religion can hardly be questioned; yet the Blaine Amendment would also have added an explicit protection against state laws abridging that liberty."). Professor Lash also notes:

> By constitutionalizing the use of the Protestant Bible and prohibiting public funds to "sectarian" institutions, the Blaine Amendment would have significantly amended contemporary First Amendment norms. For the first time, the Constitution would have recognized and protected state power to coercively indoctrinate students in the tenets of a particular religion.

Lash, *Second Adoption of the Establishment Clause*, 27 Ariz. L. Rev. at 1149. Professor Green adds that the reasons for the rejection of the Blaine Amendment were complex, including the fact that "many people viewed [it] as a crass political maneuver designed to appeal to anti-Catholic voters." Green, *Second Disestablishment* at 295. *See also* Gedicks, *Incorporation of the Establishment Clause against the States*, 88 Indiana L. Jnl. at 677–91.

88   Gedicks, *Incorporation of the Establishment Clause against the States*, 88 Indiana L. Jnl. at 713.

89   *See generally id.*

Chapter 2: Religion and the Constitution: Some Key Concepts and Cases

1   *Brown v. Allen*, 344 U.S. 443, 540 (1953) (Jackson, J., concurring in the judgment).

2   Legal Information Institute of Cornell Law School, https://www.law.cornell.edu/wex/stare_decisis. Stare decisis, the Court has said, is "the means by which we ensure that the law will not merely change erratically, but will develop in a principled and intelligible fashion." *Vasquez v. Hillery*, 474 U.S. 254, 265 (1986). The doctrine "permits society to presume that bedrock principles are founded in the law rather than in the proclivities of individuals, and thereby contributes to the integrity of our constitutional system of government, both in appearance and in fact." *Id.* at 265–66.

3   This section does not offer a comprehensive summary of Supreme Court doctrine on religion and law. Instead, it focuses on some key constitutional principles that are relevant to religion's role in public life.

4   Ron B. Flowers, Melissa Rogers, and Steven K. Green, *Religious Freedom and the Supreme Court* (Waco, Tex.: Baylor University Press 2008) at 47–63. *See also* Daniel O. Conkle, *Religion, Law and the Constitution* (St. Paul: Foundation Press 2016) 60–69.

5   *United States v. Seeger*, 380 U.S. 163, 165 (1964).

6   *Id.* at 176. A Court plurality further interpreted this exemption in a later case, saying, "What is necessary . . . for a registrant's conscientious objection to all war to be 'religious' within the meaning of [the exemption] is that this opposition to war stem[s] from the registrant's moral, ethical, or religious beliefs about what is right and wrong and that these beliefs be held with the strength of traditional religious convictions." *Welsh v. United States*, 398 U.S. 333, 339–40 (1970).

7   *Wisconsin v. Yoder*, 406 U.S. 205, 215 (1972).

8   *Thomas v. Review Bd.*, 450 U.S. 707, 713 (1981).

9   *See* Adam Bernstein, *Roy Torcaso, 96; Defeated Md. in 1961 Religious Freedom Case*, The Washington Post (June 21, 2007).

10   *Torcaso v. Watkins*, 223 Md. 49, 53 (Md. Ct. App. 1960).

11   Bernstein, *Roy Torcaso, 96*.

12   The Maryland Court said: "The petitioner is not compelled to believe or disbelieve, under threat of punishment or other compulsion. True, unless he makes the declaration of belief he cannot hold public office in Maryland, but he is not compelled to hold office." *Torcaso v. Watkins*, 223 Md. at 58 (Md. Ct. App. 1960). While the Maryland Court of Appeals found other aspects of the oath presented to Torcaso to be improper, it ruled that it was appropriate for state officeholders to be required to profess a belief in God, given the requirements of state law.

13   *Torcaso v. Watkins*, 367 U.S. 488, 495–96 (1961) (citations and footnotes omitted).

14   *See* Bernstein, *Roy Torcaso, 96*.

15   The Court said:

> [Torcaso] also claimed that the State's test oath requirement violates the provision of Art. VI of the Federal Constitution that "no religious Test shall ever be required as a Qualification to any Office or public Trust under the United States." Because we are reversing the judgment on other grounds, we find it unnecessary to consider appellant's contention that this provision applies to state as well as federal offices.

> *Torcaso v. Watkins*, 367 U.S. at 489 n.1.

16   *Epperson v. Arkansas*, 393 U.S. at 104.

17   *See, e.g., Abington Township v. Schempp*, 374 U.S. at 225 (government must "maintain strict neutrality, neither aiding nor opposing religion."). The general ban on governmental advancement of religion has arisen in the context of government-sponsored religious displays. *See below* chap. 5.

18   *Larson v. Valente*, 456 U.S. 228, 244 (1982).

19   *Gillette v. United States*, 401 U.S. 437, 452 (1971).

20   Even policies that appear to rely on secular distinctions may sometimes constitute religious discrimination. In a case involving a Minnesota charitable solicitations law, for example, the Court found that a religious exemption impermissibly discriminated against certain faith-based organizations. *See Larson v. Valente*, 456 U.S. 228. Under the Minnesota law, religious organizations that received more than half of their contributions from members or affiliated organizations were exempt from the law's registration and reporting requirements; other religious organizations were not. The Court said this rule created an impermissible religious preference. Minnesota had not chosen means that would

effectively protect its stated interest in protecting its citizens from abusive solicitations. *Id.* at 248–51. The Court also found that the configuration of the religious exemption was based at least in part on favoritism for some faiths and opposition to others. *Id.* at 246–47. Various state senators indicated that the aim of the religious exemption was to regulate "people that are running around airports and running around streets and soliciting people," not "substantial religious institutions . . . ." *Id.* at 254. Another senator wondered "why we're so hot to regulate the Moonies," referring to members of the Unification Church. *Id.* at 255.

21   *See below* chap. 4.

22   James Madison, *Memorial and Remonstrance against Religious Assessments*, in Flowers, Rogers, and Green, *Religious Freedom and the Supreme Court* at 1133.

23   Lyman H. Butterfield, *Elder John Leland, Jeffersonian Itinerant*, 62 Proc. of the Am. Antiquarian Soc'y 160, 174 (1952).

24   *Declaration of the Virginia Association of Baptists* (December 25, 1776), Founders Online, National Archives, http://founders.archives.gov/documents/Jefferson/01-01 -02-0249. Original source: *The Papers of Thomas Jefferson*, vol. 1, *1760–1776*, ed. Julian P. Boyd (Princeton: Princeton University Press 1950) 660–61.

Similarly, Massachusetts Baptist preacher Isaac Backus argued that the Massachusetts establishment diverted pastors from their most fundamental duties. Backus asked: "Has not this earthly scheme [of taxation to support churches] prevailed so far in our land as to cause many ministers, instead of taking *heed to the ministry received from the Lord* and instead of *watching for souls as those who must give an account*, rather to act as if they were not accountable to any higher power than that of the *men* who support them?" Isaac Backus, *An Appeal to the Public for Religious Liberty against the Oppressions of the Present Day*, in McLoughlin, *Isaac Backus* at 334.

25   Butterfield, *Elder John Leland*, 62 Proc. of the Am. Antiquarian Soc'y 160.

26   *Id.* at 160–61.

27   *Id.* at 154 (quoting *Ode to the Mammoth Cheese*); 214–29. The National Constitution Center provides further details on this cheese:

> Leland enlisted the ladies of his Baptist congregation to concoct the giant cheese. He reportedly barred milk from "Federalist cows" from being used in the cheese-making process. Using milk from 900 Republican cows, they used a large cider press to form the cheese. Leland also carefully ensured that no slaves were used to make the cheese.
>
> Leland's followers were Baptists in the decidedly non-Baptist New England, and the cheese was seen as a symbol of religious freedom and diversity. The cheese was engraved with the motto "Rebellion to tyrants is obedience to God."
>
> The Federalist newspapers weren't amused by the stunt, and they called it "mammoth" as an insult . . . .
>
> But the symbolism of the Mammoth Cheese was most poignant on New Year's Day in 1802, when Leland and his followers personally delivered the cheese to Jefferson at the White House. Jefferson thanked the men at a ceremony and paid them $200 for the cheese.
>
> The event may have inspired Jefferson to finish an important letter that very same day to a different group of New England Baptists.
>
> The president wrote to a group in Connecticut about the "wall of separation" in response to a letter he received from the group several days earlier.

In what became known as the Danbury Baptist letter, Jefferson stated:

> "I contemplate with sovereign reverence that act of the whole American people which declared that their legislature should 'make no law respecting an establishment of religion, or prohibiting the free exercise thereof,' thus building a wall of separation between Church and State."

Jefferson's phrase "wall of separation" was cited by the Supreme Court as the justification for the separation of church and state implied in the First Amendment. Critics point to the fact that the concept of the "wall of separation" is Jefferson's and doesn't appear in the Constitution.

National Constitution Center Staff, *A Tale of a Giant Cheese, a Loaf of Bread and the First Amendment*, Constitution Daily (March 27, 2013), https://constitutioncenter.org/blog/a-tale-of-a-giant-cheese-and-the-first-amendment.

28 John Leland, *The Government of Christ a Christocracy* (1804), reprinted in *Writings of the Late Elder John Leland* at 278. Leland continued:

> Magistrates frequently love the advantages of Christianity more than the precepts of it, and flatter themselves that they are doing much for God, and themselves, when they make laws to protect what they esteem the truth of Christianity, and to reward the preachers of that truth, but every law which they make of that complexion, proves their aversion to the scheme of pure Christianity: for, by such a procedure, they arraign either the wisdom, or good will of Christ, the Lord, for not giving enough, and the best of laws for the government of the church, at all times, and in all places. And further, they arrogate to themselves a lording over consciences, which is God's prerogative, and a favor which is not attached to their civil office.

Id.

In other writings, Pastor Leland lamented the effects of the Virginia establishment on the integrity and vitality of Anglican preachers. Virginia's Anglican preachers, Leland said, "not only plead for theatrical amusements, and what they call civil mirth, but their preaching is dry and barren, containing little else but morality." John Leland, *The Virginia Chronicle* (1790), reprinted in *Writings of the Late Elder John Leland* at 108. According to Leland, "The great doctrines of universal depravity, redemption by the blood of Christ, regeneration, faith, repentance and self-denial, are but seldom preached by them, and when they meddle with them, it is in such a superficial manner, as if they were nothing but things of course." *Id.* at 108-09.

Conversely, Leland noted, "where there has been the greatest freedom from religious oppression, where liberty of conscience is entirely enjoyed, there has been the greatest revival of religion; which is another proof that true religion can, and will prevail best, where it is left entirely to Christ." John Leland, *The Rights of Conscience Inalienable: And, Therefore, Religious Opinions Not Cognizable by Law* (1791), reprinted in *Writings of the Late Elder John Leland* at 192.

29 These tests include the "*Lemon*" test, which asks whether there is a secular purpose for governmental action; whether advancing or inhibiting religion is the primary effect of governmental action; and whether such action fosters excessive governmental entanglement with religion. *Lemon v. Kurtzman*, 403 U.S. 602 (1971); *but see Agostini v. Felton*, 521 U.S. 203, 233 (1997) (deciding that "it is simplest to recognize why entanglement is significant and treat it—as we did in *Walz* [*v. Tax Comm'n*]—as an aspect of the inquiry into a statute's effect.").

Another test is called the "endorsement" test. The test asks whether governmental action has the purpose or effect of endorsing religion. *See, e.g., County of Allegheny v. American Civil Liberties Union*, 492 U.S. 573 (1989). In cases involving religious exercises, the Court has also simply asked whether those exercises are state sponsored. *See, e.g., Santa Fe Indep. Sch. Dist. v. Doe*, 530 U.S. 290 (2000). *See also below* chap. 5.

In the *Lee v. Weisman* case, the Court used the "coercion" test, which asks whether individuals are being coerced to support religion or participate in a religious observance. 505 U.S. at 587 ("It is beyond dispute that, at a minimum, the Constitution guarantees that government may not coerce anyone to support or participate in religion or its exercise, or otherwise act in a way which 'establishes a [state] religion or religious faith, or tends to do so.'") (quoting *Lynch v. Donnelly*, 465 U.S. 668, 678 (1984)). Some justices have criticized this test, or at least versions of it, as underinclusive, *see, e.g., Lee v. Weisman*, 505 U.S. at 609–31 (Souter, J., concurring) and overinclusive, *see, e.g., Elk Grove Unified School District v. Newdow*, 542 U.S. at 45–54 (Thomas, J., concurring in the judgment).

For more on these tests and critiques of them, *see, generally* Flowers, Rogers, and Green, *Religious Freedom and the Supreme Court* at 385–1067.

In 2019, the Court upheld the constitutionality of a large, longstanding cross memorial on government land. *American Legion v. American Humanist Association*, No. 17-1717, slip. op. (2019). A Court plurality in this case said that various factors "counsel against" efforts to evaluate Establishment Clause challenges to such "longstanding monuments, symbols and practices," under the *Lemon* test. Instead, a presumption of constitutionality should attach to them. *Id.* at 15–16. *See below* chap. 5.

30 *Mitchell v. Helms*, 530 U.S. 793 (2000).

31 *See below* chaps. 6 and 7.

32 *Santa Fe Indep. Sch. Dist. v. Doe*, 530 U.S. at 302 (quoting *Board of Ed. of Westside Community Schools v. Mergens*, 496 U.S. at 250).

33 *See below* chap. 5.

34 *See* Elizabeth Winkler, *Is It Time for France to Abandon Laïcité?* The New Republic (January 7, 2016).

35 Wake Forest, *Religious Expression*.

36 *Id.*

37 *Thomas v. Review Board*, 450 U.S. 707, 715–16 (1981) (citation omitted).

38 *Hernandez v. Comm'r*, 490 U.S. 680, 699 (1989); *Presbyterian Church v. Hull Memorial Presbyterian Church*, 393 U.S. 440 (1969).

39 A "minyan" is "the quorum required for Jewish communal worship that consists of ten male adults in Orthodox Judaism and usually ten adults of either sex in Conservative and Reform Judaism." Merriam-Webster Dictionary.

40 *Hosanna-Tabor Lutheran Church v. Equal Employment Opportunity Comm'n*, 565 U.S. 171 (2012). *See also below* chap. 9.

41 *Hosanna-Tabor Lutheran Church v. Equal Employment Opportunity Comm'n*, 565 U.S. at 188-89.

42 *Walz v. Tax Comm'n*, 397 U.S. 664, 670 (1970).

43 *McDaniel v. Paty*, 435 U.S. 618 (1978).

44 *Id.* at 641 (Brennan and Marshall, JJ., concurring in the judgment).

45 *Trinity Lutheran Church v. Comer*, 582 U.S. ___, 137 S. Ct. 2012 (2017). The relevant provision of the Missouri constitution states "[t]hat no money shall ever be taken from the public treasury, directly or indirectly, in aid of any church, sect or denomination of

religion, or in aid of any priest, preacher, minister or teacher thereof, as such; and that no preference shall be given to nor any discrimination made against any church, sect or creed of religion, or any form of religious faith or worship." 137 S. Ct. at 2017.

46 *See below* chap. 7.

47 *See below* chap. 8.

48 *Employment Division v. Smith*, 494 U.S. 872, 888 (1990).

49 For further details on Free Exercise Clause standards, *see below* chap. 8.

50 *Church of Lukumi Babalu Aye v. City of Hialeah*, 508 U.S. 520 (1993).

51 42 U.S.C. Section 2000bb *et seq.* (2019). *See below* chap. 8.

52 42 U.S.C. Section 2000cc *et seq.* (2019). *See below* chaps. 8 and 10.

53 *Cutter v. Wilkinson*, 544 U.S. 709, 720 (2005).

54 *Id.* at 722.

55 *See, e.g., Thorton v. Caldor*, 472 U.S. 703 (1985). *See below* chap. 8.

56 *Walz v. Tax Comm'n*, 397 U.S. at 669. The Court has said:

> The general principle deducible from the First Amendment and all that has been said by the Court is this: that we will not tolerate either governmentally established religion or governmental interference with religion. Short of those expressly proscribed governmental acts there is room for play in the joints productive of a benevolent neutrality which will permit religious exercise to exist without sponsorship and without interference.

Id.

57 "This Court has long recognized that the government may (and sometimes must) accommodate religious practices and that it may do so without violating the Establishment Clause." *Hobbie v. Unemployment Appeals Comm'n of Fla.*, 480 U.S. 136, 144–45 (1987) (footnote omitted).

58 *Corporation of Presiding Bishop v. Amos*, 483 U.S. 327 (1987). In this case, the Court said it had "no occasion to pass on the argument [of the employers] that the exemption to which they are entitled under [Section] 702 is required by the Free Exercise Clause." *Id.* at 339 n.17.

59 *Locke v. Davey*, 540 U.S. 712 (2004).

60 This provision from Washington's constitution states:

> Absolute freedom of conscience in all matters of religious sentiment, belief and worship, shall be guaranteed to every individual, and no one shall be molested or disturbed in person or property on account of religion; but the liberty of conscience hereby secured shall not be so construed as to excuse acts of licentiousness or justify practices inconsistent with the peace and safety of the state. No public money or property shall be appropriated for or applied to any religious worship, exercise or instruction, or the support of any religious establishment.

Id. at 719 n.2.

61 *See below* chap. 7.

62 *Everson v. Board of Education*, 330 U.S. at 40 (Rutledge, J., dissenting).

63 *West Virginia State Bd. of Educ. v. Barnette*, 319 U.S. at 638.

64 Father John Courtney Murray, *Civil Unity and Religious Integrity: The Articles of Peace, Woodstock Theological Library at Georgetown University*, https://www.library.georgetown.edu/woodstock/murray/whtt_c2_1954d.

65 *Id.*

66 *See* Preamble, U.S. Const.

Chapter 3: Faith and 1600 Pennsylvania Avenue

1 David McCullough, *John Adams* (New York: Simon & Schuster 2001) 550–51.

2 *Id. See also* William Seale, *The President's House* (Washington, D.C.: White House Historical Society 1986) 1:1–2.

3 *My Dearest Friend: Letters of Abigail and John Adams*, ed. Margaret A. Hogan and C. James Taylor (Cambridge, Mass.: Harvard University Press 2007) 472–73.

4 David McCullough, *The American Spirit: Who We Are and What We Stand For* (New York: Simon & Schuster 2017) 81. *See also* John F. Kennedy, *Remarks at the Dedication of the Restored Mantelpiece in the State Dining Room of the White House*, The White House (April 2, 1962), http://www.presidency.ucsb.edu/ws/index.php?pid=8752.

5 Gary Scott Smith, *Faith and the Presidency: From George Washington to George W. Bush* (New York: Oxford University Press 2006) 27. While Washington faithfully attended church, he apparently did not take communion. *Id.*

6 Jefferson said: "I am of a sect by myself, as far as I know." *Id.* at 69 (footnote omitted). In 1821, Jefferson famously, and wrongly, predicted: "there is not a young man now living in the United States who will not die a Unitarian." *Id.* (footnote omitted).

7 For example, two days after sending his famous letter to the Danbury Baptist Association, the one in which he recognized that the First Amendment had built a wall of separation between church and state, Jefferson attended worship services held in the House of Representatives, with Baptist minister John Leland preaching. *Id.* at 77.

8 Gary Scott Smith, *Religion in the Oval Office: The Religious Lives of American Presidents* (New York: Oxford University Press 2015) 93.

9 Smith, *Faith and the Presidency* at 97.

10 Smith, *Religion in the Oval Office* at 161.

11 *Id.* at 162; C. Edward Spann and Michael E. Williams Sr., *Presidential Praise: Our Presidents and Their Hymns* (Macon: Mercer University Press 2017) 165.

12 Smith, *Faith and the Presidency* at 194.

13 *Id.* (footnote omitted).

14 *Id.* at 195 (footnote omitted).

15 Smith, *Religion in the Oval Office* at 233.

16 *Id.* at 232 (footnote omitted).

17 *Id.* at 236 (footnote omitted).

18 Smith, *Faith and the Presidency* at 221–22, 224.

19 *Id.* at 224. Kevin M. Kruse, *One Nation under God: How Corporate America Invented Christian America* (New York: Basic Books 2015) xii.

20 Smith, *Faith and the Presidency* at 223–24.

21 *Id.* at 225. Evergreen Chapel was not constructed at Camp David until the presidency of George H. W. Bush. *See below* n.31.

22 *Id.* at 262 (footnote omitted).

23 *Id.* at 268 (footnote omitted); Edmund S. Ions, *The Politics of John F. Kennedy* (New York: Routledge Library Editions: Political Science Vol. 1 1967) 89.

24 Smith, *Religion in the Oval Office* at 273–77.

25 Smith, *Faith and the Presidency* at 295.

26 Brian T. Kaylor, *Presidential Campaign Rhetoric in an Age of Confessional Politics* (Lanham, Md.: Lexington Books 2011), 33 (citation omitted).

27 *Id. See also* Eric Marrapodi, *Jimmy Carter Publishes Study Bible, Discusses Faith-Filled Life*, CNN (March 17, 2012). Amy Sullivan, *Why the Modern President Can't Belong to a Church*, Time (December 16, 2011).

28 Smith, *Religion in the Oval Office* at 335.

29 *Id.*

30 These churches included St. John's Episcopal Church, Nineteenth Street Baptist Church, Zion Baptist Church, Allen Chapel African Methodist Episcopal Church, Shiloh Baptist Church, Vermont Avenue Baptist Church, Alfred Street Baptist Church, and Metropolitan African Methodist Episcopal Church. Michael Grass, *Where the Obama Family Has Worshiped in DC*, Huffington Post (January 16, 2012).

31 *See* Michael Giorgione, *Inside Camp David: The Private World of the Presidential Retreat* (New York: Little Brown and Company 2017) at 191–203.

32 President Obama also read daily devotionals written by Joshua DuBois, who served in then-senator Obama's office and directed the White House Office of Faith-Based and Neighborhood Partnerships during the first term. Joshua DuBois, *The President's Devotional* (New York: HarperOne 2013). As DuBois has noted, however, "[s]ending the president a daily Christian reflection is not part of the White House Faith-Based director's job description . . . ." Elizabeth Dias, *Revealed: President Obama's Daily Email Devotionals*, Time (October 20, 2013).

As part of his practice of reading ten letters a day from Americans of all walks of life, President Obama read and sometimes engaged with letter writers who raised religious issues. At the beginning of his administration, President Obama said "he would like to see 10 letters a day. After that, the 10LADs, as they came to be called, were put in a purple folder and added to the back of the briefing book he took with him to the residence on the second floor of the White House each night." Jeanne Marie Laskas, *To Obama with Love, and Hate, and Desperation*, The New York Times (January 17, 2017). *See also* Laskas, *To Obama, with Love, Joy, Anger, and Hope* (New York: Random House 2018).

33 Rev. Bruce Cameron compiled President Obama's remarks at these events. *See* Cameron, *We Are Easter People* (on file with author). At the breakfast, gospel choirs sang, and sometimes a soloist did too, a few religious leaders read scripture, and a minister offered brief reflections.

34 *Van Orden v. Perry*, 545 U.S. at 723 (Stevens, J., dissenting).

35 Smith, *Religion in the Oval Office* at 162; First Inaugural Address of William McKinley (March 4, 1987), https://avalon.law.yale.edu/19th_century/mckin1.asp; Micah 6:8 ("He has showed you, O man, what is good: and what does the Lord require of you, but to do justice, and to love kindness, and to walk humbly with your God.") (RSV). When he was fatally wounded by an anarchist who shot him at close range, McKinley raised a blood-stained hand toward his assailant and said: "Let no one hurt him; May God forgive him." *Id.* at 189.

36 Smith, *Faith and the Presidency* at 228 and 250. In his inaugural address, Eisenhower said:

> My friends, before I begin the expression of those thoughts that I deem appropriate to this moment, would you permit me the privilege of uttering a little private prayer of my own. And I ask that you bow your heads. Almighty God, as we stand here at this moment my future associates in the Executive branch of Government join me in beseeching that Thou will make full and complete our dedication to the service of the people in this throng, and their fellow citizens everywhere. Give us, we pray, the power to discern clearly right from wrong, and allow all our words and actions to be governed thereby, and by the laws of this land. Especially we pray

that our concern shall be for all the people regardless of station, race, or calling. May cooperation be permitted and be the mutual aim of those who, under the concepts of our Constitution, hold to differing political faiths; so that all may work for the good of our beloved country and Thy glory. Amen.

Dwight D. Eisenhower, *1953 Presidential Inauguration*, Presidential Library, Museum and Boyhood Home, https://www.eisenhower.archives.gov/all_about_ike/presidential/1953 _inauguration.html; *see also* http://www.presidency.ucsb.edu/ws/index.php?pid=9600; *Newdow v. Bush*, 355 F. Supp. 2d 265, 287 (D.D.C. 2005) (citing Compl., App. D.). The video of Eisenhower's prayer is here: https://www.youtube.com/watch?v=DKqgFY8wmhI.

In his farewell address, Eisenhower said:

> To all the peoples of the world, I once more give expression to America's prayerful and continuing aspiration: We pray that peoples of all faiths, all races, all nations, may have their great human needs satisfied; that those now denied opportunity shall come to enjoy it to the full; that all who yearn for freedom may experience its spiritual blessings; that those who have freedom will understand, also, its heavy responsibilities; that all who are insensitive to the needs of others will learn charity; that the scourges of poverty, disease and ignorance will be made to disappear from the earth, and that, in the goodness of time, all peoples will come to live together in a peace guaranteed by the binding force of mutual respect and love.

Smith, *Faith and the Presidency* at 250; *Farewell Radio and Television Address to the American People*, Eisenhower Archives (January 17, 1961), https://www.eisenhower.archives .gov/all_about_ike/speeches/farewell_address.pdf.

Several Founding Fathers offered "supplications" to the Almighty in their inaugural addresses. *See Newdow v. Bush*, 355 F. Supp. 2d at 286–87. President Washington, for example, stated: "[I]t would be peculiarly improper to omit in this first official act my fervent supplications to that Almighty Being who rules over the universe . . . that His benediction may consecrate to the liberties and happiness of the people of the United States a Government instituted by themselves for these essential purposes." *Id.* at 287 (quoting Def. Mot. Dismiss, Ex. J (*Inaugural Addresses of the Presidents of the United States*)) at 2; *see also id.* at 22–23 (benediction of President Jefferson in 1805); *id.* at 28 (benediction of President Madison in 1809).

37   Smith, *Faith and the Presidency* at 266 (footnote omitted).

38   *Id.* at 259.

39   *See* Diane Winston, *The History of the National Prayer Breakfast*, Smithsonian.com (February 2, 2017). *See also* Todd J. Gilman, *Tyler's Louie Gohmert Puts Obama Criticism on Pause at National Prayer Breakfast*, Dallas Morning News (February 2013).

40   2 Tim 1:7 (NKJV).

41   *Remarks by the President at the National Prayer Breakfast*, The White House (February 4, 2016), https://obamawhitehouse.archives.gov/the-press-office/2016/02/04/remarks -president-national-prayer-breakfast-0. President Obama's reference to "Roma" is to Roma Downey, who served as a keynote speaker at this event. CSPAN, *Mark Burnett and Roma Downey Remarks at National Prayer Breakfast* (February 4, 2016), https://www.c-span .org/video/?c4579081/mark-burnett-roma-downey-remarks-national-prayer-breakfast.

42   Jason Horowitz, Nick Corasaniti, and Ashley Southall, *Nine Killed in Shooting at Black Church in Charleston*, The New York Times (June 25, 2015); *Remarks by the President in Eulogy for the Honorable Rev. Clementa Pinckney*, The White House (June 26, 2015), https://obamawhitehouse.archives.gov/the-press-office/2015/06/26/remarks-president -eulogy-honorable-reverend-clementa-pinckney. *See also* Amy Sullivan, *The Last 100*

Days: Theologian-in-Chief, Yahoo News (January 14, 2017). The nine victims of the attack were: Cynthia Graham Hurd, 54; Susie Jackson, 87; Ethel Lance, 70; Rev. DePayne Middleton Doctor, 49; Rev. Clementa Pinckney, 41; Tywanza Sanders, 26; Rev. Daniel Simmons Sr., 74; Sharonda Coleman-Singleton, 45; and Myra Thompson, 59. *Statement by Attorney General Loretta E. Lynch on the Sentencing of Dylann Roof,* Department of Justice (January 10, 2017), https://www.justice.gov/opa/pr/statement-attorney-general -loretta-e-lynch-sentencing-dylann-roof. *See also below* chap. 10.

43   *President Obama Narrates "The People's House"* (January 13, 2017), https://obamawhitehouse .archives.gov/blog/2017/01/13/president-obama-narrates-peoples-house-virtual-reality -tour-white-house.

44   *See Remarks by the President at Iftar Dinner,* The White House (August 13, 2010), https:// obamawhitehouse.archives.gov/the-press-office/2010/08/13/remarks-president-iftar-dinner; *Remarks by the President at Iftar Dinner,* The White House (August 10, 2012), https:// obamawhitehouse.archives.gov/the-press-office/2012/08/10/remarks-president-iftar-dinner.

45   *See* Amy B. Wang, *President Trump Just Ended a Long Tradition of Celebrating Ramadan at the White House,* The Washington Post (June 25, 2017).

46   *Id.*

47   Smith, *Faith and the Presidency* at 386.

48   *Id.* at 243.

49   Juliet Eilperin, *Passover Seder: One Last Time for an Obama White House Tradition,* The Washington Post (April 28, 2016).

50   *See, e.g., President Obama: Happy Diwali,* The White House (November 11, 2015), https:// obamawhitehouse.archives.gov/blog/2015/11/10/president-obama-happy-diwali.

51   *Statement by the President on the Celebration of Vesak,* The White House (May 20, 2016), https://obamawhitehouse.archives.gov/the-press-office/2016/05/20/statement-president -celebration-vesak.

52   *See, e.g., Statement by the President on the Birth of Guru Nanak Devi Ji,* The White House (November 6, 2014), https://obamawhitehouse.archives.gov/the-press-office/2014/11/06/ statement-president-anniversary-birth-guru-nanak-dev-ji.

53   Petula Dvorak, *Trump Brought "Merry Christmas" Back to the White House? Fact Check: Wrong,* The Washington Post (November 30, 2017).

54   Brakkton Booker, *FACT CHECK: Trump's Pledge to Restore "Merry Christmas" to the White House,* NPR (November 30, 2017).

55   Ian Schwartz, *Trump: Christmas Is Back, Bigger and Better Now than Ever Before . . . and Now We Say It with Pride,* Real Clear Politics (December 24, 2017).

56   Luz Lazo, *The National Christmas Tree Lighting Is Thursday. Prepare for a Dreadful Commute,* The Washington Post (November 28, 2017); *The National Christmas Tree,* National Park Service, https://www.nps.gov/whho/planyourvisit/national-christmas-tree .htm.

57   As President Bush and First Lady Laura Bush noted:

> A mainstay of White House Christmas decorations is the 18th century crèche that was donated to the White House by Mrs. Charles W. Engelhard, Jr. of Far Hills, New Jersey in 1967. On display in the East Room, the crèche was made in Naples, Italy of terra cotta and carved wood.

> *Holiday Decorations,* The White House, https://georgewbush-whitehouse.archives.gov/ president/holiday/decorations/03.html.

Similarly, the Obama White House noted that "this piece has sat in the East Room for the holidays for more than forty-five years, spanning nine administrations." *2015 White House Holidays—A Timeless Tradition*, The White House, Office of the First Lady (December 2, 2015), https://obamawhitehouse.archives.gov/the-press-office/2015/12/02/2015-white-house-holidays-timeless-tradition. While it was reported that an Obama administration social secretary considered not displaying this crèche in the White House during Christmas 2009, the crèche was displayed in the East Room of the White House at Christmas time throughout the Obama administration. Dvorak, *Trump Brought "Merry Christmas" Back*.

58   *See generally* Smith, *Religion in the Oval Office*; and *Faith and the Presidency*. Government officials have also sometimes wished Americans "Happy Holidays" during December to be more inclusive. Some Americans celebrate Hanukkah, not Christmas, and other Americans do not celebrate any religious holiday in December or perhaps any religious holidays at all.

59   The full statement read:

> During this season of Advent, Christians in the United States and around the world are preparing to celebrate the birth of Jesus Christ. At this time, those of us fortunate enough to live in countries that honor the birthright of all people to practice their faith freely give thanks for that blessing. Michelle and I are also ever-mindful that many of our fellow Christians do not enjoy that right, and hold especially close to our hearts and minds those who have been driven from their ancient homelands by unspeakable violence and persecution.
>
> In some areas of the Middle East where church bells have rung for centuries on Christmas Day, this year they will be silent; this silence bears tragic witness to the brutal atrocities committed against these communities by ISIL.
>
> We join with people around the world in praying for God's protection for perse-cuted Christians and those of other faiths, as well as for those brave men and women engaged in our military, diplomatic, and humanitarian efforts to alleviate their suffering and restore stability, security, and hope to their nations. As the old Christmas carol reminds us:
>
> > The Wrong shall fail,
> > The Right prevail,
> > With peace on earth, good-will to men.

> *Statement by the President on Persecuted Christians at Christmas*, The White House (December 23, 2015), https://obamawhitehouse.archives.gov/the-press-office/2015/12/23/statement-president-persecuted-christians-christmas.

60   Smith, *Faith and the Presidency* at 49. *See also below* chap. 10.

61   *Id.* at 76–77.

62   *Id.* at 199–201.

63   *Id.* at 283.

64   *See, e.g.,* Hunter Schwartz, *Obama Met with Mormon leaders on Immigration Reform—A Rare Issue They Actually Agree On*, The Washington Post (April 23, 2015); Associated Press, *Obama Discusses Immigration with Faith Leaders*, The San Diego Union-Tribune (April 15, 2014); *Readout of the President's Meeting with African American Faith Leaders*, The White House (August 26, 2013), https://obamawhitehouse.archives.gov/the-press-office/2013/08/26/readout-president-s-meeting-african-american-faith-leaders; Barb Fraze, *Christian Leaders Meet Obama, Discuss Concerns for Mideast Minorities*, Catholic

News Service (September 12, 2014); Abby Phillip, *Ebola Survivor Kent Brantly Met Obama in Oval Office*, The Washington Post (September 16, 2014).

65 Daniel Burke, *Dalai Lama to Obama: "You Are Young and Can Do a Lot,"* CNN (December 1, 2017).

66 *Remarks by the President in Conversation on Poverty at Georgetown University*, The White House (May 12, 2015), https://obamawhitehouse.archives.gov/the-press-office/2015/05/12/remarks-president-conversation-poverty-georgetown-university. Also in 2015, President Obama made remarks at the national convention of the Catholic Health Association. *See Remarks by the President at the Catholic Health Association*, The White House (June 9, 2015), https://obamawhitehouse.archives.gov/the-press-office/2015/06/09/remarks-president-catholic-health-association-conference.

67 Jake Tapper, Karen Travers, and Sunlen Miller, *President Obama Meets Pope Benedict at the Vatican*, ABC News (July 10, 2009). *President Obama's Remarks Welcoming Pope Francis to the White House*, The New York Times (September 23, 2015); Michael Gryboski, *Russell Moore Talks about His Meeting with President Obama on Prison Reform*, The Christian Post (September 20, 2016).

    Presidents Wilson, Eisenhower, Kennedy, Johnson, Nixon, Ford, Carter, Reagan, (George H. W.) Bush, Clinton, and (George W.) Bush also met with popes while they served. *See* Ines San Martin, *Those 29 Times Presidents and Popes Have Intersected*, Crux (May 19, 2017). Presidents Roosevelt, Truman, Nixon, Carter, and Ford appointed personal representatives to serve as liaisons to the Vatican. *See* Smith, *Faith and the Presidency* at 205–6, 310; Smith, *Religion in the Oval Office* at 244–46, 280. President Reagan officially established relations in 1984. *See* Smith, *Faith and the Presidency* at 341.

68 Thomas J. Reese, *Inside the Vatican: The Politics and Organization of the Catholic Church* (Cambridge, Mass.: Harvard University Press 1996) 5.

69 In 2018, the United Nations High Commission on Refugees said: "An unprecedented **68.5 million** people around the world have been forced from home. Among them are nearly **25.4 million refugees,** over half of whom are **under the age of 18.**" *Figures at a Glance*, United Nations High Commission on Refugees (June 19, 2018), http://www.unhcr.org/en-us/figures-at-a-glance.html.

70 *See How to Save the U.S. Refugee Admissions Program*, The International Crisis Group (September 12, 2018), https://www.crisisgroup.org/united-states/002-how-save-us-refugee-admissions-program. The Crisis Group report notes that "Denis McDonough, the White House chief of staff and a strong supporter of resettlement (which he had first encountered through his church's support for Vietnamese refugees as a boy growing up in Minnesota) was a particularly strong advocate, believing not just in the strategic and humanitarian benefits of the program, but that it has been 'overwhelmingly successful' in bringing to the U.S. people who have made enormous contributions to American life." *Id.*

71 *See* Bryan Walsh, *Alan Kurdi's Story: Behind the Most Heartbreaking Photo of 2015*, Time (December 29, 2015).

72 Andorra Bruno, *Refugee Admissions and Resettlement Policy*, Congressional Research Service (November 7, 2017), https://fas.org/sgp/crs/misc/RL31269.pdf.

73 *See generally Fact Sheet: Advancing Shared Values for a Better World*, The White House (September 23, 2015), https://obamawhitehouse.archives.gov/the-press-office/2015/09/23/fact-sheet-advancing-shared-values-better-world. *See also Obama Increases Number of Syrian Refugees for U.S. Resettlement to 10,000*, The New York Times (September 10, 2015; *Presidential Determination on Refugee Admissions for Fiscal Year 2016*, The White

House (September 29, 2015), https://obamawhitehouse.archives.gov/the-press-office/ 2015/09/29/presidential-determination-presidential-determination-refugee-admissions. The presidential determination for FY 2016 raised the overall ceiling for refugees by fifteen thousand. *See Presidential Memorandum—FY 2015 Refugee Admissions*, The White House (September 30, 2014), https://obamawhitehouse.archives.gov/the-press-office/2014/09/ 30/presidential-memorandum-fy-2015-refugee-admissions.

74   Jens Manuel Krogstad and Jynnah Radford, *Key Facts about Refugees to the United States*, Pew Research Center (January 30, 2017), http://www.pewresearch.org/fact-tank/2017/ 01/30/key-facts-about-refugees-to-the-u-s/.

75   *Id.*

76   *Id.*

77   *Id.*

78   *See* Denis McDonough and Ryan Crocker, *The World's System for Resettling Refugees Benefits the United States*, Foreign Policy (October 22, 2018).

79   *See* Nahal Toosi, *Trump's Refugee Crackdown Plans Put Pompeo on the Spot*, Politico (August 8, 2018), https://www.politico.com/story/2018/08/08/mike-pompeo-refugee -limit-stephen-miller-767373.

80   Timothy Morgan, *1,180 Churches Help World Relief Resettle Refugees at Record Rate*, Christianity Today (October 20, 2016).

81   *Id. See below* chap. 6.

82   *See* Kenneth Bae with Mark Tabb, *Not Forgotten: The True Story of My Imprisonment in North Korea* (Nashville: W Publishing Group 2016).

83   Corky Siemaszko, *Meet the Americans Freed from Iranian Prison*, NBC News (January 17, 2016).

84   *Remarks by the President at the National Prayer Breakfast*, The White House (February 6, 2014), https://obamawhitehouse.archives.gov/the-press-office/2014/02/06/remarks -president-national-prayer-breakfast.

85   *Id.*

86   *Id.*

87   *Id.*

88   President Obama subsequently met with Pastor Abedini's wife and children, for example. *See* David Jackson, *President Obama Meets with Wife of Pastor Jailed in Iran*, USA Today (January 22, 2015).

89   *See* Katie Zezima, *Clapper Details Trip to North Korea That Led to the Release of Two Americans*, The Washington Post (November 16, 2014).

90   *Remarks by the President at the National Prayer Breakfast*, The White House (February 5, 2015), https://obamawhitehouse.archives.gov/the-press-office/2015/02/05/remarks -president-national-prayer-breakfast.

91   *Remarks by the President at the National Prayer Breakfast*, The White House (February 4, 2016), https://obamawhitehouse.archives.gov/the-press-office/2016/02/04/remarks -president-national-prayer-breakfast-0.

92   *See* Merlin Gustafson, *The Religious Role of the President*, The Midwest Journal of Political Science 14 (1970), 708–22. Smith, *Faith and the Presidency* at 239–40.

93   Smith, *Faith and the Presidency* at 239, 109.

94   "Fox's role was not a new one; the White House had always [coordinated the religious activities of the executive offices and departments] by various means. The innovation was that *one* man had been appointed to coordinate the function and that the religious

requirements of the office had been formally recognized." Gustafson, *Religious Role of the President* at 721. Professor Gustafson also observed:

> Recent developments such as greater power in national government and centralizing tendencies in organized religion have made the religious activities of the Presidency more significant. Along with these developments, communication lines between the citizenry and executive policy-makers have become more diffuse. Under the circumstances the Office of the Presidency needs expert advice on matters religious and theological. An ombudsman for religious interests could fill a demonstrated need. Recent administrations have not continued this type of appointment, however, and the religious role of the Presidency remains for the most part unrecognized.

Id. at 721–22.

95 "Like other post-World War II presidents, [President] Clinton assigned White House staff to serve as a 'bridge to the religious communities.'" Smith, *Religion in the Oval Office* at 340.

96 Smith, *Faith and the Presidency* at 273–75.

97 *Id.* at 274.

98 Randall Balmer, *God in the White House: How Faith Shaped the Presidency from John F. Kennedy to George W. Bush* (New York: HarperOne 2008); Smith, *Faith and the Presidency* at 308–11. President Johnson apparently asked Moyers, his press secretary at the time, to offer a prayer at a White House dinner. Johnson and Moyers were seated at opposite ends of a long table, and, a few sentences into the prayer, President Johnson interrupted, saying: "Louder, Bill, we can't hear you!" Moyers responded: "I'm not talking to you, Mr. President!" James P. Moore, *One Nation under God: The History of Prayer in America* (New York: Doubleday 2005).

99 Gustafson, *Religious Role of the President* at 711.

100 The Domestic Policy Council and White House Counsel's Office are part of the Executive Office of the President (EOP), an office that President Franklin D. Roosevelt officially created in 1939 to provide him with the support he needed to govern. *See* Executive Order 8248, *Establishing the Division of the Executive Office of the President and Defining Their Functions and Duties*, 4 Fed. Reg. 3864 (September 8, 1939), https://www.archives.gov/ federal-register/codification/executive-order/08248.html. The EOP "represents an institutional response to needs felt by every occupant of the Oval Office" for "assistance and advice." Harold C. Relyea, Congressional Research Service, *The Executive Office of the President: An Historical Overview* (November 2008), https://fas.org/sgp/crs/misc/98-606 .pdf. Depending on a president's needs and wishes, the composition of the EOP can vary, but it typically includes the National Security Council (NSC); the Office of Management and Budget (OMB), including the Office of Information and Regulatory Affairs (OIRA); the White House Counsel's Office (WHCO); the National Economic Council (NEC); and the Domestic Policy Council (DPC), among other components. In 1970, President Nixon created the Office of Policy Development to coordinate the development of domestic and economic policy. *See* Federal Register, https://www.federalregister.gov/agencies/office-of -policy-development. In 1993, President Bill Clinton split this office into two components: the Domestic Policy Council and the National Economic Council. *Id.* The federal executive branch also includes various federal agencies, commissions, and committees.

101 *See* Department of Housing and Urban Development, Center for Community and Interfaith Partnerships, https://archives.hud.gov/initiatives/fbci/fbciann.cfm (archived April 9, 2010).

102 *Id.* In a HUD press release, Father Hacala described the aims of the office in the following way:

> The **goal** of this Center, which is not a new funding source at HUD, is to work directly with those of you involved in community development corporations, not-for-profit groups, community organizing activities and faith-based groups.
>
> Its **purpose** will be to focus, integrate and intensify our efforts in working WITH you, and to work together to help make the Center a more active partner in the grass-roots empowerment movement in the areas of housing and economic development.
>
> Its **objectives** include:
>
> > 1) to comprehensively and actively solicit feedback and appropriate response to HUD's outreach regarding housing and urban development issues;
> >
> > 2) to communicate HUD actively to community and faith-based constituencies, including the least-well-off;
> >
> > 3) to coordinate the use of HUD's resources, both internally and externally;
> >
> > 4) to seek new private and public partnerships on the local, regional and national levels.

  Id.
103 Smith, *Faith and the Presidency* at 387–92.
104 *Id.*
105 Melissa Rogers, *President Trump Just Unveiled a White House "Faith" Office: It Actually Weakens Religious Freedom*, The Washington Post (May 14, 2018).
106 *See* Melissa Rogers, *Religious Freedom and the Federal Executive Branch: Suggestions for Future Administrations,* 15 Univ. St. Thomas L. Jnl. 703 (2019). *Presidential Adviser Explains Mission of White House Faith-Based Office, Principles of Interaction Between Religion and Government,* Religious Communicators Council (April 10, 2015), https://www.religioncommunicators.org/presidential-adviser-explains-mission-of-white-house-faith-based-office-principles-of-interaction-between-religion-and-government.
107 *Remarks at the Launch of the Office of Faith-Based Community Initiatives,* State Department (August 7, 2013), https://2009-2017.state.gov/secretary/remarks/2013/08/212781.htm.
108 *Id.*
109 Melissa Rogers and Dana Mayber, *The Power of Partnerships,* The White House (November 29, 2016), https://obamawhitehouse.archives.gov/blog/2016/11/29/power-partnerships.
110 Smith, *Faith and the Presidency* at 243.
111 *Id.* at 275.
112 Smith, *Religion in the Oval Office* at 280.
113 *See* Lee Davidson, *Utahns Left Legacy for Leavitt to Follow,* Deseret Morning News (August 13, 2003), https://www.deseretnews.com/article/1002980/Utahns-left-legacy-for-Leavitt-to-follow.html; Frank James, *Romney Rekindles Conservative Doubts with Pick to Lead White House Transition,* NPR (June 4, 2012).
114 *See* Lauren Markoe and Brian Pellot, *Rabbi David Saperstein Will Be First Non-Christian to Serve as United States Ambassador for Religious Freedom,* Religion News Service, in The Washington Post (July 28, 2014).

115 Lori Johnston, *Trump's Evangelical Advisory Board Violates the Law, Advocacy Group Says,* The Washington Post (August 30, 2018).

116 Martin Luther King Jr., *A Knock at Midnight* (June 5, 1963), https://kinginstitute.stanford.edu/king-papers/documents/knock-midnight.

117 *See below* chap. 4. *See* Thomas J. Reese, *Thank You, Steve Bannon,* Religion News Service (September 17, 2017).

118 Michael J. O'Loughlin, *Alongside Catholic Leaders, President Trump Signs Executive Order on Religious Liberty, Health Care,* America (May 4, 2017).

119 *See* Wake Forest, *Religious Expression.*

Chapter 4: Religion, Policy, and Politics

1 *See Attorney General Sessions Delivers Remarks Discussing the Immigration Enforcement Actions of the Trump Administration,* Department of Justice (May 7, 2018), https://www.justice.gov/opa/speech/attorney-general-sessions-delivers-remarks-discussing-immigration-enforcement-actions.

2 *Id.*

3 Salvador Rizzo, *Trump's False Claim That Obama Had the Same Family Separation Policy,* The Washington Post (November 27, 2018).

4 *Id.*

5 Julie Zausmer, *From Pulpits across America, Sermons Condemn Separation of Immigrant Families,* The Washington Post (June 19, 2018).

6 Attorney General Jeff Sessions, *Attorney General Sessions Addresses Recent Criticisms of Zero Tolerance by Church Leaders,* Department of Justice (June 14, 2018), https://www.justice.gov/opa/speech/attorney-general-sessions-addresses-recent-criticisms-zero-tolerance-church-leaders.

7 Madison, *Memorial and Remonstrance,* in Flowers, Rogers, and Green, *Religious Freedom and the Supreme Court* at 1133–37.

8 *See* Katie Benner and Maggie Haberman, *Matthew Whitaker, a Trump Loyalist, Is Seen as Ascendant amid Rosenstein Chaos,* The New York Times (September 26, 2018). During his 2014 run for the U.S. Senate, Matthew Whitaker said at a forum for Republican candidates that, if elected, he would ask judicial nominees whether they were "people of faith" who had "a biblical view of justice." *Id.*

9 Alyssa Fischer, *Matthew Whitaker Once Said Judges Should Have a "Biblical View of Justice,"* The Forward (November 9, 2018), https://forward.com/fast-forward/413928/matthew-whitaker-once-said-judges-should-have-a-biblical-view-of-justice/.

10 *Id.*

11 *Id.*

12 Peter Beinart, *The Muted GOP Response to Roy Moore's Anti-Muslim Prejudice,* The Atlantic (September 28, 2017).

13 *Id.* As the Joint Statement on Religious Expression in American Public Life notes:

> Those who make an affirmation or take an oath promising to fulfill certain duties toward the government may choose to do so while placing a hand on a text that is sacred to him or her (whether the text is the Bible or something else), but this is not in any way required by the Constitution. If an elected official chooses to place his or her hand on a book while taking an oath or making an affirmation, the official may select a religious or nonreligious book. If the official wishes to use a religious book, the official may select whatever scripture is sacred to him or her,

whether that scripture is the Bible, the Torah, the Quran, the Bhagavad-Gita or something else. An officeholder may choose to add the words "so help me God" at the end of this oath or affirmation. Adding these words to the oath or affirmation, however, is not and could not be required by government.

See Wake Forest, *Religious Expression.*

14 Aaron Blake, *Did Feinstein Accuse a Judicial Nominee of Being Too Christian?* The Washington Post (September 7, 2017).

15 John H. Garvey and Amy V. Coney, *Catholic Judges in Capital Cases*, 81 Marq. L. Rev. 303 (1997–1998).

16 *Id.* at 304.

17 Michael Gerson, *Senate Democrats Show Off Their Anti-religious Bigotry*, The Washington Post (September 14, 2017).

18 Blake, *Did Feinstein Accuse? See also* 28 U.S.C. Section 455 (2018), which states in part:

(a) Any justice, judge, or magistrate judge of the United States shall disqualify himself in any proceeding in which his impartiality might reasonably be questioned.

(b) He shall also disqualify himself in the following circumstances:

(1) Where he has a personal bias or prejudice concerning a party, or personal knowledge of disputed evidentiary facts concerning the proceeding.

19 Kennedy was not the first Catholic to run for president. Alfred Smith won the Democratic nomination in 1928, but he lost badly to Herbert Hoover. Randall Balmer, *God in the White House: How Faith Shaped the Presidency from John F. Kennedy to George W. Bush* (New York: HarperOne, 2008) 8–10. Notably, Hoover, a Quaker, denounced anti-Catholicism on the campaign trail, saying he did not want support from Americans who held such views. *See* Smith, *Religion in the Oval Office* at 206.

20 Theodore H. White, *The Making of the President 1960* (New York: Athenaeum House Inc. 1962) 107–8; Sen. John F. Kennedy, Address to the Greater Houston Ministerial Association (September 12, 1960), John F. Kennedy Presidential Library and Museum.

21 In his speech, Kennedy promised not to appoint any ambassador to the Vatican and to oppose unconstitutional aid to parochial schools and boycotts of public schools, issues that had been raised as sources of concern during the campaign:

I ask you tonight to follow in that tradition—to judge me on the basis of 14 years in the Congress, on my declared stands against an ambassador to the Vatican, against unconstitutional aid to parochial schools, and against any boycott of the public schools (which I attended myself). And instead of doing this, do not judge me on the basis of these pamphlets and publications we all have seen that carefully select quotations out of context from the statements of Catholic Church leaders, usually in other countries, frequently in other centuries, and rarely relevant to any situation here. And always omitting, of course, the statement of the American Bishops in 1948 which strongly endorsed church-state separation, and which more nearly reflects the views of almost every American Catholic.

White, *Making of the President 1960*; Balmer, *God in the White House* at 8–10.

22 Here is the exchange on whether Catholics believe it is acceptable to lie in certain circumstances:

Question. B. E. Howard, Minister of the Church of Christ. First of all I should like to quote some authoritative quotations from Catholic sources and then propose a question.

"So that a false statement knowingly made to one who has not a right to the truth will not be a lie," Catholic Encyclopedia, Volume 10, P. 696. "However, we are also under an obligation to keep secrets faithfully, and sometimes the easiest way of fulfilling that duty is to say what is false or tell a lie." Catholic Encyclopedia, Volume 10, P. 195.

"When mental reservation is permissible, it is lawful to corroborate one's utterances by an oath if there be an adequate cause." Article on perjury, Catholic Encyclopedia, Volume 11, Page 696. "The truth we proclaim under oath is relative and not absolute." Explanation of Catholic Morale, P. 130.

Just recently from the Vatican in Rome this news release was given from the official Vatican newspaper, and I am quoting that of May 19, 1960, Tuesday. Stated that the Roman Catholic hierarchy had the right and duty to intervene in the political field to guide its flock. The newspaper rejected what is termed "the absurd split of conscience between the believer and the citizen." However, [L'Osservatore] Romano made it clear that its stern pronouncement was valid for Roman Catholic laymen everywhere. It deplored the great confusion of ideas that is spreading especially between Catholic doctrine and social and political activities and between the ecclesiastical hierarchy and the lay faithful in the civil field. Pope John XXIII recently gave this statement according to the St. Louis Review, dated December 12, 1958: "Catholics may unite their strength toward the common aid of the Catholic hierarchy . . ."

From the floor. I object to this. The time is running out.

Question. This is the question, sir: Do you subscribe to the doctrine of mental reservation which I have quoted from the Catholic authorities? Do you submit to the authority of the present Pope which I have quoted in these quotations?

Senator Kennedy. Let me say in the first place I have not read the Catholic Encyclopedia and I don't know all the quotation which you are giving me. I don't agree with the statement. I find no difficulty in saying so. But I do think probably I could make a better comment if I had the entire quotation before me.

But in any case I have not read it before. If the quotation is meant to imply that when you take an oath you don't mean it, or it is proper for you to make oaths and then break them, it is proper for you to lie, if that is what this states, and I don't know whether that is what it states unless I read it all in context, then, of course, I would not agree with it.

Secondly, on the question of the [L'Osservatore] Romano article, once again I don't have that in full. I read the statement of last December which was directed to a situation in Sicily where some of the Catholics were active in the Communist Party. But I am not familiar with the one of May 1960 that you mentioned. In any case the [L'Osservatore] Romano has no standing, as far as binding me. Thirdly, the quotation of Pope John of 1958, I didn't catch all of that, and if you will read that again I will tell you whether I support that or not.

Sen. John F. Kennedy, *Address to the Greater Houston Ministerial Association* (September 12, 1960), John F. Kennedy Presidential Library and Museum.

23 When he ran for president, Mitt Romney made a speech entitled "Faith in America" at the George Bush Presidential Library in College Station, Texas. Dan Balz, *In Speech on Faith, Romney Vows to Serve "No One Cause,"* The Washington Post (December 7,

2007); *Transcript: Mitt Romney's Faith Speech*, NPR (December 6, 2007), https://www
.npr.org/templates/story/story.php?storyId=16969460. Romney said that some Americans
"would prefer it if I would simply distance myself from my religion, say that it is more
a tradition than my personal conviction, or disavow one or another of its precepts." *Id.*
He responded:

> That I will not do. I believe in my Mormon faith and I endeavor to live by it. My
> faith is the faith of my fathers—I will be true to them and to my beliefs.
>
> Some believe that such a confession of my faith will sink my candidacy. If they are
> right, so be it. But I think they underestimate the American people. Americans
> do not respect believers of convenience.

24 Brad Knickerbocker, *Mitt Romney's Mormon Religion: Is It a Political Problem?* Christian
Science Monitor (June 4, 2011).

25 *See Harris v. McRae*, 448 U.S. 297, 319-20 (1980); Wake Forest, *Religious Expression* at
5–6.

26 *See Wallace v. Jaffree*, 472 U.S. 38 (1985). The *Wallace* Court held only that the Alabama
moment-of-silence law was unconstitutional, not that all such laws and policies were
unconstitutional. The Court also struck down a county's Ten Commandments display
for similar reasons. *See McCreary County v. American Civil Liberties Union*, 545 U.S.
844 (2005).

27 *Harris v. McRae*, 448 U.S. 297 (1980).

28 *Id.* at 319.

29 *Id.* (quoting *McGowan v. Maryland*, 366 U.S. at 422).

30 The Supreme Court has recognized: "Adherents of particular faiths and individual
churches frequently take strong positions on public issues . . . . Of course, churches as
much as secular bodies and private citizens have that right." *Walz v. Tax Comm'n*, 397
U.S. at 670.

31 *See, e.g.,* Jonathan Blitzer, *How Church Leaders in Charlottesville Prepared for White
Supremacists*, The New Yorker (August 15, 2017).

32 *See, e.g.,* Emily McFarlan Miller, *Religious Leaders Overwhelmingly Condemn Trump
Ending DACA*, Religion News Service (September 5, 2017).

33 *See, e.g.,* amicus curiae briefs by religious organizations in *Janus v. American Federa-
tion of State, County and Municipal Employees*, 585 U.S. ___, 138 S. Ct. 2448 (2018),
http://www.scotusblog.com/case-files/cases/janus-v-american-federation-state-county
-municipal-employees-council-31/; *Trump v. Hawaii*, 585 U.S. ___, 138 S. Ct. 2392
(2018), http://www.scotusblog.com/case-files/cases/trump-v-hawaii-3/; *National Institute
of Family and Life Advocates v. Becerra*, 585 U.S. ___, 138 S. Ct. 2361 (2018), http://
www.scotusblog.com/case-files/cases/national-institute-family-life-advocates-v-becerra/;
Masterpiece Cakeshop, Ltd. v. Colorado Civil Rights Commission, 584 U.S. ___, 138 S.
Ct. 1719 (2018), http://www.scotusblog.com/case-files/cases/masterpiece-cakeshop-ltd
-v-colorado-civil-rights-commn/.

34 *See* Katrina vanden Heuvel, *A New Poor People's Campaign Wants to Change How
Society Defines Morality*, The Washington Post (December 5, 2017). *See also* https://
poorpeoplescampaign.org/.

35 Julie Zausmer, *From Pulpits across America, Sermons Condemn Separation of Immigrant
Families*, The Washington Post (June 19, 2018).

36 *McDaniel v. Paty*, 435 U.S. 618.

37   *Id.* at 621 n.1 (quoting art. IX, sec. 1, of the Constitution of Tennessee). Although the provision spoke in Christian terms, the state argued that it was applied to clergy of all faiths.

38   "Any citizen of the state who can qualify for membership in the House of Representatives of the General Assembly may become a candidate for delegate to the convention . . . ." *Id.* at 621 (quoting ch. 848, sec. 4, of 1976 Tenn. Pub. Acts).

39   *Paty v. McDaniel,* 547 S.W.2d 897, 903 (1977). The restriction, the court said,

> simply does not impose any burden, direct or indirect upon religious belief or religious action. It is not religious belief, but the career or calling, by which one is identified as dedicated to the full-time promotion of the religious objectives of a particular religious sect, that disqualifies. Ineligibility for service in the General Assembly in no way restricts religious action—except in the law making process of government—where religious action is absolutely prohibited by the establishment clause . . . .

Id.

40   *McDaniel v. Paty,* 435 U.S. at 623–24, 626.

41   John Leland, *The Virginia Chronicle: With Judicious and Critical remarks under XXIV Heads* (Norfolk: Prentis and Baxter 1790) 43.

42   *McDaniel v. Paty,* 435 U.S. at 625.

43   The plurality opinion argued that the *Torcaso* case "d[id] not govern," because "ministerial status is defined in terms of conduct and activity rather than in terms of belief." *Id.* at 626–27. In separate opinions, however, other justices said *Torcaso* prohibited this restriction. *See generally id.* at 629–46 (Brennan and Marshall, JJ., concurring in the judgment; Stewart, J., concurring in the judgment).

44   *Id.* at 630 (Brennan and Marshall, JJ., concurring in the judgment).

45   *Id.* at 632.

46   *Id.* at 641.

47   *See* Yolanda Putnam and Joan Garrett McClane, *Civil Rights Pioneer Paul McDaniel Has Ministered to Chattanooga for 48 Years; Now He's Stepping Back,* Times Free Press (March 9, 2014).

48   Madison, *Memorial and Remonstrance,* in Flowers, Rogers, and Green, *Religious Freedom and the Supreme Court* at 1133–37.

49   *Thomas v. Review Board,* 450 U.S. at 716.

50   Cathy Lynn Grossman, *5 Faith Facts about Hillary Rodham Clinton: Social Gospel Methodist to the Core,* Religion News Service (January 29, 2016).

51   *See* Wake Forest, *Religious Expression* at 8–10; *Politics and the Pulpit 2008: A Guide to the Internal Revenue Code Restrictions on the Political Activity of Religious Organizations,* Pew Forum on Religion and Public Life, https://www.pewresearch.org/wp-content/uploads/sites/7/2008/03/politics_and_the_pulpit_2008.pdf.

52   Wake Forest, *Religious Expression* at 8–10.

53   *Id.*

54   *Id.*

55   *Id.*

56   *Id.*

57   Ruth Graham, *Religious Leaders Left Unimpressed by Trump's "Religious Liberty" Executive Order,* Slate (May 4, 2017); *Branch Ministries v. Rossotti,* 211 F.3d 137.

58   *See Marsh v. Chambers,* 463 U.S. 783 (1983).

59   *Id.* at 792.

60 The Court said that the fact that prayers were not offered at the Constitutional Convention "may simply have been an oversight." *Id.* at 787 n.6.

61 *Id.* at 794–95.

62 *Id.* at 793 n.14. In *County of Allegheny v. American Civil Liberties Union*, the Court referenced this fact, saying:

> Indeed, in *Marsh* itself, the Court recognized that not even the "unique history" of legislative prayer, can justify contemporary legislative prayers that have the effect of affiliating the government with any one specific faith or belief. The legislative prayers involved in *Marsh* did not violate this principle, because the particular chaplain had "removed all references to Christ." Thus, *Marsh* plainly does not stand for the sweeping proposition JUSTICE KENNEDY apparently would ascribe to it, namely, that all accepted practices 200 years old and their equivalents are constitutional today. Nor can *Marsh,* given its facts and its reasoning, compel the conclusion that the display of the crèche involved in this lawsuit is constitutional. Although JUSTICE KENNEDY says that he "cannot comprehend" how the crèche display could be invalid after *Marsh,* surely he is able to distinguish between a specifically Christian symbol, like a crèche, and more general religious references, like the legislative prayers in *Marsh.*

492 U.S. at 602 (citations omitted).

63 Justice Brennan wrote a dissenting opinion in which Justice Marshall joined. Justice Stevens wrote a separate dissenting opinion.

64 *Marsh v. Chambers*, 463 U.S. at 816 (Brennan, J., dissenting).

65 *Id.* at 795–823. Lower courts have cited the *Marsh* decision to uphold the longstanding practice of offering prayers at presidential inaugurations. *Newdow v. Roberts*, 603 F.3d 1019 (D.C. Cir. 2010) (quoting Steven B. Epstein, *Rethinking the Constitutionality of Ceremonial Deism*, 96 Colum. L. Rev. 2083, 2106 (1996)). Before the first inauguration, a Senate committee resolved that the president, vice president, and members of the House of Representatives and the Senate should attend a service at St. Paul's Chapel after the oath of office was administered. Epstein, *Ceremonial Deism*, 96 Colum. L. Rev. at 2106 (quoting 1 Joseph Gales, *The Debates and Proceedings in the Congress of the United States* 25 (1834)). The parties did so, and the service at St. Paul's included prayers from the Book of Common Prayer by the Senate chaplain. *See Newdow v. Bush*, 355 F. Supp. 2d at 285–87. The Senate chaplain conducted inaugural prayers in the Senate chambers of the Capitol until 1937. *See Newdow v. Roberts*, 603 F.3d at 1019 (citing App. at 20–23; Epstein, *Ceremonial Deism*, 96 Colum. L. Rev. at 2107 and n.137). In 1933, National Cathedral, which calls itself a "house of prayer for all people," hosted its first inaugural prayer service with a president—in this case, Franklin Delano Roosevelt—in attendance. Mary Schjonberg, *National Cathedral to Hold Customary Post-Inaugural Prayer Service*, Episcopal News Service (December 22, 2016), https://www.episcopalnewsservice.org/2016/12/22/national-cathedral-to-host-customary-post-inaugural-prayer-service/. National Cathedral has subsequently hosted many such services shortly after the inauguration. The incoming president also often attends a prayer service at St. John's Episcopal Church on Lafayette Square the morning of the inaugural. *See, e.g.,* Smith, *Faith and the Presidency* at 196.

Courts have also have relied on the *Marsh* decision to uphold the military chaplaincy. *See Katcoff v. Marsh*, 755 F.2d 223, 232 (2d Cir. 1985) (applying *Marsh* to uphold military chaplaincy due to "Congress' authorization of a military chaplaincy before and contemporaneous with the adoption of the Establishment Clause"). In 1963, Justice Brennan noted in a concurring opinion that failing to provide chaplains to service members might violate the Free Exercise Clause. *Abington Township v. Schempp*, 374 U.S. at 296–98 (Brennan, J., concurring). Lower courts have ruled that the government may hire chaplains to serve in state prisons in order to facilitate the free exercise of individuals who are in government custody and might be unable to exercise their faith if such chaplains were not provided. *See, e.g., Rudd v. Ray*, 248 N.W. 2d 125 (Iowa 1976).

Courts have declined, however, to uphold prayer before court sessions. *See North Carolina Civil Liberties Union Legal Found v. Constangy*, 947 F.2d 1145, 1148 (4th Cir. 1991) ("Unlike legislative prayer, there is no similar long-standing tradition of opening courts with prayer. Nor is there any evidence regarding the intent of the Framers of the Bill of Rights with regard to the opening of court with prayer."). *See above* chap. 2.

66   *Galloway v. Town of Greece*, 732 F. Supp. 2d 195, 197 (W.D.N.Y. 2010).
67   *Id.* at 197. *Town of Greece v. Galloway*, 572 U.S. 565.
68   *Galloway v. Town of Greece*, 681 F.3d 20, 23 (2d Cir. 2012).
69   *Id.*
70   *Id.*
71   *Id.*
72   *Town of Greece v. Galloway*, 572 U.S. at 615–38 (Kagan, J., dissenting).
73   *Galloway v. Town of Greece*, 732 F. Supp. 2d at 197–203.
74   *Id.*
75   *Galloway v. Town of Greece*, 681 F.3d at 24.
76   *Galloway v. Town of Greece*, 732 F. Supp. 2d at 195, 198.
77   *Id.*
78   *Galloway v. Town of Greece*, 681 F.3d at 23.
79   *Galloway v. Town of Greece*, 732 F. Supp. 2d at 197.
80   *Id.*
81   *Galloway v. Town of Greece*, 681 F.3d at 23.
82   *Galloway v. Town of Greece*, 732 F. Supp. 2d at 209.
83   *Galloway v. Town of Greece*, 681 F.3d 22.
84   *Town of Greece v. Galloway*, 572 U.S. 574–75.
85   *Id.* at 578. The fact that the Nebraska chaplain in the *Marsh* case removed from his prayers all references to Christ did not suggest that sectarian references in prayers were unconstitutional, the Court said. That reasoning was not essential to its ruling and thus was not legally binding. Further, the suggestion "was disputed when written and has been repudiated by later cases," according to Justice Kennedy. *Id.* at 579.

To hold otherwise, the Court said, would require the government "to act as supervisors and censors of religious speech, a rule that would involve the government in religious matters to a far greater degree than is the case under the town's current practice of neither editing or approving prayers in advance nor criticizing their content after the fact." *Id.* at 581.
86   *Id.*
87   *Id.*
88   *Id.*
89   *Id.* at 583. Justice Thomas wrote an opinion concurring in part and concurring in the judgment, which was joined by Justice Scalia. In his opinion, Justice Thomas once again argued that the Establishment Clause "resisted incorporation" and that the only kind of coercion that the Establishment Clause prohibits is "coercion of religious orthodoxy and of financial support by force of law and threat of penalty." *Id.* at 604, 608 (Thomas, J., dissenting) (quoting *Lee v. Weisman*, 505 U.S. at 640 (Scalia, J., dissenting)). *See also* above chap. 1.

90 *Id.* at 586 (citations omitted).

91 Chief Justice Roberts and Justice Alito joined Kennedy's opinion in full.

92 *Town of Greece v. Galloway*, 572 U.S. at 588.

93 *Id.* at 589.

94 *Id.* at 590. The prayers involved in the *Lee v. Weisman* case were different, these justices said, because of the context of a public school graduation, "where school authorities maintained close supervision over the conduct of the students and the substance of the ceremony." *Id.*

95 *Id.* at 591.

96 At the hearings, citizens were afforded opportunities "to engage with and petition their government, often on highly individualized matters." *Id.* at 622 (Kagan, J., dissenting).

97 *Id.* at 630 (Kagan, J., dissenting).

98 *Id.* (citation omitted).

99 *Id.* at 631.

100 *Id.* at 632.

101 *Id.* at 628.

102 *Id.* at 594 (Alito, J., concurring).

103 Justice Alito also said that, at most, the staff's mistakes were careless, not errors due to discriminatory intent. *Id.* at 596.

104 *Id.* at 598. According to Justice Alito, the prayers in *Greece* took place before what he called the "legislative" portion of the town board meeting, where citizens could address the board, but not before the portion of the meeting that involved "adjudicatory proceedings" over variances, for example. Thus, he argued that the proceedings prefaced by prayer were not so different than the proceedings that took place in the Nebraska legislature. *Id.* at 594.

105 *Id.* at 635 n.5 (Kagan, J., dissenting).

106 Justice Breyer said:

> [I]n a context where religious minorities exist and where more could easily have been done to include their participation, the town chose to do nothing. It could, for example, have posted its policy of permitting anyone to give an invocation on its Website, greeceny.gov, which provides dates and times of upcoming town board meetings along with minutes of prior meetings. It could have announced inclusive policies at the beginning of its board meetings, just before introducing the month's prayer giver. It could have provided information to those houses of worship of all faiths that lie just outside its borders and include citizens of Greece among their members. Given that the town could easily have made these or similar efforts but chose not to, the fact that all of the prayers (aside from the 2008 outliers) were given by adherents of a single religion reflects a lack of effort to include others.

Id. at 613 (Breyer, J., dissenting).

Likewise, the appellate court that heard this case noted that Greece "fail[ed] to recognize that its residents may hold religious beliefs that are not represented by a place of worship within the town." *Galloway v. Town of Greece*, 681 F.3d at 31. The town's duty was to serve its residents, not just the religious institutions that were located within its borders. *Id.*

107 Madison, *Memorial and Remonstrance*, in Flowers, Rogers, and Green, *Religious Freedom and the Supreme Court* at 1133–37.

108 *Thomas v. Review Board*, 450 U.S. at 716 n.6 (1981).

109 *See, e.g., Branch Ministries v. Rossotti*, 211 F.3d 137. *See also* David Saperstein and Amanda Tyler, *Trump Vowed to Destroy the Johnson Amendment: Thankfully, He Has Failed*, The Washington Post (February 7, 2018).

110 Sarah Eekhoff Zylstra, *Trump's "Greatest Contribution to Christianity": Pastors Preaching Politics*, Christianity Today (July 22, 2016).

111 *Id.*

112 *See below* chap. 5.

113 *See* Trevor Potter, *Churches Cannot Be Allowed to Become Political Dark Money Shops*, The Hill (May 4, 2017). *See also* the introduction above.

114 *See generally* Melissa Rogers, *Religious Freedom and the Federal Executive Branch: Suggestions for Future Administrations*, 15 St. Thomas L. Jnl. 703 (2019).

115 *See, e.g.,* William N. Eskridge Jr. and Robin Fretwell Wilson, eds., *Religious Freedom, LGBT Rights and the Prospects for Common Ground* (New York: Cambridge University Press 2019).

116 Martin Luther King Jr., *A Knock at Midnight* (June 5, 1963), https://kinginstitute.stanford.edu/king-papers/documents/knock-midnight.

117 Abraham Lincoln, *First Inaugural Address* (March 4, 1861), in Ronald C. White Jr., *The Eloquent President: A Portrait of Lincoln through His Words* (New York: Random House 2000).

118 McKay Coppins, *God's Plan for Mike Pence*, The Atlantic (January/February 2018) (citing polling by Public Religion Research Institute).

119 *Id.*

120 McKay Coppins, *You Need to Think about It Like a War*, The Atlantic (December 7, 2017).

121 *See* Greg Smith and Jessica Martinez, *How the Faithful Voted: A Preliminary 2016 Analysis*, Pew Research Center (November 9, 2016).

122 Christopher White, *Georgetown Panel Explores Healing in a Polarized America*, Crux (June 5, 2018); Georgetown University Initiative on Catholic Social Thought and Public Life, *Overcoming Polarization in a Divided Nation through Catholic Social Thought: Bringing the Joy of the Gospel to a Divided Nation* (June 4, 2018).

123 Bob Allen, *Videos Say What Presidential Candidates Would Do to Help the Poor*, Baptist News Global (August 6, 2015).

Chapter 5: Religious Expression on Government Property

1 *The National Mall: America's Front Yard*, PBS (April 21, 2015), http://www.pbs.org/program/national-mall-americas-front-yard/.

2 The mall is "where people come to figure out what the United States is all about," says historian Kirk Savage. Jennifer Robinson, *The National Mall—America's Front Yard*, KPBS (July 9, 2016), http://www.kpbs.org/news/2015/apr/20/national-mall-americas-front-yard/.

3 As Mike Smith, a leader of the AIDS quilt project (The Names Project Foundation, http://www.aidsquilt.org/about/the-names-project-foundation), has explained:

> There's only one place where you go to speak truth to power. There is only one place you go to air your grievances in a way that the whole country can engage in, and that's the National Mall.

Robinson, *National Mall—America's Front Yard*.

4   *See The Day the Rabbis Marched,* The David S. Wyman Institute for Holocaust Studies, http://new.wymaninstitute.org/2017/01/the-day-the-rabbis-marched-documents/.

5   *See March on Washington for Jobs and Freedom,* Martin Luther King Jr. Religion and Education Institute, Stanford University, https://kinginstitute.stanford.edu/encyclopedia/march-washington-jobs-and-freedom.

6   Tara Isabelle Burton, *The March for Life, America's Biggest Anti-abortion Rally, Explained,* Vox (January 18, 2018).

7   *See Holy Mass on the Mall,* Vatican (October 7, 1979), https://w2.vatican.va/content/john -paul-ii/en/homilies/1979/documents/hf_jp-ii_hom_19791007_usa-washington.html.

8   Annys Shin, *Remembering the Million Man March,* The Washington Post (October 12, 2017).

9   *Promise Keepers Fill Washington's Mall with Prayer,* CNN (October 4, 1997).

10   Adelle Banks, *Christian Women Gather on the Mall for Prayer,* Religion News Service (October 9, 2017).

11   *Religious Leaders March in Opposition to Trump,* NBC News (August 28, 2017).

12   Joe Hein, *American Indians from around the U.S. March on White House in Rally for Rights,* The Washington Post (March 10, 2017).

13   *Santa Fe Indep. Sch. Dist. v. Doe,* 530 U.S. at 302 (quoting *Board of Ed. of Westside Community Schools v. Mergens,* 496 U.S. at 250 (opinion of O'Connor, J.)).

14   *See* Wake Forest, *Religious Expression.*

15   *Id.*

16   *Id.*

17   *Widmar v. Vincent,* 454 U.S. 263 (1981).

18   *Chess v. Widmar,* 480 F. Supp. 907 (W.D. Mo. 1979).

19   *Id.* at 909.

20   *Id.* at 910.

21   *Id.*

22   *Id.* at 912.

23   *Widmar v. Vincent,* 454 U.S. 263 (1981).

24   *Id.* at 271 n.10. When the trial court ruled in UMKC's favor, it cited the U.S. Supreme Court's recent decision in *Tilton v. Richardson* that the government could not subsidize the construction of buildings at a church-affiliated university if those buildings would be used for religious purposes. *Id.* at 915 (citing *Tilton v. Richardson,* 403 U.S. 672 (1970)). "In light of *Tilton,*" the trial court said, "a university policy permitting regular religious services in university-owned buildings would have the primary effect of advancing religion" and thus would violate the First Amendment's Establishment Clause. *Id.* at 915–16.

   The U.S. Supreme Court rejected this argument: "We do not believe that *Tilton* can be read so broadly." *Id.* at 272 n.12. In *Tilton,* the Court was concerned that the religious college might convert federally subsidized buildings to religious uses, but "nothing in *Tilton* suggested a limitation on the State's capacity to maintain forums equally open to religious and other discussions." *Id.* Both before and after the *Tilton* decision, the Court has recognized "the right of religious speakers to use public forums on equal terms with others." *Id.*

25   In the *Widmar* case, the Court said:

> The dissent argues that "religious worship" is not speech generally protected by the "free speech" guarantee of the First Amendment and the "equal protection" guarantee of the Fourteenth Amendment. If "religious worship" were protected "speech," the dissent reasons, "the Religion Clauses would be emptied of any independent

meaning in circumstances in which religious practice took the form of speech." This is a novel argument. The dissent does not deny that speech *about* religion is speech entitled to the general protections of the First Amendment. It does not argue that descriptions of religious experiences fail to qualify as "speech." Nor does it repudiate last Term's decision in *Heffron v. International Society for Krishna Consciousness, Inc.*, which assumed that religious appeals to nonbelievers constituted protected "speech." Rather, the dissent seems to attempt a distinction between the kinds of religious speech explicitly protected by our cases and a new class of religious "speech act[s]," constituting "worship." There are at least three difficulties with this distinction.

First, the dissent fails to establish that the distinction has intelligible content. There is no indication when "singing hymns, reading scripture, and teaching biblical principles" cease to be "singing, teaching, and reading"—all apparently forms of "speech," despite their religious subject matter—and become unprotected "worship."

Second, even if the distinction drew an arguably principled line, it is highly doubtful that it would lie within the judicial competence to administer. Merely to draw the distinction would require the university—and ultimately the courts—to inquire into the significance of words and practices to different religious faiths, and in varying circumstances by the same faith. Such inquiries would tend inevitably to entangle the State with religion in a manner forbidden by our cases.

Finally, the dissent fails to establish the *relevance* of the distinction on which it seeks to rely. The dissent apparently wishes to preserve the vitality of the Establishment Clause. But it gives no reason why the Establishment Clause, or any other provision of the Constitution, would require different treatment for religious speech designed to win religious converts, than for religious worship by persons already converted. It is far from clear that the State gives greater support in the latter case than in the former.

Widmar v. Vincent, 454 U.S. at 269 n.6 (citations omitted).

26 *Id.*

27 When an entity receives direct government aid, however, the rules are different. *See below* chaps. 6 and 7.

28 Another increasingly common feature of campus life at colleges and universities, including public colleges and universities, includes multifaith or interfaith clubs or initiatives that meet on campus and carry out service work. President Barack Obama encouraged these efforts with his Interfaith and Community Service Campus Challenge, and they continue to be led by organizations like Interfaith Youth Corps. *See generally* Melissa Rogers, *Fifth Annual President's Interfaith and Community Service Campus Challenge*, The White House (September 15, 2016), https://obamawhitehouse.archives.gov/blog/2015/09/15/fifth-annual-presidents-interfaith-and-community-service-campus-challenge; Advisory Council on Faith-Based and Neighborhood Partnerships, *A New Era of Partnerships: A Report of Recommendations to the President*, The Department of Health and Human Service (March 2010), 69–95, https://obamawhitehouse.archives.gov/sites/default/files/microsites/ofbnp-council-final-report.pdf; Interfaith Youth Corps, https://www.ifyc.org/. Initiatives like these build bridges of understanding across differences through conversation and community service by students of different faiths and beliefs.

29 *Lamb's Chapel v. Center Moriches Union Free Sch. Dist.*, 508 U.S. 384 (1993).

30 *Id.* at 394.

31   In both the *Lamb's Chapel* and *Good News* cases, the Supreme Court assumed without
      deciding that the forums were nonpublic forums rather than designated public forums.
      See Wake Forest, *Religious Expression* at 13.

32   In 1995, the Court considered a case involving such an unattended display. A square
      surrounding the Ohio statehouse had been opened for nongovernmental expression,
      including unattended displays sponsored by nongovernmental organizations. The Court
      ruled that the government could not refuse to allow the Ku Klux Klan to display a cross
      there. *Capitol Square Rev. Bd. v. Pinette*, 515 U.S. 753 (1995). While the state said it
      rejected this display in order to avoid endorsing Christianity, lower courts and ultimately
      the Supreme Court found that allowing the display would not involve the state in doing
      so. The expression took place on government property that had been opened to nongov-
      ernmental speakers; the KKK requested permission through the same application and
      on the same terms required of other nongovernmental groups; and a sign appeared near
      the cross disclaiming any governmental sponsorship or endorsement. *Id.* at 762–63.

      The fact that the KKK was the speaker drew notice and protests. Immediately after
      the trial court issued an injunction ordering the state to grant the Klan's permit, a local
      council of churches that was disturbed by the Klan's speech applied for and received
      blanket permission to erect additional crosses in the square to speak for the Christian
      church. *Id.* at 792 (Souter, J., concurring in part and concurring in the judgment). In a
      separate opinion, Justice Thomas stated that he believed the Klan's message was primarily
      political, not religious. *See id.* at 770 (Thomas, J., concurring) ("In Klan ceremony, the
      cross is a symbol of white supremacy and a tool for the intimidation and harassment
      of racial minorities, Catholics, Jews, Communists, and any other groups hated by the
      Klan."). Despite the odious nature of the speaker and its message, the Supreme Court's
      decision stands as a protection for religious expression in the public square.

33   Four Supreme Court justices would have held that "[r]eligious expression cannot violate
      the Establishment Clause where it (1) is purely private and (2) occurs in a traditional
      or designated public forum, publicly announced and open to all on equal terms." *Id.* at
      770 (plurality opinion). This view did not draw the support of a fifth justice and thus
      did not become a part of the Court majority's opinion. In a concurring opinion, Justices
      O'Connor, Souter, and Breyer rejected this *"per se"* rule, saying that, even in these cases,
      the government may sometimes be required to take steps to avoid being perceived as
      supporting or endorsing a nongovernmental religious message. *Id.* at 772–83 (O'Connor,
      J., concurring in part and concurring in the judgment). These justices noted that they
      would not expect to find that the government had violated the Establishment Clause in
      cases where it permitted nongovernmental speech on equal terms "in a vigorous public
      forum that the government administered properly." *Id.* at 775. Nonetheless, the justices
      said:

> Where the government's operation of a public forum has the effect of endorsing
> religion, even if the governmental actor neither intends nor actively encourages
> that result, the Establishment Clause is violated. This is so not because of "'trans-
> ferred endorsement,'" or mistaken attribution of private speech to the State, but
> because the State's own actions (operating the forum in a particular manner and
> permitting the religious expression to take place therein), and their relationship
> to the private speech at issue, *actually convey* a message of endorsement. At some
> point, for example, a private religious group may so dominate a public forum that
> a formal policy of equal access is transformed into a demonstration of approval.
> Other circumstances may produce the same effect—whether because of the fortuity

of geography, the nature of the particular public space, or the character of the religious speech at issue, among others. Our Establishment Clause jurisprudence should remain flexible enough to handle such situations when they arise.

Id. at 777–78 (citations omitted).

34 *See Christian Legal Society v. Martinez*, 561 U.S. 661 (2010).

35 *Id.* at 683.

36 *Id.* at 694.

37 *Id.* at 699 (citations omitted). *Compare with id.* at 706–741 (Alito, J., dissenting).

38 "[T]he *advisability* of Hastings' policy does not control its *permissibility*," the Court said. *Id.* at 692.

39 *See, e.g., Business Leaders in Christ v. University of Iowa*, 2018 U.S. Dis. LEXIS 221969 (S.D. Iowa, January 23, 2018).

40 *Pleasant Grove City v. Summum*, 555 U.S. 460, 471 (2009). The Free Speech Clause restrains the government's ability to regulate private speech. It does not apply to government speech, the Supreme Court has said. *Id.* at 467–69. Otherwise, the Court has explained, the government would be hamstrung. "Every jurisdiction that has accepted a donated war memorial," for example, "may be asked to provide equal treatment for a donated monument questioning the cause for which the veterans fought." *Id.* at 480.

41 A 2010 consensus statement of current law in this area states:

> To determine whether a governmental display or monument that includes religious elements is constitutionally permissible, courts examine its purpose and primary effect. Courts also sometimes ask whether the display or monument would cause the reasonable observer to believe that the government was endorsing or disparaging religion. When courts ask these questions, they focus on factors such as the overall context of the display or monument and the facts that gave rise to its creation. If the predominant purpose or effect of a governmental display or monument is to advance religion, it will be found unconstitutional.

Wake Forest, *Religious Expression* at 15.

42 *Lynch v. Donnelly*, 465 U.S. 668 (1984). Some of the Court's most fractured church-state decisions involve cases like these that were heard from 1980 to 2005. These decisions are not simply five-to-four rulings. Some decisions produced no majority, only a plurality, with multiple concurring and dissenting opinions. Certain concurring and dissenting opinions address issues that are not essential to the resolution of the case. The issues are complex, which partially explains the divisions at the Court and the confusion the opinions sometimes created. It also appears, however, that the chief justices who presided over the Court during this period—Chief Justices Warren Burger and William Rehnquist—either made little attempt to encourage discipline at the Court or tried to do so yet were spectacularly unsuccessful.

43 The display contained the following components, all of which were owned by the city:

> In addition to the crèche, the city's display contained: a Santa Claus house with a live Santa distributing candy; reindeer pulling Santa's sleigh; a live 40-foot Christmas tree strung with lights; statutes of carolers in old-fashioned dress; candy-striped poles; a "talking" wishing well; a large banner proclaiming "SEASONS GREETINGS"; a miniature "village" with several houses and a church; and various "cut-out" figures, including those of a clown, a dancing elephant, a robot, and a teddy bear.

County of Allegheny v. American Civil Liberties Union, 492 U.S. at 596.

44 *Id.* at 678–87.
45 *Id.* at 687 (O'Connor, J., concurring). *See also County of Allegheny v. American Civil Liberties Union*, 492 U.S. at 594.
46 *Lynch v. Donnelly*, 465 U.S. at 688 (O'Connor, J., concurring).
47 *See Capitol Square Review Bd. v. Pinette*, 515 U.S. 753, 780 (1995) (O'Connor, J., concurring in part and concurring in the judgment). O'Connor explained why she "disagree[d] that the endorsement test should focus on the actual perception of individual observers, who naturally have differing degrees of knowledge." Under that approach, Justice O'Connor explained:

> [A] religious display is necessarily precluded so long as some passersby would perceive a governmental endorsement thereof. In my view, however, the endorsement test creates a more collective standard to gauge "the 'objective' meaning of the [government's] statement in the community," *Lynch, supra*, at 690 (O'CONNOR, J., concurring). In this respect, the applicable observer is similar to the "reasonable person" in tort law, who "is not to be identified with any ordinary individual, who might occasionally do unreasonable things," but is "rather a personification of a community ideal of reasonable behavior, determined by the [collective] social judgment." W. Keeton, D. Dobbs, R. Keeton, & D. Owen, Prosser and Keeton on *Law of Torts* 175 (5th ed. 1984). Thus, "we do not ask whether there is *any* person who could find an endorsement of religion, whether *some* people may be offended by the display, or whether *some* reasonable person *might* think [the State] endorses religion." *Americans United*, 980 F. 2d at 1544. Saying that the endorsement inquiry should be conducted from the perspective of a hypothetical observer who is presumed to possess a certain level of information that all citizens might not share neither chooses the perceptions of the majority over those of a "reasonable non-adherent," cf. L. Tribe, *American Constitutional Law* 1293 (2d ed. 1988), nor invites disregard for the values the Establishment Clause was intended to protect. It simply recognizes the fundamental difficulty inherent in focusing on actual people: There is always *someone* who, with a particular quantum of knowledge, reasonably might perceive a particular action as an endorsement of religion. A State has not made religion relevant to standing in the political community simply because a particular viewer of a display might feel uncomfortable.

Id. at 779–80.
48 *Lynch v. Donnelly*, 465 U.S. at 691.
49 *Id.* at 692.
50 *Id.* at 726–27 (Blackmun, J., dissenting).
51 *Id.* at 711–12 (Brennan, J., dissenting).
52 *See* Scott Bomboy, *The Supreme Court's Plastic Reindeer Rule Looms over Holiday Season*, Constitution Daily, National Constitution Center (December 10, 2014), https://constitutioncenter.org/blog/the-supreme-courts-plastic-reindeer-rule-looms-over-the-holiday-season/.
53 *Allegheny County v. American Civil Liberties Union*, 492 U.S. 573, 579 (1989).
54 *Id.* at 580.
55 *Id.*
56 *Id.* at 600.
57 *Id.* at n.50.
58 *Id.* at 582.
59 *Id.* at 620.

60 *Id.* at 623.
61 *Id.* at 637.
62 *Id.* at 655.
63 *Id.*
64 Warren Burger retired from the Court in June 1986. Linda Greenhouse has described how the longtime friendship between Chief Justice Burger and Justice Blackmun deteriorated while they served on the Court. *See generally* Greenhouse, *The Blackmun Papers—Second of 2 Articles; Friends for Decades, but Years on Court Left Them Strangers*, The New York Times (March 5, 2004). Greenhouse wrote:

> During their last years on the court, it appears that Justice Blackmun and Chief Justice Burger barely spoke, communicating mostly through memos. Justice Blackmun's notes to himself, and his annotations on memos and draft opinions from the chief justice, show annoyance, even disdain. The best man at the Burgers' wedding six decades earlier, he did not attend Elvera Burger's funeral in 1994. By the end of their long lives, the two men had become strangers.
>
> The sad dissolution of their friendship apparently had no single catalyst. Instead, Justice Blackmun's files, including a 1995 oral history, suggest that the rift resulted from a series of grievances, a clash of styles and a divergence of judicial philosophy.

Id.
65 *Allegheny County v. American Civil Liberties Union*, 492 U.S. at 594, 595.
66 *Id.* at 655 (Kennedy, J., concurring in the judgment in part and dissenting in part).
67 *Id.* at 610.
68 *Id.* at 669 (Kennedy, J., concurring in the judgment in part and dissenting in part).
69 *Id.* at 607–8.
70 *McCreary County v. American Civil Liberties Union*, 545 U.S. 844 (2005).
71 *Id.* at 881.
72 *Id.* at 860. The Court noted that "openly available data supported a commonsense conclusion that a religious objective permeated the government's action." *Id.* at 863. "[S]crutinizing purpose does make practical sense, as in Establishment Clause analysis, where an understanding of official objective emerges from readily discoverable fact, without any judicial psychoanalysis of a drafter's heart of hearts." *Id.* at 862.
73 Referencing a frieze on the walls of its courtroom, the Supreme Court said:

> We do not forget, and in this litigation have frequently been reminded, that our own courtroom frieze was deliberately designed in the exercise of governmental authority so as to include the figure of Moses holding tablets exhibiting a portion of the Hebrew text of the later, secularly phrased Commandments; in the company of 17 other lawgivers, most of them secular figures, there is no risk that Moses would strike an observer as evidence that the National Government was violating neutrality in religion.

Id. at 874.
74 *Van Orden v. Perry*, 545 U.S. 677 (2005).
75 *Id.* at 703 (Breyer, J., concurring in the judgment).
76 *Id.* at 700, 704.
77 *Id.* at 704. Justice Breyer continued:

> Such a holding might well encourage disputes concerning the removal of long-standing depictions of the Ten Commandments from public buildings across the

Nation. And it could thereby create the very kind of religiously based divisiveness that the Establishment Clause seeks to avoid.

   Id.

78 William Branigin, Fred Barbash, and Daniela Deane, *Supreme Court Justice O'Connor Retires*, The Washington Post (July 1, 2005).

79 Jan Crawford Greenburg, *Rehnquist's Stay on the Court Forced O'Connor Out*, ABC News (January 23, 2007).

80 *Id.*

81 *Id.*

82 *Id.*

83 *Bush Nominates Roberts to Supreme Court*, CNN (July 20, 2005).

84 Charles Lane, *Chief Justice William H. Rehnquist Dies*, The Washington Post (September 4, 2005).

85 Peter Baker, *Bush Nominates Roberts as Chief Justice*, The Washington Post (September 6, 2005). On October 7, 2005, President Bush nominated Harriet Miers to fill Justice O'Connor's spot on the Court. In the face of a heated backlash regarding Miers' qualifications, her nomination was withdrawn on October 28. President Bush subsequently nominated then-judge Samuel Alito, and he was confirmed as an associate justice on January 31, 2006. *See* Josh Gerstein, *Harriett Miers Papers Set for Release*, Politico (March 5, 2016).

86 *Transcript: Day Three of the Roberts Confirmation Hearing*, The Washington Post (September 14, 2005).

87 *Id.*

88 *Id.*

89 As Justice O'Connor has noted: "The Court has avoided drawing lines which entirely sweep away all government recognition and acknowledgment of the role of religion in the lives of our citizens for to do so would exhibit not neutrality but hostility to religion." *County of Allegheny v. American Civil Liberties Union*, 492 U.S. at 623 (O'Connor, J., concurring in part and concurring in the judgment). Various members of the Court have indicated that they would uphold the national motto ("In God We Trust"); the reference to God in the words that are said before the Supreme Court is seated (including the sentence, "God save the United States and this Honorable Court!"); and the word "God" in the Pledge of Allegiance ("one nation under God"). *See, e.g., Elk Grove Unified School District v. Newdow*, 542 U.S. at 33–45 (O'Connor, J., concurring in the judgment).

90 *American Legion v. American Humanist Ass'n*, 139 S. Ct. 2067 (2019).

91 *Id.* at 2085.

92 *Id.* at 2090.

93 *Id.* at 2070.

94 *Id.* at 2087.

95 *Id.* at 2091 (Breyer, J., concurring).

96 *Id.*

97 *Id.* at 2094 (Kagan, J., concurring in part).

98 *Id.*

99 *Id.* at 2093 (asterisk omitted) (Kavanaugh, J., concurring).

100 *Id.* at 2094–98 (Thomas, J., concurring in the judgment).

101 *Id.* at 2102 (Gorsuch, J., concurring in the judgment).

102 *Id.* at 2104 (Ginsburg, J., dissenting) (citation omitted).

103 *Id.* at 2112.

104 *Engel v. Vitale*, 370 U.S. 421, 425 (1962).

105 *Abington Township v. Schempp*, 374 U.S. 203 (1963).

106 *See* Stephen D. Solomon, *Ellery's Protest: How One Young Man Defied Tradition and Sparked the Battle over School Prayer* (Ann Arbor: University of Michigan Press 2007); Steven K. Green, *The Bible, the School and the Constitution: The Clash That Shaped Modern Church-State Doctrine* (New York: Oxford University Press 2012).

107 Here is a relevant exchange from President Kennedy's press conference shortly after the Supreme Court handed down its decision in *Engel v. Vitale*:

> QUESTION: Mr. President, in the furor over the Supreme Court's decision on prayer in the schools, some members of Congress have been introducing legislation for Constitutional amendments specifically to sanction prayer or religious exercise in the schools. Can you give us your opinion of the decision itself, and of these moves of the Congress to circumvent it?
>
> THE PRESIDENT: I haven't seen the measures in the Congress and you would have to make a determination of what the language was, and what effect it would have on the First Amendment. The Supreme Court has made its judgment, and a good many people obviously will disagree with it. Others will agree with it. But I think that it is important for us if we are going to maintain our Constitutional principle that we support the Supreme Court decisions even when we may not agree with them.
>
> In addition, we have in this case a very easy remedy, and that is to pray ourselves and I would think that it would be a welcome reminder to every American family that we can pray a good deal more at home, we can attend our churches with a good deal more fidelity, and we can make the true meaning of prayer much more important in the lives of all of our children. That power is very much open to us.
>
> I would hope that as a result of this decision that all American parents will inten- sify their efforts at home, and the rest of us will support the Constitution and the responsibility of the Supreme Court in interpreting it, which is theirs, and given to them by the Constitution.

John F. Kennedy Presidential Library and Museum, *News Conference #37* (June 27, 1962), https://www.jfklibrary.org/Research/Research-Aids/Ready-Reference/Press -Conferences/News-Conference-37.aspx.

108 *See Lee v. Weisman*, 505 U.S. 577 (1992).

109 *Id.* at 581.

110 *Id.* at 587.

111 *Id.* at 586.

112 *Id.* at 599. Justice Souter wrote a separate concurring opinion, in which Justices Stevens and O'Connor joined, to emphasize that the Establishment Clause applies to govern- mental practices that favor religion generally and that state coercion was not a necessary element of an Establishment Clause violation. *Id.* at 609–31 (Souter, J., concurring).

113 Kathryn Q. Seelye, *Proposed Prayer Amendment Splits the Right*, The New York Times (November 22, 1995).

114 Signatories to the document included the American Civil Liberties Union, the American Jewish Congress, Americans United for Separation of Church and State, the Baptist Joint Committee for Religious Liberty, National Association of Evangelicals, National Sikh Center, Northern American Council for Muslim Women, the Union of American Hebrew Congregations, and the United Church of Christ. *See Religion in Public Schools:*

A Joint Statement of Current Law, American Jewish Congress (April 1995), https://eric
.ed.gov/?id=ED387390.

115 Memorandum on Religious Expression in Public Schools (July 12, 1995), https://www
.govinfo.gov/content/pkg/WCPD-1995-07-17/pdf/WCPD-1995-07-17-Pg1227.pdf.

116 *1995 Speech by President Clinton on Religious Liberty*, Religious Tolerance (July 12,
1995), http://www.religioustolerance.org/clinton1.htm (part 1), and http://www
.religioustolerance.org/clinton2.htm (part 2).

117 *Id.*

118 Department of Education, *Religious Expression in American Public Schools: A Statement
of Principles* (August 1995 and June 1998), http://www.christianlaw.org/cla/media/
downloads/Download/Rel_Guidelines.pdf.

119 *Memorandum on Religious Expression in Public Schools*, The White House (July 12, 1995),
https://www.gpo.gov/fdsys/pkg/WCPD-1995-07-17/pdf/WCPD-1995-07-17-Pg1227.pdf.

120 In 2005, the Supreme Court decided a case involving a public school's policy of organizing pregame prayers at high school football games. *Santa Fe Indep. Sch. Dist. v. Doe*,
530 U.S. 290 (2000). The Court found that the policy was "invalid on its face because
it establish[ed] an improper majoritarian election on religion, and unquestionably ha[d]
the purpose and create[d] the perception of encouraging the delivery of prayer at a series
of important school events." *Id.* at 317. At the same time, the Court reemphasized that
the religion clauses of the First Amendment do not "impose a prohibition on all religious
activities in our public schools," and that "nothing in the Constitution as interpreted
by this Court prohibits any public school student from voluntarily praying at any time
before, during, or after the schoolday." *Id.* at 313.

Two sets of current or former students and their respective mothers sued the Santa Fe
school district. One family was Mormon, and the other was Catholic, and both pursued
the lawsuit under pseudonyms because they were fearful of the backlash that they would
experience. *Id.* at 294. The lower court's decision in this case described some of the
clearly unconstitutional activities involving these families that proceeded the litigation:

> [I]n April 1993, [for example,] while plaintiff Jane Doe II was attending her seventh
> grade Texas History class, her teacher, David Wilson, handed out fliers advertising
> a Baptist religious revival. Jane Doe II asked if non-Baptists were invited to attend,
> prompting Wilson to inquire about her religious affiliation. On hearing that she was
> an adherent of the Church of Jesus Christ of [Latter-day] Saints (Mormon), Wilson
> launched into a diatribe about the non-Christian, cult-like nature of Mormonism,
> and its general evils. Wilson's comments inspired further discussion among Jane
> Doe II's classmates, some of whom reportedly noted that "[h]e sure does make it
> sound evil," and "[g]ee, . . . it's kind of like the KKK, isn't it?" Jane Doe II was
> understandably upset by this incident, and two days later, her mother, Jane Doe
> I, complained to SFISD. Because Wilson's actions were concededly contrary to
> written SFISD policies barring the distribution of religious literature in class or
> the verbal abuse of any student, he was given a written reprimand and directed to
> apologize to the Does and to his class.

Doe v. Santa Fe Indep. Sch. Dist., 168 F.3d 806, 810 (5th Cir. 1999). The trial court noted
that "many [school] officials apparently neither agreed with nor particularly respected"
the court's decision to allow the challengers to sue anonymously. *Id.* at 809 n.1. About a
month after the complaint was filed, the trial court threatened school officials and others
with contempt sanctions and criminal liability if they continued to attempt to "ferret
out" the identities of the plaintiffs. *Id.*

121 Memorandum on Religious Expression in Public Schools (July 12, 1995). Equal Access
    Act, 20 U.S.C. Section 4071 *et seq.* (2019). The Supreme Court has found that the Equal
    Access Act does not violate the First Amendment's Establishment Clause. *See Board of
    Educ. v. Mergens*, 496 U.S. 226 (1990).
122 *See Religion in Public Schools: A Joint Statement of Current Law.*
123 Wake Forest, *Religious Expression*, states:

> In some instances, courts have upheld a school's decision to prohibit a student's
> distribution of religious items in the context of school-sponsored activities, conclud-
> ing that the school's actions were reasonable and directed toward preserving educa-
> tional goals. However, outside the context of school-sponsored activities, such
> as in hallways and other areas where students are normally permitted to share
> items with other students, courts generally have held that students' distribution
> of religious literature must be allowed, subject only to the same time, place and
> manner restrictions that are imposed on distributions of nonreligious literature.

See id. at 23.
124 Here is the fuller statement of the Court on these issues:

> It is insisted that, unless these religious exercises are permitted, a "religion of
> secularism" is established in the schools. We agree of course that the State may
> not establish a "religion of secularism" in the sense of affirmatively opposing or
> showing hostility to religion, thus "preferring those who believe in no religion
> over those who do believe." We do not agree, however, that this decision in any
> sense has that effect. In addition, it might well be said that one's education is not
> complete without a study of comparative religion or the history of religion and its
> relationship to the advancement of civilization. It certainly may be said that the
> Bible is worthy of study for its literary and historic qualities. Nothing we have said
> here indicates that such study of the Bible or of religion, when presented objectively
> as part of a secular program of education, may not be effected consistently with
> the First Amendment.

Abington Township v. Schempp, 374 U.S. at 225 (citations omitted).
125 *A Teacher's Guide to Religion in the Public Schools* (Nashville: First Amendment Center
    2008) 3 (footnote omitted), http://www.religiousfreedomcenter.org/wp-content/uploads/
    2014/08/teachersguide.pdf.
126 Emile Lester and Patrick S. Roberts, *Learning about World Religions in Public Schools: The
    Impact on Student Attitudes and Community Acceptance in Modesto, California* (Nashville:
    First Amendment Center 2006) 6–7, https://fsi-live.s3.us-west-1.amazonaws.com/s3fs
    -public/FirstForum_ModestoWorldReligions.pdf.
127 *Id.* at 7.
128 Howard Friedman, *Calligraphy Assignment Involving Shahada Leads to Early Winter
    Break for Virginia Students*, Religion Clause (December 19, 2015), http://religionclause
    .blogspot.com/search?q=assignment+on+islam.
129 *See, e.g., Teacher's Guide to Religion in the Public Schools*; Linda K. Wertheimer, *Faith
    Ed.: Teaching about Religion in an Age of Intolerance* (Boston: Beacon 2015).
130 The Supreme Court struck down a Kentucky statute that required the posting of a copy
    of the Ten Commandments on the wall of each public school classroom in the state,
    even though the copies were purchased with contributions made by nongovernmental
    sources. *See Stone v. Graham*, 449 U.S. 39 (1980). The Court concluded that the law had
    no secular purpose. It also noted: "This is not a case in which the Ten Commandments
    are integrated into the school curriculum, where the Bible may constitutionally be used

in an appropriate study of history, civilization, ethics, comparative religion, or the like." *Id.* at 42.

131 *ACLU and PFAWF File Lawsuit against Ector County School Board for Impermissibly Promoting Religion*, American Civil Liberties Union (May 17, 2007), https://www.aclu .org/news/texas-parents-challenge-unconstitutional-bible-class-public-schools?redirect= cpredirect/29738.

132 The Society of Biblical Literature, *Bible Electives in Public Schools: A Guide*, https://www .sbl-site.org/assets/pdfs/SchoolsGuide.pdf; *The Bible and Public Schools: A First Amendment Guide* (New York and Nashville: The Bible Literacy Project and First Amendment Center 1999), http://www.religiousfreedomcenter.org/wp-content/uploads/2014/08/ bible_guide_graphics.pdf.

133 *See* National Council for Social Studies, College, Career, and Civic Life (C3) Framework for Social Studies State Standards (June 2017), https://www.socialstudies.org/c3.

134 *Id. See also* Benjamin Pietro Marcus, *Another Historic Moment: Religious Studies Companion Document Added to a National Education Framework*, Religion & Education 44, no. 3 (2017).

135 American Academy of Religion Executive Director Jack Fitzmier put it well when he said the timing for this new resource "could not be more apt." *Religious Studies Recognized as Essential Part of K-12 Education*, Religious Freedom Center of the Freedom Forum Institute (June 12, 2017), http://www.newseuminstitute.org/2017/06/12/religious-studies -recognized-as-essential-part-of-k-12-education/.

136 Entities skilled at providing such trainings include the Freedom Forum Institute's Religious Freedom Center and the Baptist Joint Committee for Religious Liberty. *See* Religious Freedom Center, http://www.religiousfreedomcenter.org/; Baptist Joint Committee for Religious Liberty, https://bjconline.org/.

137 *See id.*

138 *See* Adelle Banks, *Religious Freedom Advocate Charles Haynes: "It's Not a Choice,"* Religion News Service (October 19, 2018).

Chapter 6: Government Partnerships with Faith-Based Organizations

1 Executive Order 13199, 66 Fed. Reg. 8499 (January 31, 2001), https://www.gpo.gov/ fdsys/pkg/FR-2001-01-31/pdf/01-2852.pdf. Executive Order 13199 was the first executive order President Bush signed.

2 William J. Galston served as deputy director of the Domestic Policy Council during the Clinton administration. William P. Marshall and Elena Kagan were among the legal scholars with expertise on church-state issues who served in the Clinton White House Counsel's Office.

3 Melissa Rogers and E. J. Dionne, *Serving People in Need, Safeguarding Religious Freedom: Recommendations for the New Administration on Partnerships with Faith-Based Organizations* (Washington, D.C.: Brookings, Wake Forest University Divinity School 2008), https://www.brookings.edu/wp-content/uploads/2012/04/12_religion_dionne.pdf.

4 *Bradfield v. Roberts*, 175 U.S. 291 (1899).

5 Another Democrat, Vice President Al Gore, also endorsed the idea of governmental partnerships with faith-based and community organizations on the presidential campaign trail. Jennifer Moore, *Gore Vows to Increase Aid to Faith-Based Groups*, The Chronicle of Philanthropy (June 3, 1999).

6   *See* Jason Horowitz, *The Catholic Roots of Obama's Activism*, The New York Times (March 22, 2014).

7   *Remarks by the President at Catholic Health Association Conference*, The White House (June 9, 2015), https://obamawhitehouse.archives.gov/the-press-office/2015/06/09/remarks -president-catholic-health-association-conference.

8   *Obama Delivers Speech on Faith in America*, The New York Times (July 1, 2008).

9   *President Obama's Remarks at National Prayer Breakfast*, The New York Times (February 5, 2009).

10 Executive Order 13498, 75 Fed. Reg. 6533 (February 9, 2009). There were three Advisory Councils on Faith-Based and Neighborhood Partnerships during the Obama administration. *See About the President's Advisory Council on Faith-Based and Neighborhood Partnerships*, The White House (2017), https://obamawhitehouse.archives.gov/administration/ eop/ofbnp/about/council.

11 *See* White House Office of Faith-Based and Neighborhood Partnerships, Inaugural Advisory Council (2009–2010), https://obamawhitehouse.archives.gov/administration/ eop/ofbnp/about/2009-2010; Karen Travers, *Obama Names 26-Year-Old Director of Faith-Based Office*, ABC News (February 5, 2009).

12 *See* Advisory Council on Faith-Based and Neighborhood Partnerships, *A New Era of Partnerships*, White House Office of Faith-Based and Neighborhood Partnerships (March 2010), https://obamawhitehouse.archives.gov/sites/default/files/partnerships-reform-office .pdf. *See* White House Office of Faith-Based and Neighborhood Partnerships, Inaugural Advisory Council (2009–2010), https://obamawhitehouse.archives.gov/administration/ eop/ofbnp/about/2009-2010.

13 *See, e.g.,* Executive Order 13559, 75 Fed. Reg. 71319 (November 17, 2010).

14 *See* Partners for Sacred Places, *The Economic Halo Effect of Historic Sacred Places*, Sacred Places: The Magazine of Partner for Sacred Places (2016), http://www.sacredplaces.org/ uploads/files/16879092466251061-economic-halo-effect-of-historic-sacred-places.pdf. A study by Partners for Sacred Places found, for example, that 87 percent of the beneficiaries of community programs and events offered by houses of worship are not members of those congregations.

15 *See* Capital Research Corporation, George Washington University, *Formative Evaluation of Jobs Clubs Operated by Faith-Based and Community Organizations: Findings from Site Visits and Options for Future Evaluation* (May 2014), https://www.dol.gov/asp/evaluation/ completed-studies/Formative_Evaluation_of_Job_Clubs_Operated_by_Faith_And _Community_Based_Organizations/FINAL_REPORT_formative_evaluation_job _clubs_operated_faith_cbo.pdf.

16 White House Office of Faith-Based and Neighborhood Partnerships, *Faith-Based and Neighborhood Partnerships: Year of Action Highlights*, The White House (December 2014), https:// obamawhitehouse.archives.gov/sites/default/files/docs/2014ofbnpyearofactionreport.pdf.

17 *Id.* at 3–4; Portia Wu, *Promising Practices and Resources for Addressing Long-Term Unemployment* (October 17, 2014), https://wdr.doleta.gov/directives/attach/TEN/TEN-12-14 _Acc.pdf, at 8 (encouraging those wishing to engage long-term unemployed, including jobs clubs, to coordinate with state unemployment insurance programs and "to provide responsive reemployment services to unemployed individuals before they reach the six-month mark").

18 Abby Phillip, *Ebola Survivor Kent Brantly Met with President Obama in the Oval Office*, The Washington Post (September 6, 2014).

19 *Id.*

20 *See* Carrie Nielsen, Sarah Kidd, Ansumana R. M. Sillah, Edward Davis, Jonathan Mermin, and Peter Kilmarx, *Improving Burial Practices and Cemetery Management during an Ebola Virus Disease Epidemic—Sierra Leone, 2014*, Center for Disease Control and Prevention, Morbidity and Mortality Weekly Report (January 16, 2015), https://www.cdc .gov/mmwr/preview/mmwrhtml/mm6401a6.htm; Amy Maxmen, *How the Fight against Ebola Tested a Culture's Traditions*, National Geographic (January 30, 2015), https://news .nationalgeographic.com/2015/01/150130-ebola-virus-outbreak-epidemic-sierra-leone -funerals/; *Note for the Media: New WHO Safe and Dignified Burial Protocol—Key to Reducing Ebola Transmission*, World Health Organization (November 7, 2014), http:// www.who.int/mediacentre/news/notes/2014/ebola-burial-protocol/en/.

21 *President Obama Speaks at National Prayer Breakfast*, US News & World Report (February 6, 2016).

22 8 U.S.C. Section 1101(a) (42) (2019).

23 Melissa May Borja, *Refugee Resettlement Is a Church-State Enterprise*, New School for Social Research (December 30, 2015), http://www.publicseminar.org/2015/12/refugee -resettlement-is-a-church-state-enterprise/.

24 *Id.*

25 *See, e.g.,* Jodi Kantor, *Warm Welcome for Syrians in a Country about to Ban Them*, The New York Times (January 28, 2017).

26 Deborah Amos, *New Jersey Church Group to Resettle Syrian Refugee Family with Special Needs*, NPR (September 14, 2016).

27 *Id.*

28 *Id.*

29 *Bradfield v. Roberts*, 175 U.S. 291.

30 *Id.* at 298.

31 *Id.* at 298–99.

32 *Bowen v. Kendrick*, 487 U.S. 589 (1988).

33 *Id.* at 594–600.

34 The trial court found that AFLA violated the Establishment Clause both on its face and as applied. *Id.* at 589–601; *Kendrick v. Bowen*, 657 F. Supp. 1547 (D.D.C. 1987). The trial court said the program had the primary effect of advancing religion and created excessive church-state entanglement. Concerns included the fact that some grantees "ha[d] included explicitly religious materials, or a curriculum that indicates an intent to teach theological and secular views on sexual conduct, in their HHS-approved grant proposals." *Id.* at 1565.

35 *Bowen v. Kendrick*, 487 U.S. at 622.

36 *Id.* at 607.

37 *Id.* at 609.

38 *Id.* at 604 n.8. Chief Justice Rehnquist expressed a dim view of the argument that the statute created excessive church-state entanglement. "[T]his litigation presents us with yet another 'Catch-22' argument," Rehnquist said. "[T]he very supervision of the aid to assure that it does not further religion renders the statute invalid." *Id.* at 615. There was no reason to presume that ensuring appropriate uses of the aid would cause a constitutional violation, the Court held.

39 *Id.* at 626 (Blackmun, J., dissenting).

40 *Id.* at 625–54.

41 *See generally* Executive Order 13279, 67 Fed. Reg. 77141 (December 16, 2002).

42   *See generally* Executive Order 13279, 67 Fed. Reg. 77141; and Executive Order 13559, 75 Fed. Reg. 71319.

43   *See* President George W. Bush's Speeches on Faith-Based and Community Initiatives, The White House (2001–2008), https://georgewbush-whitehouse.archives.gov/government/fbci/speech.html.

44   For a discussion of some of the relevant employment issues, *see below* at chap. 9.

45   John J. DiIulio Jr., *Compassion "in Truth and Action": How Sacred and Secular Places Serve Civic Purposes, and What Washington Should—and Should Not—Do to Help*, speech prepared for delivery and release before the conference of the National Association of Evangelicals, Dallas (March 7, 2001), https://georgewbush-whitehouse.archives.gov/news/releases/2001/03/20010307-11.html.

46   *See* Rogers, *President Trump Just Unveiled a White House "Faith" Office*. The Advisory Council could not agree on some important church-state issues, but members did agree that more could and should be done to protect the religious liberty of social service beneficiaries. Accordingly, the council made a slate of recommendations, and President Obama embraced these recommendations by signing them into law via Executive Order 13559 in November 2010. *See* Advisory Council on Faith-Based and Neighborhood Partnerships, *A New Era of Partnerships*, White House Office of Faith-Based and Neighborhood Partnerships (March 2010), https://obamawhitehouse.archives.gov/sites/default/files/partnerships-reform-office.pdf; *see, e.g.,* Executive Order 13559, 75 Fed. Reg. 71319. After a public notice and comment process, nine federal agencies issued final rules implementing this executive order.

47   *See* 64 Fed. Reg. 19355 (April 4, 2016).

48   *See* Rogers, *President Trump Just Unveiled a White House "Faith" Office*.

49   *See* Ron Kampeas, *Trump's Faith-Based Initiative Removes a Barrier to Proselytizing, and Some Jews Are Worried*, Jewish Telegraphic Agency (May 4, 2018).

50   At least through summer 2016, no problems had been reported to the federal government regarding these requirements. Discussion between Melissa Rogers and staff of the Department of Health and Human Services.

51   *See* Kelsey Dallas, *"Nothing Is More Powerful than God": A Look at President Donald Trump's New Faith-Based Initiative*, Deseret News (May 5, 2018).

52   42 U.S.C. Section 2000bb *et seq.* (2019). *See also* chap. 8.

53   Arguments along these lines are described in the following article: Stanley Carlson-Thies, *Trump Announces New Federal Faith and Community Initiative*, Institutional Religious Freedom Alliance (May 7, 2018), http://www.irfalliance.org/trump-announces-new-federal-faith-and-community-initiative/.

54   *Id.*

55   *Zelman v. Simmons-Harris*, 536 U.S. at 652.

56   For further discussion of these issues, *see below* chap. 7.

57   For further discussion of employment issues, *see below* chap. 9.

58   Title VII of the 1964 Civil Rights Act, 42 U.S.C. Section 2000e *et seq.* (2018).

59   *Corporation of the Presiding Bishop of the Church of Jesus Christ of Latter-day Saints v. Amos*, 483 U.S. 327 (1987). The religious organization involved in this case did not receive any government aid.

60   *Hosanna-Tabor Evangelical Lutheran Church and School v. Equal Employment Opportunity Commission*, 565 U.S. 171 (2012).

61   *Id.* at 196.

62 *See* Melissa Rogers, *Federal Funding and Religion-Based Employment Decisions*, chapter in *Sanctioning Religion? Politics, Law, and Faith-Based Public Services*, ed. David K. Ryden and Jeffrey Polet (Boulder, Colo.: Lynne Rienner 2005).

63 Executive Order 11246, 30 Fed. Reg. 12319, 12935 (September 24, 1965); Executive Order 11375, 32 Fed. Reg. 14303 (October 13, 1967)(adding "sex" to EO 11246 and substituting "religion" for "creed").

64 31 U.S.C. Section 6303(1) (2017). *See also* Sarah L. Pettijohn, *Federal Government Contracts and Grants for Nonprofits*, Urban Institute (May 2013).

65 Office of Research, University of Pittsburgh, *Federal Grants vs. Federal Contracts*, http://www.research.pitt.edu/sites/default/files/u24/Grants_vs_Contracts.pdf.

66 31 U.S.C. Section 6304(1) (2019).

67 Executive Order 13672 amends Executive Orders 11246 and 11478. *See* Executive Order 13672, 79 Fed. Reg. 42971 (July 21, 2014).

68 The full exemption states:

> The Secretary of Labor may, when the Secretary deems that special circumstances in the national interest so require, exempt a contracting agency from the require-ment of including any or all of the provisions of Section 202 of this Order in any specific contract, subcontract, or purchase order.

Section 204(a) of EO 11246. Another exemption in this same section of the order states:

> The Secretary of Labor may also provide, by rule, regulation, or order, for the exemption of facilities of a contractor that are in all respects separate and distinct from activities of the contractor related to the performance of the contract: provided that such an exemption will not interfere with or impede the effectuation of the purposes of this Order: and provided further, that in the absence of such an exemption all facilities shall be covered by the provisions of this Order.

Id. at Section 204(d).

69 The exemption states that the nondiscrimination prohibitions of the order

> shall not apply to a Government contractor or subcontractor that is a religious corporation, association, educational institution, or society, with respect to the employment of individuals of a particular religion to perform work connected with the carrying on by such corporation, association, educational institution, or society of its activities. Such contractors and subcontractors are not exempted or excused from complying with the other requirements contained in this Order.

Section 204(c) of EO 11246. *See also* 41 C.F.R. Section 60-1.5(a)(5) & (6).

70 Melissa Rogers and E. J. Dionne, *Serving People in Need, Safeguarding Religious Freedom: Recommendations for the New Administration on Partnerships with Faith-Based Organi-zations* (Washington, D.C.: Brookings, Wake Forest University Divinity School 2008), https://www.brookings.edu/wp-content/uploads/2012/04/12_religion_dionne.pdf.

71 The argument that refusals to employ or serve individuals in same-sex marriages are only objections to individuals' conduct—not their status or identity—has been rejected by the U.S. Supreme Court. When conduct is closely connected to a protected status or class, objections to conduct are treated as objections to that protected status or class, the Court has said. In the *Christian Legal Society v. Martinez* case, for example, the Supreme Court addressed similar arguments by the Christian Legal Society in the following way:

CLS contends that it does not exclude individuals because of sexual orientation, but rather "on the basis of a conjunction of conduct and the belief that the conduct is not wrong." Brief for Petitioner 35–36 (emphasis deleted).

Our decisions have declined to distinguish between status and conduct in this context. *See Lawrence v. Texas*, 539 U.S. 558, 575 (2003) ("When homosexual *conduct* is made criminal by the law of the State, that declaration in and of itself is an invitation to subject homosexual *persons* to discrimination." (emphasis added)); *Id.,* at 583 (O'Connor, J., concurring in judgment) ("While it is true that the law applies only to conduct, the conduct targeted by this law is conduct that is closely correlated with being homosexual. Under such circumstances, [the] law is targeted at more than conduct. It is instead directed toward gay persons as a class."); cf. *Bray v. Alexandria Women's Health Clinic*, 506 U.S. 263, 270 (1993) ("A tax on wearing yarmulkes is a tax on Jews."). *See also* Brief for Lambda Legal Defense and Education Fund, Inc., et al. as *Amici Curiae* 7–20.

Christian Legal Society v. Martinez, 561 U.S. 661, 689 (2010).

72 42 U.S.C. Section 2000bb *et seq.* (2019). In a 2007 opinion, the Department of Justice found that the government had the discretion under RFRA to exempt a grantee that was an evangelical organization from a grant program's religious nondiscrimination requirements so that the organization could continue to hire only co-religionists. *See* John P. Elwood, Deputy Assistant Attorney General, Office of Legal Counsel, *Application of the Religious Freedom Restoration Act to the Award of a Grant Pursuant to the Juvenile Justice and Delinquency Prevention Act*, Department of Justice (June 29, 2007), https://www .justice.gov/file/451561/download.

Even so, the Department of Justice placed a number of caveats on its opinion. DOJ said, for example, that it was not deciding whether the government could exempt grantees from other kinds of nondiscrimination requirements, like those based on race or sex. The opinion stated:

> We need not resolve whether the government would have a compelling interest in enforcing the Safe Streets Act's nondiscrimination provision with respect to a differently situated grant applicant—perhaps one without such a history to authenticate its claim that homogeneity of belief is essential to its mission, or whose hiring practices implicate compelling government interests in eradicating racial or sex discrimination. In such a case, the government might well have a compelling interest in requiring strict adherence with the Safe Streets Act's nondiscrimination requirements.

Id. at 187. Also, a DOJ opinion serves as the advice from one component of the executive branch to another. It does not have the same legal standing as a court opinion. *See* Trevor Morrison, *Stare Decisis in the Office of Legal Counsel*, 110 Columbia L. Rev. 1448 1451 (2010) ("Exercising authority delegated by the Attorney General, [the Department of Justice's Office of Legal Counsel] provides legal advice to the President and other executive components."). For a letter supporting this OLC opinion, see *Letter to President Barack Obama from Institutional Religious Freedom Alliance et al.* (September 10, 2015), http://www.irfalliance.org/wp-content/uploads/2015/09/Letter-to-President-to-maintain -OLC-memo-9-10-2015.pdf.

73 *Obergefell v. Hodges*, 576 U.S. ___, 135 S. Ct. 2584 (2015).
74 *Id.* at 2607.
75 *See, e.g., Law Professors' Analysis of a Need for Legal Guidance and Policy-Making on Religious Exemptions Raised by Federal Contractors*, Columbia University School of Law (May 10,

2016), https://www.law.columbia.edu/sites/default/files/microsites/gender-sexuality/files/olc_memo_analysis_final.pdf. *See also below* chap. 8.

76   *See* Department of Labor, *Implementing Legal Requirements Regarding the Equal Opportunity Clause's Religious Exemption*, Notice of Proposed Rulemaking, 84 Fed. Reg. 41677 (August 15, 2019). After receiving public comments on its proposed rule, DOL is expected to respond to those comments and issue a final rule.

77   Executive Order 13831, *Establishment of a White House Faith and Opportunity Initiative* (May 3, 2018), https://www.federalregister.gov/documents/2018/05/08/2018-09895/establishment-of-a-white-house-faith-and-opportunity-initiative; and Executive Order 13798, *Promoting Free Speech and Religious Liberty* (May 4, 2017), https://www.federalregister.gov/documents/2017/05/09/2017-09574/promoting-free-speech-and-religious-liberty.

78   Department of Labor, *Implementing Legal Requirements*. DOL referenced several Supreme Court decisions in its notice, including *Masterpiece Cakeshop, Ltd v. Colorado Civil Rights Comm'n*, 138 S. Ct. 1719; *Trinity Lutheran Church v. Comer*, 137 S. Ct. 2012; and *Burwell v. Hobby Lobby Stores, Inc.*, 573 U.S. ___, 134 S. Ct. 2751 (2014). *See* chaps. 7 and 8 below for further discussions of these cases.

79   *See below* chap. 8 for further discussion of these issues.

80   *See, e.g., Fulton v. City of Philadelphia*, 320 F. Supp. 3d 661 (E.D. Pa 2018); *Dumont v. Lyon*, 314 F. Supp. 3d 706 (E.D. Mich. 2018),

81   *See generally Law Professors' Analysis of a Need for Legal Guidance and Policy-Making on Religious Exemptions Raised by Federal Contractors*, Columbia University School of Law (May 10, 2016), https://www.law.columbia.edu/sites/default/files/microsites/gender-sexuality/files/olc_memo_analysis_final.pdf.

82   22 U.S.C. Section 7101 *et seq.* (2019).

83   *Id.* at Section 7101(b)(1).

84   *Id.*

85   *Id.* at Section 7105(b)(1)(B).

86   *Id.* at Section 7110.

87   *American Civil Liberties Union v. Azar*, 2018 U.S. Dist. LEXIS 175470 (N. D. Ca. 2018).

88   *Id.* at Section 7101(b)(6). *See also Statement by George H. Sheldon, Acting Assistant Secretary for Children and Families, Department of Health and Human Services, before the Committee on Oversight and Government Reform*, United States House of Representatives (December 1, 2011), https://democrats-oversight.house.gov/sites/democrats.oversight.house.gov/files/documents/Sheldon%20Testimony-Bio.pdf.

89   Some religious organizations argue that they cannot be denied aid based on the fact that they have religious or moral objections to making referrals for contraception and abortions. *See, e.g.,* Comments of U.S. Conference of Catholic Bishops *et al., Removing Barriers for Religious and Faith-Based Organizations to Participate in HHS Programs and Receive Public Funding*, HHS-9928-RFI (November 21, 2017).

90   Elaborating on its policy on grants to faith-based organizations, in 2015, HHS said:

> Consistent with the ACF Policy on Grants to Faith-Based Organizations (please see *Section III.1 Eligible Applicants* for more information), ACF is mindful that potential grantees may have religious objections to providing certain kinds of services, including referrals. ACF is committed to providing the full range of legally permissible services to people who need them, and to do so in a timely fashion and in a manner that respects the diverse religious and cultural backgrounds of those we serve. At the same time, ACF is also committed to finding ways for organizations

to partner with ACF and other grantees even if they object to providing specific services on religious grounds.

If an organization has a religious objection to providing any of the services or referrals required in the program, it may propose an approach to meeting its grant obligations consistent with ACF's faith-based policy. The alternative approach must be one that accomplishes the goal of ensuring that trafficking victims understand the full range of services available to them, including reproductive health services, and that there is a mechanism by which victims requesting such services can receive appropriate referrals. If an alternative approach is proposed, ORR will decide whether to accept the alternative approach, based upon a determination of whether the alternative approach will ensure timely referrals to all services and/or referrals for which the individual is eligible, is not burdensome to the client, and is operationally feasible for ACF.

Trafficking Victims Assistance Program, HHS-2015-ACF-ORR-ZV-0976 (August 19, 2015) 5, https://ami.grantsolutions.gov/files/HHS-2015-ACF-ORR-ZV-0976_1.pdf; *see also American Civil Liberties Union v. Azar*, 2018 U.S. Dist. LEXIS 175470.

91   *American Civil Liberties Union v. Azar*, 2018 U.S. Dist. LEXIS 175470 at *16.
92   *Id.* at *25–26.
93   *American Civil Liberties Union v. Azar*, 2018 U.S. Dist. LEXIS 175470.
94   *Id.* at *33–*42.
95   *Id.*
96   *Id.* at *42. The court "expresse[d] no opinion about whether an unaccompanied minor who may have suffered harm from being transferred or being delayed abortion services might be able to bring a claim," but said the ACLU did not have standing to make such a claim. *Id.* at *40 (citation omitted). "Because there is no evidence that government tax money has been used to subsidize religion, the ACLU's third-party-harm theory fails and cannot serve as the basis for . . . its Establishment Clause claim." *Id.* at *40–41.
97   *See* Executive Order 13559, 75 Fed. Reg. 71319.
98   Alternatively, objecting awardees may agree to refer clients or job seekers to government officials, who may then direct them to nonobjecting awardees.
99   *See, e.g.,* E. J. Dionne and Ming Hsu Chen, eds., *Sacred Places, Civic Purposes: Should Government Help Faith-Based Charity?* (Washington, D.C.: Brookings Institution Press 2001).
100 *See* the introduction and chap. 3 above.
101 McDonough and Crocker, *World's System for Resettling Refugees Benefits the United States.*
102 *See* the introduction and chap. 3 above.

Chapter 7: Faith and Federal Funds

1   Patrick Henry, *A Bill Establishing a Provision for Teachers of the Christian Religion* (January 1, 1784), in Flowers, Rogers, and Green, *Religious Freedom and the Supreme Court* at 1129–30.
2   *Id.* at 1130.
3   *Id.*
4   *Id.*
5   Madison, *Memorial and Remonstrance*, in Flowers, Rogers, and Green, *Religious Freedom and the Supreme Court* at 1133–37.
6   *Id.*

7   Thomas Jefferson, *A Bill for Establishing Religious Freedom*, in Flowers, Rogers, and Green, *Religious Freedom and the Supreme Court* at 1131–32.

8   *Walz v. Tax Commission*, 397 U.S. 664.

9   The U.S. Supreme Court held that the District of Columbia did not violate the Establishment Clause when it contracted with Providence Hospital, run by the Sisters of Charity, an order of Catholic nuns, to provide health care to D.C. residents. *Bradfield v. Roberts*, 175 U.S. 291.

10 *Everson v. Board of Education*, 330 U.S. 1.

11 *Walz v. Tax Commission*, 397 U.S. 664. The New York Constitution states that tax exemption may be granted for real or personal property used exclusively for religious, educational, or charitable purposes and owned by a nonprofit body organized or conducted exclusively for one or more such purposes. *Id.* at 666–67.

12 *Id.*

13 *Id.* at 674.

14 *Id.* at 676–77. In his concurring opinion, Justice Brennan agreed and distinguished between tax exemption and government subsidies:

> Tax exemptions and general subsidies . . . are qualitatively different. Though both provide economic assistance, they do so in fundamentally different ways. A subsidy involves the direct transfer of public monies to the subsidized enterprise, and uses resources exacted from taxpayers as a whole. An exemption, on the other hand, involves no such transfer. It assists the exempted enterprise only passively, by relieving a privately funded venture of the burden of paying taxes.

Id. at 690 (Brennan, J., concurring). In contrast to tax exemptions for religious, charitable, and educational entities, tax exemptions that are provided only to religious entities may run afoul of the Establishment Clause. *See, e.g., Texas Monthly v. Bullock*, 489 U.S. 1 (1989).

15 *Bob Jones University v. United States*, 461 U.S. 574 (1983).

16 *Bob Jones University v. United States*, 468 F. Supp. 890, 894 (D. S.C. 1978).

17 *Id.* at 894–95. BJU ended its policy against interracial dating and marriage in 2000 when that policy became an issue in the presidential race after then-candidate George W. Bush spoke at the school during the Republican primary in South Carolina. *Bob Jones University Ends Ban on Interracial Dating*, CNN (March 4, 2000).

18 *Bob Jones University v. United States*, 461 U.S. at 577–78.

19 *Id.* at 578.

20 Revenue Ruling 71–447, 1971–2 C.B. 230, https://www.irs.gov/pub/irs-tege/rr71-447 .pdf. Section 501(c)(3) organizations are exempt from federal taxation, and donations to them are generally deductible to the donor.

21 *Id.* Consistency with public policy is a requirement that arises from common law, which is often defined as law made by judicial decisions, not statutes.

22 *Id.*

23 *Id. See also Bob Jones University v. United States*, 461 U.S. at 578 (the Internal Revenue Service decided that it could "no longer legally justify allowing tax-exempt status [under Section 501(c)(3)] to private schools which practice racial discrimination" and that it could no longer treat gifts to such schools as tax-deductible to the donor).

24 *Bob Jones University v. United States*, 461 U.S. at 582.

25 *Id.*

26 *Id.* at 583.

27 *Bob Jones University v. United States*, 461 U.S. at 592.

28 *Id.*

29 *Id.*

30 *Id.* at 583.

31 The schools did not persuade the Court when they argued that only Congress, not the IRS, could make a judgment that revocation of tax-exempt status was appropriate. "Congress cannot be expected to anticipate every conceivable problem that can arise or to carry out day-to-day oversight, [so] it relies on the administrators and on the courts to implement the legislative will." *Id.* at 597. Federal legislators had failed to modify the relevant IRS rulings, the Court said, and had enacted similar policies. *Id.* at 601 (citing a provision that denied tax-exempt status to social clubs that had a policy of discrimination on the basis of race, color, or religion). The Court stressed that the IRS was not empowered to make such judgments on its own. Instead, the IRS relied on the judgments that Congress, the executive branch, and the courts had made about the evil of racial discrimination in the context of education.

Justice Powell wrote an opinion concurring in part and concurring in the judgment. He agreed that the denial of tax exemptions did not violate the First Amendment, but he expressed concern about the Court's explanation of the justification for tax exemptions for charitable organizations. *Id.* at 606–12 (Powell, J., concurring in part and concurring in the judgment). Powell feared that the majority opinion suggested that "the primary function of a tax-exempt organization is to act on behalf of the Government in carrying out governmentally approved policies." *Id.* at 609. That would conflict with the notion that tax exemption helps to encourage "diverse, indeed often sharply conflicting, activities and viewpoints." *Id.* Powell also was not confident that the schools involved in the case "necessarily contribute[d] nothing of benefit to the community." *Id.* In any case, Powell said, Congress should set policy here, not judges or the IRS.

Justice Rehnquist dissented. "To the extent that the Court states that Congress in furtherance of this policy could deny tax-exempt status to educational institutions that promote racial discrimination, I readily agree," Rehnquist said, but the Court "should not legislate for Congress." *Id.* at 612, 622 (Rehnquist, J., dissenting). Rehnquist also made it clear that, if Congress took such a step, he would not find that it had violated the schools' First Amendment rights. *Id.* at 622 n.3.

32 *Id.* at 604.

33 *Id.*

34 *Id.*

35 *Id.* at 605.

36 *Id.*

37 *Id.* at 604 n.29.

38 Alderson Reporting Company, *Transcript of Oral Argument in Obergefell v. Hodges* (April 28, 2015) at 38, https://www.supremecourt.gov/oral_arguments/argument_transcripts/2014/14-556q1_l5gm.pdf.

39 *Id.*

40 *Bob Jones University v. United States*, 461 U.S. at 604.

41 *Id.* at 595. Also, the Court specifically noted that Bob Jones University was a religious school, not a church. *Id.* at 604 n.29.

42 Office of Senator Mike Lee, *IRS Commissioner Commits Not to Target Religious Institutions* (July 30, 2015), https://www.lee.senate.gov/public/index.cfm/press-releases?ID=b237c7ed-b6fa-4268-93b9-0465057a3b3b.

43 *Obergefell v. Hodges*, 576 U.S. __, 135 S. Ct. 2584.

44 *Id.* at 2607.
45 *Remarks by the President on the Supreme Court Decision on Marriage Equality*, The White House (June 26, 2015), https://obamawhitehouse.archives.gov/the-press-office/2015/06/26/remarks-president-supreme-court-decision-marriage-equality. President Obama included similar sentiments in his statement welcoming the Court's ruling in *Windsor v. United States*, which struck down the Defense of Marriage Act as unconstitutional. Responding to the *Windsor* decision, President Obama said:

> On an issue as sensitive as this, knowing that Americans hold a wide range of views based on deeply held beliefs, maintaining our nation's commitment to religious freedom is also vital. How religious institutions define and consecrate marriage has always been up to those institutions. Nothing about this decision—which applies only to civil marriages—changes that.

Statement by the President on the Supreme Court Ruling on the Defense of Marriage Act, The White House (June 26, 2013), https://obamawhitehouse.archives.gov/doma-statement.
46 *Lemon v. Kurtzman*, 403 U.S. at 612.
47 *See, e.g.,* Green, *Bible, the School and the Constitution; Separation of Church and States: An Examination of State Constitutional Limits on Government Funding for Religious Institutions*, 2 First Amend. L. Rev. 1-198 (2003).
48 George F. Will, *When the Separation of Church and State Leads to Children with Scraped Knees*, The Washington Post (April 14, 2017).
49 *Everson v. Board of Education*, 330 U.S. 1.
50 *Id.* at 15–16.
51 *Id.* at 18.
52 *Id.* at 17–18.
53 *Id.* at 18.
54 *Id.*
55 *Id.* at 46 (Rutledge, J., dissenting).
56 *Id.* at 60.
57 *Id.* at 46.
58 *Id.* at 31–32.
59 *Id.* at 23–24 (Jackson, J., dissenting).
60 *Id.*
61 *Lemon v. Kurtzman*, 403 U.S. 602.
62 *Id.* at 607–9.
63 *Id.* at 609–11.
64 *Id.* at 612 (citation omitted).
65 *Id.* at 612–13 (citations omitted).
66 *Id.* at 613.
67 *Id.* at 613–14.
68 *Id.* at 616.
69 *Id.* at 619.
70 *Id.* at 625.
71 *Id.* at 649 (quoting *Abington Township v. Schempp*, 374 U.S. at 259 (Brennan, J., concurring)).
72 *Id.* at 651–52.
73 Justice Lewis Powell was confirmed as a Supreme Court justice in December 1971, taking the place of Justice Black. *See* Flowers, Rogers, and Green, *Religious Freedom and the*

Supreme Court at 1139–66; George Clemon Freeman Jr., *Justice Powell's Constitutional Opinions*, 45 Wash. and Lee L. Rev. 411 (1988). The Court handed down its decision in *Lemon* in June 1971, so Justice Black, not Justice Powell, sat on the Court when that case was decided. *See Lemon v. Kurtzman*, 403 U.S. 602.

74 *See above* chap. 1.

75 *Agostini v. Felton*, 521 U.S. 203, 209–10 (1997).

76 *Id.* at 212.

77 *Aguilar v. Felton*, 473 U.S. 402 (1985).

78 *Agostini v. Felton*, 521 U.S. at 222.

79 The Court no longer believed that the placement of public employees on the grounds of religious schools "inevitably results in the impermissible effect of state-sponsored indoctrination or constitutes a symbolic union between government and religion." *Id.* at 223. Also, the current Court did not assume that any government aid that directly supported the educational function of religious schools was unconstitutional or that the mere presence of public employees on religious schools' premises created a forbidden "symbolic union" between religion and government. Further, the Title I program did not necessarily result in excessive church-state entanglement. The fact that religious schools and government had to cooperate to make the Title I program work, or that the program might create "political divisiveness," did not create such entanglement, the Court said.

80 *Id.* at 233.

81 *Id.* at 222–37.

82 *Id.* at 240 (Souter, J., dissenting).

83 *Id.* at 240–41.

84 *Mitchell v. Helms*, 530 U.S. 793 (2000).

85 *Id.*

86 *Marks v. United States*, 430 U.S. 188, 193 (1977) (citations omitted) ("When a fragmented Court decides a case and no single rationale explaining the result enjoys the assent of five Justices, 'the holding of the Court may be viewed as that position taken by those members who concurred in the judgment on the narrowest grounds . . . . '") (quoting *Gregg v. Georgia*, 428 U.S. 169 n.15 (1976)).

87 *Mitchell v. Helms*, 530 U.S. at 808 (plurality opinion).

88 *Id.* at 809.

89 *Id.* at 828.

90 *Id.*

91 *Id.* at 827–28.

92 *Id.* at 829.

93 *Id.* at 837 (O'Connor, J., concurring in the judgment).

94 *Id.* at 843–44.

95 *Id.* at 902 (Souter, J., dissenting).

96 *Id.* at 912.

97 *Id.* at 870–73.

98 Rebecca T. Rosen, *Neal Katyal: Senate's Obstruction of Merrick Garland "Was Unforgiveable*,*"* The Atlantic (June 27, 2017).

99 Melissa Rogers, *Six Observations about the Supreme Court's Trinity Lutheran Case*, The Christian Century (July 6, 2017).

100 *Trinity Lutheran Church v. Comer*, 582 U.S. ___, 137 S. Ct. 2012 (2017).

101 *Id.* at 2022.

102 *Id.* at 2024–25.

103 *Id.* at 2029 (Sotomayor, J., dissenting).

104 *Id.* at 2040.

105 *Id.* at 2041.

106 *Id.* at 2024 n.3.

107 The four justices were: Chief Justice Roberts and Justices Kennedy, Alito, and Kagan. In an opinion concurring in part, Justice Gorsuch, joined by Justice Thomas, commented on this footnote, saying:

> Of course the footnote is entirely correct, but I worry that some might mistakenly read it to suggest that only "playground resurfacing" cases, or only those with some association with children's safety or health, or perhaps some other social good we find sufficiently worthy, are governed by the legal rules recounted in and faithfully applied by the Court's opinion. Such a reading would be unreasonable for our cases are "governed by general principles, rather than ad hoc improvisations." *Elk Grove Unified School Dist. v. Newdow*, 542 U.S. 1, 25 (2004) (Rehnquist, C. J., concurring in judgment). And the general principles here do not permit discrimination against religious exercise—whether on the playground or anywhere else.

Id. at 2026 (Gorsuch, J., concurring in part).

108 *Id.* at 2027 (Breyer, J., concurring in the judgment).

109 *Id.*

110 *See, e.g.,* Supreme Court Order Vacating and Remanding Decisions regarding School Vouchers for Further Consideration in Light of *Trinity Lutheran v. Comer* (June 27, 2017), https://www.supremecourt.gov/orders/courtorders/062717zr_6537.pdf.

111 *See Zelman v. Simmon-Harris*, 536 U.S. 639, 649 (2002).

112 *Id.* at 645.

113 *Id.* at 643–49.

114 *Id.* at 652.

115 *Id.* at 668 (O'Connor, J., concurring).

116 *Id.* at 670.

117 *Id.* at 686 (Souter, J., dissenting).

118 *Id.*

119 *Id.* at 711.

120 *Id.* at 717.

121 *Id.* at 707.

122 *Id.* at 717.

123 The Court had earlier determined that government vocational aid that flows to individuals may be used by those individuals to attend Bible colleges without restriction and without violating the First Amendment's Establishment Clause. *See Witters v. Washington Department of Services for the Blind*, 474 U.S. 481 (1986). In *Witters*, the Court noted that aid recipients had a "huge variety of possible careers, of which only a small handful are sectarian." *Id.* at 488. The Court also said that "nothing in the record indicates that . . . any significant portion of the aid expended under the [government program] as a whole will end up flowing to religious education." *Id.*

124 *Bob Jones University v. United States*, 461 U.S. 574, 604.

125 *Id.* at 595.

126 *See above* introduction at n.69.

Chapter 8: Religious Exemptions and Accommodations

1 Mary Ann Glendon, *A World Made New: Eleanor Roosevelt and the Universal Declaration of Human Rights* (New York: Random House 2001) ix.

2 *Id.* at 33.

3 *Id.* at xv.

4 *Id.*

5 *Id.* at xvi.

6 *Id.* at xviii.

7 *Id.*

8 *Id.* at xxi.

9 Universal Declaration of Human Rights, United Nations, Article 1, http://www.un.org/en/universal-declaration-human-rights/. *See also Punta del Este Declaration on Human Dignity for Everyone Everywhere: Seventy Years after the Universal Declaration on Human Rights* (December 2018), https://www.dignityforeveryone.org/wp-content/uploads/2018/12/Punta-de-Este-Declaration-on-Human-Dignity.pdf.

10 Universal Declaration of Human Rights, at Preamble.

11 *Id.* at Article 18.

12 J. Brent Walker, *A Primer on Governmental Accommodation of Religion*, Journal of Church and State 49 (2007) 409–21, https://bjconline.org/a-primer-on-governmental-accommodation-of-religion/.

13 Joseph Hincks, *The U.S. Army Just Made It Easier for Religious Troops to Wear Beards, Hijabs and Turbans,* Time (January 7, 2017).

14 *West Virginia Board of Education v. Barnette*, 319 U.S. 624 (1943).

15 Katherine Franke, *Religious Freedom for Me, but Not for Thee,* The Washington Post (September 28, 2018); Rafael Carranza, *Clergy, Volunteers Leaving Water for Border Crossers in Arizona Desert Face Higher Risks,* Arizona Central (August 5, 2018); Rory Carroll, *Eight Activists Helping Migrants Cross Brutal Desert Charged by US Government,* The Guardian (January 24, 2018); Jacob Gershman, *Aid for Immigrants on Desert Trek Stirs Religious-Freedom Fight,* Wall Street Journal (December 6, 2018).

16 Alan Goldenbach, *When Rules Run Up against Faith,* The Washington Post (January 16, 2008).

17 William A. Galston and Melissa Rogers, *Health Care Providers' Consciences and Patients' Needs: The Quest for Balance,* The Brookings Institution (February 23, 2012), https://www.brookings.edu/wp-content/uploads/2016/06/0223_health_care_galston_rogers.pdf.

18 Duarte Geraldino and Frank Carlson, *More Churches Are Opening Their Doors to Undocumented Immigrants Facing Deportation,* PBS NewsHour (January 15, 2018). *See also* Thomas Scott-Railton, *A Legal Sanctuary: How the Religious Freedom Restoration Act Could Protect Sanctuary Churches,* 128 Yale L. Jnl. 408 (2018).

19 Jaeah Lee, *It's Not Just Hobby Lobby: These 71 Companies Don't Want to Cover Your Birth Control Either,* Mother Jones (April 2, 2014).

20 *See, e.g., Adorers of the Blood of Christ v. Federal Energy Regulatory Commission*, No. 17–3163 (July 25, 2018), http://www2.ca3.uscourts.gov/opinarch/173163p.pdf; Robinson Meyer, *The Last-Ditch Attempt to Stop the Dakota Access Pipeline: Can Religious Freedom and* Hobby Lobby *Block the Black Snake?* The Atlantic (February 10, 2017).

21 *Masterpiece Cakeshop, Ltd. v. Colorado Civil Rights Comm'n*, 584 U.S. ___,138 S. Ct. 1719 (2018).

22 John C. Moritz, *La Lomita Mission Site Should Not Be Used for Planned Border Wall, Bishop Says*, Corpus Christi Caller Times (November 16, 2018); John C. Moritz, *Catholic Diocese Fights to Keep Historic Site from Being Used in Trump's Border Wall*, Corpus Christi Caller Times (November 27, 2018).

23 *See* Douglas Laycock and Oliver Thomas, *Interpreting the Religious Freedom Restoration Act*, 73 Tex. L. Rev. 209 (1994); Flowers, Rogers, and Green, *Religious Freedom and the Supreme Court* at 95–293. Using these Free Exercise standards, the Court upheld the right of religious individuals to receive unemployment compensation when they were fired due to conflicts between job requirements and their faith. *Sherbert v. Verner*, 374 U.S. 398 (1963); *Thomas v. Review Bd.*, 450 U.S. 707 (1981); *Hobbie v. Unemployment Appeals Commission of Florida*, 480 U.S. (1987); *Frazee v. Illinois Employment Security Department*, 489 U.S. 829 (1989). The Court also ruled in favor of Amish parents who requested an exemption from compulsory education requirements for their children past the eighth grade. Doing so would not harm the children's mental or physical health or "public safety, peace, order, or welfare," the Court said. *Wisconsin v. Yoder*, 406 U.S. 205, 230 (1972).

24 *Cutter v. Wilkinson*, 544 U.S. at 722–24; *Presiding Bishop v. Amos*, 438 U.S. 327, 338 (1987) ("Where, as here, government acts with the proper purpose of lifting a regulation that burdens the exercise of religion, we see no reason to require that the exemption come packaged with benefits to secular entities.").

25 *Cutter v. Wilkinson*, 544 U.S. at 720.

26 Michael W. McConnell, *Free Exercise Revisionism and the Smith Decision*, 57 University of Chicago Law Rev. 1109, 1145 (1990) (quoting Letter from James Madison to Edward Livingston (July 10, 1822), in Gaillard Hunt, ed., *The Writings of James Madison*, vol. 9 (G. P. Putnam's Sons, 1901) 100), https://chicagounbound.uchicago.edu/cgi/viewcontent .cgi?referer=https://www.google.com/&httpsredir=1&article=12578&context=journal _articles; Founders Online, National Archives, https://founders.archives.gov/documents/ Madison/04-02-02-0471.

> Here is the relevant excerpt from the James Madison's letter:

> > I observe with particular pleasure the view you have taken of the immunity of Religion from Civil Jurisdiction, in every case where it does not trespass on private rights or the public peace. This has always been a favorite point with me: and it was not with my approbation, that the deviation from it took place in Congress when they appointed Chaplains to be paid from the national Treasury. It would have been a much better proof to their Constituents of their pious feelings, if the members had contributed for the purpose, a pittance from their own pockets. As the precedent is not likely to be rescinded, the best that ⟨can⟩ now be done may be, to apply to the Constitution, the maxim of the law, de minimis non curat.

27 *Cutter v. Wilkinson*, 544 U.S. 709, 722.

28 *See, e.g., Thornton v. Caldor*, 472 U.S. 703 (1985).

29 *Id.* at 708–9.

30 *Id.* at 710.

31 *United States v. Lee*, 455 U.S. 252 (1982).

32 *Id.*

33 *Id.* at 260–61. The exemption states:

> (g) MEMBERS OF CERTAIN RELIGIOUS FAITHS

> > (1) EXEMPTION Any individual may file an application (in such form and manner, and with such official, as may be prescribed by regulations under

this chapter) for an exemption from the tax imposed by this chapter if he is a member of a recognized religious sect or division thereof and is an adherent of established tenets or teachings of such sect or division by reason of which he is conscientiously opposed to acceptance of the benefits of any private or public insurance which makes payments in the event of death, disability, old-age, or retirement or makes payments toward the cost of, or provides services for, medical care (including the benefits of any insurance system established by the Social Security Act). Such exemption may be granted only if the application contains or is accompanied by—

(A) such evidence of such individual's membership in, and adherence to the tenets or teachings of, the sect or division thereof as the Secretary may require for purposes of determining such individual's compliance with the preceding sentence, and

(B) his waiver of all benefits and other payments under titles II and XVIII of the Social Security Act on the basis of his wages and self-employment income as well as all such benefits and other payments to him on the basis of the wages and self-employment income of any other person, and only if the Commissioner of Social Security finds that—

(C) such sect or division thereof has the established tenets or teachings referred to in the preceding sentence,

(D) it is the practice, and has been for a period of time which he deems to be substantial, for members of such sect or division thereof to make provision for their dependent members which in his judgment is reasonable in view of their general level of living, and

(E) such sect or division thereof has been in existence at all times since December 31, 1950. An exemption may not be granted to any individual if any benefit or other payment referred to in subparagraph (B) became payable (or, but for section 203 or 222(b) of the Social Security Act, would have become payable) at or before the time of the filing of such waiver.

26 U.S.C. Section 1402(g)(2019).

34 *United States v. Lee*, 455 U.S. at 261. *See also Alamo Foundation v. Secretary of Labor*, 471 U.S. 290 (1985) (rejecting claim that First Amendment prevented application of Fair Labor Standards Act to workers engaged in commercial activities of a religious foundation); Thomas C. Berg, *Religious Exemptions and Third-Party Harms*, Federalist Society Review 17, no. 3 (2016), https://fedsoc.org/commentary/publications/religious-exemptions-and-third-party-harms.

After the Supreme Court handed down its decision in the *Lee* case, Congress changed the Social Security laws to exempt any employer or partnership consisting of members of any "recognized religious sect" that is "conscientiously opposed to acceptance of the benefits of any private or public insurance" from paying payroll taxes for any employee "who is also a member of such a religious sect or division and an adherent of its established tenets or teachings . . . ." The full provision states:

(a) IN GENERAL Notwithstanding any other provision of this chapter (and under regulations prescribed to carry out this section), in any case where—

(1) an employer (or, if the employer is a partnership, each partner therein) is a member of a recognized religious sect or division thereof described in

> section 1402(g) (1) and an adherent of established tenets or teachings of such sect or division as described in such section, and has filed and had approved under subsection (b) an application (in such form and manner, and with such official, as may be prescribed by such regulations) for an exemption from the taxes imposed by section 3111, and
>
> (2) an employee of such employer who is also a member of such a religious sect or division and an adherent of its established tenets or teachings has filed and had approved under subsection (b) an identical application for exemption from the taxes imposed by section 3101, such employer shall be exempt from the taxes imposed by section 3111 with respect to wages paid to each of the employees thereof who meets the requirements of paragraph (2) and each such employee shall be exempt from the taxes imposed by section 3101 with respect to such wages paid to him by such employer.

26 U.S.C. Section 3127 (2019).

35 *See* Ira C. Lupu and Robert W. Tuttle, *Secular Government, Religious People* (Grand Rapids: Eerdmans 2014) 177–210; Michael W. McConnell, *Free Exercise Revisionism and the Smith Decision*, 57 Univ. of Chicago L. Rev. 1109, 1127 & n.89 (1990) ("In most areas of constitutional law, the Court's supposed 'compelling interest test' falls far short of that."). *See, e.g., Bowen v. Roy*, 476 U.S. 693 (1986); *Lyng v. Northwest Indian Cemetery Protection Assoc.*, 485 U.S. 439 (1988); *Goldman v. Weinberger*, 475 U.S. 503 (1986); *O'Lone v. Estate of Shabazz*, 482 U.S. 342 (1987).

36 *Employment Division v. Smith*, 494 U.S. 872 (1990). Notably, the Court did not overrule any precedents in *Smith*, but it did try to distinguish some of them. The Court said, for example, that the "only decisions in which this Court has held that the First Amendment bars application of a neutral, generally applicable law to religiously motivated action are distinguished on the ground that they involved not the Free Exercise Clause alone, but that Clause in conjunction with other constitutional protections." *Id.* at 881. Also, the *Smith* majority argued that the Court's previous decisions regarding unemployment compensation merely "stand for the proposition that where the State has in place a system of individual exemptions, it may not refuse to extend that system to cases of 'religious hardship' without compelling reason." *Id.* at 884. None of those cases, however, had involved "an across-the-board criminal prohibition on a particular form of conduct," the *Smith* majority said. *Id.* For critiques of these and other aspects of the *Smith* opinion, *see generally* Michael W. McConnell, *Free Exercise Revisionism and the Smith Decision*, 57 Univ. of Chiciago L. Rev. 1109 (1990); Douglas Laycock, *The Remnants of Free Exercise*, 1990 Sup. Ct. Rev. 1 (1990).

37 *Id.* at 874.

38 *Id.*

39 *Id.*

40 *See generally Sherbert v. Verner*, 374 U.S. 398 (1963); and *Thomas v. Review Board*, 450 U.S. 707.

41 *See generally* Laycock and Thomas, *Interpreting the Religious Freedom Restoration Act*, 73 Tex. L. Rev. 209.

42 *Church of the Lukumi Babalu Aye v. City of Hialeah*, 508 U.S. at 531.

43 *Employment Division v. Smith*, 494 U.S. at 888.

44 *Id.*

45 *Church of the Lukumi Babalu Aye v. City of Hialeah*, 508 U.S. 520, 533–34 (1993).

46   *Id.* at 543–44. For a view that challenges aspects of this interpretation, *see* Jim Oleske, *Masterpiece Cakeshop and the Effort to Rewrite Smith and Its Progeny*, Take Care (September 2, 2017), https://takecareblog.com/blog/masterpiece-cakeshop-and-the-effort-to-rewrite -smith-and-its-progeny.

47   *Employment Division v. Smith*, at 890.

48   *Id.* at 891 (O'Connor, J., concurring in the judgment).

49   *Id.* at 894 (citations omitted).

50   *Id.* at 908–9 (citations omitted) (Blackmun, J., dissenting).

51   Laycock and Thomas, *Interpreting the Religious Freedom Restoration Act*, 73 Tex. L. Rev. 209.

52   *See* Baptist Joint Committee, *The Religious Freedom Restoration Act: Twenty Years of Protecting Our First Freedom* (2013), https://bjconline.org/wp-content/uploads/2014/ 04/RFRA-Book-FINAL.pdf.

53   *Id.*

54   42 U.S.C. Section 1996a (2019).

55   *Id.* at 1996a(b)(1).

56   42 U.S.C. Section 2000bb *et seq.* (2019). RFRA states:

> (a) IN GENERAL Government shall not substantially burden a person's exercise of religion even if the burden results from a rule of general applicability, except as provided in subsection (b).
>
> (b) EXCEPTION Government may substantially burden a person's exercise of religion only if it demonstrates that application of the burden to the person—
>
> > (1) is in furtherance of a compelling governmental interest; and
> >
> > (2) is the least restrictive means of furthering that compelling governmental interest.

Id. at Section 2000bb-1.

57   *Burwell v. Hobby Lobby Stores, Inc.*, 573 U.S. 682, 747 (2014) (Ginsburg, J., dissenting) (citing 139 Cong. Rec. 26178 (statement of Sen. Kennedy)).

58   *See* Senate Report No. 103–111, p. 8 (1993); *see also* H. R. Rep. No. 103–88, pp. 6–7 (1993). For a critique of RFRA, *see* Ira C. Lupu, *The Failure of RFRA*, 20 Ark. Little Rock L. Rev. 575 (1998).

59   *City of Boerne v. Flores*, 521 U.S. 507 (1997).

60   *See generally* Laycock and Thomas, *Interpreting the Religious Freedom Restoration Act*, 73 Tex. L. Rev. 209; Christopher Lund, *RFRAs, State RFRAs and Religious Minorities*, 53 San Diego L. Rev. 163 (2016).

61   *Swanner v. Anchorage Equal Rights Commission*, 874 P.2d 274, 280 n. 9 (1994).

62   *Id.*

63   *Swanner v. Anchorage Equal Rights Commission*, 115 S. Ct. 460 (1994) (Thomas, J., dissenting).

64   *Id.* at 461.

65   *Id.*

66   *Id.* at 462.

67   42 U.S.C. Section 2000cc (2019). *See below* chap. 10 for more information on RLUIPA.

68   *Id.*

69   For a more detailed explanation of these matters, *see* Timothy Jost, *On Objections to Contraception Coverage, Trump Administration Appears Set to Reverse Obama Approach*,

Health Affairs (June 2, 2017), https://www.healthaffairs.org/do/10.1377/hblog20170602
.060408/full/. As the Jost piece notes, the contraception coverage requirement also covers
health insurance offered to students by certain institutions of higher education.

70   National Academies of Science, Engineering and Medicine, http://www.nationalacademies
.org/hmd/.

71   Preventive Care Benefits for Women, https://www.healthcare.gov/preventive-care-women/.

72   76 Federal Register 46626 (August 3, 2011).

73   *Burwell v. Hobby Lobby*, 573 U.S. 682.

74   *Id.* Coverage of Certain Preventive Services under the Affordable Care Act, 78 Fed. Reg.
39870 (July 2, 2013).

75   Another closely held business run by the same family who owns Hobby Lobby also was
involved in the lawsuit—Mardel, an association of thirty-five Christian bookstores. *Id.*
at 702.

76   *Id.* at 706 n.18 ("Even if RFRA simply restored the status quo ante, there is no reason to
believe, as HHS and the dissent seem to suggest, that the law was meant to be limited to
situations that fall squarely within the holdings of pre-*Smith* cases."). *See also* Martin S.
Lederman, *Reconstructing RFRA: The Contested Legacy of Religious Freedom Restoration*,
125 Yale L.J. Forum 416 (2016); Marty Lederman, *Hobby Lobby Part XVIII—The one
(potentially) momentous aspect of Hobby Lobby: Untethering RFRA from free exercise doctrine*,
Balkinization (July 6, 2014), https://balkin.blogspot.com/2014/07/hobby-lobby-part
-xviii-one-potentially.html.

77   *Burwell v. Hobby Lobby*, 573 U.S. 682, 696.

78   *Id.* at 714 (citations omitted).

79   *Id.* at 749 (Ginsburg, J., dissenting). Justice Ginsburg wrote for the dissenters. Two of the
dissenters—Justices Ginsburg and Sotomayor—argued that for-profit corporations were
not persons under RFRA because neither the Act's text nor its legislative history mentions
for-profit corporations and no prior Court decision had extended a religious exemption
to such a corporation, either under the First Amendment or RFRA. Because they agreed
that the challenge to the contraception mandate should not prevail, Justices Breyer and
Kagan noted that they did not need to decide whether either for-profit corporations or
their owners could bring claims under RFRA, so they did not decide that issue. All four
dissenters said the objecting businesses had not shown that the contraception mandate
substantially burdened their religious exercise—there was only a weak link between
the corporate owners' religious objections and the ultimate use of contraception by
their covered employees or their dependents, they said. The dissenters also credited the
government with demonstrating that the mandate advanced compelling governmental
interests in public health and women's well-being by the means that were least restrictive
of religious exercise. The Court's proposed settlement of the issues—that the accommodation the government made available to religious nonprofits be extended to closely
held for-profits like Hobby Lobby—was not one that the challengers had suggested, so
the government had not had the opportunity to address it. Noting many other religious
objections that might be raised, the dissenters said they feared the Court "ha[d] ventured
into a minefield by its immoderate reading of RFRA." *Id.* at 771–72.

80   *Id.* at 746–47 (citations and footnote omitted).

81   *Id.* at 747–50 (citations and footnote omitted). Here is the response of the Court majority
to these arguments:

> RFRA, by imposing a least-restrictive-means test, went beyond what was required
> by our pre-*Smith* decisions. Although the author of the principal dissent joined

the Court's opinion in [*City of Boerne v. Flores*], she now claims that the statement was incorrect. For present purposes, it is unnecessary to adjudicate this dispute. Even if RFRA simply restored the status quo ante, there is no reason to believe, as HHS and the dissent seem to suggest, that the law was meant to be limited to situations that fall squarely within the holdings of pre-*Smith* cases.

Id. at 706 n.18 (citations omitted).

82 Writing for the Court majority, Justice Alito also tried to distinguish *United States v. Lee*, saying it was "a free exercise, not a RFRA, case," and that the case's language about commercial entities, "if taken at face value, is squarely inconsistent with the plain meaning of RFRA." *Id.* at 735 & n.43. The dissenters, however, insisted that *Lee* was "[a]mong the pathmarking pre-*Smith* decisions RFRA preserved . . . ." *Id.* at 768 (Ginsburg, J., dissenting). For arguments by the majority and the dissent about the least restrictive means test, see *id.* at 728–30 and 764–68 (Ginsburg, J., dissenting).

83 *Id.* at 731 ("We do not decide today whether an approach of this type complies with RFRA for purposes of all religious claims."). *Compare with id.* at 767 (Ginsburg, J., dissenting) (noting this reservation and the fact that the Court imposed the accommodation even though the businesses had never said such an arrangement was acceptable to them, and even though the government had never had the opportunity to react to the proposal).

84 At the time, due to Justice Antonin Scalia's death, the Supreme Court included only eight justices. Republican presidents nominated four of those justices, and Democratic presidents nominated the other four justices. The Court may have been deadlocked in this case, thus prompting them to take the unusual step of requesting supplemental briefing and seeking to prompt the parties to settle the case rather than ruling on its merits.

85 *Zubik v. Burwell*, 578 U.S. ___, 136 S. Ct. 1557, 1560 (2016).

86 *See FAQs about Affordable Care Act Implementation Part 36*, Department of Labor, Employee Security Benefits Administration (January 9, 2017), https://www.dol.gov/sites/default/files/ebsa/about-ebsa/our-activities/resource-center/faqs/aca-part-36.pdf; Ira C. Lupu, *Hobby Lobby and the Dubious Enterprise of Religious Exemptions*, 38 Harv. Journal of Law and Gender 35 (2015).

87 Executive Order 13798, *Promoting Free Speech and Religious Liberty*, 82 Fed. Reg. 21675 (May 9, 2017).

88 *Trump Administration Issues Final Rules Protecting Constitutional Rights in Health Insurance*, Department of Health and Human Services (November 7, 2018), https://www.hhs.gov/about/news/2018/11/07/trump-administration-issues-final-rules-protecting-conscience-rights-in-health-insurance.html.

89 *Id.*

90 *See, e.g., Commonwealth of Pennsylvania v. Trump*, No. 17–4540 (E.D. Pa. 2017), https://assets.documentcloud.org/documents/4329962/COMMONWEALTH-of-PENNSYLVANIA-v-TRUMP-Et-Al.pdf.

91 *See generally Masterpiece Cakeshop, Ltd. v. Colorado Civil Rights Comm'n*, 584 U.S. ___, 183 S. Ct. 1719.

92 Co. Rev. Stat. Section 24-34-601 (2019).

93 *Mullins v. Masterpiece Cakeshop, Inc.*, 370 P. 3d 272, 277 (Colo. Ct. App. 2015).

94 The Colorado Court of Appeals said:

> Masterpiece thus distinguishes between discrimination based on a person's status and discrimination based on conduct closely correlated with that status. However, the United States Supreme Court has recognized that such distinctions are generally inappropriate. *See Christian Legal Soc'y Chapter of Univ. of Cal., Hastings Coll.*

of Law v. Martinez, 561 U.S. 661, 689 (2010) ("[The Christian Legal Society] contends that it does not exclude individuals because of sexual orientation, but rather 'on the basis of a conjunction of conduct and the belief that the conduct is not wrong.' . . . Our decisions have declined to distinguish between status and conduct in this context."); *Lawrence v. Texas*, 539 U.S. 558, 575 (2003) ("When homosexual conduct is made criminal by the law of the State, that declaration in and of itself is an invitation to subject homosexual persons to discrimination."); *Id.* at 583 (O'Connor, J., concurring in the judgment) ("While it is true that the law applies only to conduct, the conduct targeted by this law is conduct that is closely correlated with being homosexual. Under such circumstances, [the] law is . . . directed toward gay persons as a class."); *see also Bob Jones Univ. v. United States*, 461 U.S. 574, 605 (1983) (concluding that prohibiting admission to students married to someone of a different race was a form of racial discrimination, although the ban restricted conduct). Further, in *Obergefell v. Hodges*, 576 U.S. ___, 135 S. Ct. 2584 (2015), the Supreme Court equated laws precluding same-sex marriage to discrimination on the basis of sexual orientation. *Id* at ___, 135 S. Ct. at 2604 (observing that the "denial to same-sex couples of the right to marry" is a "disability on gays and lesbians" which "serves to disrespect and subordinate them"). The Court stated: "The nature of marriage is that, through its enduring bond, two persons together can find other freedoms, such as expression, intimacy, and spirituality. This is true for all persons, whatever their sexual orientation." *Id.* at ___, 135 S. Ct. at 2599 (emphasis added). "Were the Court to stay its hand . . . it still would deny gays and lesbians many rights and responsibilities intertwined with marriage." *Id.* at ___, 135 S. Ct. at 2606.

In these decisions, the Supreme Court recognized that, in some cases, conduct cannot be divorced from status. This is so when the conduct is so closely correlated with the status that it is engaged in exclusively or predominantly by persons who have that particular status. We conclude that the act of same-sex marriage constitutes such conduct because it is "engaged in exclusively or predominantly" by gays, lesbians, and bisexuals. Masterpiece's distinction, therefore, is one without a difference. But for their sexual orientation, Craig and Mullins would not have sought to enter into a same-sex marriage, and but for their intent to do so, Masterpiece would not have denied them its services.

   Id. at 280–81.
95   *Id.* at 282.
96   *Id.* at n.8.
97   *Id.* at 283.
98   *Id.*
99   *See Masterpiece Cakeshop, Ltd. v. Colorado Civil Rights Comm'n*, 584 U.S. ___, 138 S. Ct. at 1724.
100 The Court questioned a comment by another commissioner that Phillips could not act on his religious beliefs if he wanted to do business in the state. Instead, the commissioner said, Phillips "needs to look at being able to compromise." The Court said:

   Standing alone, these statements are susceptible of different interpretations. On the one hand, they might mean simply that a business cannot refuse to provide services based on sexual orientation, regardless of the proprietor's personal views. On the other hand, they might be seen as inappropriate and dismissive comments showing lack of due consideration for Phillips' free exercise rights and the dilemma he faced.

Given the other commissioner's subsequent comment about "despicable pieces of rhetoric," however, the Court said that "the latter [interpretation] seems the more likely." *Id.* at 1729.

101 *Id.*

102 *Id.*

103 *Id.* at 1731.

104 *Id.* at 1727 (citing *Newman v. Piggie Park Enterprises, Inc.*, 390 U.S. 400, 402, n.5 (1968) (per curiam)).

105 *Id.* at 1732.

106 *Id.* at 1733 (Kagan, J., concurring).

107 *Id.*

108 *Id.* at * (Kagan, J., concurring).

109 *Id.* at 1735. (Gorsuch, J., concurring).

110 Even if Jack Phillips, the owner of Masterpiece, refused to make and sell a wedding cake to the gay couple's straight mother because the cake would be used at a same-sex wedding, that act would still violate CADA. CADA prohibits business practices that would, directly or indirectly, refuse "the full and equal enjoyment" of goods and services to particular customers because of their sexual orientation. Vikram David Amar and Alan E. Brownstein, *Attitudinal and Doctrinal Takeaways from Masterpiece Cakeshop Case*, Verdict: Justia (June 15, 2018), https://verdict.justia.com/2018/06/15/attitudinal-and-doctrinal-takeaways-from-the-masterpiece-cakeshop-case.

111 *Masterpiece Cakeshop, Ltd. v. Colorado Civil Rights Comm'n*, 584 U.S. ___, 138 S. Ct. at 1736 (Gorsuch, J., concurring).

112 *Id.* at * (Kagan, J., concurring).

113 *Id.*

114 *Id.* at 1747–48 (2018) (Thomas, J., concurring in part and concurring in the judgment) (citations omitted).

115 *Id.* at 1751–52 (Ginsburg, J., dissenting) (citations omitted).

116 *Id.* at 1750 n.7.

117 *Id.* (citation omitted).

118 *Id.*

119 Justice Gorsuch said:

> In *Employment Div., Dept. of Human Resources of Ore. v. Smith,* this Court held that a neutral and generally applicable law will usually survive a constitutional free exercise challenge. 494 U.S. 872, 878–879 (1990). *Smith* remains controversial in many quarters. *Compare* McConnell, *The Origins and Historical Understanding of Free Exercise of Religion*, 103 Harv. L. Rev. 1409 (1990), with Hamburger, *A Constitutional Right of Religious Exemption: An Historical Perspective*, 60 Geo. Wash. L. Rev. 915 (1992).

> *Id.* at 1734. In a subsequent statement on another case, Justices Alito, joined by Justices Thomas, Gorsuch, and Kavanaugh, noted that "the Court drastically cut back on the protection provided by the Free Exercise Clause" in the *Smith* ruling. *Kennedy v. Bremerton Sch. Dist.*, 139 S. Ct. 634, 637 (2019).

120 The roster and breakdown of the justices in the *Employment Division v. Smith* case was as follows:

> SCALIA, J., delivered the opinion of the Court, in which REHNQUIST, C.J., and WHITE, STEVENS, and KENNEDY, JJ., joined. O'CONNOR, J., filed an opinion concurring in the judgment, in Parts I and II of which BRENNAN,

MARSHALL, and BLACKMUN, JJ., joined without concurring in the judgment. BLACKMUN, J., filed a dissenting opinion, in which BRENNAN and MARSHALL, JJ., joined.

121　*See, e.g.,* William P. Marshall, *The Case against Constitutionally Compelled Free Exercise Exemptions,* 40 Cas. W. Res. L. Rev. 357 (1989).

122　*Cutter v. Wilkinson,* 544 U.S. at 722–24.

123　It is rare, but not unprecedented, for free exercise claims to be found to be insincere. *See, e.g.,* Frederick Mark Gedicks, *"Substantial" Burdens: How Courts May (and Why They Must) Judge Burdens on Religion under RFRA,* 85 Geo. Wash. L. Rev. 94 (2017). Public servants should never assume that such claims are insincere.

124　*Cutter v. Wilkinson,* 544 U.S. at 720.

125　*Id.* at 722.

126　*See, e.g., Thornton v. Caldor,* 472 U.S. 703. *See generally* Micah Schwartzman, Nelson Tebbe, and Richard Schragger, *The Costs of Conscience,* University of Virginia School of Law Research Paper No. 2018–14, Cornell Law School Research Paper No. 18–35 (2018). *See also* Christopher C. Lund, *Religious Exemptions, Third-Party Harms, and the Establishment Clause,* 91 Notre Dame L. Rev. 1375 (2016).

127　*See* Schwartzman, Tebbe, and Schragger, *Costs of Conscience* at 903-06. Professor Tebbe seeks to distinguish this case by arguing, for example, that draftees may be ineligible for any number of reasons, including health and student status. Thus, "[f]or any particular draftee, it may be impossible to draw a causal connection between being sent to the battlefield and another citizen's conscientious objection." *Id.* at 904.

128　*See below* at chap. 9.

129　*See* Lund, *Religious Exemptions,* 91 Notre Dame L. Rev. at 1379–80.

130　*See generally id.*; Berg, *Religious Exemptions*; Schwartzman, Tebbe, and Schragger, *Costs of Conscience*; Frederick Mark Gedicks and Rebecca G. Van Tassell, *Of Burdens and Baselines: Hobby Lobby's Puzzling Footnote 37,* in Schwartzman, Flanders, and Robinson, *Rise of Corporate Religious Liberty.*

131　*See* Gedicks and Van Tassell, *Of Burdens and Baselines,* in Schwartzman, Flanders, and Robinson, *Rise of Corporate Religious Liberty* at 332–36.

132　As Professor Fred Gedicks and Rebecca Van Tassel explain:

> The proper baseline for measuring third-party burdens by permissive accommodations in the for-profit workplace can only be the distribution of workplace burdens and benefits immediately preceding the accommodation. There is no waiting period before the loss of government entitlements and protections "vests" as a burden, harm, or cost.

Id. at 336.

133　Some other free exercise tests, like those in some state RFRAs, also ask whether there is such a substantial burden.

134　Professor Gedicks explains:

> RFRA's "substantial burden" element is commonly disaggregated into two conceptual parts: (1) the suffering of "substantial *religious* costs" if the claimant complies with the burdensome law, and (2) the suffering of "substantial *secular* costs" if the claimant violates it. Courts may properly adjudicate the question of "secular costs"—that is, whether the legal sanctions for disobeying a burdensome law are "substantial." The Supreme Court held in *Burwell v. Hobby Lobby Stores, Inc.,* however, that judicial review of the substantiality of "religious costs" is precluded

by the Court's "religious-question" doctrine, which bars courts from adjudicating issues of theology, doctrine, or belief. Courts may adjudicate whether claimants are "sincere" in alleging religious costs, whether they honestly believe a law interferes with religious practice, but courts may not rule on the substantiality of those costs.

Courts and commentators are divided over the correctness and wisdom of this limitation on judicial review.

Gedicks, *"Substantial" Burdens*, 85 Geo. Wash. L. Rev. at 96–97 (quoting Ira C. Lupu and Robert W. Tuttle, *Secular Government, Religious People* (Grand Rapids: Wm. B. Eerdmans 2014) 241–42).

135 *Id.* at 98.
136 *Id.* at 96–97.
137 *See id. See also* Brief of the Baptist Joint Committee for Religious Liberty as *Amicus Curiae* in Support of Respondents, *Zubik v. Burwell*, United States Supreme Court (February 15, 2016) (citing primary sources), http://www.scotusblog.com/wp-content/uploads/2016/02/Zubik-BJC-Amicus-Final.pdf.
138 Gedicks, *"Substantial" Burdens*, 85 Geo. Wash. L. Rev. at 117–22 (citing primary sources).
139 Brief of the Baptist Joint Committee for Religious Liberty as *Amicus Curiae* in Support of Respondents, *Zubik v. Burwell*, at 1, 8–12.
140 *Id.* at 16–17 (citing 42 U.S.C. Section 2000bb(a)(5)).
141 Douglas Laycock, *How the Little Sisters of the Poor Case Puts Religious Liberty at Risk*, The Washington Post (March 20, 2016). Professor Laycock says:

Only the believer can say what is a substantial burden religiously. But courts must say what is a substantial burden legally. Believers should get substantial deference on that question, but they cannot get absolute deference, and they never have. Courts decide the cases and set the outer boundaries.

Another wrongheaded notion is that the government violates the Free Exercise Clause if it does not exempt all organizations that have religious objections from laws and policies whenever the government exempts houses of worship. This approach could have the perverse effect of actually discouraging the government from exempting churches and other houses of worship from certain legal obligations. *See* Laycock, *How the Little Sisters of the Poor*. Professor Laycock says:

This argument is a mortal threat to an essential and widespread source of protection for religious liberty. There are thousands of specific religious exemptions in U.S. law. If legislators and administrative agencies cannot enact a narrow religious exemption without it being expanded to become all-inclusive, many of them will not enact any religious exemptions at all. And they will start repealing the exemptions they have already enacted.

Id. See also Brief of the Baptist Joint Committee for Religious Liberty as *Amicus Curiae* in Support of Respondents, *Zubik v. Burwell*.

142 *See generally id.* As Professor Gedicks has explained, reserving room for a legal evaluation of the substantiality of a burden on religious exercise in many cases is not inconsistent with the Supreme Court's holding in the *Hobby Lobby* case. Gedicks, *"Substantial" Burdens*, 85 Geo. Wash. L. Rev. at 149 ("*Hobby Lobby* left courts free to measure the substantiality of religious costs without violating the religious-question doctrine when the claimant is not as directly involved in the religiously objectionable conduct as the claimants would have been in *Hobby Lobby*, so long as they do so by reference to relevant secular law.").

143 *Id.* at 115.

144 *Id.* at 115–17.

145 *Id.* at 149–50.

146 42 U.S.C. Section 2000bb(a)(5) & 2000bb(b)(1)(2019); *The Religious Freedom Restoration Act*, Hearing before the Committee on the Judiciary of the United States Senate, 102nd Congress (Second Session) on S. 2969, *A Bill to Protect the Free Exercise of Religion*, Senate Hearing 102–1076 (September 18, 1992) (Washington, D.C.: U.S. Government Printing Office 1993) at 2, https://www.justice.gov/sites/default/files/jmd/legacy/2014/02/13/hear-j-102-82-1992.pdf (Senator Kennedy states that RFRA "simply restores the long-established standard of review that had worked well for many years and that requires courts to weigh free exercise claims against the compelling State interest standard."). *See also* Lederman, *Reconstructing RFRA*, 428–41 (2016) (citing primary sources).

147 42 U.S.C. Section 2000bb(a)(5) (2019). *See also* Lederman, *Reconstructing RFRA*, 428–41 (2016) (citing primary sources).

148 *See above* at Recommendation 3.

149 *See, e.g., Burwell v. Hobby Lobby*, 573 U.S. 682, 729 n.37 (2015) ("It is certainly true that in applying RFRA 'courts must take adequate account of the burdens a requested accommodation may impose on nonbeneficiaries.'"); *United States v. Lee*, 455 U.S. at 257–61; *Thornton v. Caldor*, 472 U.S. 703, 708-10.

150 42 U.S.C. Section 2000bb-1(b)(2) (2019).

151 *See, e.g.,* Lederman, *Reconstructing RFRA*, 433–41; Andrew Koppelman and Frederick M. Gedicks, *Is Hobby Lobby Worse for Religious Liberty than Smith?* 9 U. St. Thomas J. L. & Pub. Pol'y 223 (2015).

152 42 U.S.C. Section 2000bb(a)(5) (2019).

153 For a thoughtful and measured discussion of some of the problematic aspects of the Court's opinion in *Burwell v. Hobby Lobby*, see Alan Brownstein, *Hobby Lobby: A Unnecessarily Broad Opinion*, Religious Freedom Institute (June 30, 2016), https://www.religiousfreedominstitute.org/cornerstone/2016/6/30/hobby-lobby-a-unnecessarily-broad-opinion.

154 Department of Labor, *Implementing Legal Requirements Regarding the Equal Opportunity Clause's Religious Exemption*, Notice of Proposed Rulemaking, 84 Fed. Reg. 41677 (August 15, 2019). *See also* Directive on Executive Order 11246 Section 204(c), Religious Exemption, Department of Labor Office of Federal Contract Compliance Programs (OFCCP) (August 10, 2018), https://www.dol.gov/ofccp/regs/compliance/directives/Dir2018-03-ESQA508c.pdf. *See above* chap. 6 and introduction.

155 *Burwell v. Hobby Lobby*, 573 U.S. 682, 693 ("The effect of the HHS-created accommodation on the women employed by Hobby Lobby and the other companies involved in these cases would be precisely zero."); *Id.* at 739 (Kennedy, J., concurring) (accommodations for religious exercise may not "unduly restrict other persons, such as employees, in protecting their own interests, interests the law deems compelling.").

156 Berg, *Religious Exemptions*.

157 *Id.*

158 *See Burwell v. Hobby Lobby*, 573 U.S. 682 (ruling under RFRA that closely held businesses with religious objections to Affordable Care Act's contraception mandate must be permitted to access the accommodation provided for religious organizations).

159 Closely held businesses are not necessarily small businesses. *See* Kiel Brennan-Marquez, *A Business Can Exercise Religion, but Hobby Lobby Still Gets It Wrong*, Boston Review (July

7, 2014). *See also* James David Nelson, *Conscience, Incorporated*, 2013 Mich. St. L. Rev. 1565 (2013), https://papers.ssrn.com/sol3/papers.cfm?abstract_id=2247051. *See generally* Schwartzman, Tebbe, and Schragger, *Costs of Conscience*; Lund, *Religious Exemptions*, 91 Notre Dame L. Rev. 1375.

160 *Masterpiece Cakeshop, Ltd. v. Colorado Civil Rights Comm'n*, 584 U.S.___, 138 S. Ct. at 1734 (Kagan, J., concurring).

161 Transcript of Oral Argument before the United States Supreme Court in *Masterpiece Cakeshop, Ltd. v. Colorado Civil Rights Commission* (December 7, 2017) at 32; *see also* Amicus Brief of the General Synod of the United Church of Christ *et al.* in *Masterpiece Cakeshop, Ltd. v. Colorado Civil Rights Commission*, https://www.scotusblog.com/wp -content/uploads/2017/11/16-111_bsac_general-synod-of-the-unitedchurchofchrist.pdf.

162 138 S Ct. at 1723. The Court said:

> One of the difficulties in this case is that the parties disagree as to the extent of the baker's refusal to provide service. If a baker refused to design a special cake with words or images celebrating the marriage—for instance, a cake showing words with religious meaning—that might be different from a refusal to sell any cake at all. In defining whether a baker's creation can be protected, these details might make a difference.
>
> The same difficulties arise in determining whether a baker has a valid free exercise claim. A baker's refusal to attend the wedding to ensure that the cake is cut the right way, or a refusal to put certain religious words or decorations on the cake, or even a refusal to sell a cake that has been baked for the public generally but includes certain religious words or symbols on it are just three examples of possibilities that seem all but endless.

Id. Professors Dale Carpenter and Eugene Volokh have said that cases involving wedding musicians and photographers who object to participating in same-sex wedding ceremonies merit different treatment under the First Amendment's Free Speech Clause because the work of these service providers fits neatly into categories the Court has already recognized to be expressive. *See Masterpiece Cakeshop, Ltd. v. Colorado Civil Rights Commission*, Brief of American Unity Fund and Profs. Dale Carpenter and Eugene Volokh as Amici Curiae in Support of Respondents, http://www.scotusblog.com/wp-content/uploads/2017/11/ 16-111_bsac_american_unity_fund.pdf. Also, these scholars have noted:

> To be sure, cakes often do convey messages in the writing or graphics on the cake itself. Cake-makers might indeed have a First Amendment right to decline to include such written or graphic messages on a cake. The cake itself, though intended for use in a ceremony, is not itself generally expressive of any message (other than perhaps the fact that "this cake is intended for use in this ceremony").

Id. at 10.

163 *See also* Melissa Rogers, *Religious Freedom and the Federal Executive Branch: Suggestions for Future Administrations*, 15 St. Thomas L. Jnl. 703 (2019).

Chapter 9: Faith and the Workplace

1 *See Equal Employment Opportunity Commission v. Abercrombie & Fitch*, 575 U.S. __ , 135 S. Ct. 2028 (2015).

2 *Equal Employment Opportunity Commission v. Abercrombie & Fitch*, 798 F. Supp. 2d 1272 (N.D. Okla. 2011).

3   *Id.* at 1275.
4   *Id.* at 1272–79.
5   *Id.*
6   42 U.S.C. Section 2000e (2019).
7   Adam Liptak, *Muslim Woman Denied Job over Head Scarf Wins in Supreme Court,* The New York Times (June 1, 2015).
8   *Equal Employment Opportunity Commission v. Abercrombie & Fitch,* 575 U.S. ___, 135 S. Ct. at 2033.
9   *Id.* at 2031, 2032 (citing 42 U.S.C. 2000e-2(m), which states: "Except as otherwise provided in this subchapter, an unlawful employment practice is established when the complaining party demonstrates that race, color, religion, sex, or national origin was a motivating factor for any employment practice, even though other factors also motivated the practice.").
10 *Id.* at 2034.
11 *Id.*
12 Court of Justice, *Samira Achbita v. G4S Secure Solutions,* Case C-157/1 (March 14, 2017), http://curia.europa.eu/juris/document/document.jsf?text=&docid=179082&pageIndex= 0&doclang=EN&mode=lst&dir=&occ=first&part=1&cid=678370.
13 *Id.*
14 *Id.*
15 42 U.S.C. Section 2000e *et seq.* (2019).
16 EEOC, *Fact Sheet on Religious Garb and Grooming in the Workplace,* https://www.eeoc .gov/eeoc/publications/fs_religious_garb_grooming.cfm.
17 *Id.*
18 *See* Wake Forest, *Religious Expression.*
19 *Guidelines on Religious Expression and Religious Exercise in the Federal Workplace,* The White House (August 14, 1997), https://clintonwhitehouse2.archives.gov/WH/New/ html/19970819-3275.html.
20 *Id.*
21 *Id.*
22 42 U.S.C. Section 2000e(j) (2019).
23 Requests for accommodation may include requests for time off for religious observance or approval of shift swaps. Employees may seek exceptions from company garb or grooming policies or requirements for participation in certain work activities. Workers may ask if they can use workspace for prayer. EEOC, *Questions and Answers: Religious Discrimination in the Workplace,* https://www.eeoc.gov//policy/docs/qanda_religion.html (last modified January 31, 2011).
24 *Trans World Airlines v. Hardison,* 432 U.S. 63, 75 (1977).
25 *Id.* at 69.
26 *Id.* at 84.
27 *Id.* The Court said that the duty to accommodate religious practices does not take precedence over collective-bargaining contracts and the seniority system. *Id.* at 79. Title VII does not require an employer to "deny the shift and job preference of some employees, as well as deprive them of their contractual rights, in order to accommodate or prefer the religious needs of others . . . ." *Id.* at 81. Absent discriminatory intent, the Court said, "the operation of a seniority system cannot be an unlawful employment practice even if the system has some discriminatory consequences." *Id.* at 82.
28 *Id.* at 86–87 (Marshall, J., dissenting).
29 *Id.* at 88.

30   *Id.* at 87.

31   *Id.* at 95–96.

32   William J. Clinton, *Memorandum on Religious Exercise and Religious Expression in the Federal Workplace*, U.S. Government Publishing Office (August 14, 1997), https://www .govinfo.gov/content/pkg/PPP-1997-book2/pdf/PPP-1997-book2-doc-pg1104.pdf; *Religious Expression in Federal Offices*, C-SPAN (August 14, 1997), https://www.c-span.org/ video/?89280-1/religious-expression-federal-offices.

33   *Guidelines on Religious Expression and Religious Exercise in the Federal Workplace*, The White House (August 14, 1997), https://clintonwhitehouse2.archives.gov/WH/New/ html/19970819-3275.html (quoting *Ansonia Board of Education v. Philbrook*, 479 U.S. 60, 71 (1986)).

34   *Id. See also Ansonia Board of Education v. Philbrook*, 479 U.S. 60.

35   EEOC, *Questions and Answers: Religious Discrimination in the Workplace*, https://www .eeoc.gov//policy/docs/qanda_religion.html (last modified January 31, 2011).

36   *See* Senator John Kerry, *Workplace Religious Freedom Act of 2013* (S. 3686) (December 17, 2012), https://www.govtrack.us/congress/bills/112/s3686; Lauren E. Bohn, *Workplace Religious Freedom Bill Finds Revived Interest*, Religion News Service (July 3, 2010). An accommodation is not reasonable, according to the bill, unless it removes the conflict between the workplace practice and the religious observance. *Id.*

37   42 U.S.C. Section 2000e-1(a) states:

> This subchapter shall not apply to an employer with respect to the employment of aliens outside any State, or to a religious corporation, association, educational institution, or society with respect to the employment of individuals of a particular religion to perform work connected with the carrying on by such corporation, association, educational institution, or society of its activities.

38   Michael Wolf, Bruce Friedman, and Daniel Sutherland, *Religion in the Workplace: A Comprehensive Guide to Legal Rights and Responsibilities* (Chicago: American Bar Association 2008) 20.

39   42 U.S.C Section 2000e-2(e) (2) (2019) states:

> [I]t shall not be an unlawful employment practice for a school, college, university, or other educational institution or institution of learning to hire and employ employees of a particular religion if such school, college, university, or other educational institution or institution of learning is, in whole or in substantial part, owned, supported, controlled, or managed by a particular religion or by a particular religious corporation, association, or society, or if the curriculum of such school, college, university, or other educational institution or institution of learning is directed toward the propagation of a particular religion.

Further, Title VII contains a religious exemption that can be claimed by *any* employer, not just religious employers, but it is extremely narrow. The statute allows employers to prefer employees of a particular religion if religion is a bona fide occupational qualification. 42 U.S.C. Section 2000e-2(e) (1) (2019) states:

> Notwithstanding any other provision of this subchapter, (1) it shall not be an unlawful employment practice for an employer to hire and employ employees, for an employment agency to classify, or refer for employment any individual, for a labor organization to classify its membership or to classify or refer for employment any individual, or for an employer, labor organization, or joint labor-management committee controlling apprenticeship or other training or retraining programs to

admit or employ any individual in any such program, on the basis of his religion, sex, or national origin in those certain instances where religion, sex, or national origin is a bona fide occupational qualification reasonably necessary to the normal operation of that particular business or enterprise . . . .

Called the "BFOQ" exception, this exception is rarely claimed by employers, and it is even more rare for courts to hold that the exemption is properly invoked. *See* Wolf, Friedman, and Sutherland, *Religion in the Workplace* at 23–26. A lower court has recognized, for example, that the BFOQ exception allows a university that did not qualify for a religious exemption but had historical roots as a Jesuit institution to consider only Jesuits for several positions within the school's philosophy department. *Id.* at 24–25.

40 *See* Rogers, *Federal Funding and Religion-Based Employment Decisions*, in Ryden and Polet, *Sanctioning Religion?* at 108–9.

41 *Id.*

42 *Id.*

43 *Id.*

44 *Corporation of Presiding Bishop v. Amos*, 483 U.S. 327.

45 Mayson did not contest the assertion that the entities that ran the gym—the Corporation of the Presiding Bishop of the LDS Church and the Corporation of the President of the LDS Church—were religious organizations for purposes of Title VII's 702 religious exemption. *Id.* at 330.

46 *Amos v. Corporation of Presiding Bishop*, 594 F. Supp. 791, 802 (D. Utah 1984) ("Specifically, the plaintiff's duties included the following. He had to maintain the swimming pools and chlorinating equipment, the whirlpools, exercise machines, athletic equipment, locks and lockers, electric motors, air compressors, air conditioners, furnaces, washer and dryer, showers and other plumbing and the electrical system. In addition, he was responsible for ordering the custodial and certain other supplies.").

47 *Corporation of Presiding Bishop*, 483 U.S. at 330 n.4.

48 In their various opinions, Justices Brennan, Marshall, Blackmun, and O'Connor concurred only in the judgment in this case. *Id.* at 340, 346.

49 *Id.* at 334.

50 *Id.* at 336–37.

51 *Id.* at 337.

52 *Id.* at 339.

53 *Id.* at n.17. The Court also did not address the question of whether the Constitution requires or permits the government to allow religious organizations to make religion-based employment decisions regarding government-funded jobs. The case did not raise this issue, as there was no suggestion that the LDS organization received any financial assistance from the state. *See* Rogers, *Federal Funding and Religion-Based Employment Decisions*, in Ryden and Polet, *Sanctioning Religion?* at 111–13.

54 *Corporation of Presiding Bishop v. Amos*, 483 U.S. at 349 (O'Connor, J., concurring in the judgment).

55 *See* EEOC, *Questions and Answers: Religious Discrimination in the Workplace.*

56 *See, e.g., Hall v. Baptist Memorial Health Care Corp.*, 27 F. Supp. 2d 1029 (W.D. Tenn. 1998); *LeBoon v. Lancaster Jewish Community Center Ass'n*, 503 F.3d 217 (3d Cir. 2007); *Spencer v. World Vision*, F.3d (9th Cir. 2010).

57 *See, e.g., Equal Employment Opportunity Commission v. Kamehameha Schools/Bishop Estate*, 990 F.2d 458 (9th Cir. 1993); *Fike v. United Methodist Children's Home*, 547 F. Supp. 286 (E.D. Va. 1982).

58   *See Equal Employment Opportunity Commission v. Townley Engineering & Manufacturing Company*, 859 F.2d 610 (9th Cir. 1988).

59   *Id.* at 619.

60   *Curay-Cramer v. Ursuline Academy*, 450 F.3d 130 (3d Cir. 2006).

61   *See, e.g., Little v. Wuerl*, 929 F.2d 944 (3d Cir. 1991).

62   *Id.*

63   *Id.* at 946.

64   *Id.* at 951.

65   *Id* at 948–51.

66   *See, e.g.,* Wolf, Friedman, and Sutherland, *Religion in the Workplace* at 223–30; EEOC, *Questions and Answers: Religious Discrimination in the Workplace*; *Rayburn v. General Conference of Seventh-day Adventists*, 772 F.2d 1164, 1166 (4th Cir. 1985) ("While the language of [Section] 702 makes clear that religious institutions may base relevant hiring decisions upon religious preferences, Title VII does not confer upon religious organizations a license to make those same decisions on the basis of race, sex, or national origin") (citations omitted). A federal district court addressed the question in the following way:

> [Religious employers] argue that whether or not plaintiff's pregnancy was the precipitating event which led to her termination, the underlying decision to fire plaintiff was a *religious* one, based upon a widely recognized and sincerely held belief that extramarital sex is a sin. Firing her, therefore, does not implicate Title VII, or at the very least falls within the exception to Title VII for religious organizations.
>
> However, it is clear that Title VII *generally* applies when a wom[a]n has been terminated for pregnancy, regardless of the *reason* put forth by the employer as to why that pregnancy justifies termination.

    Vigars v. Valley Christian Center, 805 F. Supp. 802, 806 (N.D. Ca. 1992).

67   Wolf, Friedman, and Sutherland, *Religion in the Workplace* at 19; note that in *EEOC v. Pacific Press Publishing Association*, the Ninth Circuit Court of Appeals held that a religious publishing house violated an employee's rights under Title VII when it denied her monetary allowances that it paid to similarly situated male employees. 676 F.2d 1272 (1981). In that case, the Ninth Circuit also found that such a holding did not infringe on the religious body's free exercise rights because the body said it did not believe in discriminating against women or minority groups. *Id.* at 1279. The religious publishing house had argued that (1) Title VII did not apply to the house and (2) if Title VII did apply, that application violated the First Amendment's religion clauses. The Ninth Circuit rejected both arguments. *Id.* at 1278–83.

68   *See Curay-Cramer v. Ursuline Academy*, 450 F.3d at 141. The Third Circuit explained its reasoning on this point:

> [W]e agree with the District Court's determination that applying the [Pregnancy Discrimination Act] and Title VII raises a substantial constitutional question under the First Amendment's Religion Clauses. Curay-Cramer contends that she was fired because she is a woman and that similarly situated male employees have been treated less harshly for substantially similar conduct. In order to assess this claim of the relative harshness of penalties for "similar conduct," we would have to measure the degree of severity of various violations of Church doctrine.
>
> In determining whether there is a substantial constitutional question, we are guided by the Supreme Court's analytical framework in *Catholic Bishop*, 440 U.S. at 490, 99 S. Ct. 1313. In *Catholic Bishop*, the Supreme Court was faced with the question

whether the National Labor Relations Act should be read to grant the National Labor Relations Board jurisdiction over religious schools. 440 U.S. 490, 99 S. Ct. 1313, 59 L.Ed.2d 533 (1979). In holding that the statute did not confer such jurisdiction, the Court set forth an analytical process to determine whether a statute presents "a significant risk that the First Amendment will be infringed." *Id.* at 502, 99 S. Ct. 1313. First, a court must determine whether applying the statute raises "serious constitutional questions." *Id.* at 501, 99 S. Ct. 1313. Second, if it does, a court must discern whether there is a "clear expression of an affirmative intention" on the part of Congress to have the act apply in the situation presented. *Id.* at 504, 99 S. Ct. 1313. Finally, if such an affirmative intention is shown, the court will determine whether the statute violates the Constitution as applied to the facts presented in the case. *Id.* at 507, 99 S. Ct. 1313. The purpose of this test is to avoid addressing constitutional questions absent clear legislative intent to apply the statute in a way that raises a significant risk of infringing constitutional rights. *Geary*, 7 F.3d at 324.

Id. at 137–38 (citations omitted).

69 Curay-Cramer also claimed that her termination violated the Pregnancy Nondiscrimination Act. The court assumed, without deciding, that Curay-Cramer had a colorable claim under this act, but it rejected her claim: "We conclude that Curay-Cramer did not engage in protected activity when she signed a pro-choice advertisement that did not mention employment, employers, pregnancy discrimination, or even gender discrimination." *Id.* at 134.

70 *Id.* at 137–42.

71 *Id.* at 140.

72 *Id.* at 141.

73 *Id.* at 142.

74 *Hosanna-Tabor Evangelical Lutheran Church and School v. Equal Employment Opportunity Commission*, 565 U.S. 171.

75 *Id.* at 177.

76 *Id.* at 181.

77 The Court also noted:

Perich continues to seek frontpay in lieu of reinstatement, backpay, compensatory and punitive damages, and attorney's fees. An award of such relief would operate as a penalty on the Church for terminating an unwanted minister, and would be no less prohibited by the First Amendment than an order overturning the termination. Such relief would depend on a determination that Hosanna-Tabor was wrong to have relieved Perich of her position, and it is precisely such a ruling that is barred by the ministerial exception.

Id. at 194.

78 *Id.*

79 *Id.* at 196.

80 *Id.*

81 *Id.*

82 *See* Alex Vandermaas-Peeler, Daniel Cox, Maxine Najile, and Molly Fisch-Friedman, *Wedding Cakes, Same-Sex Marriage and the Future of LGBT Rights in America*, Public Religion Research Institute (August 2, 2018), https://www.prri.org/research/wedding-cakes-same-sex-lgbt-marriage/ (71 percent of Americans support laws that would protect LGBT people from discrimination in jobs, housing, and public accommodations). Views on these issues have not shifted significantly in the last few years, PRRI says. *Id.*

83 Erik S. Thompson, *Compromising Equality: An Analysis of the Religious Exemption in the Employment Non-Discrimination Act and Its Impact on LGBT Workers*, 35 B.C.J.L. & Soc. Just. 285 (2015).

84 42 U.S.C. Section 2000ee *et seq.*

85 Erik S. Thompson, *Compromising Equality: An Analysis of the Religious Exemption in the Employment Non-Discrimination Act and Its Impact on LGBT Workers*, 35 B.C.J.L. & Soc. Just. 285 (2015).

86 Dena Sher and Ian Thompson, *Why ENDA's Religious Exemption Must Be Narrowed*, American Civil Liberties Union (April 30, 2013), https://www.aclu.org/blog/lgbt-rights/why-endas-religious-exemption-must-be-narrowed.

87 *Id.*

88 *See* The United States Conference of Catholic Bishops, *Questions and Answers about the Employment Non-Discrimination Act*, http://www.usccb.org/issues-and-action/human-life-and-dignity/labor-employment/upload/enda-backgrounder-2013.pdf. This publication states:

> 9. Does ENDA threaten religious liberty?
>
> Yes. Except for a relatively narrow subset of religious employers, ENDA provides no religious liberty protection of any kind for any stakeholder. Thus, for-profit employers, nonprofit employers having no religious affiliation, solely-owned and closely-held businesses, and even some religious employers would be subject to ENDA, even if they have a religious or moral objection to same-sex sexual behavior, or to the provision of fringe benefits to persons based on their having a sexual relationship with their employees outside of a marriage between a man and a woman. In addition, ENDA does not protect the speech or religious convictions of employers and co-workers on matters of sexual ethics and sexual identity.

Id.

89 Another way in which prohibitions on LGBT discrimination in employment (and other venues) might be instituted is through court decisions interpreting existing statutory prohibitions on gender discrimination to encompass discrimination based on sexual orientation or gender identity. *See below* at n.92.

90 *See below* at chap. 7.

91 Compare the Equality Act (H.R. 2282) (2017), https://www.govtrack.us/congress/bills/115/hr2282 (2017); with a proposal called Fairness for All, Council of Christian Colleges and Universities (Spring 2017), https://www.cccu.org/magazine/fairness-for-all/. *See also Senator Lee Introduces the First Amendment Defense Act*, Office of Senator Mike Lee (March 8, 2018), https://www.lee.senate.gov/public/index.cfm/2018/3/sen-lee-introduces-first-amendment-defense-act; the First Amendment Defense Act (S. 2525)(2018), https://www.congress.gov/115/bills/s2525/BILLS-115s2525is.pdf.

In 2015, the Obama administration announced its support for a version of the Equality Act that had been introduced in Congress, while also noting that it "look[ed] forward to working with Congress to ensure that the legislative process produces a result that balances both the bedrock principles of civil rights … with the religious liberty that we hold dear in this country." Juliet Eilperin, *Obama Supports Altering Civil Rights Act to Ban LGBT Discrimination*, The Washington Post (November 10, 2015). This Washington Post report said:

> The White House endorsed legislation Tuesday that would amend the 1964 Civil Rights Act to ban discrimination on the basis of sexual orientation or gender identity.

White House press secretary Josh Earnest said the Obama administration had been reviewing the bill "for several weeks."

"Upon that review it is now clear that the administration strongly supports the Equality Act," he said. "That bill is historic legislation that would advance the cause of equality for millions of Americans.

"We look forward to working with Congress to ensure that the legislative process produces a result that balances both the bedrock principles of civil rights ... with the religious liberty that we hold dear in this country," Earnest added.

> *Id.*

92   *See* Amy Howe, *Court to Take Up LGBT Rights in the Workplace* (updated), Scotusblog (April 22, 2019).

93   *See* Melissa Rogers, *The Court Has Spoken. Now What? Hosanna-Tabor Evangelical Lutheran Church and School v. Equal Employment Opportunity Commission,* Sojourners (February 14, 2012).

94   *See, e.g., Trans World Airlines v. Hardison,* 432 U.S. 63 (Marshall, J., dissenting).

95   *See* Kerry, *Workplace Religious Freedom Act of 2013;* Bohn, *Workplace Religious Freedom Bill.*

Chapter 10: Religious Discrimination and Hate Crimes

1   Moses Seixas, *George Washington's Mount Vernon,* http://www.mountvernon.org/digital-encyclopedia/article/moses-seixas/.

2   *Id.*

3   Patrick Glass, *Rhode Island Ratifies Constitution, May 29, 1790,* Politico (May 29, 2014).

4   Seixas, *George Washington's Mount Vernon.*

5   *Id.*

6   *Id.*

7   *Town of Greece v. Galloway,* 572 U.S. at 637 (Kagan, J., dissenting).

8   *From George Washington to the Hebrew Congregation in Newport, Rhode Island, 18 August 1790,* Founders Online, National Archives, http://founders.archives.gov/documents/Washington/05-06-02-0135 (last modified February 1, 2018). (Original source: *The Papers of George Washington,* Presidential Series, vol. 6, *1 July 1790–30 November 1790,* ed. Mark A. Mastromarino (Charlottesville: University Press of Virginia 1996) 284–86.)

9   Roxanne Dunbar-Ortiz, *An Indigenous Peoples' History of the United States* (Boston: Beacon 2014) 107–14; *see also* Tisa Wenger, *Religious Freedom: The Contested History of an American Ideal* (Chapel Hill: University of North Carolina Press 2017) at 101–42.

10   Dunbar-Ortiz, *An Indigenous Peoples' History of the United States* at 112.

11   *Id.* at 113.

12   *Id.*

13   *See* Smith, *Religion in the Oval Office* at 148–55.

14   As Professor Angela R. Riley has noted: "A vast body of scholarship has detailed the wrongs committed against Indian people: broken treaties, land dispossession, genocide, disease, bounties placed on Indian 'skins,' abusive boarding schools, religious persecution, denial of voting rights, and removal of Indian children from Indian homes (among other things) were all promoted by American law and policy." Riley, *Native Nations and the Constitution: An Inquiry into "Extra-Constitutionality,"* 130 Harv. L. Rev. Forum 173, 180–81 (2017).

15   *See, e.g.,* Joel W. Martin, *Native American Religion* (New York: Oxford University Press 1999).

16   Brief of Scholars of Mormon History & Law as *Amici Curiae* in Support of Neither Party, *Trump v. Hawaii* (March 2018) at 6, https://www.supremecourt.gov/DocketPDF/17/ 17-965/38276/20180308221409148_Mormon%20Scholars%20Amici%20Brief%20-%20Hawaii%20v%20Trump%202018.pdf.

17   *Id.* at 6–7.

18   *Id.* at 9–13.

19   Brief *Amicus Curiae* of the United States Conference of Catholic Bishops, Catholic Charities, USA, Catholic Legal Immigration Network, Inc. in Support of Respondents (March 30, 2018) at 15, https://www.supremecourt.gov/DocketPDF/17/17-965/41839/ 20180330170127467_No.%2017-965%20Amicus%20Brief%20ISO%20Respondents %20Final.pdf.

20   *Id.* at 17.

21   *See, e.g.,* Linda Gordon, *The Second Coming of the KKK: The Ku Klux Klan of the 1920s and the American Political Tradition* chap. 8 (New York: W. W. Norton 2017).

22   *Id.*

23   *Id.*; *Pierce v. Society of Sisters*, 268 U.S. 510 (1925).

24   42 U.S.C. Section 1996 *et seq.* (2019).

25   These laws are usually based on the Constitution's clause giving Congress the power to regulate interstate commerce. U.S. Const., Art. 1, Sec. 8, Cl. 3.

26   *From George Washington to the Hebrew Congregation in Newport, Rhode Island, 18 August 1790.* President Washington's remarks drew on the following verses from the book of Micah:

> But in the last days it shall come to pass, that the mountain of the house of the Lord shall be established in the top of the mountains, and it shall be exalted above the hills; and people shall flow unto it.
>
> And many nations shall come, and say, Come, and let us go up to the mountain of the Lord, and to the house of the God of Jacob; and he will teach us of his ways, and we will walk in his paths: for the law shall go forth of Zion, and the word of the Lord from Jerusalem.
>
> And he shall judge among many people, and rebuke strong nations afar off; and they shall beat their swords into plowshares, and their spears into pruninghooks: nation shall not lift up a sword against nation, neither shall they learn war any more.
>
> But they shall sit every man under his vine and under his fig tree; and none shall make them afraid: for the mouth of the Lord of hosts hath spoken it.

Micah 4:1–4 (King James Version).

27   *See, e.g., Church of the Lukumi Babalu Aye v. City of Hialeah*, 508 U.S. 520; *Larson v. Valente*, 456 U.S. at 244 ("The clearest command of the Establishment Clause is that one religious denomination cannot be officially preferred over another.").

28   *Church of the Lukumi Babalu Aye v. City of Hialeah*, 508 U.S. at 532.

29   *Id.*

30   "The principle that government may not enact laws that suppress religious belief or practice is so well understood that few violations are recorded in our opinions," the Court has said. *Id.* at 523.

31   Beliefs of Jehovah's Witnesses, http://thejehovahswitnesses.org/flag.php.

32   *Id.* Jehovah's Witnesses cite the following Bible verses for their beliefs:

> Thou shalt not make unto thee any graven image, or any likeness of any thing that is in heaven above, or that is in the earth beneath, or that is in the water under the earth.

> Thou shalt not bow down thyself to them, nor serve them: for I the LORD thy God am a jealous God, visiting the iniquity of the fathers upon the children unto the third and fourth generation of them that hate me.

Exod 20:4-5 (KJV).

33   The Pew Research Center has found that .8 percent of Christians in the United States are Jehovah's Witnesses. *See* Pew Research Center: Religion and Public Life, *Religious Landscape Study*, http://www.pewforum.org/religious-landscape-study/#religions.

34   *Minersville School District v. Gobitis*, 310 U.S. 586 (1940).

35   *Id.*

36   *Id.*

37   319 U.S. 624 (1943).

38   *Id.* at 638.

39   *Niemotko v. Maryland*, 340 U.S. 268 (1951).

40   *Niemotko v. State*, 194 Md. 247, 251 (Md. Ct App. 1950).

41   *Id.*

42   *Niemotko v. Maryland*, 340 U.S. at 268.

43   *Id.* at 272.

44   *Id.* at 272–73.

45   *Id.* at 273. *See also Fowler v. Rhode Island*, 345 U.S. 67 (1953).

46   *Church of the Lukumi Babalu Aye v. City of Hialeah*, 508 U.S. 520, 524.

47   *Id.*; *Church of the Lukumi Babalu Aye v. City of Hialeah*, 723 F. Supp. 1467, 1469–71 (S.D. Fl. 1989).

48   *Church of the Lukumi Babalu Aye v. City of Hialeah*, 723 F. Supp. at 1469.

49   *Id.* at 1469–70.

50   *Id.* at 1470–71.

51   *Church of the Lukumi Babalu Aye v. City of Hialeah*, 508 U.S. at 525 (citations omitted).

52   *Id.*

53   *Id.* at 526.

54   *Id.* at 526–27.

55   *Id.* at 527–28.

56   *Id.* at 541–42 (citations omitted). Justice Kennedy included these excerpts from the transcript of the city council meeting in his opinion in *Lukumi Babalu Aye v. City of Hialeah*, although only Justice Stevens joined this part of Kennedy's opinion.

57   *Id.* at 530.

58   *Id.* at 538.

59   *Id.* at 543.

60   *Id.* at 545.

61   *Id.* at 543.

62   *Id.* at 547.

63   Christina Cassady, *Hate Crimes against Muslims Highest since 9/11*, Associated Press (November 14, 2016).

64   Jenna Johnson and Abigail Hauslohner, *"I Think Islam Hates Us": A Timeline of Trump's Comments about Islam and Muslims*, The Washington Post (May 20, 2017).

65   *Id.*

66   Michael Schmidt and Richard Perez-Pena, *FBI Treating San Bernardino Attack as Terrorism Case*, The New York Times (December 4, 2015).

67   Johnson and Hauslohner, *"I Think Islam Hates Us."*

68   *Id.*

69 *Id.*

70 *Id.*

71 *Id.*

72 Executive Order 13769, *Protecting the Nation from Foreign Terrorist Entry*, 82 Fed. Reg. 8977 (January 27, 2017), https://www.whitehouse.gov/presidential-actions/executive-order-protecting-nation-foreign-terrorist-entry-united-states/.

73 *Id.* at Section 5(b). "Where necessary and appropriate, the Secretaries of State and Homeland Security shall recommend legislation to the President that would assist with such prioritization," the executive order also said.

74 *Id.* at Section 5(e).

75 *Id.* at Section 1.

76 *Id.* at Section 10(iii).

77 *International Refugee Assistance Project v. Trump*, 265 F. Supp. 3d 570, 586 (D. Md. 2017).

78 In his January 27 interview with the Christian Broadcasting Network, President Trump had the following exchange:

> DAVID BRODY: "Persecuted Christians, we've talked about this, the refugees overseas. The refugee program, or the refugee changes you're looking to make. As it relates to persecuted Christians, do you see them as kind of a priority here?"
>
> PRESIDENT TRUMP: "Yes."
>
> DAVID BRODY: "You do?"
>
> PRESIDENT TRUMP: "They've been horribly treated. Do you know if you were a Christian in Syria it was impossible, at least very tough to get into the United States? If you were a Muslim you could come in, but if you were a Christian, it was almost impossible and the reason that was so unfair, everybody was persecuted in all fairness, but they were chopping off the heads of everybody but more so the Christians. And I thought it was very, very unfair. So we are going to help them."

Brody File Exclusive: President Trump Says Persecuted Christians Will Be Given Priority as Refugees, Christian Broadcasting Network (January 27, 2017).

79 Amy B. Wang, *Trump Asked for a Muslim Ban, Giuliani Says—and Ordered a Commission to Do It Legally*, The Washington Post (January 29, 2017).

> Giuliani said: "When [Trump] first announced it, he said, 'Muslim ban.' He called me up. He said, 'Put a commission together. Show me the right way to do it legally.'"
>
> Giuliani said he assembled a "whole group of other very expert lawyers on this," including former U.S. attorney general Michael Mukasey, Rep. Mike McCaul (R-Tex.) and Rep. Peter T. King (R-N.Y.).
>
> "And what we did was, we focused on, instead of religion, *danger*—the areas of the world that create danger for us," Giuliani told [Fox News host Jeanine Pirro]. "Which is a *factual* basis, not a religious basis. Perfectly legal, perfectly sensible. And that's what the ban is based on. It's not based on religion. It's based on places where there are substantial evidence that people are sending terrorists into our country."

Id.

80 Hillel R. Smith and Ben Harrington, Congressional Research Service, *Overview of "Travel Ban" Litigation and Recent Developments* (January 19, 2018), https://fas.org/sgp/crs/homesec/LSB10017.pdf.

81 *State of Washington v. Trump*, 2017 U.S. Dist. LEXIS 16012 (W. D. Wa. 2017); *Aziz v. Trump*, 234 F. Supp. 3d 724 (E.D. Va. 2017).

82   *State of Washington v. Trump*, 847 F.3d 1151 (9th Cir. 2017).

83   *Id.* at 1168.

84   Executive Order 13780, *Protecting the Nation from Foreign Terrorist Entry*, 82 Fed. Reg. 13209 (March 6, 2017), https://www.whitehouse.gov/presidential-actions/executive-order -protecting-nation-foreign-terrorist-entry-united-states-2/.

85   *International Refugee Assistance Program v. Trump*, 883 F.3d 233, 267 (4th Cir. 2018) (citations omitted). The Fourth Circuit noted:

> Senior Policy Advisor Stephen Miller similarly explained that the changes to EO-2 were "mostly minor technical differences," and promised that they would result in "the same basic policy outcomes for the country." Then–White House Press Secretary Sean Spicer confirmed that "[t]he principles of the [second] executive order remain the same."

Id. (citations omitted). The Fourth Circuit also observed that President Trump

> continued to express his interest in returning to "the original Travel Ban," rather than "the watered down, politically correct version." On June 5, 2017, President Trump stated that the "Justice Dept. should ask for an expedited hearing of the watered down Travel Ban before the Supreme Court—& seek much tougher version!" and that "The Justice Dept. should have stayed with the original Travel Ban, not the watered down, politically correct version they submitted to [the Supreme Court]." The very next day, then–White House Press Secretary Spicer explained that President Trump's tweets are "official statements by the president of the United States."

Id. (citations omitted).

86   *See, e.g.,* Smith and Harrington, *Overview of "Travel Ban" Litigation and Recent Developments.*

87   *International Refugee Assistance Program v. Trump*, 857 F.3d 554, 635 (4th Cir. 2017).

88   *Id.* at 596 n.17.

89   *Id.*

90   Fred Barbash, *Muslim Ban Language Suddenly Disappears from Trump Campaign Website after Spicer Questioned*, The Washington Post (May 9, 2017).

91   *International Refugee Assistance Program v. Trump*, 883 F.3d at 267 (citations omitted).

92   *Id.*

93   *Id.*

94   Presidential Proclamation 9645, *Presidential Proclamation Enhancing Vetting Capabilities and Processes for Detecting Attempted Entry Into the United States by Terrorists or Other Public Safety Threats* (September 24, 2017), https://www.whitehouse.gov/presidential -actions/presidential-proclamation-enhancing-vetting-capabilities-processes-detecting -attempted-entry-united-states-terrorists-public-safety-threats/. "Upon completion of the first . . . review period, the President, on the recommendation of the Secretary of Homeland Security, determined that Chad had sufficiently improved its practices, and he accordingly lifted restrictions on its nationals." *Trump v. Hawaii*, 585 U.S. ___, 138 S. Ct. 2392, 2406 (2018) (citation omitted).

95   Smith and Harrington, *Overview of "Travel Ban" Litigation and Recent Developments.*

96   *International Refugee Assistance Program v. Trump*, 883 F.3d at 267 (citations omitted).

97   *Id.* (citations omitted).

98   *Id.* (citations omitted).

99   *International Refugee Assistance Program v. Trump*, 883 F.3d 233.

100 *Id.* at 263 (citations omitted).

101 *Id.* at 264.

102 *Id.* at 268.

103 *Id.* at 269.

104 *Trump v. Hawaii*, 585 U.S. ___, 138 S. Ct. 2392 (2018), http://www.scotusblog.com/case-files/cases/trump-v-hawaii-3/. Among the parties filing friend-of-the-court briefs in the case were legal scholars who are also experts in the history of the Church of Jesus Christ of Latter-day Saints (LDS Church). They filed a brief in support of neither party. These scholars noted that members of the LDS Church were the targets of "widespread hostility" in the nineteenth century due to the fact that they were viewed as "potentially dangerous outsiders." Brief of Scholars of Mormon History & Law as *Amici Curiae* in Support of Neither Party, *Trump v. Hawaii* (March 2018) at 9–13, 6–7. Nineteenth-century officials described members of the LDS Church as a "community of traitors, murderers, fanatics and whores." *Id.* at 6. Also, "[t]he government responded to this popular animus by initiating a variety of legal measures targeting Mormons, including executive actions designed to cut down Mormon immigration to the United States." *Id.* at 7.

The United States Conference of Catholic Bishops (USCCB) filed on behalf of the challengers of the proclamation's constitutionality. The USCCB brief noted that some colonial charters prohibited Catholics from holding public office and that the majority of schools in the nineteenth century required students to listen and read from the Protestant King James Version of the Bible, or suffer expulsions or beatings. Brief *Amicus Curiae* of the United States Conference of Catholic Bishops, Catholic Charities, USA, Catholic Legal Immigration Network, Inc. in Support of Respondents (March 30, 2018) at 15, 17.

105 *Trump v. Hawaii*, 585 U.S. ___, 138 S. Ct. at 2420.

106 *Id.* at 2421.

107 *Id.*

108 *Id.*

109 *Id.* at 2423.

110 *Id.* at 2424 (Kennedy, J., concurring).

111 *Id.* at 2424.

112 *See* Marty Lederman, *Contrary to Popular Belief, the Court Did Not Hold that the Travel Ban Is Lawful—Anything But,* Just Security (July 2, 2018).

113 *Trump v. Hawaii*, 585 U.S. ___, 138 S. Ct. at 2430 (Breyer, J., dissenting).

114 *Id.* at 2433.

115 *Id* at 2439 n.4 (citations omitted).

116 *Id.* at 2445.

117 *See* chap. 8 above.

118 *Trump v. Hawaii*, 585 U.S. ___, 138 S. Ct. at 2447 (Sotomayor, J., dissenting) (citations omitted).

119 *Id.* at 2448.

120 *See* Saeed Ahmed, Ed Lavandara, and Catherine Shoichet, *Alleged Kansas Jewish Center Gunman Charged with Murder,* CNN (April 5, 2014).

121 Jewish Telegraph Agency, *KC JCC Shooter Sentenced to Death,* The Jerusalem Post (November 10, 2015).

122 *See* Catherine Shoichet, *Kansas City Shooting: 3 Lives Defined by Love, Taken by Gunman's Rage,* CNN (August 31, 2015).

123 *See FBI Releases 2017 Hate Crime Statistics,* Federal Bureau of Investigation (November 13, 2018), https://ucr.fbi.gov/hate-crime/2017/resource-pages/hate-crime-summary;

David K Li, *Hate Crimes in America Spiked 17 Percent Last Year, FBI Says,* NBC News (November 13, 2018).

124 *See id.;* Anti-Defamation League, *ADL Calls on Leaders to Redouble Efforts to Counter Hate after FBI Reports Hate Crimes Jumped 17%* (November 13, 2018), https://www.adl .org/news/press-releases/adl-calls-on-leaders-to-redouble-efforts-to-counter-hate-after -fbi-reports-hate.

125 Anti-Defamation League, *ADL Calls on Leaders to Redouble Efforts to Counter Hate after FBI Reports Hate Crimes Jumped 17%* (November 13, 2018).

126 *See* Isabel Fattal, *A Brief History of Anti-Semitic Violence in America,* The Atlantic (October 28, 2018).

127 *Id.*

128 *See* Yonat Shimron and Jack Jenkins, *Pittsburgh Suspect's Hatred of Jews, HIAS Part of Larger Anti-immigrant Surge,* Religion News Service (October 29, 2018). Zaimov, *Robert Bowers, Shooter Who Killed 11 at Synagogue*; Serwer, *Trump's Caravan Hysteria Led to This.*

129 *See Protecting Religiously Affiliated Institutions Act of 2018,* Senate Report 115–325, 115th Congress, 2d Sess., S. 994, https://www.govinfo.gov/content/pkg/CRPT-115srpt325/pdf/ CRPT-115srpt325.pdf.

130 *See* Sikh Coalition, *New Wave of Hate Crimes Demand Vigilance* (March 9, 2018), https:// www.sikhcoalition.org/blog/2018/new-wave-hate-crimes-demands-vigilance/.

131 *See* New America, *Anti-Muslim Activities in the United States: Violence, Threats and Discrimination at the Local Level,* https://www.newamerica.org/in-depth/anti-muslim -activity/.

132 *See* generally Uddin, *The Latest Attacks on Islam* and *When Islam Is Not a Religion.*

133 Colin Atagi, *14 Dead in San Bernardino, and We Still Don't Know Why One Year Later,* USA Today (December 1, 2016); Ralph Ellis, Ashley Fantz, Faith Karimi, and Eliott C. McLaughlin, *Orlando Shooting: 49 Killed, Shooter Pledged ISIS Allegiance,* CNN (June 13, 2016).

134 *See* Zaimov, *Robert Bowers, Shooter Who Killed 11 at Synagogue*; Kiran Khalid, *Some Experts See Fatwa as Significant Blow to Terrorist Recruiting,* CNN (March 3, 2010).

135 DeNeen L. Brown, *We Are Armed Now: In Kentucky, Shootings Leave a Black Church and the White Community around It Shaken,* The Washington Post (November 11, 2018).

136 *Id.*

137 *Id.*

138 Taryn Finley, *The Charleston Shooting Was at Least the 91st Violent Attack on a Black Church since 1956,* The Huffington Post (December 6, 2017).

139 Church Arson Prevention Act, 18 U.S.C. Section 247 (2019), https://www.justice.gov/ jmd/ls/church-arson-prevention-act-1996-pl-104-155.

140 *Id.* The law also simplified the interstate commerce requirement. In 2018, Congress passed and President Trump signed a bill that extended this law to protect property owned by religiously affiliated groups, not just religious organizations (*Protecting Religiously Affiliated Institutions Act of 2018*). Before the bill passed, federal protection was lacking when Jewish community centers, for example, were hit with bomb threats. The bill also increases penalties for these crimes in certain cases. *See id.*

141 *Statement of Eric Treene, Special Counsel for Religious Discrimination, Civil Rights Division before the United States Senate Committee on the Judiciary,* Department of Justice (May 2, 2017), https://www.justice.gov/crt/speech/statement-eric-treene-special-counsel-religious -discrimination-civil-rights-division.

142 18 U.S.C. Section 249 (2019).

143 *Statement of Eric Treene, Special Counsel for Religious Discrimination*.

144 *Statement by Attorney General Loretta E. Lynch on the Sentencing of Dylann Roof*, Department of Justice (January 10, 2017), https://www.justice.gov/opa/pr/statement-attorney -general-loretta-e-lynch-sentencing-dylann-roof. Roof was sentenced to death in January 2017, the first time a death penalty verdict was rendered in a federal hate crimes case. Emily Shapiro, Anne Emerson, and Kristen McFann, *Dylann Roof Sentenced to Death, First to Get Death Penalty for Federal Hate Crimes*, ABC News (January 10, 2017).

145 *See* Robert Ghianni, *Tennessee Man Sentenced over Plot to Attack Muslim Community*, Reuters (June 15, 2017).

146 *See* Title IV of the Civil Rights of 1964, 42 U.S.C. Section 2000d *et seq.*

147 *See* Title II of the Civil Rights of 1964, 42 U.S.C. Section 2000a(b) (2019).

148 *See* Title III of the Civil Rights of 1964, 42 U.S.C. Section 2000b (2019).

149 According to the Department of Justice, the act "covers instances of overt discrimination against members of a particular religion as well less direct actions, such as zoning ordinances designed to limit the use of private homes as a place of worship." The act exempts noncommercial housing operated by a religious organization that is reserved for persons of the same faith. *See* Department of Justice, *The Fair Housing Act*, https:// www.justice.gov/crt/fair-housing-act-1.

150 15 U.S.C. Section 1691 *et seq.* (2019).

151 42 U.S.C. Section 2000cc *et seq.* (2019).

152 *Islamic Society of Basking Ridge v. Township of Bernards*, No. 3:16-cv-01369-MAS-LHG (D.N. J.), http://s3.amazonaws.com/becketpdf/3-ISBR-Proposed-Amicus-Brief-AS-FILED.pdf.

153 The Becket Fund, *Christians, Jews, Sikhs and Hindus Defend New Jersey Mosque: Muslim Congregation Seeks Right to Assemble amidst Local Opposition* (May 11, 2016), https:// www.becketlaw.org/media/christians-jews-sikhs-hindus-defend-new-jersey-mosque/.

154 *See Islamic Society of Basking Ridge v. Township of Bernards*, No. 3:16-cv-01369-MAS-LHG.

155 *See Update on the Justice Department's Enforcement of the Religious Land Use and Institutionalized Persons Act (2010–2016)*, Department of Justice (July 2016), https://www .justice.gov/crt/file/877931/download.

156 *Id.*

157 *Id.*

158 *See* Timothy Williams, *The Hated and the Hater, Both Touched by Crime*, The New York Times (July 18, 2011).

159 *Id.*

160 *Id.*

161 *See* Associated Press, *Mark Stroman Executed for 9/11 Dallas-Area Revenge Killings*, The Dallas News (July 2011).

162 *See* A World Without Hate, http://worldwithouthate.org/.

163 *Id.*

164 *Id.*

165 *See* Melissa Rogers, *Combating Religious Discrimination Today*, The White House (July 22, 2016), https://obamawhitehouse.archives.gov/blog/2016/07/22/combating-religious -discrimination-today.

166 For more information about the *Know Your Neighbor* initiative, *see* http://knowyourneighbor .us/; and https://ing.org/kyn-campaign/.

167 *See* Michelle Boorstein, *How the National Prayer Breakfast Sparked an Unusual Meeting between Muslims and Evangelicals*, The Washington Post (February 8, 2018).

168 *See* Anti-Defamation League, https://www.adl.org/education-and-resources/resources
     -for-educators-parents-families/educational-programs-training.
169 *See* Mona Chalabi, *Americans More Likely to Like Muslims if They Know One*, FiveThirtyE-
     ight (February 13, 2015), https://fivethirtyeight.com/features/americans-are-more-likely
     -to-like-muslims-if-they-know-one/. To be clear, one should not have to know or even
     like a person in order to seek to protect his or her rights. At the same time, promising
     avenues that might move people from the sidelines to active engagement on behalf of
     their neighbors should be pursued.
170 Projects like these have been spurred by findings that Americans need to do more to
     ensure that attitudes are aligned with constitutional promises. In 2015, a poll found
     that 82 percent of Americans said it was very or extremely important that Christians be
     permitted to practice their religion freely in the United States, but only 61 percent said
     the same is true for Muslims. *See* Associated Press–NORC Center for Public Affairs
     Research, *Americans Evaluate the Balance between Security and Civil Liberties* (December
     2015), http://www.apnorc.org/projects/Pages/HTML%20Reports/americans-evaluate
     -the-balance-between-security-and-civil-liberties1222-4187.aspx. The same survey found
     that just 72 percent of Americans said it was important to protect the religious liberty of
     Jewish people, and only 67 percent said it is important to protect the religious freedoms
     of members of the Church of Jesus Christ of Latter-day Saints.
171 Melissa Rogers, *Uniting to End Anti-Semitism*, The White House (November 26, 2014),
     https://obamawhitehouse.archives.gov/blog/2014/11/26/uniting-end-anti-semitism.
172 *Berlin Declaration, 2004*, Organization for Security and Co-operation in Europe (OSCE),
     https://www.osce.org/cio/31432.
173 *Id.*
174 *American Civil Rights Delegation to Urge OSCE Nations for Greater Hate Crimes Protections
     at Berlin Anti-Semitism Conference*, The Leadership Conference on Civil and Human
     Rights (November 10, 2014).
175 *Id.*
176 *Id.* President Barack Obama also sent a delegation to the 2014 conference, which was
     led by U.S. Ambassador to the United Nations Samantha Power. Other members of
     the delegation included Abraham Foxman; Ambassador to Germany, John Emerson;
     Organization for Security and Co-operation in Europe Ambassador Daniel Baer; Dr.
     Deborah Lipstadt; Ira Forman, Special Envoy to Monitor and Combat Anti-Semitism
     at the State Department; and me. *See* Rogers, *Uniting to End Anti-Semitism*.
177 *Remarks by the President at the Islamic Society of Baltimore*, The White House (February
     3, 2016), https://obamawhitehouse.archives.gov/the-press-office/2016/02/03/remarks
     -president-islamic-society-baltimore.
178 *Combatting Religious Discrimination Today*, Department of Justice (July 2016), https://
     www.justice.gov/crt/file/877936/download.
179 *See* Anti-Defamation League, https://www.adl.org/; *Post-Charlottesville Hate Crimes
     Recommendations to the Department of Justice*, Leadership Conference on Civil and Human
     Rights (September 15, 2017), https://civilrights.org/post-charlottesville-hate-crime
     -summit-coalition-recommendations-department-justice/; *Mayors Compact to Combat
     Hate, Extremism and Bigotry*, Anti-Defamation League (2017), https://www.adl.org/
     mayors-compact-to-combat-hate-extremism-and-bigotry; Human Rights First, https://
     www.humanrightsfirst.org/.
180 Letter to John M. Gore, Assistant Attorney General of the Civil Rights Division of the
     Department of Justice, Hate Crimes Coalition Policy Recommendations (September 15,

2017), https://www.adl.org/sites/default/files/documents/final-post-Charlottesville-DoJ
-hate-crime-summit-coalition-recommendations.docx.pdf.

181 *See* Peter Beinart, *Trump Shut Programs to Counter Violent Extremism*, The Atlantic (October 29, 2018). "[T]he FBI concluded [in 2017] that white supremacists killed more Americans from 2000 to 2016 than 'any other domestic extremist movement.'" *Id*. Nevertheless, the Trump administration canceled two grants made during the Obama administration to organizations that addressed white supremacy. *Id*. Peter Beinart has reported:

> In an interview in 2017, White House Deputy Assistant to the President Sebastian Gorka declared that there "has never been a serious attack or a serious plot [in the United States] that was unconnected from ISIS or al-Qaeda." When critics cited the 1995 Oklahoma City bombing, Gorka responded, "It's this constant 'Oh, it's the white man. It's the white supremacists. That's the problem.' No, it isn't."
>
> Gorka's wife, and frequent co-author, Katharine Gorka, shares his Islamo-centric view of terrorism. She has proposed that the U.S. close "radical mosques" and bar Al Jazeera from broadcasting in the United States. "American and Western leaders," she's declared, "have preemptively shut down any debate within Islam by declaring that Islam is the religion of peace." These views matter because although Sebastian has left the Trump White House, Katharine still serves as an adviser to the secretary of Homeland Security. In the months following Trump's election, according to *The Forward*, she asked for the names of employees working on CVE. She led a team that proposed changing the mission from *countering violent extremism* to *countering radical Islamist extremism*. That didn't happen. But Eric Rosand, a former senior State Department official, told *Buzz-Feed* that Gorka "played a significant role in denying CVE grant funding to groups that work to de-radicalize neo-Nazis and other far right extremists."

Id.

182 *See* Astead W. Herndon, *Some Critics Say Trump's Selective Silence Is Deafening*, The Boston Globe (June 19, 2017); Philip Bump, *Why Won't Donald Trump Rush to Tweet Criticism of Attacks against Muslims?*, The Washington Post (June 19, 2017).

183 *Id*.

184 *See generally* Thomas C. Berg, *There Is Religious Bigotry behind Trump's Travel Ban: The Supreme Court Should Have Known Better*, America (June 28, 2018).

185 *See generally* Ilya Somin, *The Supreme Court's Indefensible Double Standard in the Travel-Ban Case and Masterpiece Cakeshop*, Vox (June 27, 2018).

186 In the *Masterpiece Cakeshop* case, the Court majority said: "The official expressions of hostility to religion in some of the commissioners' comments—comments that were not disavowed at the Commission or by the State at any point in the proceedings that led to affirmance of the order—were inconsistent with what the Free Exercise Clause requires." 584 U.S. at ___, 138 S. Ct. at 1732.

187 *See generally* Joshua Matz, *Free Exercise in Peril*, The Pennsylvania Gazette (August 23, 2018). Matz, a former clerk for Justice Kennedy, wrote:

> Although many justices wrote separately in *Hawaii*, two opinions stand out. The first is by (retired) Justice Anthony M. Kennedy, who wrote a concurrence that will forever dishonor his legacy. Kennedy had devoted his career to an extraordinarily robust conception of the judicial role in protecting fundamental rights. But here, faced with one of the most open and notorious assaults on religious liberty in modern American history, he blinked. And then he shone a spotlight on his own lack of conviction by effectively begging Trump to follow the law: "An anxious world must know that our Government remains committed always to the liberties the Constitution seeks to preserve and protect, so that freedom extends outward,

and lasts." These are noble words. It's a shame that they were written to excuse judicial inaction, rather than to justify vindication of religious liberty.

Id.

188   *See* Anti-Defamation League, https://www.adl.org/education-and-resources/resources -for-educators-parents-families/educational-programs-training.

189   *See above* at pp. 218–21.

Conclusion

1   *President Obama Attends Righteous among Nations Ceremony,* Yad Vashem (January 28, 2016), http://www.yadvashem.org/events/28-january-2016.html.

2   *Remarks by the President at Islamic Society of Baltimore,* The White House (February 3, 2016), https://obamawhitehouse.archives.gov/the-press-office/2016/02/03/remarks -president-islamic-society-baltimore.

3   2 Tim 1:7 (NKJV).

4   U.S. News Staff, *Obama Speaks at National Prayer Breakfast,* U.S. News & World Report (February 4, 2016).

5   *Remarks of the President at Islamic Center,* The White House (September 17, 2001), https:// georgewbush-whitehouse.archives.gov/news/releases/2001/09/20010917-11.html.

6   *Id.*

7   John Meacham, *A Leader Should Appeal to Their People's Best Instincts: Donald Trump Appeals to the Worst,* Time (November 1, 2018).

8   *Id.*

9   *See* chaps. 4 and 10 above.

10   *Abington Township v. Schempp,* 374 U.S. at 256 (Brennan, J., concurring).

11   *See above* chap. 8.

12   McDonough and Crocker, *World's System for Resettling Refugees Benefits the United States.*

13   *See, e.g., Letter from Evangelical Immigration Table* (August 7, 2018) http:// evangelicalimmigrationtable.com/citing-religious-liberty-evangelical-leaders-urge -trump-administration-to-support-refugee-resettlement/; *Policy Experts, Refugees and Religious Leaders Call on President Trump to Raise Refugee Cap,* Refugee Council USA (September 18, 2018), http://www.rcusa.org/blog/policy-experts-refugees-and-religious -leaders-call-on-president-trump-to-raise-refugee-cap; Rhina Guidos, *Catholic Religious Call on Congress to Support Refugee Resettlement,* Catholic News Service (April 4, 2017), https://www.ncronline.org/news/politics/catholic-religious-call-congress -support-refugee-resettlement; *More than 5,000 Religious Leaders Sign Letter Supporting Refugee Resettlement,* Interfaith Immigration Coalition (March 10, 2017), http://www .interfaithimmigration.org/5000religiousleaderletter/.

14   Imani Perry, *May We Forever Stand: A History of the Black National Anthem* (Chapel Hill: University of North Carolina Press 2018) 3–4.

15   *Id.* at 73.

16   *Id.* at 1, 6.

17   *Id.* at xvi.

18   *Id.* at 7.

19   *Id.* at 19.

20   *Id.* at 20. Dr. Imani Perry says that "speak[ing] to black life by using a devotional frame made perfect sense":

> For James Weldon Johnson "Lift Every Voice" was "a hymn for Negro people." We should understand this designation, proffered by a man who declared himself

agnostic, as an acknowledgment of the importance of hymnody in black cultural life. To speak to black life by using a devotional frame made perfect sense, given that churches were the earliest black American institutions, and given that at the core of black American culture was the distinct form of Christianity that black Americans created on these shores. In particular the idea of faith as a practical repository, and as an intellectual and ideological orientation looking toward freedom that stood in the face of enslavement and Jim Crow and all manner of violence faced by black America, was deeply rooted in black life in the late nineteenth century.

Id.

21   *Id.* at 32.
22   *Id.* at 37.
23   *Id.* at 24.
24   *Id.* at 25.
25   *Id.* at 38.
26   *Id.* at 110.
27   *Id.* at 157–60.
28   *Id.* at 218–19.

INDEX OF UNITED STATES SUPREME COURT CASES
AND SELECTED FEDERAL STATUTES

Selected Federal Statutes

SELECTED BIBLIOGRAPHY

Books

Akhil Reed Amar, *The Bill of Rights: Creation and Reconstruction* (New Haven: Yale University Press 1998).

C. Antineau, A. Downey, and E. Roberts, *Freedom from Federal Establishment: Formation and Early History of the First Amendment Religion Clauses* (Milwaukee: Bruce 1964).

Kenneth Bae with Mark Tabb, *Not Forgotten: The True Story of My Imprisonment in North Korea* (Nashville: W Publishing Group 2016).

Randall Balmer, *God in the White House: How Faith Shaped the Presidency from John F. Kennedy to George W. Bush* (New York: HarperOne 2008).

Catherine Drinker Bowen, *Miracle at Philadelphia: The Story of the Constitutional Convention May to September 1787* (Boston: Little, Brown 1966).

Gerard V. Bradley, *Church-State Relationships in America* (Westport, Conn.: Greenwood 1987).

Jeff Broadwater, *George Mason: Forgotten Founder* (Chapel Hill: University of North Carolina Press 2006).

Alan Brownstein, ed., *The Establishment of Religion Clause: Its Constitutional History and the Contemporary Debate* (Amherst, N.Y.: Prometheus Books 2008).

Daniel O. Conkle, *Religion, Law and the Constitution* (St. Paul: Foundation Press 2016).

E. J. Dionne and Ming Hsu Chen, eds., *Sacred Places, Civic Purposes: Should Government Help Faith-Based Charity?* (Washington, D.C.: Brookings Institution Press 2001).

Joshua DuBois, *The President's Devotional* (New York: HarperOne 2013).

Roxanne Dunbar-Ortiz, *An Indigenous Peoples' History of the United States* (Boston: Beacon 2014).

William N. Eskridge Jr. and Robin Fretwell Wilson, eds., *Religious Freedom, LGBT Rights and the Prospects for Common Ground* (New York: Cambridge University Press 2019).

Noah Feldman, *The Three Lives of James Madison: Genius, Partisan, President* (New York: Random House 2017).

Ron B. Flowers, Melissa Rogers, and Steven K. Green, *Religious Freedom and the Supreme Court* (Waco, Tex.: Baylor University Press 2008).

Michael Giorgione, *Inside Camp David: The Private World of the Presidential Retreat* (New York: Little Brown and Company 2017).

Mary Ann Glendon, *A World Made New: Eleanor Roosevelt and the Universal Declaration of Human Rights* (New York: Random House 2001).

Linda Gordon, *The Second Coming of the KKK: The Ku Klux Klan of the 1920s and the American Political Tradition,* (New York: W.W. Norton 2017).

Steven K. Green, *The Bible, the School and the Constitution: The Clash That Shaped Modern Church-State Doctrine* (New York: Oxford University Press 2012).

Steven K. Green, *The Second Disestablishment: Church and State in Nineteenth-Century America* (New York: Oxford University Press 2010).

Margaret A. Hogan and C. James Taylor, eds., *My Dearest Friend: Letters of Abigail and John Adams* (Cambridge, Mass.: Harvard University Press 2007).

Edmund S. Ions, *The Politics of John F. Kennedy* (New York: Routledge Library Editions: Political Science Vol. 1 1967).

Robert Jones, *The End of White Christian America* (New York: Simon & Schuster 2016).

Brian T. Kaylor, *Presidential Campaign Rhetoric in an Age of Confessional Politics* (Lanham, Md.: Lexington Books 2011).

Kevin M. Kruse, *One Nation under God: How Corporate America Invented Christian America* (New York: Basic Books 2015).

Jeanne Marie Laskas, *To Obama, with Love, Joy, Anger, and Hope* (New York: Random House 2018).

Alexander Leitch, *A Princeton Companion* (Princeton, N.J.: Princeton University Press 1978).

John Leland, *The Writings of the Late Elder John Leland: Including Some Events in His Life*, ed. L. F. Greene (New York: G. W. Wood 1845).

Ira C. Lupu and Robert W. Tuttle, *Secular Government, Religious People* (Grand Rapids: Eerdmans 2014).

James Madison, *Debates on the Adoption of the Federal Constitution*, ed. Jonathan Elliot (Washington, D.C.: 1845).

James Madison, *The Federalist No. 52*, in *James Madison: Writings* (New York: The Library of America 1999).

Joel W. Martin, *Native American Religion* (New York: Oxford University Press 1999).

David McCullough, *John Adams* (New York: Simon & Schuster 2001).

David McCullough, *The American Spirit: Who We Are and What We Stand For* (New York: Simon & Schuster 2017).

William McLoughlin, ed., *Isaac Backus on Church, State and Calvinism, Pamphlets, 1754–1789* (Cambridge, Mass.: Harvard University Press 1968).

James P. Moore, *One Nation under God: The History of Prayer in America* (New York: Doubleday 2005).

Imani Perry, *May We Forever Stand: A History of the Black National Anthem* (Chapel Hill: University of North Carolina Press 2018).

Thomas J. Reese, *Inside the Vatican: The Politics and Organization of the Catholic Church* (Cambridge, Mass.: Harvard University Press 1996).

David K. Ryden and Jeffrey Polet, eds., *Sanctioning Religion? Politics, Law, and Faith-Based Public Services* (Boulder, Colo.: Lynne Rienner 2005).

Micah Schwartzman, Chad Flanders, and Zoe Robinson, *Rise of Corporate Religious Liberty* (Oxford University Press 2016).

William Seale, *The President's House* (Washington, D.C.: White House Historical Society 1986).

Gary Scott Smith, *Faith and the Presidency: From George Washington to George W. Bush* (New York: Oxford University Press 2006).

Gary Scott Smith, *Religion in the Oval Office: The Religious Lives of American Presidents* (New York: Oxford University Press 2015).

Steven D. Smith, *Foreordained Failure: The Quest for a Constitutional Principle of Religious Freedom* (New York: Oxford University Press 1995).

Stephen D. Solomon, *Ellery's Protest: How One Young Man Defied Tradition and Sparked the Battle over School Prayer* (Ann Arbor: University of Michigan Press 2007).

C. Edward Spann and Michael E. Williams Sr., *Presidential Praise: Our Presidents and Their Hymns* (Macon: Mercer University Press 2017).

Asma Uddin, *When Islam Is Not a Religion: Inside America's Fight for Religious Freedom* (New York: Pegasus Books 2019).

Tisa Wenger, *Religious Freedom: The Contested History of an American Ideal* (Chapel Hill: University of North Carolina Press 2017).

Linda K. Wertheimer, *Faith Ed.: Teaching about Religion in an Age of Intolerance* (Boston: Beacon 2015).

Ronald C. White, Jr., *The Eloquent President: A Portrait of Lincoln through His Words* (New York: Random House 2000).

Theodore H. White, *The Making of the President 1960* (New York: Athenaeum House Inc. 1962).

John Witte Jr., *Religion and the American Constitutional Experiment: Essential Rights and Liberties* (Boulder, Colo.: Westview 2000).

Michael Wolf, Bruce Friedman, and Daniel Sutherland, *Religion in the Workplace: A Comprehensive Guide to Legal Rights and Responsibilities* (Chicago: American Bar Association 2008).

JOURNAL ARTICLES AND JOINT STATEMENTS

Thomas C. Berg, *Religious Exemptions and Third-Party Harms*, Federalist Society Review 17, no. 3 (2016).

The Bible and Public Schools: A First Amendment Guide (New York and Nashville: The Bible Literacy Project and First Amendment Center 1999).

Gerard V. Bradley, *The No Religious Test Clause and the Constitution of Religious Liberty: A Machine That Has Gone of Itself*, 37 Case W. L. Rev 674 (1987).

Kiel Brennan-Marquez, *A Business Can Exercise Religion, but Hobby Lobby Still Gets It Wrong*, Boston Review (July 7, 2014).

Lyman H. Butterfield, *Elder John Leland, Jeffersonian Itinerant*, 62 Proc. of the Am. Antiquarian Soc'y 160, 174 (1952).

Daniel O. Conkle, *The Establishment Clause as a Federalism Mandate*, 82 Northwestern L. Rev. 1129 (1988).

Robert L. Cord, *Church-State Separation: Restoring the "No Preference" Doctrine of the First Amendment*, 9 Harv. Jnl. Law & Pub. Pol'y 129 (1986).

Steven B. Epstein, *Rethinking the Constitutionality of Ceremonial Deism*, 96 Colum. L. Rev. 2083 (1996).

Noah Feldman, *The Intellectual Origins of the Establishment Clause*, 77 N. Y. U. L. Rev. 346 (2002).

George Clemon Freeman Jr., *Justice Powell's Constitutional Opinions*, 45 Wash. and Lee L. Rev. 411 (1988).

John H. Garvey and Amy V. Coney, *Catholic Judges in Capital Cases*, 81 Marq. L. Rev. 303 (1997–1998).

Frederick Mark Gedicks, *Incorporation of the Establishment Clause against the States: A Logical, Textual, and Historical Account*, 88 Indiana L. Jnl. 669, (2013).

Frederick Mark Gedicks, *"Substantial" Burdens: How Courts May (and Why They Must) Judge Burdens on Religion under RFRA*, 85 Geo. Wash. L. Rev. 94 (2017).

Steven K. Green, *Blaming Blaine: Understanding the Blaine Amendment and the No-Funding Principle*, 2 UNC First Amendment L. Rev. 107 (2003).

Kent Greenawalt, *Common Sense about Original and Subsequent Understandings of the Religion Clauses*, 8 Pa. J. Const. L. 479 (2006).

Merlin Gustafson, *The Religious Role of the President*, The Midwest Journal of Political Science 14 (1970).

Philip Hamburger, *A Constitutional Right of Religious Exemption: An Historical Perspective*, 60 Geo. Wash. L. Rev. 915, 916 (1992).

Andrew Koppelman and Frederick M. Gedicks, *Is Hobby Lobby Worse for Religious Liberty than Smith?* 9 U. St. Thomas J. L. & Pub. Pol'y 223 (2015).

Kurt T. Lash, *The Second Adoption of the Establishment Clause: The Rise of the Non-Establishment Principle*, 27 Ariz. St. L. Jnl. 1085 (1995).

Kurt T. Lash, *The Second Adoption of the Free Exercise Clause: Religious Exemptions under the Fourteenth Amendment*, 88 Northwestern Univ. L. Rev. 1106 (1994).

Douglas Laycock, *"Nonpreferential" Aid to Religion: A False Claim about Original Intent*, 27 Wm and Mary L. Rev. 875 (1986).

Douglas Laycock, *The Remnants of Free Exercise*, 1990 Sup. Ct. Rev. 1 (1990).

Douglas Laycock and Oliver Thomas, *Interpreting the Religious Freedom Restoration Act*, 73 Tex. L. Rev. 209 (1994).

Martin S. Lederman, *Reconstructing RFRA: The Contested Legacy of Religious Freedom Restoration*, 125 Yale L.J. Forum 416 (2016).

Christopher C. Lund, *RFRAs, State RFRAs and Religious Minorities*, 53 San Diego L. Rev. 163 (2016).

Christopher C. Lund, *Religious Exemptions, Third-Party Harms, and the Establishment Clause*, 91 Notre Dame L. Rev. 1375 (2016).

Ira C. Lupu, *The Failure of RFRA*, 20 Ark. Little Rock L. Rev. 575 (1998).

Benjamin Pietro Marcus, *Another Historic Moment: Religious Studies Companion Document Added to a National Education Framework*, Religion & Education 44, no.3 (2017).

William P. Marshall, *The Case against Constitutionally Compelled Free Exercise Exemptions*, 40 Cas. W. Res. L. Rev. 357 (1989).

Michael W. McConnell, *Free Exercise Revisionism and the Smith Decision*, 57 Univ. of Chicago L. Rev. 1109 (1990).

Michael W. McConnell, *The Origins and Historical Understanding of Free Exercise of Religion*, 103 Harv. L. Rev. 1409 (1990).

Father John Courtney Murray, *Civil Unity and Religious Integrity: The Articles of Peace*, Woodstock Theological Library at Georgetown University (1954).

James David Nelson, *Conscience, Incorporated*, 2013 Mich. St. L. Rev. 1565 (2013).

Note, *An Originalist Analysis of the No Religious Test Clause*, 120 Harv. L. Rev. 1649 (2007).

Punta del Este Declaration on Human Dignity for Everyone Everywhere: Seventy Years after the Universal Declaration on Human Rights (December 2018).

Religion in Public Schools: A Joint Statement of Current Law, American Jewish Congress (April 1995).

Religious Expression in American Public Life: A Joint Statement of Current Law, Wake Forest University Center for Religion and Public Affairs (January 2010).

Angela R. Riley, *Native Nations and the Constitution: An Inquiry into "Extra-Constitutionality,"* 130 Harv. L. Rev. Forum 173 (2017).

Melissa Rogers, *Religious Freedom and the Federal Executive Branch: Suggestions for Future Administrations*, 15 Univ. St. Thomas L. Jnl. 703 (2019).

Micah Schwartzman, Nelson Tebbe, and Richard Schragger, *The Costs of Conscience*, University of Virginia School of Law Research Paper No. 2018–14, Cornell Law School Research Paper No. 18–35 (2018).

Thomas Scott-Railton, *A Legal Sanctuary: How the Religious Freedom Restoration Act Could Protect Sanctuary Churches*, 128 Yale L. Jnl. 408 (2018).

Separation of Church and States: An Examination of State Constitutional Limits on Government Funding for Religious Institutions, 2 First Amend. L. Rev. 1–198 (2003)

Erik S. Thompson, *Compromising Equality: An Analysis of the Religious Exemption in the Employment Non-Discrimination Act and Its Impact on LGBT Workers*, 35 B.C.J.L. & Soc. Just. 285 (2015).

J. Brent Walker, *A Primer on Governmental Accommodation of Religion*, Journal of Church and State 49 (2007).